As Good as a Marriage

Manchester University Press

Frontispiece Anne Lister 1791–1840, Shibden Hall

As Good as a Marriage

The Anne Lister Diaries 1836–38

Jill Liddington

Manchester University Press

Published by Manchester University Press
Oxford Road, Manchester M13 9PL

www.manchesteruniversitypress.co.uk

British Library Cataloguing-in-Publication Data
A catalogue record for this book is available from the British Library

ISBN   978 1 5261 5735 5   hardback
ISBN   978 1 5261 7641 7   paperback

First published 2023

Typeset
by New Best-set Typesetters Ltd

She said it would be as good as a marriage.
'Yes', said I, 'quite as good or better.'
Anne Lister's diary, Thursday 27 September 1832

CONTENTS

FIGURES AND MAPS

MAPS

ACKNOWLEDGEMENTS

This book is a companion volume to *Female Fortune* (1998) and I would like to thank Rivers Oram for commissioning that book when interest in Anne Lister was still limited; I certainly also appreciate Elizabeth Fidlon's publishing a new edition in 2019 when *Gentleman Jack* was first broadcast.

At my new publisher, Manchester University Press, I am immensely grateful to my editor Emma Brennan. From the start she believed in this sequel to *Female Fortune*. I relish having a publisher in the north, and one with excellent distribution networks in the US and beyond, vital given *Gentleman Jack*'s global impact. So huge thanks to everyone at MUP who has guided this book through: Emma Brennan of course, also Paul Clarke and Adam Noor, and the copy-editor Andrew Kirk.

No book on Anne Lister would be conceivable without West Yorkshire Archive Service, custodians of the magnificent Anne Lister diaries. So I thank Ruth Cummins and Jenny Wood for their professional support, especially during the difficult COVID lockdown. In Local Studies at Halifax Library, I am grateful to Sarah Rose for access to its treasures. And in the Calderdale Museums Service which runs the Shibden Museum, I would like to thank Richard Macfarlane, Eli Dawson and Steve Crabtree, as well as Bobsie Robinson who oversees the service.

Huge gratitude must go to scriptwriter Sally Wainwright, without whose creative genius there would be no *Gentleman Jack*, and the readership for everything Anne Lister would be infinitely smaller. So thank you, Sally, especially for your warm words at the launch of the *Female Fortune* new edition in March 2022!

Research on Anne Lister and Ann Walker has grown phenomenally in the three years since *Gentleman Jack* first aired, and I would particularly like to thank Ian Philp of Lightcliffe for all his research on the Crow Nest estate, and for coordinating my Calderdale Heritage Walks.

Since 2019 and *Gentleman Jack*, a growing army of Anne Lister fans have become involved in research, too many to name; but I would particularly like to thank Packed with Potential. For expert pre-Darwinian geological advice, I am most grateful to Mike Leeder and Tim Atkinson; and also to Tim for sharing his mountaineering wisdom, guiding us up Vignemale in 2003. For reading and commenting on draft chapters, I would particularly like to thank friends and colleagues Laura Johansen, Mike Leeder, Dave Russell and especially Kerry McQuade. And huge appreciation to Mike Barrett for skilfully designing the maps, as well as Ann Walker's family tree.

I'd also like to applaud two local bookshops: the Book Corner in Halifax Piece Hall, expertly managed by Sarah Shaw and colleagues; and the Book Case in Hebden Bridge, run by Kate Claughan who, with her son Jango, wheeled umpteen boxes of *Female Fortune* into the Minster for ALBW 2022!

Writing something complex like *As Good as a Marriage* could have been isolating, especially during the endless COVID lockdowns. So there are a few people I feel hugely grateful to for keeping me going as I changed publishers and as this book slowly took shape. In particular, thanks to my sister and niece, Annie and Georgia Moseley, for listening over the years. And as always, I remain grateful beyond words to my partner, Julian Harber, for his (nearly) inexhaustible store of patience with Anne Lister, and for keeping this particular writer going during the bad times and the good.

Two Anne Lister fans deserve special thanks. The first is Pat Esgate in the US, lead organizer of the Anne Lister Birthday Week (ALBW). Pat has believed in me and in this book from the very start. I remain enormously grateful for the loyal support of both

Pat and her partner Bren. Nearer home, and over a longer period, I greatly appreciate the work of Rachel Lappin. She was the perfect travelling companion when Pat invited me to do a small US book tour with *Female Fortune* in December 2019. And she helped me in my battle with computer technology, after I discovered that my 1993 diary transcripts were accessible on paper, but not on my computer. Rachel also helped me with editing my earlier audio-visual recordings and, during COVID, editing my Anne Lister talks on Zoom. She now works as Calderdale's Senior Visitor Engagement Officer, the perfect person to welcome Anne's many fans to Halifax. Also involved in running ALBW, I would like to thank administrator Cheryl MacDonald and photographer Joanne Bartone.

For permission to include images, I thank Eli Dawson, Curator, Calderdale Museums; Tim Whitehead of Happy Valley Pride, based in Hebden Bridge; Sarah Rose, Local Studies Librarian, Halifax; Mike Barrett of frogsdesign in Bradford; and Ruth Cummins, West Yorkshire Archive Service (WYAS), Calderdale. Anne Lister's diaries 1836–38 are reproduced by kind permission of West Yorkshire Archives Service (SH:7/ML/E/19–21). I am most grateful to Alan Betteridge for all his earlier archive support and now for permission to reproduce the 1835 Halifax map.

Finally, many thanks to everyone at the Society of Authors for their invaluable help, especially Sarah Baxter and Nicola Soloman.

ANNE LISTER AND ANN WALKER: THEIR WORLD

LIVING AT SHIBDEN HALL

Anne Lister *born* 1791, inherited the estate from her Uncle James, 1826

Aunt Anne Lister *born* 1765

Ann Walker *born* 1803, inherited half the Crow Nest estate in 1830; moved into Shibden 1834

By 1837, servants included Cookson and Oddy; housemaid Anne, kitchen maid Sarah and a cook; also footman Robert, groom George and general servant John Booth

ANN WALKER'S RELATIVES

Aunt Ann Walker, Cliff Hill, Crow Nest estate, Lightcliffe; Ann Walker visited her regularly

Elizabeth Sutherland, Ann's sister; she married Captain Sutherland; lived at Udale, Scotland

William Priestley, Ann's older cousin, and his wife Eliza, Lightcliffe. Ann Walker's aunt Elizabeth had married John Priestley, near Sowerby

Edwards family, Pye Nest, Sowerby Bridge. Ann's mother Mary Edwards had married John Walker. When Ann was 19, her father died and her mother soon after. John Walker's will appointed nephew William Priestley and brother-in-law Henry Edwards as trustees to protect the interests of Ann and Elizabeth

Christopher Rawson, JP, Hope Hall, banker, magistrate and coal owner. His younger brother W. H. Rawson married Mary Priestley, Ann Walker's older cousin

Catherine Rawson, Ann's close friend; daughter of Stansfield, one of the many Rawson brothers

Henry Priestley and his wife Mary, Haugh End near Sowerby; Mary was related to Mariana Lawton

Note: for further information, see Appendix, p. 305

Key estate employees

Samuel Washington, lived at Crow Nest; land steward for both Anne Lister and Ann Walker

James Holt, coal steward

Joseph Mann, master miner and under coal steward

Robert Mann, 'out-works at home' and colliery banksman

Mr Husband, clerk-of-works; later also David Booth

Lawyers, doctors, clergy, architects, bankers and landowners

Robert Parker and Thomas Adam, Halifax lawyers; offices by the Piece Hall

Jonathan Gray, York lawyer

Mr Jubb, family doctor; visited Shibden regularly

Dr (Steph) Belcombe, York, Mariana Lawton's brother; helped treat Ann Walker

Revd Musgrave, Vicar of Halifax; married to Ellen Waterhouse

Revd Wilkinson, elderly curate, Lightcliffe; also headmaster of Heath School, Halifax

Samuel Gray, landscape garden designer

John Harper, York, eminent architect

John Horner, Halifax, artist

Mr McKean, Halifax banker

Hammersleys, London bankers

Michael Stocks, JP, Radical, landowner in upper Shibden valley and coal owner

Anne Lister's friends

Isabella Norcliffe, Langton Hall, beyond York

Lady Stuart, elderly aunt of Hon. James Stuart Wortley, MP for Halifax to 1837; and of Hon. John Stuart Wortley, candidate for the West Riding, 1837

Lady Stuart de Rothesay, Lady Stuart's daughter-in-law and wife of the ex-ambassador to France; in 1830 she visited France with Anne

Lady Vere Cameron, Lady Stuart's great-niece, recently married
Lady Gordon, a friend of Lady Stuart
Mariana Lawton, lived in Cheshire, married to landowner Charles
  Lawton. M~ in the diaries

KEY SHIBDEN TENANTS

Matty Pollard, a reliable source of practical female knowledge
Note: For a fuller list of names of enfranchised tenants voting in the
  1837 election, see Appendix, p. 308

Preface

This book was born of the COVID-19 pandemic when, after the March 2020 lockdown, we all had to self-isolate. Countries across the globe each experienced COVID differently, as did each of the four nations of the UK. In England, the North felt itself particularly hard hit, especially after the government introduced its tier system. Those of us placed in higher tiers, such as West Yorkshire and our local authority, Calderdale, felt harshly treated and often very confused.

Until that woeful point in late March my Anne Lister life was set fair, as was that of others immersed in her diaries. Almost twelve months earlier, in spring 2019, Sally Wainwright's *Gentleman Jack* (BBC1/HBO) had had huge popular impact, both in the UK and the US. Anne Lister fans began to head over to Halifax from Europe and the US. So, popular demand grew for anyone involved in Anne Lister research. This reached a crescendo in July 2019 when Helena Whitbread and I spoke to a packed audience in Halifax Minster, Helena on early Anne Lister, me on Anne in the 1830s. At the end, an American woman (who I now know to have been Pat Esgate from upstate New York) suddenly stood up and paid heartfelt and generous tribute to Helena and myself for our work. 'You have changed women's lives and I thank you', she said. The atmosphere in the Minster was electric, the applause spontaneous.[1]

By mid-2019 Rachel Lappin was helping me edit the video recording of the Anne Lister blue plaque unveiling at Shibden Hall in April. Then Pat Esgate invited us to the US in December and organized a small yet very enjoyable book tour. In February 2020, to celebrate LGBTQ+ History Month, I gave a sell-out talk at Manchester's wonderful Portico Library, as well as two public lectures, all three on 'Writing Anne Lister: An LGBTQ+ History'. And then, to plan a talk in our local Hebden Bridge Town Hall, Rachel and I met the Happy Valley Pride organizer.

Indeed, my spring 2020 diary was packed with walks, talks and book signings, especially for the Anne Lister Birthday Weekend (ALBW) organized by Pat Esgate in early April. And on 11 March I attended Sally Wainwright's Freedom of the Borough ceremony in Halifax Town Hall. It was a joyful affair. Yet this turned out to be our last Anne Lister event. For then coronavirus suddenly hit the UK. Almost overnight, everything planned was cancelled. My Happy Valley Pride talk for 18 March was not going to happen. I almost wept at I gazed wistfully at the stunning poster.

1 Happy Valley Pride poster, Hebden Bridge, March 2020

We all reeled at this drastic change to our world. No one had experienced a pandemic like this before. For Anne Lister fans, Pat Esgate had just given a final polish to her impressive ALBW plans, organizing Americans and Europeans to visit Halifax. Now, suddenly, no planes. Pat, however, was indomitable. If air travel and public gatherings were now impossible, she would turn to the new-fangled Zoom. She rapidly arranged online interviews with Sally Wainwright and Suranne Jones, then with Helena Whitbread, and on 3 April, Anne Lister's birthday, with me.

We were all new to interviews recorded on Zoom. However, I was put at ease by Pat's friendly professionalism. She asked about the pioneer editors – John Lister, Muriel Green and Phyllis Ramsden – to whose earlier work Anne Lister followers are deeply indebted.[2] I then talked about how in 2001 I had met Sally Wainwright, who had been given *Female Fortune* as a present by a mutual friend; and how we soon started working together on script ideas. However, 2001 was too early in Sally's career. It would be another fifteen years before *Gentleman Jack* could take shape.[3]

Then came the inevitable question from Pat: 'So are you working on another Anne Lister book?' Like everyone else, I was still reeling emotionally from the impact of the lockdown, all my plans punctured. So I cautiously replied: 'No, but I hope others will continue the Anne Lister story.' Meanwhile, we all watched the grim reports of packed intensive care wards and mounting deaths, in the UK and round the world.

For me, however, two things then happened. First, the public response to my ALBW interview (especially from 'Lister Sister' fans) was so warmly enthusiastic that I began to feel far more positive about plunging further into the diaries. And second, contrary to our optimistic hopes, it was becoming grimly clear that the COVID lockdown was *not* going to end any time soon. Like so many others, I would be locked in at home for months, facing a completely blank diary and desperately needing to improvise something – anything – to keep despondency at bay.

So, within a week, I had changed my mind. I decided to expand my work on Anne Lister: from May 1836, when *Female Fortune* ended, to mid-1838. Looking around, I could not spot other researchers working on all the voluminous diary entries for these two years. There were the impressive 'Anne Lister Codebreakers', organized by West Yorkshire Archive Service (WYAS). However, they often focused on pre-1836, on the coded passages, and on Anne's extensive travels – especially to France in the late 1820s, and, most exotically, to Russia in 1839.[4] Other researchers tracked the story from Anne's death in West Georgia in 1840, after which Ann Walker faced the unenviable task of arranging for body and coffin to be transported back to Halifax for burial; and the vexatious litigation that dogged Ann afterwards.[5]

So, if I did not do this work myself, who else would?[6] Anne Lister fans often said that they were hungry for a complete edition of the diaries (little did they know the scale of this task!) The lockdown had put all my other Anne Lister plans on hold; so much so that I had to invent a depressing new verb: to re-cancel. So I took a very deep breath and set to work.

Overnight, I found myself plunging back twenty-seven years. I gazed at my faded diary printouts for May 1836 to May 1838. And dating from 1993–94, at my handwritten and typed transcripts. These I had saved on large floppy discs; but of course, over a quarter of a century, computer technology had changed out of all recognition. Scholarly understanding of Anne Lister along with public fascination with her had also changed dramatically, most particularly since *Gentleman Jack*. Here, I draw together these two worlds, old and new, to pull together what we know of Anne Lister for these twenty-four months.

THE NEGLECTED YEARS: ANNE LISTER 1836–38

Why do we know so little about Anne Lister for these years? I decided to dig down, deeper than my 1993–94 original reading of the diaries. I plunged right back to the very beginning to check what pioneer editors had written. What could they tell us, what had they omitted – and why? This meant going back to the 1880s.

John Lister's father, Anne's indirect descendant, had inherited Shibden Hall. John himself was an assiduous scholar with a growing interest in politics. In 1887 he began publishing his lengthy selections from the diaries in the *Halifax Guardian*.[7] He opened with the 1837

General Election and how Anne Lister and Ann Walker, though of course both voteless, exerted political pressure as landowners on their enfranchised tenants. On 23 July they visited Ann's tenants, who enquired 'if A~ would be contented to let them split their votes? No! ... Better give a plumper for Wortley, and then talk about staying' in their cottages.[8]

From 1887 to 1892 John Lister continued for 121 gripping instalments. He knew Halifax history extremely well, illuminating how prudently Anne weighed her various entrepreneurial interests, agriculture and land-based industry. However, of course, at this stage he was unable to crack Anne's secret code.[9]

By the time John reached the mid-1830s, he had produced no fewer than ninety instalments. For the 1835 election, he described in compelling detail the damage done in what became known as 'the window-breaking election'.[10] However, 1836 was not an election year, and he skipped over it briefly. So we read little of Anne's aunt's death or of Mariana Lawton's visit to Shibden. John Lister was keen to reach 1837, another election year, to which he devoted seven instalments, much of it detailing Anne and Ann's electoral bullying of their tenants. Then for 1838, he again scurried over 4½ months (January to mid-May), leaving considerable gaps.[11] Yet it would surely be ungenerous to chide the assiduous John Lister for these omissions.

John ended his *Halifax Guardian* instalments in October 1892. And it was at about this time that, aided by fellow antiquarian Arthur Burrell, he managed to crack Anne's secret code. Legislation against male homosexuality had become more harsh in 1885, and the coded passages understandably shocked both men.[12] John died in 1933, taking to his grave his knowledge of the coded diaries. He had contributed hugely to Anne Lister scholarship, yet has left us wanting to know more about Anne in 1836–38.

After his death, the Halifax librarian's daughter took on the task of sorting the vast jumble of papers at Shibden. Muriel Green decided to focus on Anne's letters rather than her diaries. She systematically catalogued the correspondence, and in 1938 completed her librarianship dissertation. 'A Spirited Yorkshirewoman' is an impressive transcription of 395 letters, just one fifth of those now preserved in Calderdale Archives.[13] So, for mid-1836 to mid-1838, what does Green offer? Like John Lister, she was very methodical – and she has left all scholars in her debt. However, also like John Lister, she eventually grew wearied by the scale of her task. Her dissertation runs to 542 pages, yet she does not reach May 1836 until page 489, by which time gaps are growing. Indeed, she skips completely over four months in winter 1836–37.[14] Again, it would be churlish to remonstrate. However, what we do miss are many of Anne's 1836–38 letters, usually to her elite women friends, which offer a rather different picture from the diaries.[15]

All the while, Anne's secret code, cracked nearly half a century earlier, remained unknown: the key to this code was locked in the Halifax librarian's safe. Indeed, it was not until 1958, long after John Lister's death, that local historian Dr Phyllis Ramsden began transcribing the diaries. Working with her friend Vivien Ingham, she was provided with the key to the code. Around 1966 they seemed to have transcribed the diaries' coded passages. But tragically, only their summaries of these coded sections survive.[16] However, for the very first time, for May 1836 to May 1838, we get a tantalizing glimpse of Anne's marriage to Ann Walker, the key theme of this book.

Their brief summaries leave the researcher gasping for the candidly revealing detail in Anne Lister's diary. For instance, they noted a 'long passage' in July 1837, summarized tersely merely as 'more scenes'; and in February 1838, there are seven lines summarized just as Ann Walker 'remembers her 4th anniversary with a widening rift between the 2 Annes'.[17] However, bending to local censure, they often expurgated certain passages. The Sexual Offences Act 1967 had decriminalized male homosexual activity, but a culture of silence, even for women, continued. Ramsden died in 1985; and it seems that she probably destroyed her transcripts of the coded passages shortly before her death.[18] It remains a huge tragedy that Ramsden's painstaking transcriptions never reached a wide readership.

*

And there Anne Lister's later years rested for another quarter-century. In *Female Fortune* (1998), I took her story up to May 1836, with the death of her father and the effective banishment of sister Marian from Shibden. Meanwhile, a new generation was opening up the diaries for the late 1830s. Cat Euler, an American student at York University, titled her DPhil 'Moving between Worlds: Gender, Class, Politics, Sexuality and Women's Networks in the Diaries of Anne Lister of Shibden Hall, Halifax, Yorkshire, 1830–1840' (1995). This remains a very impressive piece of research. Like John Lister a century earlier, Euler chose to focus on the three election years: 1832, 1835 and 1837, following local politics with informed attention. So her discussion of 1836 and especially 1838 was inevitably sparse. Additionally, unlike other scholars, Euler's approach was thematic rather than chronological, so her thesis does not have the flow of Anne Lister's words as she wrote them, as she lived them. She is also more critical of Anne than many writers. She opened with the inspired words of Virginia Woolf writing of her lover Vita Sackville-West: 'At heart [she] was nothing but an old Tory squire ... with an incurable Tory soul.'[19] Crucially, Euler's towering contribution is her intellectually sophisticated analysis of intersectionality: notably gender, class and sexuality. So researchers remain in her debt.[20]

HOW HAS THE ANNE LISTER WORLD CHANGED THIS CENTURY?

This takes us, nearly twenty-five years later, into the new century and the *Gentleman Jack* era.[21] The first book to be shaped by the imminent arrival of Sally Wainwright's drama was written by German biographer Angela Steidele. *Anne Lister: Eine Erotische Biographie*, published in Berlin in 2017, was reissued in 2018 as *Gentleman Jack: A Biography of Anne Lister: Regency Landowner, Seducer and Secret Diarist*. The book caused some controversy. Steidele wrote critically of Anne as 'a beast of a woman'. And the book was almost entirely reliant on secondary sources: Whitbread on the young Anne Lister, myself on the 1830s, and Ramsden for Anne's amazing travels.

So what does Steidele offer for the late 1830s? After the end of *Female Fortune*, she relied largely on Ramsden's summarized coded passages, Green's letters transcription, Vivien Ingham's article on Anne's climbing Vignemale in the Pyrenees, and Ramsden's travel typescripts, notably the visit to Russia.[22] However, it is important to remember what Steidele *did* achieve. She read all the available secondary sources on Anne Lister; and hers is the only volume as yet to compress all of Anne's incredible life between one set of covers.

By the time Steidele's *Gentleman Jack* came out in 2018, the Anne Lister world was changing. All antennae were alerted to Sally Wainwright's television drama, to be aired the following spring. And the world of Lister research had changed out of all recognition too. Long gone were the days of reading the diaries on microfilm in the archives, then printing out grey-on-grey pages. Digitization had changed all that. Pages of the complete diaries (between four and five million words) were now available to download for anyone with a computer, anywhere across the world. And they did![23] WYAS's Anne Lister Codebreakers was a particularly significant innovation. The project was launched in July 2019, with volunteer transcribers from across the globe assigned diary pages. By May 2022, 1,250,000 words (1806–24) had been transcribed and made available online.[24] Alongside this, 'Packed with Potential', formed in late 2019 and entirely digital, encouraged participation from everyone passionate about Anne Lister.

Second was the extraordinary explosion of social media, notably on Facebook and Twitter. This has accelerated communication and conversations about everything Anne Lister. What is extraordinary is that an early nineteenth-century landowning lesbian should have almost overnight become a social media megastar. There are now at least fourteen Facebook pages, including ALBW Chat, Gentleman Jack Fans and The Hunt through History for Anne Lister and Ann Walker. I was a late convert to Twitter but now can receive a dozen Anne Lister tweets a day. So what had been a relatively quiet research space for Helena Whitbread, Cat Euler and myself in the 1990s has since 2019 suddenly witnessed an explosion of fans around the world who are gripped by the diaries.

However, does this social media explosion have a few downsides? Given Twitter's word limit, for instance, there are many very short diary tweets, often of coded passages. This can be brilliant, inspiring even more Anne Lister fans round the globe. Yet might it also be irksome for those who wish fully to understand Anne by placing her diary entries in their rich historical context?[25] Sally Wainwright gets this: *Gentleman Jack* series 2 is drenched in essential background detail: coalmining, canal shares, electioneering and wills. Last night I watched the final episode, listening with great interest to the dialogue between Captain Sutherland and lawyers in both Halifax and York.

*

Then came the 2020 lockdown, putting paid to most travel. For Anne Lister researchers, archival sources became divided between what was digitized (and so remained available) and what still required a visit to Calderdale Archives when they reopened.[26] Luckily for me, I had printed out from microfilm many diary pages from May 1836 onwards a quarter of a century earlier.

Summer 2020 proved difficult. Calderdale, like other northern local authorities, was placed under tighter lockdown restrictions. All in-person events were cancelled.[27] However, I now had more time to progress plans for this new Anne Lister 1836–38 volume. I was in touch with Manchester University Press, which had published my most recent book.[28] My mood soon lifted when I signed the MUP contract with my editor Emma Brennan in August, a moment all authors relish. All set fair again? The upside was getting more used to Zoom. I was interviewed from Baltimore on 'A History of Researching Anne Lister';[29] and I gave a Zoom talk to Sorbonne students in Paris on 'Anne Lister of Shibden Hall: Gender, Social Class and Sexuality'. That autumn, the downside was that many research locations remained closed. WYAS, open just one day a week, inevitably had long queues to book a place.[30] In December, some events for the following spring began to be planned. Then there was the third lockdown, and they too had to be cancelled.[31]

Mid-1836 to mid-1838 seemed to be the Anne Lister years that nobody wanted us to read about! John Lister, other than the 1837 election months, skimmed, as did Muriel Green. Phyllis Ramsden sadly published little, as this was not a period of Anne's great travels. And after *Gentleman Jack*, it is likely that Anne Lister fans glanced at Ramsden's stark summaries – 'more rows', 'widening rift' – and moved on to Vignemale and Russia. Another reason, I suggest, is that during these twenty-four months Anne remained largely rooted at Shibden: researchers who do not live near Halifax soon find themselves immersed in a quagmire of local place names. So here I aim to make accessible all this complex Halifax detail. For these two years are crucial to understanding the dynamics of Anne and Ann's marriage. And it is those dynamics that are the central theme of this book.

*

I began writing this book aware that so much had changed since *Female Fortune*. Here I highlight two differences. First, there were now so many fans around the globe doing research. As noted, most were not working on 1836–38, though a few were, especially the coded passages; and I have opted to include those that are significant to my Anne Lister narrative.[32]

Second, there has been a shift in the political and historical context. The Black Lives Matter movement has gained huge international attention since 2020. Alongside this, a major historical research project, the Legacies of British Slave-ownership, based at University College London, has compiled an invaluable database; and this compelling academic research attracted huge media interest.[33]

So did Anne Lister have any connection to the slave economy? There are no known links. In the UK, slavery activity was mainly concentrated in ports such as Bristol and Liverpool, as well as rural areas little touched by industrialization.[34] In contrast, Halifax had few slave trade links. With easy access to coal and canals, steam-powered industry was a much readier wealth-creator than slavery.[35] So Anne Lister and Ann Walker could live on rents from their farming tenancies, small stone quarries and even smaller coal mines. There were, however, connections through Ann Walker's Scottish brother-in-law. Captain Sutherland had inherited slaves in the Caribbean from his uncle. Thus, in 1834, on the sugar cane plantation on St Vincent island, he owned 289 slaves.[36]

*

Transcribing has proved daunting: Anne recorded in almost obsessive detail exactly how an army of men laboured at her estate improvements. As I wrote nearly forty years ago: 'some of the barrowing, channelling and culverting details are tedious to all but a landscape historian collecting data'.[37] Most readers would fervently agree. And the dense legal language can feel confusing. Yet we need her rich social and economic hinterland to know Anne Lister. Here, as in *Female Fortune*, good editing is a fine balance between what the reader wants to know and what they need to know, the trick being to let go of the rest!

Particularly after August 1837, with the General Election over, I felt like an intrepid explorer. It seemed that few others had really trodden here, even assiduous editors having left gaps.[38] So Anne Lister's tremendous achievements as a businesswoman long remained obscure. Yet this was when she was at her most adroit legally, her skills as a social operator most impressive, writing deftly to her elite women correspondents, assisting Ann Walker on business matters. She was at her most powerful from mid-1836 onwards, her marriage to Ann now embedded at Shibden. During these twenty-four months, Anne and Ann, almost entirely based at home, had the run of the house. This book explores whether (and if so, how) it was 'as good as a marriage' – in other words, as good as heterosexual marriages in the early nineteenth century.[39]

So, here we are! The diaries from 1836 onwards remain particularly challenging. They require a grasp of 1830s politics as early Chartism bubbled up, and of pre-Darwinian geology; familiarity with the Shibden estate and its tenants; with Ann Walker's sprawling Crow Nest estate and her complex kinship networks; plus the intimate psychology of a dissident lesbian marriage. This, of course, requires familiarity with Anne's secret code, to shine a uniquely powerful light on this key unorthodox relationship.

These original diaries may seem impenetrable to anyone new to Anne Lister or unfamiliar with Halifax. So here, both for *Gentleman*

Jack fans and expert historians, I aim to open up Anne's world at a time when she and Ann could enjoy their marriage on their own at Shibden, and when Anne was at her most powerful. The diaries record how, wherever Anne turned – whether to her relationship with Ann or her coalmining expansion – she came up against Ann's many relatives. They were often hostile, notably Christopher Rawson and William Priestley. She had to deploy all her piercingly sharp intelligence and extraordinarily broad expertise to maintain her superior position in the world. So what was uppermost in her mind day-to-day? Was it Ann or was it her own elite friends? Was it their marriage or was it embellishing Shibden and somehow sustaining the Listers' dynastic destiny? Did she (and if so, how) manage to 'maintain the upper hand'? Anne Lister's many fans would call her tactics deft, adroit and, towards Ann, loving and romantic. Her critics might name them manipulative, economical with the truth and possibly cruel, even at times towards Ann.

*

Nothing had prepared us for the global impact of Sally Wainwright's mega-drama. And again, nothing had prepared us, just nine months later, for the global devastation of COVID, causing untold deaths and altering how we experience the world. The effects of the epidemic were totally unsettling for some authors, with book events cancelled and school visits postponed; for others – including myself – the ensuing lockdown, while isolating and unsettling, did at least provide quiet months required for writing.[40]

This book is written especially for those who watched *Gentleman Jack* series 2 but have not necessarily read much about Anne Lister yet.[41] I was writing this preface in April 2021, just after the lockdown in England had eased. That afternoon I walked across our hillside to the local pub and sat outside in the sunshine to gaze across our wonderful Calder Valley, a stunning Pennine view. Never again would I take the ordinary for granted.

Then, in May 2022, I watched the last dramatic episode of *Gentleman Jack* on BBC1, followed immediately by a torrent of tweets from fans demanding another series about Anne and Ann:

'Please PLEASE continue their story.'[42] With *As Good as a Marriage*, I hope I offer readers just that.

When feeling despondent during lockdown, I sometimes asked myself 'how would Anne Lister have coped?' Always energetic and resourceful, she was no stranger to plague times. We meet her now in the middle of the 1831–32 cholera epidemic.

Jill Liddington
30 May 2022

INTRODUCTION

ANNE LISTER AND ANN WALKER 1832–34: WOOING, SEDUCING, MARRYING

Anne Lister spent the winter of 1831–32 in Hastings on the south coast. Here she set up house with the well-connected Vere Hobart, elderly Lady Stuart's great-niece (whom Anne had earlier escorted to Paris).[1] However, 1831–32 were also years when cholera stalked the land. It particularly ravaged the lives of people in congested cities where working-class housing lacked access to clean water. Yet down in healthy Hastings, Anne escaped, though kept abreast of local cholera news. She wrote to her aunt at Shibden that 'people are full of the subject – some talk of barricading themselves in their houses'. Not so Anne, always an indefatigable walker. She added: 'to me such a remedy would be almost as bad as the disease. I should at least die of vapours if I could not get out. I have had some very pretty country walks.'[2] However, her old friend Mrs Norcliffe wrote from York to tell Anne in that small yet congested city, cholera 'now attacks a more respectable set of people ... the bookseller's wife ... the school mistress's daughter ... the spirit merchant ... are among the 127 already dead. People are afraid to venture to York.'[3]

However, the epidemic remained four miles from Halifax.[4] Indeed, it was not cholera that drove Anne back home in spring 1832. It was a personal tragedy. She found herself betrayed by yet another woman's conventional marriage plans. First, Mariana Belcombe (M~ in the diaries) had married a wealthy older man, Charles Lawton. This was probably the bitterest disappointment for Anne, with Charles showing little sign of dying. And Vere Hobart now married too, becoming Lady Cameron.

So, in May 1832, her exciting travels behind her, Anne made her forlorn way back to Shibden. She knew her romantic youth was over, as one by one her women friends had opted for hetero-sexual marriage. And unlike most other women, she had no extended family and scarcely any immediate family to confide in and rely on for support.

Compared to the houses of her elite women friends, Shibden now seemed old-fashioned and even shabby. Her family was equally dispiriting. Her elderly ex-soldier father shambled around rather than running the estate effectively. Her younger sister Marian was particularly irritating. Arguments flared. As in any impecunious landed family, these were often about inheritance. Irksomely, Marian was far more likely than her unorthodox sister to enter a conventional marriage that produced an heir. It was only Anne's loving aunt who possessed a deep understanding of her talented niece, even if Aunt Anne could not put the unconventionality into words.

To keep melancholy at bay, Anne retreated to Shibden's well-stocked library. She began reading: French and geology, theology and travel, gardening books plus the journalism of the day. She could spend whole days in the library. However, as a woman with an indomitable will, Anne soon renewed her commanding energies. She would remodel herself from high-society flirt and European traveller into respected inheritor of Shibden's ancient acres. She would redesign its old-fashioned patchwork of small fields into an elegant country park.[5] She might have a shorter purse than her grand friends, but she soon started work on that part of the estate immediately visible from the Hall. Yet one vital ingredient was still missing.

Jane Austen's *Pride and Prejudice* (1813) has an unforgettable opening. Two decades later, Anne could well have subtly adapted Austen's words to her own purposes: 'It is a truth universally acknowledged that a single woman in need of a good fortune must be in want of a wife.' Yet Anne had returned home empty-handed. Moreover, she was saddled with a predatory reputation, both among Halifax friends with long memories and among her elite social circle in York. She would need to proceed with care. To her advantage, Shibden, hidden from prying eyes down in Halifax, provided a comparatively safe rural space. And in July 1832 a chance reacquaintance with a neighbouring heiress, Ann Walker of Lightcliffe, changed her life forever.

*

So, what was Ann Walker's story? She lived a fairly isolated life, her parents dying when she was 19. Her older sister Elizabeth planned to marry a Captain Sutherland of the 92nd Highlanders. Her uncle, Henry Edwards, grimly warned Elizabeth that 'Captain S~ has no fortune' and added 'Captain S~ is a perfect stranger to us'. Yet, in November 1828, she did marry the captain, and was whisked up to distant Udale in northern Scotland; here their daughter Mary was born the following year.[6] Captain Sutherland, as it turned out, was not without fortune: he had inherited from his uncle, who died in 1828, properties in the Caribbean. The St Vincent island estates had sugar cane plantations worked by slaves, and were highly profitable. Captain Sutherland dropped vague but plausible allusions to Scottish money. However, it seems very unlikely that Elizabeth knew of this source of family wealth, and certainly Ann Walker did not.[7]

The Walker family was wealthier than the Listers, even if theirs was 'new money' rather than ancient acres. And in 1830, after the tragic death of their brother John, sisters Ann Walker and Elizabeth Sutherland unexpectedly each inherited half of the family's vast Crow Nest estate in Lightcliffe. Overnight, the wealth of the two sisters expanded enormously. This meant that Ann now owned land stretching far, far wider than the more compact Shibden estate; and, as we shall soon see, her tenants yielded much greater rentals.

So, in 1832, Ann was living on her own, with her servants, at Lidgate, a medium-sized house on the edge of Crow Nest estate. Aged 29, Ann was twelve years younger than Anne Lister. She might have inherited unexpected wealth, yet she possessed neither

Anne's impressive intellectual self-confidence nor her business acumen. Lonely and isolated, with just her elderly aunt for company, she had money but not the means to enjoy it.[8] So the prospect of friendship with the enthralling Anne Lister was enticing. It could introduce lonely Ann into elite society, well beyond her family's mercantile origins. And for Anne Lister, Ann might be 'new money' but it was at least money. All that was needed was deft courtship and wooing, something at which she was so practised.

*

Shibden's land sloped from the Hall down to Red Beck, beyond which lay Lightcliffe (see map p. 8). Anne's plans to redesign the ancient pocket-handkerchief fields into a 'landscape of desire' included making an elegant walk. Half-way down, Anne would now build a *chaumière* or 'moss hut'. It would be out of sight from the prying eyes both of Anne's own family, and Ann Walker's inconvenient relatives – such as the Rawsons down in Halifax, who knew Anne's reputation of old. The secluded moss hut would surely provide a conveniently intimate female space for courtship.

Anne set about wooing and seducing with impressive energy. However, while she was certain of her own sexuality and its God-given nature, Ann was much more conventional and was wracked by religious guilt. Yet Anne was coolly persistent and persuasive. She wrote all the details of the courtship in her diary, mainly of course in her secret code. So, on Thursday 27 September 1832, Anne set off early (7.30 a.m.) to Lidgate for a lengthy visit to Miss Walker. Then in the afternoon:

> We were off for her to see my walk... Sauntered ... rested in the hut & must have sat there a couple of hours...

> Dinner at 7 ... then wrote the above of today. *Miss W~ & I very cozy & confidential... She sat & sat in the moss house, hardly liking to move. Of course I made myself agreeable, & I think she already likes me even more than she herself is aware...*

> *I really did feel rather in love with her in the hut, & as we returned. I shall pay due court for the next few months... 'Well', said I to myself as I left her,*

'She is more in for it than she thinks – she likes me certainly.' We laughed at the idea of the talk our going abroad would [stir]. She said it would be as good as a marriage. 'Yes' said [I], quite as good or better.'

However, some of Ann Walker's many relatives began to be suspicious. Later on the very same day, when Mrs Stansfield Rawson, mother of Ann's friend Catherine, called at Lidgate, Anne recorded in her diary: *'Mrs Stansfield Rawson looked odd on find me there.'*[9] Likewise, and living very near Lidgate, were Ann's older cousin William Priestley and his wife Eliza. Eliza and Anne Lister had been friendly, but now Eliza became watchful. One afternoon in October 1832 she surprised Anne and Ann while they were kissing passionately at Lidgate. Anne wrote afterwards: *'I had jumped in time ... but Ann looked red and I pale, and Mrs P~ ... looked vexed, jealous and annoyed.'*[10] Suspicions were not helped by William Priestley being a trustee, appointed under Ann's father's will. John Walker's 48-page will also appointed his brother-in-law, Henry Edwards of Pye Nest, as the other trustee: both men were to look after the interests of the daughters, protecting them against unscrupulous fortune-hunting suitors.

So, in September 1832, Anne Lister, courting Ann Walker, recognized that Ann would have to be isolated from these troublemakers; she was pleased to note of the Edwards and the Walkers, *'I see there will be no cordiality again between them; this will not suit me the less well.'*[11] However, in spring 1834, as the courtship and seduction progressed to betrothal and marriage, escaping proved easier said than done. Both trustees, cousin William Priestley and uncle Henry Edwards, continued to be vigilant – to Anne's irritation.[12]

Anne was not one to be deterred.[13] By then she had not only persuaded herself that Ann should be her 'life companion', but she had also charmed and beguiled vulnerable Ann to commit to the relationship. Indeed, on 10 February, in bed together, 'our union' seemed settled, despite Ann's suspicious relatives and her own feelings of guilt:

She was ... by and by roused up & during a long grubbling said often we had never done it so well before. I was hot to washing-tub wetness... We talked & never slept till five... [I said she had] *better make up her mind at once, or what could I do? She agreed it was understood that she was to consider herself as having nobody to please, & being under no authority, but mine... Well, then, is it really settled or not?*[14]

Their marriage did seem reasonably settled for both Anne and Ann. They would each rewrite their wills, leaving the other woman a life interest in their own estate. And by 12 February the betrothal seemed agreed: '*She is to give me a ring & I her one, in token of our union as confirmed on Monday.*' Indeed, in York on Easter Sunday, 30 March:

Three kisses – better to her than to me... At Goodramgate church at 10.35; Miss W~ and I and Thomas [servant] staid [for] the sacrament... *The first time I ever joined Miss W~ in my prayers – I had prayed that our union might be happy – she had not thought of doing as much for me.*[15]

Ann Walker's hesitancy can be understood. Criticisms of the newly wed couple already circulated. Old friends such as the Norcliffes, whose Langton estate lay the other side of York, knew Anne Lister's seductive skills of old – and were cynical about Ann Walker. '*They said she was crazy.*' However, Anne adroitly, if slightly cynically, countered this by murmuring '*two fortunes are better than one*'.[16]

So, in September, Ann Walker moved into Shibden to share the home with Anne and the Lister family. Ann now seemed to feel confident about this move: she let her Lidgate house and land on a ten-year lease to a tenant, Mr Lamplugh Hird.[17] Indeed, other than regular dutiful visits to her elderly aunt living nearby at Cliff Hill, Ann had left Crow Nest for Shibden Hall and the Listers. Yet her extended family – the Priestleys, the Rawsons and the Edwards – felt they should keep a watchful eye on what Anne Lister might be planning and plotting up at Shibden. It might be a marriage for Anne and even Ann, but it was of course a 'marriage' recognized by neither Church nor state, nor indeed by society.

So, from the 1832 courtship and seduction, and the 1834 betrothal and marriage, followed shortly by Ann Walker's moving to live at Shibden, Anne Lister's social landscape expanded locally – first east out to Lightcliffe, and then west beyond Sowerby.

PEOPLE AND PLACES: THE SHIBDEN AND CROW NEST ESTATES

Anne Lister's Shibden estate was compact, encircling the Hall. It was also extremely well documented. Along with her own diaries and accounts, her efficient land steward Samuel Washington was also systematic, compiling an 'Estate Summary 1833'. And this allows the reader to walk the land with Anne and eavesdrop on the conversations she held with tenants. They were mainly small-time farmers, amplifying their income with, say, stone quarrying. At the top of steep Southowram Bank above Halifax lived John Bottomley and his family, a small farmer who had to renew his lease every year (see Map I). Then along the road immediately above Shibden, the reader passes Thomas Greenwood, who was both farmer and cabinet-maker. Further down was Charles Howarth, a farmer and joiner; in 1832 Anne got him to build the moss hut for her below Shibden Hall. Opposite lived John Oates, a self-taught man who had a tiny primitive coal pit nearby; Anne valued his opinion on mining.[18]

Further down this road, immediately below Shibden, lay Mytholm on Red Beck. Here, conveniently out of sight of Shibden's windows, were the badlands, with rural-industrial tenancies. Here, her tenant George Robinson had a small water-powered wire mill, wire being used for card-making for wool processing.[19] Also at Mytholm stood Jonathan Mallinson's Stag's Head pub. A well-placed inn on the edge of Shibden land was acceptable; but when Anne heard that he had allowed 'the [stone] Masons' and Delvers' Union fortnightly meetings at his house', she visited the Stag's Head and made it plain that he must 'give up the meetings or leave the house'.[20] The Mallinsons chose the safer option.

High up on the Southowram hillside above the Hall itself lay Marsh; the profitable extractive industry here was stone quarrying, mainly small-time quarriers. Samuel Freeman's well-situated

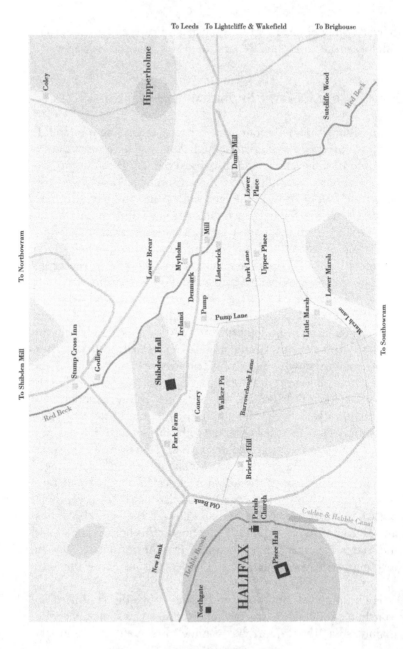

Map I Halifax and Shibden, based on Myers' map of the Parish of Halifax, 1834–35

quarrying business made him a key stone merchant. Moreover, he was a reliable 'Blue' voter, so Anne preferred to negotiate with Freeman about buying stone than with the truculent 'Yellow' Samuel Sowden on the eastern edge of her estate.[21]

So the Shibden estate could be easily walked by a woman as energetic as Anne. The only outlying property of any significance was Northgate House in the centre of rapidly expanding Halifax. And Anne, cannily observant of Halifax's rising land prices, began to plot and plan.

*

The difference between Anne Lister's Shibden estate and Ann Walker's Crow Nest estate could not be more dramatic. Yes, both centred on key buildings. The core of the Crow Nest estate were the two key Lightcliffe houses, Cliff Hill and Crow Nest, plus the land surrounding them. However, Shibden was built in the early fifteenth century, while Crow Nest dated back only to 1788. Secondly, the Crow Nest land holdings stretched far beyond Lightcliffe: north-east up towards Queensbury; south-east down towards Brighouse; north-west past Hipperholme and then curving up the beautiful Shibden valley, plus significant properties in Halifax. Also, dramatically far-flung, Ann had inherited land out west above Elland, climbing up into the Pennines, to the old townships of Stainland and Greetland (see Map II). The final difference between the Shibden and Crow Nest properties was that, unlike Shibden, the Crow Nest estate is very poorly and patchily documented, at least for the 1830s – despite their employing the same trusted land steward, Samuel Washington.[22]

Particularly after September 1834 when Ann Walker moved from her Lidgate home and into Shibden, Anne Lister was on a steep learning curve about the dimensions and complexities of Ann's lucrative estate. Anne was no slouch when it came to financial calculations, her mental arithmetic abilities being phenomenal. So, her diaries offer considerable detail of Ann's estate business dealings, always helped of course by Washington. Ann's tenanted land was, like Shibden, predominantly agriculture, often combined with stone quarrying and small-scale coalmining. It also included

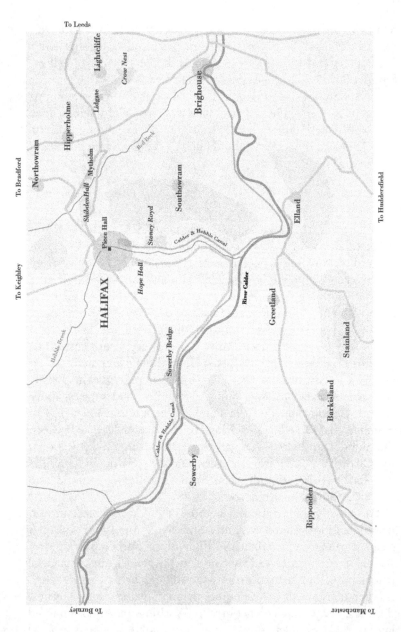

Map II Crow Nest estate: Lightcliffe to Stainland, based on Myers' map of the Parish of Halifax, 1834–35

textile mills and manufacture, plus urban rented properties, both industrial and domestic, in Hipperholme and Halifax. Owning both coal mines and textile mills, Ann encountered male rivalries just as Anne did. The difference was that, in the case of the Rawsons' mines, she was related to these men. And, unlike Anne, she did not thrive on the cut-and-thrust of entrepreneurial competition.

*

So here, as with the walk round Shibden in *Female Fortune*, I offer a quick tour round the Crow Nest estate.[23] Starting with the properties lying nearest to Crow Nest itself, they form a fairly compact yet large circle (see Map II).[24] Attractive Lidgate House, Ann's home until September 1834, stood in its own grounds on the road from Hipperholme to Lightcliffe. After Ann moved into Shibden, it was rented to Lamplugh Hird for ten years, which suggests that she did not plan to return. Further along, New House was home to William Priestley and his wife Eliza. And stretching off towards Brighouse are the elegant carriage roads leading to Crow Nest itself and to Cliff Hill, both now guarded by lodges on the road.[25] Additionally, there were a dozen farms, and a few pubs, including The Travellers and Sun Inn opposite the church. Most of the remaining property were cottages and terraced houses in Hipperholme itself.

Stretching up to the north-east corner of Northowram township, Crow Nest holdings reached towards Queensbury. Here, at Bouldshaw and Shugden, small-scale coalmining added to the property value. Lower down in Northowram township, at Shibden Mill in Shibden valley itself, Widow Bottomley lived with her sons, and paid a sizeable rent (£72.5.0d), plus smaller amounts including coal rent at £15. This earlier water-powered mill had been used for wool scribbling and carding, a good example of a modestly profitable traditional rural enterprise.[26]

Moving into Halifax town itself, Ann also owned rows of small cottages, including at Hatters Fold next to the Piece Hall, the tenants' rents being modest but often sufficient to give them a vote.[27] And at the edge of town, at Shaw Syke, William Throp ran his nursery: here Anne Lister bought her plants and shrubs. Throp was always politically deferential towards her and the Blue interest: at the 1835 election, 'he promised to use what influence he might have with non-promisers [i.e. undecided voters] to get them to vote for Wortley'. Given that the canal had arrived only recently, this part of town was expanding significantly, with eagle-eyed opportunists circling avidly.[28]

However, probably most surprising is that Crow Nest estate extended about six miles south-west of Halifax, into the steep Pennine hillsides high above Elland (see Map II). Up around Stainland, Ann owned various modest-sized properties. Why? With land and timber plentiful, plus access to a swift-running river, the potential for water-powered economic development was significant; and from the mid-1820s, transport improved with a new turnpike road. These properties might be far-flung, yet such tenants needed regular visiting, both Samuel Washington's routine estate monitoring, and of course, at election time, for Ann to check that her enfranchised tenants were voting in the 'Blue' interest.

Of particular fascination to Anne Lister was Benjamin Outram, an innovative wool entrepreneur. His mill lay alongside Black Brook, in the valley below Stainland. In November 1835 Anne recorded that Outram visited Shibden 'to shew us his lama-hair shawl and cloak pieces. He seems an ingenious man. Had him in our little dining-room to take wine... I bought £7.10s worth... I told him his prices should have been set higher for the London market. He has 2,000 yards ready.'[29] This was a time for which Ann Walker's own diary has survived, and she also recorded the visit, noting that 'he had a long conversation with drt [dearest] about introducing his things in town'. At this point, when Ann had been living at Shibden for about a year, it is unclear if Anne was aware that he was one of Ann's many tenants.[30] However, Anne noted that – more unusually – Outram was a scientist: he observed 'many of Sir Issac Newton's discoveries not sufficiently followed up', piquing her curiosity further. So, when Mariana Lawton visited Shibden in 1836, what better countryside tour was there than a visit up to Stainland, including a shopping trip to the intriguing Mr Outram?

ANNE LISTER AND ANN WALKER 1835–36: FIRST YEARS OF MARRIAGE

Ann Walker was now living with Anne Lister at Shibden. Yet her family networks were not neglected; and when formal social visits were made by carriage, Anne would accompany Ann. And it seems that, for Anne and Ann, while this round of calls always included a visit to the Edwards family at Pye Nest, it was formal rather than friendly.[31] Likewise Anne, and especially Ann, would call regularly and dutifully on elderly aunt Ann Walker at Cliff Hill (though no longer the neighbouring William Priestleys). However, the friendliest visits were to the various Priestley households on the hillsides beyond Sowerby.

Particular favourites of Anne's were Major Henry Priestley and his wife Mary, who lived at elegant Haugh End near Sowerby. Their house, alongside dignified stables, servants' quarters and warehouses, boasted enviable views over the Ryburn valley. For Anne, this friendship stretched back a long way, for Mary was related to Mariana Lawton. So Anne's first visits were with Mariana, and now with Ann. Anne enjoyed many pleasant visits to Haugh End.[32] It offered a good (if rare) example of a happy heterosexual marriage.

By contrast, the Rawson brothers' multiple commercial interests placed them on the very margins of Tory respectability for Anne.[33] So when W. H. Rawson's wife, Anne's cousin Mary, called at Shibden with her two daughters, Anne and Ann 'were civil but rather stately', the visit lasting a mere twenty minutes. As always, the exception was elections, when Anne noticed how the Edwards and the Rawsons, notably William Henry, were very usefully 'making a great many votes' for the 'Blue' candidate.[34]

Ann Walker now shared Shibden with Anne's elderly father, her younger sister Marian and her loving aunt. Anne had referred to her relationship with Ann as 'our union', both at the betrothal in February 1834 and at Goodramgate church that Easter. Was it, as far as they understood, a lesbian marriage? Well, yes. Yet of course, theirs had to be a purely private ceremony. Additionally, some of Ann's extensive kin, notably William Priestley and Christopher Rawson, grew increasingly suspicious of Anne's designs on heiress Ann and her money.

By 1835, with 'our union now settled' and so with less need for wooing and seduction, the diaries become less sexually charged, with fewer lines in Anne's secret code. Her relationship secured, Anne now became more outward-facing, looking to improve Shibden and to influence Halifax politics. Ever proactive when the situation demanded, by January 1835 she was less focused on practical estate work and more on political imperatives, given that a General Election loomed. As well as the vast West Riding constituency, Halifax now had the right to elect two MPs of its own. With both Anne and especially Ann owning property in the town, they counted up their enfranchised tenants.

As might be expected, the Blues – Anne Lister and Ann Walker's relatives, notably the Rawsons – all set to work to increase support for the Tory candidate, James Stuart Wortley. As women, Anne and Ann might not have the parliamentary vote; but with no secret ballot yet, that mattered little. Both women began actively persuading their tenants to vote for the Blue candidates – in both the Halifax and West Riding constituencies. Indeed, resolute Anne Lister informed one tenant that: 'I had made up my mind to take none but blue tenants'; and if not, 'I must try to change [their minds] myself'.[35]

By dint of such coercive tactics, Wortley won Halifax by just a single vote. He was elected, along with a Whig for the town's other seat. The Whigs were absolutely furious that Wortley had scraped into Parliament by these decidedly dubious means. This was not how Anne Lister saw it. On 7 January, her letter to her friend Lady Vere Cameron was revealing: 'What a hard run race!' she wrote, adding 'the town is in sad turmoil'. This was an understatement. In the destruction that ensued, Christopher Rawson's carriage was broken up, and the two front doors of the vicarage were smashed. Indeed, it became known as the 'window-breaking election'.[36]

Were Anne and Ann, hidden away up at Shibden out of sight of the town, protected from the turmoil below? Well, only for a few days. On Saturday 10 January, trusted land steward Samuel Washington arrived. He hesitatingly produced the *Leeds Mercury* with its marriage announcements: 'At the Parish Church, Halifax,

Captain Tom Lister of Shibden Hall to Miss Ann Walker, late of Lidgate.' This was a direct personal attack on their relationship; yet Anne maintained her elite woman's sang-froid. However, Ann, always thinner skinned, '*did not like the joke*'. Then it got worse. The *Halifax Guardian* reprinted this malicious 'mock marriage' announcement, feeding more local gossip. And an anonymous letter arrived at Shibden, directed to 'Captain Lister'. It stated: 'we beg to congratulate the parties on their happy connection'. Anne confided to her diary: '*A~ did not like the joke – suspects the* [Whigs] *– so does my aunt.*' It was aimed to humiliate, and Anne found Ann in tears.[37]

Was the aim of their political enemies publicly to 'out' this lesbian couple? Possibly. But more probably the main motive was political. The West Riding Whigs were appalled by the coercive electoral tactics of these two 'Blue' women landowners. It seems that these Whig grandees were mocking the unorthodox (though not illegal) relationship to warn off Anne and Ann from taking such an active role in future elections. So how effective was this public lampooning? Readers must wait for the 1837 election to find out.

*

Did this barbed humiliation dissuade Anne and Ann from showing their relationship in public in Halifax? Apparently not. Anne had inherited elegant Northgate House in the town centre (see figure 2). She decided to exploit the economic potential of this well-positioned property, so convenient for the Manchester–Leeds carriage trade. Ambitious to turn it into a hotel, she needed to obtain a licence. So, just three months after the 'mock marriage' jibe, Anne visited her Halifax lawyer, Robert Parker, who advised her to get the local magistrates on her side.[38] Christopher Rawson? No! Too tricky. He might be the leading magistrate, but he was also related to Ann, as well as being a bitter rival over their adjoining coal mines.

Anne never wasted time. Soon, an old-fashioned Tory country magistrate, a Mr Dearden, visited Shibden. With symbolic cordiality,

2 Northgate House, Halifax, 1779

he was offered wine and sandwiches, 'both of us <u>very</u> civil to each other'. When Anne showed him her ambitious Northgate plans, Dearden seemed delighted. Anne told him: 'A good Inn and large handsome rooms were much wanted [in the town] ... I had a pride in the thing.' It would be a casino.[39] Dearden assured her of his support and of that of his son. However, he did ask her for a subscription for the Wortley election. Anne laughed: 'Well! If you will secure me the licence, I will put my name down for £50', then a sizeable sum. 'Yes!' he replied. Later, a note arrived from Dearden, requesting that she use her influence with her enfranchised tenants in the West Riding constituency.[40] That was how business was then done.

Within months, a licence was granted. The building would be renamed the Northgate Hotel. The foundation stone would soon be laid, in full public view. What form of ceremony would be appropriate? With the 'mock marriage' lampooning only eight months behind them, Anne and Ann courageously decided that the ceremony would represent public acknowledgement of the solidity of their relationship. Indeed, Ann herself would formally lay the foundation stone. Jonathan Gray, their York lawyer who was then visiting, even *wrote a speech for A~ to make to Mr Nelson, the master builder*.[41]

After breakfast on 26 September, the two women prepared: *'A~ getting off her speech for the first stone-laying and I writing mine – put on my new pelisse and had my hair done.'* Marian planned to attend the ceremony; but, as her sister noted tersely, she 'got nervous and staid at home'. Nevertheless, Anne and Ann set off by carriage 'with our two men behind'. At Northgate, a crowd of about a hundred had gathered. Ann opened the proceedings: 'Mr Nelson, I have been requested by my friend, Miss Lister, to lay the 1st stone of a Casino...' Anne Lister's speech then enlarged on this theme: 'Mr Nelson, my friend Miss Walker had done us a great honour... I am very anxious that this Casino with its annexed Hotel should be an accommodation ... [in] this my native town in whose prosperity I have ever felt, and shall ever feel, deeply interested.' At the end, some people gave three cheers and the two women hurried back into their carriage. The ceremonial wording, also written by Jonathan Gray and recorded in Anne's diary, was slightly more revealing: 'The first stone of a spacious Casino ... was laid ... by Miss Ann Walker ... at the request of her particular friend, Miss Anne Lister of Shibden Hall.'[42] They then drove to Cliff Hill, where the Sutherlands were visiting. Here Ann showed her sister the casino inscription: 'Mrs Sutherland seemed pleased – in short, we are capital friends.' So, within Halifax and immediate family, all seemed fine.

That is probably as far as Anne and Ann could go in public, deploying polite conventional ceremony and language. However, why had Marian stayed at home? And how reconciled now was Ann to the realities of their relationship? Anne's diary suggested reservations: *'Attempted a kiss last night. A~'s manner leading to it, but she called out in the middle of it that she was too weak and I stopped immediately.*[43] Nevertheless, the Northgate ceremony helped embed a public respectability for Anne and Ann's relationship. Anne Lister had won this round.

*

General Elections happened only every few years, and stone-laying ceremonies even less frequently. By contrast, industrial activity on the Shibden estate remained a constant background thrum. Financially, the two women had become more intimately entwined. Anne was now aided by access to Ann's considerable income stream. For instance, Ann loaned Anne £1,000, and there were regular small gifts of money.[44] This helped progress Anne's coalmining ambitions. First, Walker pit (named in honour of Ann), standing high above Shibden, was, despite inevitable drainage problems, finally sunk in June 1835. However, a persistent problem was its closeness to the Rawsons' Swan Bank pits down by the canal. Anne remained suspicions about what they were up to. By 1836 there was talk of trespassing underground, though that was hard for Anne to prove. Instead, she began a whispering campaign against Christopher Rawson (his brother had after all married one of Ann's cousins).[45] The coalmining rivalry grew bitterly intense and even more complex.

The arrival of the canal extension right into Halifax meant that the economic value of local land rose, prompting dodgy business deals. It all focused on an unprepossessing strip of land called Bailey Hall, where the canal ended. Just to the east of Hebble brook, this strip stretched from the Parish Church, along the foot of the steep Southowram hillside, past the Rawsons' Swan Bank mine, to congested rows of terraced housing called Caddy Fields (see Map III). This unpromising strip of land had been purchased by the Walkers of Crow Nest in 1786. Within a couple of generations, its 1,300 acres supported no fewer than six mills, ten crofts (small agricultural holdings) and ten stables, rented out to a variety of tenants. Then, in 1831, after the death of Ann's brother John, it was inherited by Captain Sutherland and his wife Elizabeth,

Ann's sister.[46] (The mid-1830s might have been a challenging time financially for the Sutherland family. After the abolition of slavery in 1833, reparations were paid to former slave owners. Reparation documents indicate that in 1834 the Sutherlands' two estates on St Vincent island owned approximately 530 slaves, half male, half female, for which they were entitled to claim compensation. However, it seems that Captain Sutherland may not received any compensation, the money claimed going mainly to creditors and lawyers.)[47]

Back to Halifax: the following year, September 1835, this Bailey Hall land seemingly passed from the Sutherlands to 'the said Ann Walker herein described of Cliff Hill ... Spinster', adding 'to the use of the said Ann Walker her heirs and assigns for ever', with the Sutherlands surrendering their claim.[48] The wheels of property law transactions grind slow. However, eventually, on 24 March 1836, the deed was officially registered at Wakefield. Some tenancy details were recorded; for instance 46 Bailey Hall was occupied by a Matthew Paterson, and included 'houses, dyehouses, mill, engine, warehouse, two dwelling-houses, barn, gardens, yards', plus eleven acres of land.[49]

Such legal language is arcane and the property transactions complex. But the nub here seems to be that this increasingly strategically situated land continued to rise in value year on year. And for some reason, possibly because it was industrial rather than the more elegant rural part of the Crow Nest estate, the Sutherlands apparently wished to pass it to Ann – who did at least live much nearer than Udale.[50]

So, certainly from March 1836, Ann owned the Bailey Hall land. This included Water Lane mill down by the Hebble brook. This mill, right by the canal, lay immediately below Christopher Rawson's elegant Hope Hall, near his brother Jeremiah's house, and immediately opposite their mother, the elderly Mrs Rawson's Stoney Royd estate. Indeed, the Rawsons might claim to own this part of Halifax, where industry met country, near the canal and lawless badlands, the terrace-house slum of Caddy Field. Map III shows Hope House (centre), and below it, Water Lane which runs down to the canal and river – beyond which the edge of Caddy Fields housing is just visible.

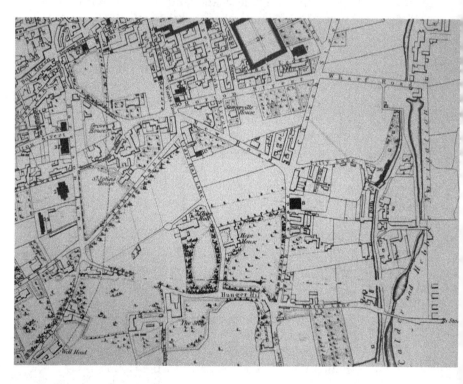

Map III James Day's map of Halifax, 1835 (detail)

3 Hope Hall, Halifax, home of Christopher Rawson, John Horner, 1835

Local tongues already wagged about Anne's recently accelerated economic activity. How exactly was she funding it? And was it really appropriate for Anne Lister, through her unorthodox relationship with Ann Walker, to have any material interest in Water Lane mill? The tension erupted obliquely yet very dramatically in early March 1836. Damage had been done to a well next to Water Lane. Was this well owned by Ann Walker or was it a public well? After the recent cholera epidemic, public access to fresh water had risen high up the political agenda in urban areas such as Halifax. If it could be proven that it was hers, poisoning this well would turn opinion against Ann – especially for those critical of her intimacy with Anne, notably Christopher Rawson. On Thursday 24 March Anne recorded in her diary that 'we both agreed A~ was ill-used by Mr Rawson ... it was a spite against [her]. Rawson irritated against me about the coal.'

Here was a golden opportunity for Christopher Rawson to deploy righteous rhetoric from the magistrates' bench.[51] This industrial-personal melodrama quickly came to a head. As so often happened, news from down in Halifax soon made its way up to

Shibden. On Sunday 27 March Joseph Mann, Anne's master miner, arrived. Very unusually, he stayed for 1½ hours. Anne's diary is revealing:

> Had the coal plan down… [Christopher] Rawson now stealing my upper-bed [coal]… Joseph Mann to get what information he could about A~'s Water-Lane well – some hope of proving that Mr Rawson set the people on, & treated them to the rum-tea-drinking. The tea-drinking last Monday, he thinks it was – and the people burnt A~ & me in effigy, he thinks it was last Tuesday. Strange piece of business on the part of Mr Rawson.[52]

This was surely a considerable understatement, given that Rawson was both a magistrate and deputy lieutenant of the county. The melodramatic tale was repeated when they visited Ann's aunt at Cliff Hill: 'I told the story of Mr Rawson & his mob – tea-drinkers with 12 pints of rum in their tea, & did not spare him.' After they got home, Joseph Mann again arrived, now with new hearsay gossip about the well-poisoning and effigy-burning. Joseph 'says they burn A~ & me in effigy on Tuesday… Rawson and Stocks [another rival coal owner] [have] cottages in Caddy-town.'[53] Had Christopher Rawson's tirades and whipping up the mob with rum worked? Did it mean that Anne and Ann were now effectively warned off their coalmining expansion? Or could they, owning the land in question, just continue as before? We will see.

Anne remained seemingly unperturbed, keeping her gaze well above these 'Caddy town' melodramatic rumours. She thrived on this whirligig of industrial rivalry and underground espionage against Rawson. Not so the sensitive Ann, more the butt of public accusations. Later that day, Anne noted that after they got home from Cliff Hill: '*A~ very low all today & begins to look wretchedly & will hardly take wine, fearing to take too much.*' By Thursday 31 March Anne was writing: '*No kiss.* [A~] *got up at six saying prayers and crying as for several mornings past.*' This melancholy mood continued into April: '*A~ so low and in tears… Really I know not how it will end. At this rate I must give* [her] *up – she is getting worse.*'[54] In the sense of destabilizing their relationship, Christopher Rawson had been effective. A mocking newspaper announcement within the first two years of their marriage was bad enough. But surely reportedly being burned in effigy was far more terrifying?

*

Meanwhile, the ups and downs of family life at Shibden continued. On Sunday 3 April Anne's elderly father died very peacefully ('death could not have come more gently, more easily', she noted). It was, however, her birthday, and she added: 'a melancholy birthday today!' Yet it was Anne – rather than Marian – who made business-like arrangements for their father's formal funeral at Halifax Parish Church. It was a sobering time.

On Wednesday 4 May Anne again recorded philosophically in her diary:

> *No kiss. A~ very low – had been crying for over an hour… 'Well' thought I to myself, 'I will do the best I can. Her being with me will not be forever. If we can get on together, travelling or what not, for a year or two till my own affairs are rather more settled, I can arrange things well enough. Heaven will order this matter, as all others – that is, for the best.'*[55]

Anne could always reassure herself that Heaven – and her own Anglican certainties – would order such matters 'for the best'. Meanwhile, just a month after their father's death, on Tuesday 10 May, Marian left to go and live at Market Weighton in the East Riding, where her mother's family had property.[56] Had she actually been banished by her elder sister? Or did she no longer feel welcome at Shibden without her father there? With her aunt virtually bed-ridden, Anne and Ann had full run of the house and estate at last.

Note on the Text

Anne Lister's diaries run to just under five million words.[1] Roughly one sixth was written in her secret code. The journals start as brief schoolgirl diaries in 1806, growing to their fullest in the late 1830s. In addition, there are also other key archival sources for 1836–38. Most important are Anne's letters, here written to her titled women friends. She used her correspondence as we might use Facebook or Twitter: to present an outward-facing persona to the elite world. Because these 1836–38 letters are so revealing of Anne, I have quoted from them more generously than in *Female Fortune*.[2] The other significant source, given that Anne's life was now intimately entwined with Ann Walker's, is of course the Crow Nest papers. Their quagmire of detail can be riveting. However, they also present the editor with huge frustrations, notably their substantial archival gaps.[3] So, the late 1830s diaries present a stupendous editorial challenge.

As Anne matured, and particularly after she returned to Shibden in 1832 and grew more powerful, so her daily journal entries lengthened. From the point when *Female Fortune* opens in December 1833, Anne wrote nearly half a million words over the following two and a half years.[4] And from when *As Good as a Marriage* begins in May 1836, and for the next two years to May 1838, Anne's daily diary entries grow even longer. Over these two years she wrote roughly half a million words. Hence Anne's diary writing grew from about 500 to at least 650 words per day, giving the transcriber an even more daunting task. *Female Fortune* selected roughly 10 per cent of the 1833–36 diaries. *As Good as a Marriage* is a longer book, and so I offer slightly fuller extracts, approximately 150 words per day.[5]

The other slight shift from *Female Fortune* is that the passages written in code occur less frequently. The wooing, seducing and marrying had all been settled. The coded passages here mainly record the pleasures and vicissitudes of a clandestine lesbian marriage in 1830s Yorkshire. As yet we do not have Ann's diary volume for these years.[6] So of course, what we hear most clearly is the confident voice of the dynamic Anne Lister, rather than the softer tones of the more conventional Ann Walker. *She* understandably still had qualms about moving from her family home into Shibden. Sexual activity was less frequent. In 1836 Anne's most repeated coded words were, perhaps rather glumly: '*No kiss*'. I have retained these coded words as they remind us what Anne was *thinking*, if not actually doing. Other passages in code include Mariana's visit to Shibden in November 1836, and the triangular relationship between the three women. The coded passages *do* record intimate sexual and romantic moments, but also the tensions and arguments between Anne and Ann, though these were often made up soon after. I have retained almost all of these, reflecting the title *As Good as a Marriage*.

As before, I have often relied on the signposts left by earlier editors, from John Lister onwards; yet, as we know, they do leave large gaps. And, despite the social media explosion since *Gentleman Jack*, most of these gaps remain, and these I have aimed to fill.[7]

From May 1836 to May 1838, Anne was essentially rooted at Shibden, her hopes for wider travels deferred. This has some real advantages for an editor, particularly if they live locally and know Halifax's geography and political landscape. However, with Anne now writing slightly more each day than previously, much of what her diaries record consists of arcane details of work to improve her estate. Anne recorded every boulder shifted, every tree planted, or pit sinking negotiated. This was directed by skilled men, with the hard work carried out by nameless labourers, represented just as '+ 2' or '+ 4'. It was a world of male muscle and one-horse carts. I have been ruthless in cutting this dispiriting data, assuming that if it does not interest me, it probably will not interest readers.[8]

Anne's business and banking dealings often grew dismayingly complex, and I have exercised a firm editorial hand here too. Other repetitive details omitted include some of Anne's prodigious reading.[9] Where material has been omitted this is indicated by ellipses.[10] As in *Female Fortune*, where omissions are significant, these are recorded in the notes. References have also been kept to a minimum, mainly to indicate archival sources or to suggest other possible interpretations. Square brackets in the text are used to indicate that a word or phrase has been inserted to aid clarity.

As in *Female Fortune*, I want to present here a coherent narrative thread, reflecting the central theme of 1836–38, 'as good as a marriage'. As well as the relationship between Anne and Ann, also key is how the local community (notably Ann's extensive family network) perceived this clandestine marriage.[11] To grasp this, we need to know their cultural landscape: who was who, and what were their social, economic and political interests. So, from this key intimacy, the narrative broadens to include a wide cast of relatives and friends, tenants and the many others who relied upon Anne and Ann for part of their livelihood; and the many *Gentleman Jack* fans will know that Sally Wainwright did this too.[12]

Transcribing the diaries remains extremely challenging. Anne's own handwriting often presents far more difficulty than the coded passages, partly because it is so very heavily abbreviated. For instance, there are many place names, incomprehensible to a new reader, which she shortened.[13] So, her abbreviations have been extended: 'H-x' is written as 'Halifax'; and their land agent 'Mr S. W.' is written as 'Mr Samuel Washington'. Anne's informal punctuation includes frequent dashes, and her style has been broadly retained. However, to enhance clarity, some punctuation has been added, with major breaks in subject matter indicated by a new sentence or paragraph.

I want the text to be as accessible as possible to the general reader. So how Anne recorded the time has been modernized (e.g. 3.25/″ is shown as 3.25).[14] I have, however, retained 'A~' for Ann Walker and 'M~' for Mariana Lawton, to remind us – as Anne constantly did – that these were her two most intimate relationships: part-sexual, part-emotional, part-friendship (over

4 Anne Lister diary page, 30–31 May 1836

many years in Mariana's case). I also wanted to preserve a sense of distance – of time past, over 180 years. For Anne's world was not our world, and can only be understood from this perspective. Thus I have retained many of her spellings (for example, 'shew' rather than 'show').

As in *Female Fortune*, the origin and status of sections of text are indicated by distinct typefaces. So, passages from the diaries are indented and prefaced in bold by the year and month, plus the date and day of the week. Coded passages are distinguished by being printed in italics. Passages written by people other than Anne Lister (for example, Crow Nest documents) are without indentation. And my editorial introductory and linking passages are distinctive from the rest of the text by being printed in bold. As these diaries are often so complex and obscure, I have added my editorial voice to guide readers, both to clarify what Anne wrote and also to signpost diary entries coming up that are particularly opaque.

Finally, so that readers may make best sense of this enticing yet dense material, I present the 1836–38 diaries in eleven broad chronological chapters, each reflecting the most significant theme for those months: Anne's dynastic ambitions for Shibden; her energetic coalmining; her political strategizing at elections; her prodigious reading and exotic travel plans; her correspondence with elite women friends, notably the aristocratic Stuarts; and, of course, living her marriage to Ann, with the Walker relatives encircling Shibden. All these themes are interwoven into the main narrative. Readers, now is the time to plunge into Anne's magnificent diaries. I hope you enjoy them.

THE ANNE LISTER DIARIES

I

LIVING MARRIED LIFE AT SHIBDEN

MAY–AUGUST 1836

MAY 1836

After the death of her elderly father and with her inconvenient sister Marian now gone from Shibden, Anne's only remaining relative was her much-loved aunt. Almost bed-ridden now, Aunt Anne's most frequent visitor was the family doctor, Mr Jubb. Meanwhile, across at Cliff Hill, Ann Walker's own elderly aunt also needed regular visits.

Anne and Ann now had the run of Shibden.[1] Like other settled couples, there were evening rituals: Ann 'did her French', Anne skimmed the newspaper. She also continued her remarkably impressive reading: everything from the Roman Empire and travel to cutting-edge geology and current politics. On Sundays, Anne and Ann read prayers to Aunt Anne. Then in the afternoon they attended Lightcliffe church, before visiting Cliff Hill. Additionally, Anne was still busy with estate work while Ann remained preoccupied with her school. So their day-to-day pattern of life together was now well established: shared activities, plus separate daytime tasks, adopting often recognizably masculine and feminine roles.[2]

WEDNESDAY 11 *No kiss*... A~ & I siding [i.e. arranging] in the house... Dinner at 7 – coffee – with my aunt – siding [in] the cellar, removing the port, sherry, madeira, Bucellas, & old raisin wine into the old oak-cupboard...[3] Tea at 10.30 – sat talking near an hour – very fine day.

SUNDAY 15 *No kiss*... She & I read prayers to my aunt at 12... I then was burning old Northgate account books & bills till 5.[4]

Meanwhile, Anne was starting to discover how distant lay some of Ann's properties, almost ten miles from Shibden. Travelling up steep winding roads into the Pennines, a routine estate visit might take two days. Of these tenants, Anne found the most interesting remained Benjamin Outram, who had earlier visited Shibden with his 'lama-hair shawl and cloak pieces'. Now the business concerned altering his tenancy agreement.

MONDAY 16. *No kiss*... Mr Washington came at 9... Mr W~ & George in the rumble [i.e. seated behind the carriage] & A~ & I in the carriage (the brown one), & off at 9.45 to make the round of A~'s Stainland property. Went first to Mr Outram's – had wine & sandwiches & oranges.[5] Looked at cloak & shawl pieces & walked over the land. Went all along the line of present [agreement], and that of proposed, goit. A~ made no objection to ... their long rigmarole ... thought it had best be shortened ... to which Outram agreed. And all went on well. 2¼ hours there – too long, considering what we had to do.[6] Then walked up the hill to where we had left the carriage waiting (in the high road) & walked back to [another tenant's] house, built in A~'s uncle's time...[7]

Up here, Samuel Washington seemed to know these winding country roads, for they never got lost (see Map II). Then it was a short drive down to:

Beestonley, Charles Law's – looks like a thriving tradesman, & a <u>neat</u> farmer... We then drove to Moulson Place (Levi Sykes)... Levi S~ wants A~ to mend the road to the house – why should she? Not her business – it must be the township that should mend it...

A~ very much tired. About an hour at Moulson Place – drove off to bait [i.e. feed] the horses & men. At 5.30 stopt at the Royal Oak, a little public house by the roadside... A~ laid down on a bed upstairs & I sat by her about an hour. She & I & Samuel Washington then ... off home at 7, and returned by Ainley top & Elland (Mr S Washington left us at Elland bridge end) & Halifax, & [we] got back at 8.55.[8]

This Stainland trip vividly illustrated the outer limits of Ann's estate.[9] A second trip was soon needed to complete the business.

Meanwhile, Anne received a significant loan (£4,000) through her lawyer Robert Parker from Mr Wainhouse, Halifax textile manufacturer.[10] This would certainly help finance her more ambitious plans for improving Shibden.

TUESDAY 17 *No kiss*... Down Old Bank to Mr Parker's office – he said he had had the £4,000 since the 13th... Signed the bond dated the 13th inst for £4,000 at 4¼ per cent to Mr Wainhouse... A~ to sign the Bouldshaw [Northowram tenancy] coal-lease... From Mr Parker's went to the Bank ... paid into the bank £3,850 & left my banking book to be settled.

In addition to stone and coal, wood was a key industrial component. Moulson Wood up near Stainland had valuable firs and larches.

WEDNESDAY 18 *No kiss*... A~ & I off at 7.25 on the ponies, & George on the gray, to Moulson [Wood] to meet Mr William Keighley... Rode thro' Halifax & turned off soon after Salterhebble as before... Off from Moulson Place at 2, & in ½ hour at Hard Platts, Joseph Taylor's... A~ pleased to see her wood looks so well after a bit of thinning.

THURSDAY 19 *No kiss*... A~ off on her pony to Cliff Hill ... [I], finding my aunt in the garden & very well, called Frank to help us (to push forward the wheel-chair) & got my aunt as far as the Lodge. She was wheeled into the high road, to see all sides of the Lodge, & then was wheeled into the barn & saddle room, & looked about her, & seemed to enjoy her peregrination, & was not at all tired...

Yet while Aunt Anne enjoyed looking round Shibden, higher up on the estate the bitter coal rivalry rumbled on. There was now not just friction with the Rawsons but also with Lightcliffe coal merchant Hinscliffe.[11]

Joseph Mann met us. They had holed this afternoon [i.e. had cut through] the whole coal (lower bed) into the hollow on the way towards the trespass made by Hinscliffe & Co & Messrs Rawson.

FRIDAY 20 *No kiss*... At 12, A~ set off by herself to Conery to speak to Matty [Pollard] about a washerwoman, & I went with Holt... All going on well – the coal holed yesterday afternoon. About 60 yards length to get up to Mr Rawson – should do about 6 yards in a week (i.e. day & night) & that as fast as they could.

SATURDAY 21 *No kiss*... To meer... A~ came to us [David Booth, her clerk-of-works, Mr Husband and John Oates] & we remained till 2. *She is too low to like to be without me, so came rather than be alone.*

Ann Walker sometimes felt lonely when Anne strode off with others on estate business, and so sometimes accompanied her. Such work conversations tended to be short, for Anne was highly efficient at managing her land. Nevertheless, all these complexities pressed upon her, made yet more tricky by their much-talked-of travel plans. These would impact on the household during their absence, and Anne confided a heartfelt plea to her diary:

> **TUESDAY 24** *No kiss...* Oh! That I could be in all places & have eyes everywhere at once, just for a few months or a year to come! ...
>
> Came in about 12.30 – with A~, with Mrs Briggs who had been dusting books in little parlour cupboards. Desired the books be put back again till I could place them upstairs. Miss Briggs will take charge of dusting my library... [To] get new servants on our return from abroad. I do not like this – why not have a comfortable proper establishment to return to?[12]

Ann and even Anne experienced melancholy. Would travel ('getting off') cure their lowness?[13] Meanwhile, Anne kept low spirits at bay with hyperactivity at Shibden. Her plans included complex financing of ambitious estate improvements plus coalmining, while suspecting that Washington was a 'sneaking man sort of man'.

> **WEDNESDAY 25** Out at 11 ... Holt & Samuel Washington measuring... S. W.'s excuses lame – said it would be shewn now when the colliery was opened & when we got up to Rawsons. 'Yes!' said I, 'but who is to pay me...?'
>
> Read ... my aunt's letter to Marian... Finished my letter to M~, begun on Friday. *Punctuated A~'s letter to her sister...*

While Ann was at Cliff Hill, Anne was increasingly sustained by her correspondence. She found particular solace in writing to Mariana.[14] This intimate letter was emotionally honest:

> Said she would see how I was subject to interruptions – begged [her] ... to be assured of my steady friendship & regard... Thought to be off for Paris last Saturday week – unsettled again as ever – nothing fixed. M~ to believe nothing till she hears it from <u>me</u>. Too much on my hands – 'one thing drags on another'. Can't explain clearly on paper. 'Come & see [me] whenever you like, but not just yet unless you give me a few days' warning.' Household troubles – 'the late dynasty did not make the rough places plain'.[15] Only 2 women servants – 'a

cook who can't cook or wash & a kitchen girl in her teens to do her own work, & housemaid's work. And I have got the widow of my [late] steward Mr Briggs to keep house, & her daughter to take care of her. Can you help us?' Does M~ know of a housekeeper? ... [We] shall be off as soon as we can... Mrs Briggs not having lived in a gentleman's house, does not know how to set us up. M~ to tell us 'how much beer should the men be allowed at breakfast, dinner & supper, and how much the women [be allowed] of tea, & sugar & butter & heaven knows what. Again, God bless you! I wish I had all knowledge. Teas, sugars, water-wheels, hotels & collieries – all crowd together in my poor brain. Oh! For a goodly cadeau of the Jardin des Plantes at Paris, or some Alpine pass, or balcony breeze upon the Aegean wave! Oh! That I could fly away for a little while & be as rest! My favourite wanderings would be rest to me... I hope to [send] date to you from the other side of the water [i.e. Channel?] – be it when or where it may, I shall always be, with unchangeable sincerity, very faithfully & especially yours A.L~.' I told her ... of my aunt's being amazingly well, & of her being wheeled ½ a mile from the house.

Anne poured out her frustrations and yearnings to Mariana, thinking of where the two of them might have been, perhaps able to give her feelings freer rein because Ann was away.

THURSDAY 26 A~ at Cliff Hill. *Incurred a cross thinking of M~ just before eight.* Fine morning... Talking to Oddy ... to be cook eventually? ... A~ here from 12 to 1.30... Undecided about staying at Cliff Hill ... [I said] charity begins at home. A~ should take care of herself. Decided her to be here to dine tomorrow & return to her aunt on Sunday after church & be home again on Tuesday to dine. [She] *half repenting her purchase* [of expensive Lower Crow Nest] *because she must borrow the money...* Told A~ we must go over to York again & settle all with Mr Gray. A~ must republish her will. A~ off at 1.30 to Cliff Hill again, to be in time for her aunt's dinner at 2.

Did 'decided her' hark back to the betrothal, when Ann had agreed 'she was ... under no authority but mine' so that Anne could now make all decisions in their marriage? [16] While it was easy to say charity began 'at home', could Ann be quite sure any more where 'home' really was: Shibden or Crow Nest? [17] And, given that Anne currently entertained more erotic thoughts of Mariana than of Ann, did reminders of that relationship strengthen Anne's sense of her own 'authority' in the marriage?

FRIDAY 27 A~ at Cliff Hill. *Incurred a cross at seven thinking of M~*. Very fine morning F54° at 8.35...

[Out and] sauntered towards home. Met A~ returning from Cliff Hill, coming in at the gate at 5.15 & then with her – dinner at 6.15 – coffee. She did her French as usual. She had Mr Washington at 9 for ½ hour... Agreed to send to the bank the 1st thing tomorrow morning, & send George over to Crow Nest with the money.[18] *A~ wrong about* [it] *– not in a good temper ever since her return this afternoon. And my getting forty five pounds of hers to pay Joseph Mann did her no good. Poor soul – her mind is not very large. And shall we split up on* [i.e. over] *money matters at last? Well, be it so. I shall get on well without her.*

Ann Walker remained plagued by both her expensive land purchase, and by a much smaller payment to Anne's master miner. Again, they fell out over money, with Ann getting 'wrong about it', and Anne sounding patronizing about the smallness of her mind.

Transactions such as Ann's land purchase went through local lawyer Robert Parker, as did political imperatives. For it is clear that, since the 1835 'window-breaking' election, protest continued to rumble on in Halifax. Disillusionment with the 1832 Reform Act grew, along with political grievances against the new Poor Law. In London, a Working Men's Association was planned, a sign of early Chartism. As always, when political unrest threatened, an order would go out for all local gentlemen to be sworn in as special constables.[19]

SATURDAY 28 *No kiss*... Came in about 12 to Mr Washington – he had received the £1,000 in Bank of England bills ... for the Lower Crow Nest estate [purchase]. He also brought me a note he had in his pocket, & should have delivered last night (from Mr Parker), to say John [Booth] & Frank [Day] & Joseph Mann should be at the magistrates' office not later than 12 today. It was 12 ... when I received the note. Told Washington he was not a person to send notes by – annoyed more particularly as he did not ... even say he was sorry. But [I] took it very well, & set off, then called [on] John & Frank & went after Joseph Mann – found his son ... sent him ... to send his father off... Told Frank's wife not to leave the place till I had got somebody else there...

Came in to A~ at 2 and with her 1½ hours till she rode off to Cliff Hill... Dinner at 6.30 – coffee. [I] had too much cider (¾ bottle) & slept till near 9.[20] Read the newspaper – with my aunt ½ hour till 10.05 – very fine day F48° now at 10.10. John Booth & Frank Day & Joseph [Mann] sworn in [as] special constables this morning, or rather afternoon – though [they had] not [arrived] at the magistrates' room till 1 or after, they had still, they said, a long while to wait.

Brooking no delay, Anne had speedily rounded up her three men, in the face of growing political unrest. And in Halifax, Radicals were critical of the magistrates, who would direct special constables to maintain law and order. Anne had every political reason in the world to want to be seen as a patriotic defender of the country, as would virtually every member of the landed gentry, other than the Radical Michael Stocks.[21]

SUNDAY 29. *No kiss...* A~ & I read prayers to my aunt in bed, & Oddy & George in about 25 minutes. Then sat with A~, low at going away for the next 3 days & irresolute [i.e. indecisive] about fixing a day for going to York to arrange with Mr Gray about the purchase made of [Lower Crow Nest]. Said off-hand as we drove to church, 'Shall I go to York while you are at Cliff Hill & settle the matter?' The manner of [her] answering 'I don't know' struck [me]. I said no more on the subject but turned it over rapidly in my own mind, & as I drove home decided to go. Mr Wilkinson ... preached 28 mins... I was asleep almost all the while...

An hour at Cliff Hill – [I] talked the whole time to Mrs A. Walker... Left A~ [there], home in 20 mins at 6.35. Poor A~ low – would rather have returned with me?

Poor Ann indeed, who perhaps already suspected how canny Anne was concerning her property.

Dinner at 7 – coffee. Letter (3 pages & ends) from M~, Leamington – good about helping me get a housekeeper ... thought of me gone abroad... Packing till 11.30pm.

So Anne set off for York by herself, picking up Cookson *en route*.

MONDAY 30 A~ at Cliff Hill... Preparing to get ready to go to York. Pick up Cookson at Leeds. To York... Dr Belcombe came ... gave formula for pills (especially good for A~). And on my mentioning her *irregularity, advised her taking twelve drops of tincture of cantharides in a little cold water twice a day, ten or twelve days before monsieur* [i.e. her period] *ought to come.* Much talk about Paris & French morals etc. Thought A~ & I should not get off till after the 11th of July...[22] A~ had much to gain from a warmer climate... Read ... last *Quarterly Review* ... [on] geology while Cookson curled & brushed my hair.

TUESDAY 31 *Incurred a cross after seven, thinking of A~, and her probable excitement on taking the cantharides.*[23]

The tone of Anne's second letter to Mariana had now shifted more towards Ann Walker.

Read over my letter to M~. 'It would be difficult to tell you my plans... All I know is that I should like to be off about the 11th of July... I know my wanderings are not over – there are many places faraway I wish & hope to see... Adney likes travelling as much as I do... [I] would be willing to give £30 a year to a good housekeeper ... £16 to a cook who would do without kitchen-maid... John Booth the only man to be left in the house, 'cowhand & gardener & fetcher-of-things from Halifax'. 'George is our footman & travelling servant, & a clever out-of-doors ... grooms, & cleans the carriages. There is certainly a degree of hugger-mugger about all this that I do not like... Marian is gone to Market Weighton – I have had no influence with her – she acts on her own judgement not mine – I have been grieved & mortified & annoyed [by her]. But there is a time for all things, & I have driven the subject from my mind...'

So, even to Mariana, Anne wrote disingenuously about what had gone amiss with her sister. Otherwise, the letter was a cool discussion of servant arrangements, plus Anne's desire to continue 'my wanderings', this time with Ann. Meanwhile, Anne had considerable complex legal business to transact in York:

Mr Gray ... explained about A~'s purchase [of Lower Crow Nest] estate... Gray had observed that in the Election business for [local candidates], Messrs Parker & Adam sent in a very high bill – while some, in the true spirit of toryism, charged as little as they could, giving their trouble for the good of the cause... After Mr Gray went away, wrote the above of today...

Anne's York conversations were particularly complex, because of course Dr Belcombe was Mariana's brother.

Just named [i.e. mentioned] to Dr Belcombe, that M~ & her friends were about organizing an establishment 'for the Training [of] Servants', & were for buying some building for the purpose... Gave no hint ... of M~'s ... going to be [financially] risked, & charged Dr Belcombe not to appear to know anything on the subject of the proposed establishment. He thought my advice to M~ very good, & shook his head, & said he did not like speculation. *He brought the half-ounce of tincture of cantharides for A~...*

York was *the* city for the best lawyers and doctors. So here, Anne got a good deal of business done, including about Ann's tenants.

Left with Mr Gray A~'s copy of a long rigmarole agreement about Outram's lease... Gray said his son had had a letter ... in which A~ said (by the way) that Mr Rawson, having now settled about his banking concern, would attend to the business of Gray's client (meaning myself). I said Gray's letter had answered all the purpose I wished, i.e. had stopt the Assafortida burning.[24] Commented a little on the banking concern – said it was perhaps not very creditable to Rawson – no people of property had joined, merely small tradesmen had been content to enter the concern... But if there was a failure, these small people would be ruined, but the general & great commerce of the town would not be stopt.

I went to the post, my letter to M~, Leamington... Changed my dress at 1.45 – off from the George Inn, York at 2.30. Home at 7.25 – tea at 7.45 – with my aunt till 9.30.

So while talking to Gray, Anne finessed her whispering campaign against Rawson's underground trespassing (with asafoetida burning) plus his doubtful banking initiative. She might be away in York, miles from Halifax, but Anne still managed to pursue her strategic goals. The Rawsons should not forget this!

JUNE 1836

Back home, Anne Lister was impatient to progress her ambitious building work, both at Northgate and also landscaping above Shibden Hall. Eminent architect John Harper oversaw her expensive plans and offered professional advice.

WEDNESDAY 1 A~ back at 11.10 from Cliff Hill... Mr Jubb came about 2 – thinks my aunt going on very well... Took A~ out to the Rockwork, the meer & about. Mr Harper set out the terrace wall – mentioned what I wished doing – temporary brewhouse & laundry... [Says I] can build a mill to use up my (spare) 15 horse-power for £1,000. The west tower was ordered... I may say the total = £1,000, this & what is doing out-of-doors & the colliery expense are quite enough...

A~ impatient – came to her at 6.30 – read her letter to her sister & to Mr Gray (both which she sent this evening), enclosing in the latter the agreement for [Lower Crow Nest] estate – begged Mr Gray to have all ready by 1 August... Dinner at 6.45 – coffee. I went out from 8 to 9 – at the Lodge, cascade bridge & about. Found A~ with my aunt.

So while Anne oversaw her estate improvements with Mr Harper, it was Ann who kept Aunt Anne company. At night, Anne saw that all was not well:

THURSDAY 2 *No kiss. A~ very low – I heard her crying but took no notice – did not seem to awake till eight. Thought I, 'we must be off'. Kept her in bed talking gently. She took two pills last* [night]... Breakfast... A~ cut out night-things [i.e. night-clothes] for me, & I out at 11.45... Told [Booth] I should have 15 horse-power to spare – to get me a good tenant [for a mill] – to get to know what I could let power for at Listerwick. He agreed [if] it was worth £20 a year per horse[-power] at Halifax, it should be worth £15 here. Harper thought £800 would built a good mill for 15 horse-power...

Home at 2.30 – A~ & I dressed. Mr Musgrave came at 3.25 & staid ½ hour – administered the sacrament to my aunt, A~, myself, Oddy, Cookson, Rachel Sharp & George. A~ & I then re-changed our dress & went out...

Despite all Anne's estate work, her travel plans had not been forgotten:

Letter to Hammersley's [London bankers] ... postpone leaving home for 5–6 weeks longer... 'I shall also be much obliged if you would be so good as [to] get my passport signed by the Saxon minister [i.e. ambassador?]...' A~ did her French... Looking over my clothes – sorting out things for the journey – with my aunt 25 minutes...

I see we must get off from home as soon as we can – immediately after the rent day. A~'s first rent day 11 July. Can we get off on the 13th? Think today it would be well to steam it from Hull to Hamburg & then post it (of course, [in] our own carriage) to Berlin, Dresden, Toplitz, Carlsbad, to Vienna etc., home by Paris. *On going to bed found my cousin was come gently.*

Significantly, the key date was Ann Walker's rent day, not Anne's. The Crow Nest rentals would help finance such an ambitious European tour. However, had Ann now grasped Anne's calculations?

FRIDAY 3 *No kiss. A~ <u>very low</u>...* Read Watt on 'Joint Stock Banking'.

SATURDAY 4 *No kiss. A~ not quite so low as yesterday or the day before...*[1] Took A~ out with me at 8.15 to Robert [Mann] + 4 ... at farmyard entrance doors ... [A~] to go on her pony to Cliff Hill... Dinner at 6.20 – coffee – A~ did her French. Came upstairs at 8, & wrote the whole of this page... *A terribly* [low] *all today.* Looking over Journal of 1833 till 9.45. Note tonight from the Halifax Philosophy Society – paper to be read on Monday 'on the phenomenon of Solar Eclipses'.[2]

SUNDAY 5 *No kiss. Is she rather better this morning?...* A~ & I read prayers to my aunt, & Oddy & Cookson & George at 11.25 in 32 minutes. With A~ at her luncheon. At the school in 25 minutes at 2.20 – 40 minutes there, hearing the children [say] their catechism. I took the first class as usual.[3] Mr Wilkinson did all the duty – heard the boys their catechism in 10 minutes – preached 19 mins from John iii. I thinking of other things – whether to hurry off immediately to Paris, & be back to for the rent day – leave the carriage all the while in London – from London to Calais by steam[boat] – thence by diligence [i.e. public stage-coach] – [or] from London to Hamburg by steam. Anxious to get A~ off.

An hour at Cliff Hill... Home at 6.25 – dinner at 7 – ten minutes with my aunt (A~ & I) till 8, then coffee – siding. Letter tonight from M~, 3 pages & ends – kind letter – has written about a cook-housekeeper after all. Thinking it best, on considering that A~ & I are not likely to settle at home for some years to come, & the fewer servants we leave behind the better... No wine or spirits allowed in the housekeeper's room.[4]

Letter also from Messrs Hammersleys... The Russian embassy declines signing my passport without having the names of my servants – & says I had better get my passport on entering the territories of Russia. Yes! Good! But they shall sign it here, if giving the names of my servants will satisfy the people.[5]

MONDAY 6 No kiss... Had Mr Husband at 9 – mentioned ... the temporary laundry. Breakfast at 9.15. *A~ terribly low, did a little French while I breakfasted. All in vain – could not stop her tears. What shall I do with her? We must get off. At this moment she is lying down – what a miserable thing it is.*

Had just written so far of today at 10.55 – then wrote & sent by George to Messrs Whitley & Booth, Booksellers etc Halifax: 'Miss

Lister will be obliged to Mr Booth to bind … Bakewell's *Geology*,[6] & Taylor's *Roman Empire*, & the German Grammar in very strong material, half-binding (leaves not much cut). All to be done by the evening of this day week…'

This extravagant expenditure partly reflected Anne's preparation for European travel, and partly her thirst for intellectual stimulation, whatever the cost.

With A~ at luncheon… *Found her at luncheon fretting at having taken more wine after I left her. Always harping on its being wrong for her to eat & drink. Afraid she shall drink. In good truth, I am afraid so too. But I do not own it. I have put her to bed. She will sleep, I hope. The fact is, she has had three or four glasses, & so much is too much. Poor thing. What waste of happiness. What will become of her? We must get off.*

TUESDAY 7 *No kiss. But a very* [good] *attempt at play last night, & grubbling this morning – she owning it was not that she disliked it, or that she did not like me, but she thought it wrong. I did not say much, but we should both be better* [if] *I could bring monsieur again.*[7] *It will end in our getting together again?*

Meanwhile, they both were progressing their estate plans. Samuel Washington came to speak to Anne about 'the coal plan'. Meanwhile, Ann, whose Crow Nest estate included three pubs, thought about another public house on the road down to Brighouse.

Sat with A~ at her luncheon – she off on horseback at 4 … to Cliff Hill, & I out… Had the Halifax agent of the Bowling iron works, and paid him for iron work for the Casino [i.e. Northgate] floor.[8]

Anne was adept at absorbing male expertise when needed. She consulted a man 'who well understands mills' about valuing her horsepower:

WEDNESDAY 8 [He] said … I might value mine at Listerwick at £22 if constant (if water enough) … asked if the situation was a good one for getting hands [i.e. labour]. I said I could have cottages enough – there would be a little village at Listerwick on account of the colliery. Why not? The village & mill & colliery will be far enough from here? Holt values A~'s Shibden mill coal at housefire coal [prices] £140 per acre…[9]

Meanwhile, life at Shibden now meant enjoying expensive wines and spending more time with Anne's aunt.[10]

42

Ordered from wine merchant in York 3 dozen port, 2 dozen sherry & 2 dozen marsala... Dinner at 6.25 – coffee – A~ did her French – from 8.45 to 10.15 with my aunt. A~ skimmed the newspaper, I looked over & sorted loose copies of business letters.

THURSDAY 9 *A~ bad as ever. Stood about three-quarters hour talking to her before I was washed. She frets over my laying out so much money here for* [i.e. from] *her – with the impression she has on her mind that we shall never be blessed together.*[11] *She said she should never be happy with me – she dared not. Of course, I said this* [problem] *might be got over any time. She had only to order horses – go any time she liked. But I said she was foolish. Why could she not wait till I myself could get off abroad & leave her.*[12] *'Oh I can wait', she answered. Much more passed, but I took it quietly. The fact is, she wants to leave me. Well, be it so. I must only think of my own concerns & do the best I can for myself. I shall see about her. Perhaps it is all for the best. I shall be at liberty again by & by. I will not trouble my head much about her but suit my own convenience...*

This was a stark contrast to Anne's hopes two years earlier for 'our union'. Was it too much to ask a lonely young woman like Ann to move away from home to live with a woman so focused on her own ambitious plans? This, combined with Ann's sexual guilt, might surely reduce the chances of a loving relationship working smoothly.[13]

Breakfast at 9. Poor A~ sorry – all made up again. But how will it all end? Poor thing, she is under my finger & thumb. I must do the best I can, but never depend upon her...

Down Old Bank ... to the bank – got £50 & a check [i.e. cheque] ... Mentioned the talk of [a local] exchange. If ever a good plan proposed & any of my ground proposed [i.e. Northgate], I would help the thing forward as far as I prudently could; but I would never put, or have put, an ugly building on any part of my land. Principle people for the exchange are the proprietors of the new assembly rooms... I said, 'let there be only what the trading [i.e. business] interest requires, & then the exchange might be accomplished'. Mentioned the Paris exchange as being, under proper modifications, a good model for us. Then to Mr Parker's office – saw Mr Adam.

Clearly, Anne, now finding herself at the centre of significant commercial plans in Halifax, strategized, wanting to burnish her own reputation before she set off, including useful French name-dropping.[14]

SUNDAY 12 *No kiss...* A~ & I read prayers... Off to the school at 2.10 – I sat in the carriage 25 mins, while A~ was at the school... Cookson & Oddy walked to Lightcliffe church (1ˢᵗ time) & sat behind, Mr Samuel Washington having given Mr Hird notice that I should now want the pew.[15] A~ & I an hour at Cliff Hill.

TUESDAY 14 *No kiss. Thought we should have had one last night – got her to come to me, but then she said it was too hot & begged off & thanked me for giving up!* ... A~ had just had Mrs Waterhouse & Mrs John Edwards for ¼ hour – all very civil.[16]

WEDNESDAY 15 *No kiss...* Then siding in the hall chamber – burnt 3 old account books belonging to my (great) uncle Japhet.

These old Northgate House account books were unwelcome reminders of the earlier Listers' closeness to manufacturing.[17] Meanwhile, Anne's improvements to Shibden were now taking place on a fairly lavish scale, and included a West Tower and battlements in Norman style. Architect John Harper was by now a key player across Yorkshire.[18]

THURSDAY 16 *No kiss...* [Major] Norcliffe's house not finished. Charlotte Norcliffe still there ... house alterations – Mr Harper engaged... Set off at 4 with A~ to Spa House [in Northowram]... Saw A~'s tenant Mrs Wilson – very poorly – weakness. A~ recommended sheep's foot, stewed down to jelly, & promised a bottle of currant wine – the poor woman.

This was a classic example of a landowner caring about the deserving poor. Meanwhile, coal was now rising in value.

FRIDAY 17 *No kiss...* At the Lodge, Mr Husband & Mallinson there – only 2 [stone-]hewers – the cornice done all 1 or 2 pieces but waiting for 50 foot of stone for the battlement...

With A~ putting her deeds in the tin boxes, & sat with her at luncheon. Had Holt between 3 & 4 for ½ hour – all going on well... Mr Rawson has bid 500 guineas for [coal up at Marsh]... Holt has not agreed for Mr Walker Priestley's coal – Walker Priestley wants £180 per acre for both beds.[19]

SATURDAY 18 *No kiss...* Up Pump Lane to [Little Marsh]... Widow of his son Thomas [Hall] fretting... I would ask A~ to let her [daughter] go to Knowle Top school [Lightcliffe] – [she was] much obliged...

Again, this suggests Anne's sympathy for tenants fallen on hard times. Up at Marsh, her miners were above Swan Bank, and thus well positioned above the Rawsons.

> Towards the top of the hill – [they] have been 3 weeks & 2 days doing this = 20 days in doing 25 yards. In about 3 weeks more we shall be at the turn round 'the nook' & by Xmas shall know whether Rawson has trespassed or not.
>
> A~ & I talked over the establishment [i.e. household] – George wanted to speak to me – afraid he was all wrong [i.e. unhappy] & that it would end in his giving warning [i.e resignation]. Had him in my study above ½ hour – agreeably surprised to find not much the matter. *He thought it right to tell me Mrs Briggs had been crying at dinner & Miss B~ fretting to see her mother fret – because Miss Walker spoke to her, Mrs Briggs, in such a way she could not bear it. Would leave at an hour's warning, but her own house not ready. I was silent a moment or two, then gently said this was not the right way for Mrs Briggs to go on. It was at least unlucky* [i.e. unfortunate?]. *All* [a] *mistake. Nobody kinder in reality than A~. Said I could take no notice of what George told* [me], *but could easily set all right if Mrs B~ spoke to me. I much obliged to her etc. Poor George saw that there was no good* [i.e. nothing] *to be done against A~. But I see they all dislike her. A~ came to me –* [I] *turned all off very nicely & all seemed satisfied.*

Here Anne was adroit in managing household relationships. It was challenging because Marian, previously responsible for domestic affairs, had left only six weeks before. Anne loyally defended Ann Walker, but saw that the servants did not like her. Her first loyalty at Shibden was to Ann, though this could be tricky.

SUNDAY 19 *A's cousin come last night on her going to bed. No kiss…* Read the Footman's guide that came from Whitley's last night…

Then Anne's painstakingly precise arithmetic offers an invaluable shaft of light on housekeeping:

> Looking over Mrs Briggs's book… My aunt paid Marian £80 per annum. A~ & I paid £144. £224 [divided by] 52 [weeks] = £4.6.1… *A~ on the sofa asleep ever since coming upstairs. Low, so gave* [her] *three & a quarter glasses of wine, she nothing loth & this quietened her.*

Given that this was almost a bottle of wine, did Anne wish to get Ann drunk? Nevertheless, the next day they took a long circular walk around part of Ann's estate, ending up in Halifax:

MONDAY 20 *No kiss...* To Water Lane mill... A~ said [tenant] Bairstow must be the person to prevent the mill people above from throwing more ashes into the brook. Bairstow or Bray or the person actually in possession of the mill (whichever of them it might legally be) must get the blacksmith out of the little shop under the end of the mill next [to] the road... The (Rawson) tea-drinking women declare they will pull the [mill's] engine boiler down as soon as it is built up. They (Mr Rawson at their head?) claim the bit of ground the blacksmith's shop stands on as waste [i.e. common land].

So, in the Halifax badlands, the well-poisoning and effigy-burning melodrama of three months earlier still rumbled on. Here, country met town, ancient met modern – with a vengeance! For steam power (and so engines and boilers) rather than fields now represented the economic future for Halifax.

A~ & I returned up the Old Bank & came in at 2... Mr Parker called on A~... A~ tore in pieces before him (Mr Parker) the note of hand I gave her for £1000, witnessed by Mr Parker & dated 26 January 1835.

Here was another instance of the complex financial transactions between Anne and Ann. In January 1835 Ann had effectively loaned Anne £1,000. Ann now tore up the note recording this, suggesting that no repayment was expected. It was a substantial gift![20]

At 4, A~ on the pony & I on foot picked up Joseph Mann at Listerwick wheel race & went to Hipperholme Lane-ends to see about the water. Joseph M~ to sink a hole 4 ft diameter ... to see if plenty of water could not be found there & carried down to the public house cottages A~ has lately bought.

The implication was that Ann had become entrepreneurially active like Anne. Then, after these flurries of estate business, writing to her elite women friends offered Anne welcome relief. First, she wrote to Lady Stuart:

Shibden Hall, Thursday 23 June 1836.

Since your so very kind letter ... five or six weeks ago, I have written to you, my dearest Lady Stuart, my letter more than once, and destroyed my letter because all the [travel] plans I had told you were upset... I have been so unsettled, and harassed, and unknowing what I could, or should do, for the last two months, that I have not ventured to pother you with my troubles.[21] I am determined not to enlarge upon them just now.

At last, I really do hope that nothing at present unforeseen will prevent my leaving here about the 10th of next month. If you will be at home about that time, I am counting upon spending a day with you… I fear I shall be obliged to be at home before Xmas, to stay at least a few week, but surely I shall have something amusing to tell you after my tour.

My present plan of route is, Paris – cross to Mount Cenis [by French–Italian border] to Turin. There leave the carriage and all unnecessary baggage, and par courir the Vaudois valleys. Then make the best use we can of what time remains.[22] I shall be delighted to take, or bring back, or do for you, anything I can.

Where is dear Vere? If she is at Brafield house [Buckinghamshire], I will make it in my way, and spend a couple of hours with her. I feel that I have now so little time to spare, that I dare not loiter long by the way.

I wish their (the Camerons') travelling servant was at liberty, or you happened to know of one likely to suit me. I have written to ask Lady Stuart de Rothesay if she knows anyone she herself, or any of her friends, can recommend.

I look forward with great pleasure to seeing you. Believe me always, dearest Lady Stuart, very truly and very affectionately yours,

A. Lister[23]

Rather disingenuously, Anne had virtually erased Ann, the pronouns mysteriously morphing from 'I' to 'we' near the end. Also, her references to Lady Vere Cameron and Lady Stuart de Rothesay artfully give the impression that she was practically a member of the minor aristocracy. All coalmining, trespassing and Water Lane wrangles are also erased from view. Then just four days after this letter to Lady Stuart, Vere Cameron herself wrote to Anne.[24]

Brafield House, Olney
June 27th [1836]

Dear Miss Lister,

How are you this long time? What are you doing with yourself and your house, your Hotel, and your coal pits, your roads and bridges, your plans and your what-nots? And above all, how is your aunt? These are questions enough for at least one page of answer in your neat business-like shorthand, which I have had such pleasing experience of in my time?

One more question, do you ever mean to come & see me again, or I should rather say, to come and see me at all, in my own house? Or, are you putting off till I am established in my very own home at Achnacary?[25] Oh, delay not, I expect to be in my bed by the 1st of August, and if I am permitted to rise again, being the mother of three children, I shall still be here till next summer, and even then we do not expect to make Achnacary fit to receive anybody but ourselves & trapped in a very hugger-mugger way; so you see it will be two years from now that you 'put off' you visit to, if you despise Brafield...

My daughter completes her third year on the 4th of July. She is a nice little girl ... but is very backward in many respects. Not so my son and heir, a bolder finer Highlander was never seen... He just begins to toddle alone & many a thump & bump in the consequence. Donald will be with me I hope by the 10th or 12 July – he is as busy as a bee, digging, trenching, draining, carrying soil etc etc for the new garden whose wall alas will not be built till next year, for he is a cautious Scotchman...

How happy you must be with 4 vols of Mr Lyell's *Geology*...[26] In the meantime, [my nephew] is going to Turin with his 3 Foster cousins to pass the summer & see his sister who is with my Sister. It is a very nice thing for him.

Now my dear Miss Lister write to me soon and believe me,

Ever affectionately yours,

Vere Cameron[27]

What a very artful letter from Vere! Elderly Lady Stuart must have communicated with her great-niece. Vere seems well aware of all Anne's entrepreneurial activities, up to and including coal pits. There is a brush-off about visiting; and again, there is absolutely no reference to Ann Walker (or indeed how Anne was paying for her 'what-nots'). Vere ticked all the conventional family boxes. Should we read this letter as a wealthy heterosexual woman rubbing in her superiority to a dissident lesbian?

July 1836

The Water Lane mill farrago rumbled on, growing ever more complex. There was no immediate link to the effigy-burning drama of a few months earlier, as it did not directly involve the Rawsons or coal trespassing. It was, however,

all on the same small spot of unprepossessing land, with its many small tenants (such as Haley) and small occupiers (such as Blamire).

SATURDAY 2 A~ did her French. Between 7 & 8 she had Mr Abraham Haley, calling himself the owner of blacksmith's shop [which] allowed him to build up against Water Lane mill. He evidently wanted to be bought off, but A~ would not hear of giving him anything. [He] would try it at York [i.e. go to law], cost what it might... A~ & I left him to consider. I then went back – he had laid out £12 & more – wanted A~ to pay him £12. I said £5, on condition of his pulling down the [blacksmith's] place, & thus securing A~ in quiet possession. 'No! It was not worth pulling down for that.' 'Well!' said I, 'then £5 = 10 of your days, and you will not soon gain that by [going to] law.' Wished him goodnight, having told him among other things that the present occupier (Blamire) has as much right to the place as he (Haley) had. Haley could show no title [deed] to it – Blamire had possession. He owned [i.e. admitted] Blamire had never paid him any rent for 3 years... He owned that only the anvil & 1 or 2 things were his. [I] told A~ she had better send for Mr Parker or Mr Adam to come at 9.30 am tomorrow. Perhaps if no time was lost, Blamire might be managed – or we should know what ought to be done.

This confirmed that Ann's Water Lane property lay on the edgy badlands. Also, that when estate business grew complex, Ann could rely on Anne Lister's clear mind. Unsurprisingly, when summoned, their Halifax lawyers jumped to:

SUNDAY 3 *No kiss*. Fine morning... Mr Adam came ... [agreed] the occupier of the smithy (Blamire) was the man to be dealt with – would see what could be done with him... Said Adam, 'if Haley was paid, Blamire would still be to manage'.

Anne must have been mightily relieved that, unlike Ann, she did not have to deal with so many small dodgy tenants and such vexatious properties.

I told Mr Adam that what I had hinted at about Mr S Washington (his being <u>tipped</u> i.e. taking a bribe or douceur) had not been substantiated. I therefore could not believe or act upon it, and had therefore told S. Washington to receive my rents as usual. But I thought Parker & Adam had better finish the Northgate ... might also settle the colliery account...

So Samuel Washington was cleared and reinstated as land steward. It was nevertheless helpful to be on sociable terms with a sympathetic magistrate, especially one whose family, the Waterhouses, had earlier owned Shibden. And Mr Waterhouse represented a key member of the traditional 'Blue' Halifax elite.

Dinner at 6.15 – Mr Waterhouse came just as we were eating our strawberries... Received him very civilly – we had our coffee and Mr Waterhouse port wine and water. Took him into the drawing room to my aunt for a few minutes, and then A~ & he and I walked out – to the low fish pond ... and up the fields home – Waterhouse delighted [with what he saw]...

Before we went out (in the drawing room), he had taken up the *Halifax Guardian*, and his observation brought to mind the Water Lane mill business on which, poor fellow! I and then A~ coming in, gave him a fair roasting. It was, however, handsomely done and I think he ended up by feeling that the business had been too hastily settled by the magistrates, and too ill, too stupidly ill, managed by A~'s attorneys. Waterhouse seems sorry and perhaps ashamed? And would have been glad had the thing been settled less harshly upon A~. He disclaimed Mr Rawson's intemperance, and seemed annoyed at it. He said it was not yet too late for York. 'No!' said I, 'but it would not go there, the better for your magisterial dogma upon it.' He owned [i.e. admitted] this. However, he was under my own roof, and I would not press him too hard.

Mr Waterhouse was trusted; but could he be wholly trusted about the Water Lane mill affair on the magistrates' bench?[1]

He staid till 8.45... He says the navigation income goes on improving, 5 or 6 thousand pounds more last year than the year before... He thinks it cannot be hurt by the rail-road for 5 or 6 years (the rail-road cannot be travel-able [before] this time), & afterwards there will always be traffick enough to keep up the concern [i.e. canal business]. The railroad from Halifax into the great Manchester and Leeds railroad may, or may not, be made. There is still a thought of a railroad from Halifax to Leeds – supported by influential people at Leeds – Mr Marshall, Mr William Beckett etc. To have their station somewhere about Northgate... I said I did not wish for it at Northgate, but if it was for the good of the town I should not oppose it – or make any difficulties about it. Some talk about the Northgate hotel.

So John Waterhouse stayed 2½ hours. Like Anne Lister, he revealed himself as 'old money', still the canal generation. Even Anne, an acute businesswoman, could not quite wean herself off canals to venture into the new-fangled railways. She saw railways rather as she saw textile mills: all right, but best kept well out of sight of her houses.[2]

Meanwhile, the size of one's rent book clearly indicated the weight of one's rentals. And Ann's rent book was considerably larger than Anne's.

MONDAY 4 *No kiss.* Very fine morning… Had Washington – ordered rent and cash book – A~'s rent book to have 220 to 230 leaves, & my rent book 150 leaves… Had A~'s Beestonley tenant Charles Law to pay his rent – ordered him cold meat & beer… Mr Horner came about 3.30 & A~ took her lesson in sketching from about 3.45 to 6 – again sketched the rocks & tinted them…

Dinner at 6.30. A~ had note from Mr Adam … to say they had at last brought Blamire to consent to give up the place [Water Lane smithy] for £7.10.0 … if A~ would consent. She wrote back by the bearer of the note that she authorized Messrs Parker & Adam to agree with Blamire on the above terms.

So had the Water Lane mill dispute been settled at last?

TUESDAY 5 *No kiss…* From 2 to 4.30 with Mr Harper – giving orders – explained the plan of house (useful) alterations (cellars, coach house into laundry, saddle-room into brewhouse, phaeton house into housekeeper's bedroom, lately intended brewhouse into saddle-room, with groom's sleeping room over it…). Mr Harper agreed with Mr Husband that £100 would do the whole… Messrs Harper & Husband set out the west tower…[3] Came in about 5 for an hour at my accounts. Mr Adam sent up a man soon after A~ went, to ask for workmen to pull Blamire's smithy down. Mr Husband agreed to give the man Mr Adam sent here, 10/- to get the place pulled down.

Then Ann and Anne got busy with their bankers.

WEDNESDAY 6 *No kiss.* Heavy thunder… A~ to order Messrs Briggs to honour Mr Harper's drafts [for] … £500 for Water Lane mill & £250 for the 4 Hatters Fold cottages. I to order the Yorkshire District Bank to honour Mr Parker's drafts under the orders of Mr Harper to the amount of £3,000. He (Harper) thinks £200 will carry Booth on till Xmas. Long talk about the Northgate hotel… Said what I should like best would be to get a good tenant... Harper to manage it. I would not object to a lease of 5 years... Harper to send me a sketch of the hotel...

A little while with A~ sketching & tinting the rocks again with Mr Horner... Wrote all the above of today till A~ came in at 6.25, at which hour came also Mr Samuel Washington. Sat by us while we dined & took coffee with us & staid settling with me after the rent day & reading over A~'s Outram [tenancy] drain-agreement. Then had Thomas Greenwood (who had been with my aunt some time) to pay his rent & he sat talking till 10.30 pm.[4]

THURSDAY 7 *No kiss. Went to bed again to A~ for half an hour.* Fair but dull morning... Had Mr Husband – ordering about the house alterations till off at 10, & out all the day making calls...

Anne and Ann scurried over the social calls in Halifax itself, but beyond Pye Nest, their visits became more leisurely. With many of Ann's relatives living beyond Sowerby, they felt more accepted socially by this rural elite.[5] At elegant Haugh End in the pretty Ryburn valley, Mary Priestley remained one of their favourites.

Then to Haugh End about 1.30 – Mrs Henry Priestley at dinner (early because busy in the nursery with her little boy)... She would have us sit down & partake of her mutton chop & cold roast etc, a good family dinner; & her own good humour & quiet good-heartedness made all agreeable. Mr Henry Priestley came in about ¼ hour, and we staid 50 minutes. A~ too was comfortable – & I am always more at ease at Haugh End than anywhere else hereabouts. Then to Thorpe, and sat 10 minutes with Mr John Priestley. A~ does and always did like him far the best of all <u>her</u> Priestley set. Then to [W. H. Rawson's] Mill House – nobody at home.

Anne carefully timed these visits: best not to waste time on the merely social. Then they headed back towards Halifax:

To Wellhead [the Waterhouses], nobody at home... Walked ... while the horses baited [i.e. fed] – the carriage to wait for us at Whitley's... Got into the carriage at Whitley's door. Then a long while shopping at Nicholson's [drapers], frocks for the Sunday school girls etc, & scissors for them at Roper's [ironmonger].

This people-packed day can be mapped in two ways. First geographically, by their route. And second, by Ann's family networks spreading up past Sowerby, notably the well-established Priestleys and Rawsons.

Also on this busy Thursday, a hastily scrawled letter arrived from Anne's sophisticated friend, Lady Stuart de Rothesay in London:

Carlton Terrace, Wednesday July 5th

My dear Miss Lister

I have been very long without answering your letter about your travels, so much so that we may expect them to have already commenced! But I have been here & there, & busy filling up chinks of time... My married child ... and her husband embarked by steam for a Highland Tour. We are left very dismal, in the midst of our gaiety, & may soon betake ourselves to Highcliffe [Castle]... Lady Stuart is really well & always wishing to go somewhere to be <u>better</u>. Vere will soon be <u>less well,</u> we expect... I am writing in so much haste! ...

Very truly yours, E Stuart de Rothesay

Given how close they had grown during their 1830 French travels, this seems a rather casual letter.[6]

MONDAY 18 *No kiss* – read prayers to A~ in bed... The Northgate carts (a little gravel, chiefly soil) here again today... Dinner at 6.20 – coffee – sat talking till after 9. Then had John above an hour in the Low Kitchen chamber firing my little gun – putting a new flint in etc. Tried the gunpowder he bought this morning. He got me a percussion pistol too this morning, but it was too late to try it tonight. I fired one of my brass pistols (with powder only) twice in the Kitchen chamber.

THURSDAY 21 *No kiss*... Sat with A~ while she took a glass of wine & a biscuit... Had Booth & 1 of his men preparing for sinking the steps & making the communication tunnel between the beer cellar & phaeton-shed cellar – till 4... I walked to Matty [Pollard's] to see her make leavened bread, kneaded in a piece...[7]

Letter tonight (3 pages & ends) from M~ (Lawton) – she has been laid up 'with inflammation on the wind-pipe for which blistering & severe remedies were used so as to leave me very weakened & debilitated'.

[Mariana] thinks of taking her sister Ann & joining them [at Wiesbaden, the German spa town]. Not to pother myself about M~'s account. Thinks she will only want fifty pounds at Xmas as she always intended & no more.

It is clear that Anne was giving sums of money to Mariana, suggesting that they too were financially entwined.[8]

It was indeed a busy day for catching up on correspondence, Anne writing to Lady Stuart, Lady Stuart de Rothesay and Lady Gordon. With these friends contemplating visits to Highcliffe Castle or Wiesbaden, this whetted Anne's own hunger for travel, enquiring whether these friends could help her find a courier.

FRIDAY 22 *No kiss...* Sent off George with my letters written last night (will be in London at 7am tomorrow by the new mail...) A~ did her French. We set out at 9.10 to the Conery – left A~ with Matty to try to make puff-pastry – made a gooseberry tart, Matty having bought butter [so] that the experiment might not be known at home...[9]

Sat with A~ in the blue room... Wrote 3 pages and ends to M~ (Lawton) – thanks for her letter ... sorry to hear she had such suffering from inflammation... *A~ copied my letter.*[10]

The letter to Mariana was telling:[11]

Change of air would do you more good than anything. I know Wiesbaden, it is a nice little place. You may get there quickly [advised travelling via Paris]... Versailles – the court is not there, and the sort of difference this makes is intelligible [i.e. noticeable?]. But the elite of society in Paris, as in London, is fastidious. The same sort of credentials are required in both places – connections, rank, wealth, or beauty – or talent, if agreeable, & of that sort which mixes well with fashionable life. In short, my dearest Mary, I should as soon hope to prescribe successfully for hydrophobia 'as [advise on how] to get into society'. Living at a hotel [in Paris is] ... not the cheapest... It is a good thing to know some compatriot settled in Paris whose rank is not too much above your own, that is, one who will take the trouble to be useful...

You know I would do anything in the world if [I] could oblige, or serve, or profit you in <u>any</u> way. Thank you very much for your answers to my domestic questions. You are right that I should not leave home without informing you. Our plans are of necessity changed. It is just determined that we cannot get off much before Xmas.

Was Anne, who had 'got into' society in Paris, being purposely unhelpful to Mariana, implying that she had little hope? Perhaps she saw her relationship with Mariana as past, now that she herself had access to her wife's income stream, and so could travel in style. Given Anne's own titled friends, Mariana might now seem sadly to lack the right 'credentials'.

SATURDAY 23 *No kiss...* A~ to taste the gooseberry tart...[12] A~ to Cliff Hill... With my aunt & sat reading the Halifax & London papers.

Anne kept herself up-to-date with both local and national politics. Meanwhile, she planned to take on more staff, including a footman.

SUNDAY 24 *No kiss...* Sat reading Gilly's *Vandois Valleys* in the blue room with A~ till prayers at 12.30 in 25 minutes, to my aunt, Cookson & Oddy & George. Then sat a little with my aunt & with [A~] – she'd wine & biscuits – till after 2. At church ... at 3. A stranger from Wakefield did all the duty – preached (very fairly) 17 mins from 2 Corinthians iii 17. 35 minutes at Cliff Hill – Mrs A~ very well & in good spirits.

MONDAY 25 *No kiss – but incurred a cross on my chair in my dressing room last night on getting ready for bed. I did the same a fortnight ago & about that time incurred a cross in bed, A~ being asleep.*[13] Fair but dull morning... Poor Robert Mann, Frank brought word last night was worse yesterday & had 8 leeches on.

So July 1836 ended with Anne Lister keeping a foot in two worlds: in the Shibden world of gooseberry tart and traditional remedies such as leeches; and in the cosmopolitan world of her titled friends – visiting and travelling, for which an Italian courier or Swiss travelling servant, she noted in a letter to Lady Stuart de Rothesay, would be so useful.[14]

AUGUST 1836

While Anne Lister kept herself well briefed on political news, it did not yet surface much in her diary: the urgent swearing in of her three men as special constables earlier was the exception. Yet nationally, increased state intervention into economic activity (for example, limits on child labour) had major repercussions locally. Indeed, Richard Oastler who lived nearby had earlier campaigned against child slavery in Yorkshire.[1] Anne tended to keep her gaze well above such matters, yet she must have noticed this report in the *Halifax Guardian* on 6 August:

Factories Regulations Act. Public Meeting of Mill-owners and Occupiers at Halifax.

On Wednesday last ... a very considerable number of gentlemen met ... at the Old Cock Inn ... to procure for the manufacturers the revision of such parts of [the Factory Act] as were alleged to be vexatious to the mill-owners & injurious to the operatives. A decided feeling of hostility to the bill... Many of the frames in the mills were standing still [i.e. idle] owing to the regulations of the act, which only allows the employment of children from 9 to 13 years of age for 8 hours per diem.

About 100 men with placards attended. Their sarcastic resolution attacked the government's supposed paternal anxiety about the protection of children. They complained of serious inconvenience to their mills and were highly critical of Oastler, who 'was actuated by party purpose'. There were also complaints about the inspector, and immediate steps were demanded. At the same time the very beginnings of early Chartism began to be felt locally, with a first visit to Halifax scheduled for Feargus O'Connor, the flamboyant Irish orator.[2]

Meanwhile, for Anne Lister high above the town, correspondence with her titled friends still occupied much of her time and attention, even if she had to be surreptitious about it.

MONDAY 1 No kiss... [Wrote] to Lady Gordon and ... to Lady Vere Cameron ... ready for me at Achnacary. *After finishing my letters, crept out of my study. Nobody finding [me], I had been there all this while, came in as if I had been out.* Some while with A~ ... then with my aunt... What cold rainy windy weather we have had of late!

TUESDAY 2 Mr Gray ... prefers to employ Sam Washington than Parker & Adam... Read the paper.

WEDNESDAY 3 *No kiss...* Mr Sam Washington came to set up our new rent books. Mr George Robinson ... came about the notice to quit... Mrs Vietch [local family friend] ... had reproached [A~] with forsaking her old friends! A~ annoyed or low upon it.

SATURDAY 6 *No kiss...* Reading Italian grammar... A~ did a little French... A~ tired after drawing – gave her a glass of wine & biscuit... Saw A– off to Cliff Hill... *And washed & burnt two of the cousin papers.* Rolled

out ... a piece of diaper [linen] 51 yards at 12.30 ... & spent from
[then] doing the tent room & north chamber... A~ read me several
paragraphs from the London paper... Sat reading Rennie's *Alphabet
of Gardening*, while A~ wrote her journal.[3]

SUNDAY 7 *No kiss*... Thomas Greenwood came ... long talk about
Northgate... I mentioned the railroad passing [above Northgate] –
Thomas Greenwood at the moment advised me to oppose it – said
it would do no good to the town – would be a disadvantage to small
traders – people could then ship off to Liverpool & buy wool & get
it back in a few hours!!! I made no answer but simply [said] that
things should be well considered...

A~ had read the prayers to my aunt... At church at 2.50... ¾
hour at Cliff Hill & home at 6½. Wrote all the above of today till
6.55 – dinner at 7 – coffee – A~ & I walked in the garden (on the
flags) from 8.15 to 9.15[4] – then sat with my aunt & read the papers
till 10.15.

[marginalia] Let Listerwick mill.

It was time for another long journey up to Stainland to visit Ann's distant
tenants. This was a reminder, if Anne needed it, of how productive the Crow
Nest estate was for coal, stone and wood, all crucial to the local economy:

MONDAY 8 *No kiss*... Off on the pony with A~ at 8.35 – spoke to the
tenants Stott & Charles Law in passing, & at Moulson Place at 10.45.
At 10.55 began felling William Keighley & 1 of his men [in Moulson
Wood?] felled 20 larches & 3 Scotch firs, containing about 100 cubic
foot of wood – 3¾ hours felling, A~ & I standing by...

Home at 7 – dinner 7.35 – coffee. Left A~ asleep about 8 ... then
35 mins with my aunt till 10.15... While A~ wrote her journal (till
11.35), sat reading Rennie's *Alphabet of Gardening*.

THURSDAY 11 *No kiss*... At the rocks till 12 when A~ came to me – walked
with her in the walk & about till after 1.[5] Then sat with her at wine
& biscuit... Dinner at 7.05 – coffee – A~ did her French. Kind letter
from Lady Vere Cameron – recommending a gardener... Vere's
accouchant [i.e. lying-in] so delayed beyond her expectation – she is
tired of waiting ... directly asks me to be sponsor [i.e. godparent] for
her next child... If a boy, to be called George Vere after V~'s father
– & if a girl, Vere only, after mamma.

Anne apparently did not comment on this request, even in code. Her relationship with Vere still remained rather uneven. This contrasted with Mariana, where conversational letters were about house improvements and domestic servants:

FRIDAY 12 'Shibden is all in an uproar just now. Did I not tell you we were making some … alterations in the cellars; and the hall stairs are in process of widening… Do you know of any nice person who wants a lady's maid… [Charlotte Booth] is about 20, steady and trustworthy and gentle-tempered… I paid 3 guineas for her apprentice-fee and have paid for her clothes since. She seems at least grateful, and I hope she will be valuable to her employer. I have no longer any thought of taking her myself; Cookson suits us too well for us to think of parting with her…'[6] Sent off my letter this evening to Mrs Lawton, Lawton Hall, Lawton, Cheshire.

SATURDAY 13 *No kiss…* With my aunt from 9.30 to 10.15 during which time [I] read the London newspaper & A~ looked over the *Halifax Guardian*.

Anne also corresponded with a servants' agency in Derby:

SATURDAY 20 *No kiss…* Engaging Hudson [footman?] at £30 and Mary Whiteley [lady's maid?] at ten guineas per annum, I to pay their [travel] expenses here – they to arrive both together on Tuesday… A~ off to Cliff Hill at 3 & back at 5… Then had Booth till after 6, planning addition to the is-to-be beer cellar (late milk cellar) – & to enter the wine-cellar into a [new] cellar to be dug under the middle of the hall – 6 foot wide.[7]

SUNDAY 21 *No kiss…* Breakfast at 9 – A~ read a little French aloud, her vocabulary – walked a little in the garden for ¼ hour till 10.50… Came in at 12.40. With my aunt – A~ & I read prayers to my aunt & Oddy & Cookson & George at 12.20 in 27 minutes. I slept ¼ hour… At church at 3 – Mr Wilkinson did all the duty – preached 18 minutes … to work out our salvation with[out?] fear & trembling… Home at 5.15.

So, on this note of household routine and domestic tranquillity, August ends this 'Living Married Life' chapter. All the while, Anne and Ann kept their gaze on radical politics and the early rumbles of Chartism down in Halifax.

What is the overall narrative of this section? Anne remained very busy with estate business at Shibden. And linked to this, she could now – thanks to Ann's disposable income – progress some of her other ambitious plans. In the house itself, there would be conspicuous expenditure on luxury goods, notably footmen and a wine cellar. This prompted the purchase of serious numbers of bottles of expensive wine, as in so many other well-financed marriages.

II

The Last of her Generation

September–October 1836

September 1836

Anne was still in the midst of house improvements. And with her aunt increasingly frail, she also kept in touch with old friends, sending game to Isabella Norcliffe.

York Tuesday September 13th 1836

Very much obliged to you for [the moor-game]. We are still in the midst of dirt and confusion... The drawing room floor has been obliged to be taken up... For my part, I am heartily tired of the business... I called to see Eliza Raine the other day, who is much better than she was the last time I saw her, though still a most painful object to look at. When do you think of going abroad? ... I hope your Aunt continues pretty well; give my best love to her, & with kindest regards to Miss Walker, ever believe me. I remain your affectionate – Friend, Isabella.[1]

Then, with new servants arriving at Shibden, some shuffling around was needed to accommodate them.

Tuesday 20 *No kiss...* Looking over ... kitchen chamber for John Booth to sleep [in]... Just before dinner, had the courier about A~'s Hatter's Fold cottage no 1. A~ agreed to let him have it... Get a respectable tenant for the two rooms of cottage no 2 at £5 a year. Dinner at 7.10 – made our own coffee... Mr Jubb came ... thought my aunt better – I do not think her better... Read tonight's paper ... anarchy in Portugal now, as in Spain.

WEDNESDAY 21 *No kiss*... Wrote 3 pp to M~... M~'s friends going to Paris... Shall be delighted to see M~ the end of next month... [Asked] for a pattern of the footman's dirty [i.e rough work] suit of clothes.

Anne also sought Mariana's advice about hierarchy among the enlarged servant body:

Is the wash[er] woman to have tea & sugar & beer or what? The housemaid and kitchen maid to have anything extra on a washing day? How is the washing to be divided amongst them?... God bless you, my dearest Mary – never despair of happiness... always very affectionately & especially yours A. L~

Anne probably put so many household queries to Mariana partly because her sister, who had overseen such arrangements, had gone. With access to Ann's income stream, Shibden now employed a more ambitious ensemble of domestic servants, among whom a footman was the symbolic key. And Mariana was the only woman to whom Anne could pose these vital etiquette questions. To her titled correspondents, Anne must appear as if she knew it all anyway and certainly could not be seen to ask.[2]

Meanwhile, around rural Shibden, old customs were still enjoyed:

Booth & his son not here – Northowram fair. Booth gone to sell a cow! Terrible to have his men left here without a master – [they were] civil & doing their best, but should have somebody over them... With the masons till drinking time at 4.30 – then took Matty [Pollard] to see the Lodge – [she was] well satisfied – herself fixed to get into it the end of next week... Home again at 5.15 – the 3 servants from [domestic service agency] (housemaid, footman & groom) had arrived. Then a minute or 2 with A~. Spoke to both the new men & to the housemaid while ... with A~.

With Anne's aunt's health deteriorating, Mr Jubb was now a regular visitor. And as her aunt neared the end of her life, Anne's thoughts inevitably turned to Lister genealogy.

WEDNESDAY 28 Dinner ... sat looking over genealogical maps [i.e. family trees]... Aunt looks very much altered & very ghastly ... weaker & weaker... She has never named Mr Musgrave, & says nothing indicative of her thought of being in such imminent danger.

The prestigious vicar of Halifax might well have been expected to visit local gentry families as death approached. After all, the Book of Common Prayer included clear guidance that the minister of the parish shall visit a sick person's house and recite 'The Order for the Visitation of the Sick'. However, Aunt Anne was very self-effacing, and of course her servants were attentive:

THURSDAY 29 *No kiss.* Oddy alarmed about my aunt... Sarah, at Oddy's request, to sleep with her (Oddy)...

Letter (3 pages) tonight from Marian dated ... Scarborough, 28 Sept ... 'as to my going to Shibden, I do not know what to say, for unless my aunt had a wish to see me, the visit would be a particularly distressing one; though perhaps remarks might be made if I did not go, which I should not like to be the cause of. But I really do not feel very capable of judging that, [so] I shall be much obliged if you will say what you think it will be best to do.' Then [she] begs me to tell my aunt, if well enough, how comfortably she (Marian) had spent 3 weeks at Scarbro' – will be at home Market Weighton on Friday & if I write in the morning, she will get the letter at 10 pm.

This seems crystal clear: even in her dying days, their aunt might not particularly wish to see her younger niece Marian. It was Anne she had always favoured, and it remained Anne who could control her sister's visit.

FRIDAY 30 *No kiss...* Letter to Miss Marian Lister, Market Weighton. 'Shibden Hall Fri 30 Sept 1836. My dear Marian – my aunt has got over the night better than we expected; but it does not seem probable that she can continue many days. She speaks with difficulty ... & appears anxious to be as little disturbed as possible. With regard to your coming over ... I think you [are] quite at liberty to consult your own feelings. I see no necessity to compel, no duty to induce, no comfort to recompense your coming. My aunt might or might not be able to take notice of your being with her... It is difficult for me to give an opinion; but I think, & feel, that, were I in your place, I should not come. I am glad you have spent 3 weeks so agreeably at Scarbro', and hope you have received great benefit from the sea breezes. Miss Walker joins me in love to yourself & remembrances to your friend.[3] Believe me, my dear Marian, always affectionately yours A.L~'

Anne deftly dissuaded her sister from visiting, even though Marian did seem to want to see her aunt for one last time. This is Anne's letter writing at its most artful, deploying all her classic rhetorical manipulations. After all, she had strong reasons for not wanting Marian to visit. In Halifax tongues would have wagged; and perhaps Mr Abbott and others, noticing Marian's presence, might have paid a call at Shibden. That would be fatal![4] Then, without pausing, Anne continued with estate business:

> Holt (James) never came to Walker pit last Tuesday… I said I would write to him – I must have him or somebody else to look after the [Walker pit] concern. Then … with John Booth in the cowhouse giving orders … thinks the pig may be killed…
>
> With my aunt till Mr Jubb came … my aunt's pulse 120 last night, 96 this morning, & 84 tonight! … [She] told me I was a very good nurse… A~ had Mr Thomas of the firm of Thomas & Holt who are making her Water Lane [mill] steam engine…

For her Water Lane property, Ann seemed to be learning more about industrial enterprise from Anne's example. Meanwhile, game remained the ideal gift exchange with friends.

> Letter from Lady Vere Cameron, Braford house – Lady Stuart with her, & the 2 brace of moorgame sent. The baby very fat & well ditto ditto Vere herself. 'The dean of Windsor, my friend Lady Broadhead & Miss Cameron are sponsors [i.e. godparents] – & she is to be called Vere Julia…' Vere Julia! Not interesting to me. No news from the Stuart de Rothesays beyond Cologne… Old Lady Stuart does not know the address of the courier – *n'importe*.

Anne's friends would keep producing babies: so irksome! Indeed, September ended with a tangible coolness between herself and Vere. Anne definitely did not want to be a godparent. Babies did not greatly interest her. Rather, Anne's priority was now her beloved aunt, who had just days to live. Even references in the diary to Ann now grow thin. Anne's overriding focus was dynastic: the Listers of Shibden.

October 1836

By now, Anne and Ann's financial intimacy, as in other marriages, involved regular banking transactions. Anne's Halifax bank was now the Yorkshire District Bank.[1]

SATURDAY 1 *No kiss*... Note to Yorkshire Bank in Halifax, enclosing £50 I got in exchange from A~ last night... Out about 11 ... at Walker pit ... & into Pump Lane. At the wheel-race (nobody there) at Mytholm. Returned along Lower Brea wood ... and along the walk & home at 3.15...[2]

Anne's keenest focus remained developments at the Listerwick colliery at Mytholm. The challenge was to get the coal up to the main road.

Found Robert Mann waiting for me – long talk, walking up and down the flags in front of the house (my feet very wet) about the colliery ... & [having] a small high-pressure engine to bring the coal out... Told him to calculate the expense & whether it would pay [i.e. be profitable] ... and to calculate also the expense of driving the 2 heads [i.e. openings] (3 foot 6 inches high & could not be less than 4 foot wide at the bottom) up to Walker pit...[3]

Anne was, however, already losing interest in the isolated Walker pit. Certainly Listerwick down at Mytholm was far better situated for transport – and hence price.

Told him to consider about all this ... & to consider about the value of the coal, that I might keep this in mind at the letting [i.e. leasing] day. Coal is rising. [A local man] had told Robert it would be 11d a load this winter. I said it would be a shilling, what with rail-roads, steam engines & 1 thing or another... [He] agreed that 1d per load clear profit was quite enough. 'Yes!' thought I... Suppose 4 loads per yard = 16.60 loads per acre at ½d = £33.13.4 clear profit per acre...

Anne, who thrived on mental arithmetic, was particularly impressive when calculating profit per acre. Meanwhile, she now had two invalids on her hands.

A~ very poorly – very bad cold coming on – dinner at 7. Mr Jubb came at 7.30 – my aunt much the same, but her pulse 112 tonight. Mr Jubb saw A~. She had a great deal of fever – had eaten no dinner. To send for medicine & get her to bed, after having had her feet in hot [water] 20 minutes. She took ½ a cup of tea – backwards & forwards with her & my aunt.

SUNDAY 2 *No kiss*. Ready at 10 when Mr Jubb came... If [A~'s] bowels not acted upon by 2pm to send to Mr Jubb for something to produce immediate effect – luckily this afterwards proved unnecessary... [Mr Jubb thinks] my aunt may continue some time...

Backwards & forwards with my aunt or A~. At 12.15 read prayers to my aunt & Cookson & Oddy & the housemaid in ½ hour, & sat with my aunt while Oddy dined... Then backwards & forwards – from 3 to 5 stood reading the *Halifax Guardian* of Saturday, partly aloud to A~. Then in the blue room skimmed over last night's London paper... A~ ... had a little veal broth & dry toast ... dinner at 7.10 in 35 minutes,

What persuaded Anne to spend *two hours* reading the *Halifax Guardian*? She did not record what she read. However, a glance at the paper for 1 October suggests that it was probably about radical reformer Richard Oastler and the likely impact of the Ten Hour Bill on employers of children in local mills. Politics was certainly warming up, with a 'Great Radical Dinner' planned in Halifax. The speakers would be Edward Protheroe (unsuccessful Radical candidate in the Halifax 'window-breaking' election) and also Feargus O'Connor.[4] That Anne made no comment is revealing: as a 'Blue' member of the local landed gentry her silence spoke volumes. She surely saw that radical fervour was rising, but preferred not to acknowledge this. It was as if there were two parallel narratives: one spoken and the other silent. And she did, after all, have other things on her mind.[5]

Some very heavy showers in the afternoon so that none of the servants could get to church... A~ got up & came & lay on the sofa (in her dressing gown & cloak) in the blue [room]. She would not take tea which I had made for her...

MONDAY 3 *No kiss*... Mr Jubb came about 10. My aunt had had a restless night, but Oddy thought her no worse. The moment I saw her countenance & tongue, my own opinion was fixed. I told Mr Jubb so, & he owned he thought me right, and said for the first time he thought she could not rally this time. When once the tongue [was] in that state, not one in 20 recovered... I see death in her look & hardly expect her continuing this week out. A~ better but not to get up till evening...

Had Mr Husband ... spoke about [master builder] Nelson's doing the East tower...[6] Then getting madeira for my aunt & cowslip wine & see her take one glass...

Went to A~ for a minute or 2. Then wrote as follows, to go by the groom (after dinner) to 'Mrs Walker, Cliff Hill... My dear madam.

I hope you will not be uneasy at our not being at church yesterday... Miss Walker ... got cold on Saturday... [I] think my aunt very poorly, and have given up all hope of her rallying. Believe me, my dear madam, very truly yours, A. Lister'.[7]

The small Walker pit produced modest amounts of coal, and it also presented other problems.[8]

[Men] at Walker pit helping to fill the carts... Had Joseph Mann & paid him... A~ low ... gave her a glass of liquid (lukewarm) jelly & a biscuit... Out again at 5 & went to Walker Pit – found Holt there & Joseph Mann... Hinscliffe's is a large trespass...

In the past, James Hinscliffe and Anne would settle down for convivial mining gossip. A coal merchant rather than coal owner, he was not in direct competition with her. But surely he was not to be trusted now if – like the Rawsons – he was trespassing?[9]

William & Matty Pollard left the Conery & moved into the Lodge today...[10] A~ low – but read to her (& amused her) the article in the *Quarterly Review* just come (came yesterday) on Captain Hall's new work, *A Winter in Lower Styria.*

The widely travelled Captain Basil Hall wrote of this mountainous region in southern Austria, undoubtedly whetting Anne's appetite 'to get off'.

TUESDAY 4 *No kiss...* With A~ till she got up after 9. Then had her tenant Bairstow to pay the last ½ year's rent for Water Lane mill, & A~ paid him the last year's poor rate £7.17.6d, though the lease settles that the tenant is to pay all taxes – but Mr S. Washington had paid them?! A~ will pay not more – this well understood by Bairstow now...

With Anne at her elbow, Ann managed her tenants firmly, even regarding the disputatious Water Lane mill.

Went downstairs to Holt ... [about] Hinscliffe's trespass... Walked with Holt to the wheel-race, & went down to the bottom [of Listerwick] & examined the engine-pit ... to appoint Joseph Mann to look after it for him... Told Holt to give me a regular plan of his way [i.e. method] that he thought best to work the Colliery... To be hurrying gates, 4 foot wide & 3 ft 4 inches or as I said 3 ft 6 ins high; [11] & still says the coal will pay for driving... He owned [that] 3 acres a year could not be pulled up at Listerwick unless I had 2 pits close together, which plan he seemed much to approve.[12]

So Anne finessed her Listerwick plans with James Holt. Meanwhile, there was also commercial rivalry over stone quarrying, particularly above Shibden at Marsh. This, of course, was near Rawsons' coal trespass which still rumbled on below. Naturally, great quantities of stone were needed for Shibden's architectural embellishments.

WEDNESDAY 5 *No kiss*... Looking after the 2 invalids ... cold meat & teaspoonful of madeira...

Stone working – Booth & Joseph Sharpe & 2 or 3 lads at the West tower – laid the 1st cellar steps this afternoon... With my aunt from 9 to 10 – sat reading – my aunt very poorly but very quiet – never spoke or stirred.

THURSDAY 6 *No kiss*... Came in at 1.30 – Mr Jubb came soon afterwards. A~ better – my aunt not worse, but very weak & exhausted. A~ & I talking – would rather have a housekeeper than ... a cook... *Poor A~ is anything but agreeably decided one way or other & [she] ended, as is often the case, by getting low & crying – so took her downstairs...* Then saw her to bed (to lie down) & out again at 3 – went to the Lodge ... I see the Lodge is more beautiful than convenient...

Dressed – dinner at 7 – A~ sat down with me & enjoyed the moor-game – then left me & I sat asleep the last ¼ hour afterwards – *she having been rather peevish with me, so I staid downstairs. She is always sorry afterwards & makes it up...*

Tensions between Anne and Ann so often sprang from organizing the servants.[13]

Meanwhile, Anne's coalmining developments required a small army of workmen:

Charles & James Howarth making Listerwick engine-pit-frame – 4 York joiners since some days past.

FRIDAY 7 *No kiss*... Mr Washington came to enter his accounts of this year in my new cash book... Settled with Mr S. Washington & paid him £40.4.2 in full... Did up A~'s parcel, received this morning. *A* *cashmere black embroidered scarf, with … familiar note from Lieutenant Peterson, Eleventh Dragoons, Burlington… A~ indignant at both [the] note & present. Sent back the latter tonight by Frank, directed by me to the Lieutenant etc Wakefield, 7 October. Not a line or syllable written in answer – & burnt the note after dinner.*

Ann was being courted by a lieutenant in the Dragoons. Who was this man and how did he know her address? One possible suspect was Captain Sutherland. Ann certainly saw the gift as highly presumptuous.[14]

SATURDAY 8 *No kiss…* Cookson must have leeches applied to her side for fear of pleurisy… Jubb … would send the leech woman to Cookson (8 leeches)…[15]

Longish talk out of doors with the 2 Manns – I agreed I had better not spend much more money … at Walker pit to find out Mr Rawson's trespass. To ascertain Hinscliffe's [trespass], & then get the little bit of coal I can safely. Serve myself & sell the rest, & have the [horse?] gin etc ready for Listerwick.[16] Asked the Manns to give me their value of the coal to let [i.e. lease] – & also what they thought it would make if I kept it in my own hands & gave an agent a certain percentage on the clear profit account…

So Anne might give up her direct involvement in the small Walker pit in favour of the better-placed Listerwick. Here massive industrial energy could be more profitably expended.

Sat with A~; she read 2 pages of French & I read *Encyclopaedia of Geology* article till 9.10, then came to my aunt… She was sitting up in bed, and spoke a little… Her thoughts are now principally about the house. Though she hints at not being likely to continue long, no mention of Mr Musgrave nor any other subject of religion; she is too ill to talk of these matters.

Significantly, Aunt Anne's end-of-life thoughts dwelt on Shibden Hall itself, the home she had known all her life.
That same day, the *Halifax Guardian* ran a very lengthy report on the town's 'Great Radical Dinner', with Feargus O'Connor and Edward Protheroe speaking, attacking the oppressive new Poor Law.[17] But of course, Anne's own thoughts were necessarily far closer to home.

SUNDAY 9 *No kiss…* Mr Jubb sat with my aunt… Then sat with A~ while she took her arrowroot & gave her a small wineglass full of malmsey madeira which she seemed to enjoy... [My aunt's] great change since morning – very weak but restless... Oddy to lie down for 2 or 3 hours while the housemaid watches... A~ sat by me from about 9 to 10.30. I read at intervals the *Alphabet of Physical Geology* & tonight's paper...[18] Lay down with my clothes on – quite dressed, ready to get up at any moment.

Anne Lister could not have been more caring about her beloved aunt's final hours.

MONDAY 10 *No kiss*... Changed my pelisse – went to my aunt... Mr Jubb, as he sat by her bedside, said (at 10.20) that her pulse was gone – her feet were getting cold... Mr Jubb ... tried to give her brandy & water, but she could not swallow it... The last thing she took (& that with great difficulty) was a jelly about noon yesterday...

A~ came for me, & I was just in time to see my poor aunt in her last moment of life in this world. It was just 5 minutes from my return upstairs to her breathing her last at 1.05 pm. For an instant her mouth had an expression of pain, but that expression was gone... The last breath ... was a slight catch but no groan or sigh. The last intelligible words were last night, 'I don't know what to do' and this morning (I think it was) 'I must go out'... As death approaches – her countenance was tranquil...

I remember [my] feelings on the loss of my uncle, the death of my father is quite recent. But my aunt is the last of the generation. She was always good & kind to me – none will ever think so highly of me – none was more interested in my interest – none... I <u>thought</u> till the tears started – my head began to ache & I came in to write letters. Changed my pelisse etc – a few minutes with A~. At my desk at 4.40 and wrote quickly the letter to Lady Stuart. Then went & sat by A~ and wrote the other 3 letters with less ease because she talked to me.

Anne's letters confirm her social priorities. She had always had strong affection for older women. Now, her aunt's death left an emotional chasm. Who could fill those shoes? Anne immediately turned to Lady Stuart, Ann Walker seemingly just an interruption to this correspondence:

Letter to: my dearest Lady Stuart ... you will not be surprised to learn that my poor dear aunt is no more... She expired at five minutes past one this afternoon, so quietly that I was hardly aware of it at the moment. My great anxiety is removed – its removal is a blessing to her; but with me it leaves a strange feeling of bereavement – dearest Lady Stuart, very truly & very affectionately yours, A Lister.[19]

After Lady Stuart, Anne wrote to Mariana, the woman closest to her throughout her life. To Mariana, Anne spared no details:

Shibden Hall. My dearest Mary… Perhaps you have at this moment your house full of company – ours is again in mourning – my aunt's sufferings seem to have decreased with her strength for the last week; yet the fatal change did not positively appear to be taking place till about noon yesterday, from which time to about nine this morning she was restless, without, however, seeming to be in great pain… At five minutes after one, breathed [her] last so gently, that I was not, at the moment, quite certain she was gone, & that her place [i.e. Shibden] should know her no more. The last of the last generation is now slipt away. Mary! You & I, and those we love, must now stand foremost in the gap. You know how good & kind my poor aunt always was to me. She has not lived to profit by the alterations begun so soon [i.e. recently] on her account & at her own request. The house is in sad uproar – this makes it look more forlorn, & casts a deeper shade over our bereavement. We shall expect you at the end of the month – surely we shall then be more able to give you the common comforts of home. Cookson is laid up – the kitchen maid is gone away ill – the housekeeper we had hired died (did I not tell you?) very suddenly, a few days before she ought to have come. God bless you, Mary – always very especially & affectionately yours, A. L~.

Here we have Anne's most intimate letter on her aunt's death. It suggested that the bereavement was also a bereavement for the house and its improvements.
   Anne's letter to her sister Marian, her one surviving relative, came a poor third in the correspondence, focusing only on their aunt's physical decline towards death.

Shibden Hall… my dear Marian – you would suppose from my not writing again that my aunt continued much in the same state as when I wrote to you last… We had no reason to suppose she might not have continued longer – till about yesterday noon or afternoon, when her strength seemed failing faster than it had done before… From 8 to 10 this morning … she became more quiet, & breathed her last at

5 minutes past one, so gently that I was not quite certain at the moment that all was over. The sad state of confusion the house is in only adds to our melancholy. Our remembrances to your friend [Miss Inman?], & love to yourself, & believe me, my dear Marian, always affectionately yours, A.L~

There is no mention of the funeral, nor any suggestion that Marian should attend. Finally, Anne wrote hurriedly to her old friend Isabella Norcliffe. So, in the hierarchy of intimate friendships, Mariana topped it over poor Marian and Isabella.[20]

Shibden Hall... my dearest Isabella – after my aunt's long & severe sufferings you will not be surprised to hear of her release... Alas, she for whom the alterations were so hurried on, has not lived to benefit by them. We should have asked you to come [to visit] now, but we have hardly room for ourselves, or people to do the work we are in absolute need of. Cookson is laid up... We are expecting Mrs Lawton at the end of the month, if we can manage it. Can you tell us of any trusty person to come & help us.? Give my love to Mr & Mrs Duffin, and tell them of our trouble. My great anxiety is gone; but it is a great bereavement. Love to Charlotte. Ever very faithfully & affectionately yours A.L~.

At 6.50 had sealed & given A~ for the Letter bag my letter to 'the honourable Lady Stuart, Brafield house', to 'Mrs Lawton, Lawton hall', & 'Miss Marian Lister, Market Weighton' & to 'Miss Isabella Norcliffe, Petergate, York'.

Back at Shibden, Matty Pollard was a good woman in a crisis: she had known Aunt Anne so long.[21]

Went with Matty Pollard into my aunt's room for 10 minutes. How changed since morning. Said Matty, 'a more respectable Lady did not live anywhere'. All looked solemn – I might have said, 'It is good for us to be here.' It is a relief to me to have written my journals. Dinner at 7 – coffee upstairs.

On this Monday, Anne had written over three pages in her diary. It was such a significant day: death and then bereavement correspondence. It was followed, of course, by Anne's making the formal arrangements for her aunt's ceremonial funeral.

Tuesday 11 *No kiss...* A~ read a little French. Had Mr Duncan, the undertaker at 11 – gave the necessary direction for my aunt's funeral at 9 am next Monday. The sexton to come up[22] – [Thomas] Greenwood to make the coffin... [I] said I was dissatisfied with the clothes chosen for the footman & groom...

Then sat with A~. On telling Mr Duncan to invite the vicar, he said he was not at home. I then told him (Duncan) to invite the curate – talked over to A~ the propriety of my writing to the vicar & asking him to come over... During breakfast wrote out list of people to have gloves & biscuits for the funeral...

Anne's funeral list gives us the texture of her local world. It is four pages long and starts with the names of the eight men who would bear the coffin. All were Shibden tenants, starting with George Naylor of Upper Place, and including Charles Howarth of Ireland plus George Robinson of Lower Brea. There are four mutes, including two of Charles Howarth's sons.[23] Then the long list of 'Tenantry to have gloves and biscuits' (38 men) included John Bottomley of Brierley Hill and John Oates of Pump. Next came five 'Servants occupying Cottages', starting with John Booth at Mytholm and William Pollard at the Lodge.[24] The final list was 'Employees to have gloves & biscuits': first, Samuel Washington, steward at Crow Nest; Lawrence Husband, clerk-of-works; also James Holt coal steward; Robert and Joseph Mann; and Joseph Crossley, Halifax hairdresser. The first few female names now appear, including Miss Hebden, dressmaker. Finally came the vicar, three curates, a clerk, Mr Jubb, the undertaker and the sexton.[25]

Then walked with [A~] 25 minutes on the flags. Mr Harper came about 3.30, & with him (in and out) about an hour. Mentioned my intention of getting off from here as soon as I could, and proposed having Mr & Mrs Husband in the house.[26] Harper thought this plan good – will find out for me what addition I should make to Mr Husband's salary on this account... Mentioned leaving him (Mr Harper) to overlook Husband's payments of workmen of all sorts, including Colliers.

No tidings [i.e. news] of Mr Gray. Harper thinks if he does not come we can do without him. Much to do at Northgate – [he] will be here all tomorrow & till Thursday evening... Approves my plan of palisading off the upper & lower parts of the farmyard, leaving the coach house open & driving through it as one does in the north of Germany.

Looking for papers respecting my uncle's funeral – in vain... Dinner at 7 in 25 mins & then hurried upstairs to write to ... 'the Reverend

Charles Musgrave, Whitkirk vicarage, Leeds' ... 'My dear Sir –
remembering with gratitude your very kind attentions to my aunt
during the last few years of her long & painful illness ... I hope that,
should no particular engagement put it out of your power, you will
come over to her funeral. Your doing so will afford me a melancholy
satisfaction. Mr Duncan has been instructed to invite your officiating
curate, & to make the necessary arrangements for nine on Monday
morning; but if this hour should be inconvenient to you, a later [time]
shall be fixed. Miss Walker begs you to present her kind regards along
with my own to Mrs Musgrave. Believe me very truly yours, A Lister'.

**Anne Lister believed that, in honour of her aunt, the vicar of Halifax should
conduct the funeral service. After all, his wife's family, the Waterhouses, had
owned Shibden in sixteenth century.[27]**

Coffee... A~ read French & we looked over geological map of Sweden
& Denmark.[28]

**So, just a day after Anne's beloved aunt had died, Ann Walker remained
almost invisible, other than sending kind regards to the vicar's wife. There
appears little of the intimate conversations of condolence and grief that might
be expected when one partner in a marriage had just lost a dear relative.
Indeed, did Anne seem to confide more in her correspondence with friends
than in Ann?[29]**

WEDNESDAY 12 *No kiss*... Wrote & copied notes to The Editor of the
Halifax Guardian & to the Editor of the *Halifax Express* newspaper ...
& to Mr Duncan, tailor, Halifax... Wrote little note to Mr Booth,
Bookseller, Halifax, for a quire of black-edged notepaper & ½ stick
of black sealing wax, & 2 bottles of ink. A~ wrote in my name for
Miss Hebden, to send [her] to measure 2 of the servants for mourning
– sent off John Booth with all the above notes after his dinner...
    Dinner at 6.55 – coffee upstairs – A~ read French. Till 9.50 wrote
all but 1st lines of today. Letter tonight 1 ½ pages from Marian, Market
Weighton – hopes to hear from me again after next Monday, on
which day she concludes the funeral will be... 'My dear Anne – I
received your letter this morning which conveyed to me the melancholy
intelligence I had been daily expecting since I last heard from you. I
can now only trust that yourself & Miss Walker may continue well,
& when the harass[ment] of the present is over, you may enjoy peace

& comfort, & that your alterations at Shibden, & your many concerns may all realize their most sanguine expectations. Perhaps you will write again sometime next week, for I shall take it for granted the Funeral will be on Monday, but I feel wishful to hear again from you when you feel a little more settled. Miss Inman begs her remembrances to yourself & Miss Walker, & with my love to both, believe me, my dear Anne, very affectionately yours, Marian Lister.'

Not a word on my advice – or rather, on my observation that, were I in her place, I thought & felt she should not come. But her letter is very well done – no humbug about my poor aunt whom she disliked, under-valued and whose loss she could not consistently pretend to deplore [i.e. lament].

Surely Marian *was* following Anne's advice not to come? Did Marian really dislike their aunt or was she just aware that Anne was obviously the favoured niece?

Very civil letter from Mrs Musgrave tonight saying ... Mr Musgrave [was] at Scarbro' would not return till Saturday but ... she was sure he would come over & perform the last offices [i.e. funeral] for Mrs Lister. All this very civil & very comfortable & proper – and my aunt would have been pleased, could she have been conscious of the thing.

THURSDAY 13 *No kiss...* Came upstairs at 10, from then to 1.30 looking for the papers respecting my uncle Lister's funeral & making out list of bearers etc. Had just finished the 1ˢᵗ copy when Mr Duncan's son came (at 1.30) – gave him my rough sheet – to be sent back tonight.

From 2 to 4 had Mr Harper – settled about the East tower... The garden wall to be done as set out by the gardener – 9 foot high – lined with brick – will cost about 20/- per r[unn]ing yard – will take (70 yards long) about 10,000 bricks. The east tower will take 12,000 to line it... Mr Husband under (the control of) Mr Harper – the bank to honour Mr Harper's checks to a fixed amount. Advises the [Northgate] hotel being let before beginning to build the shops – agreed to.[30] Leave the alterations in the house to Mr Harper – every room to be made decent – the present kitchen to be the manservants' sleeping room...

So Anne intended to be off from Shibden soon after her aunt's funeral, and continued her very expensive plans for the estate.[31]

After Mr Harper went, a few minutes with Robert Mann + 4 preparing the road (scraping – spading-off clay, ready for rubble) for the funeral procession on Monday... Then walked with A~ in the walk about ¾ hour till 5 – then a few minutes with Mr Husband in the hall...

Home at 6.30 – dressed – sent off my letter ... to the Editor of the *Morning Herald*... Letter tonight, 1¾ pages, commonplace kind condolence from Miss Norcliffe, Petergate, York.[32]

Anne now found Isabella's condolences merely 'commonplace'.

Friday 14 *No kiss*... Called in to Mr Jubb at 12 – he went with me to see my aunt – I perceived a change last night – Matty sent to speak to me (through Cookson) this morning. Mr Jubb thinks the coffin had best come tonight, & my poor aunt be soldered up – the corpse may be [i.e. smell] offensive before tomorrow morning... Sat with A~ talking & helping her to measure & cut out 3 servants' hall table cloths...[33]

Holt came [about coal up at Marsh]... Mr Rawson has just offered £400.[34] Holt had offered £500 to be paid in ten years...

Matty Pollard, Duncan & Greenwood [came] with these people ... to solder up [the coffin] – ordered the corpse to be left upstairs – would not have the body in the drawing room tomorrow while the joiners are hammering at the hall floor. Matty came for me to see my aunt – A~ wished to go with me and, though rather nervous & in tears, behaved better than I expected.[35] My poor aunt looked so little changed, & all agreed (Matty said) that there was no necessity for soldering up for several days, that I would have it done. But had the lead coffin placed on the bed & all made tidy. To have the corpse in the house & be unable to see it, is doubly melancholy...

Very kind nice letter from Lady Stuart, Brafield House – 'The melancholy event you wrote to acquaint me of having taken place, I trust & hope you look on rather as a blessing; for one gone, so loved, should be released from her long suffering!' Hopes I shall after a short time be able to leave home – kindly hopes to see me in London or Richmond Park, as may suit me best. Stuart de Rothesays at Berne – going to Turin – give up Geneva on account of cholera...

Letter 2½ pages from M~ Lawton... She seems sorry, perhaps shocked, at not having seen my poor aunt once again! Her 1st impulse was to come, 'but a second thought made me pause, perhaps you have all at this moment [that] you best desire, & if you had a wish you would have expressed it. In perfect confidence that your friend of your youth & affection is always ready to share your sorrows & rejoice in your comforts. Call upon me as you may, & when you may, I am always ready. Events have indeed made a wide gap in your affections, but those you have loved best press forward to help to fill up the void, & whilst many [are] left, there is yet one to love you "dearly fondly & faithfully"... I am sad, I feel very very sad – but F[red?] I am faithfully & affectionately yours, Mariana.'

This is surely the most loving letter 'a friend of your youth and affection' could write.

SUNDAY 16 *No kiss...* Walked with A~ on the flags ... then a little while in the drawing room tidying – all ready prepared for the coffin being brought down into the drawing room tonight. Went to see my aunt about 2.30 pm – saw no change in her appearance. Sat with A~ till 3 then went down to read prayers... From 3.15 to 4, A~ & I read the evening service... It is good for us to be [together] in affliction ... very good – all the [five] women & the 3 men came in, & all seemed attentive to & impressed by the sermon...

With A~ in the storeroom... My cold still very bad but better than yesterday or the day before – I begin yesterday to wear an additional piece of flannel across my chest & this seems to have done me good. I read with less difficulty or rather with more ease than I expected.[36]

Went to see my aunt – her appearance changed – stood looking perhaps a minute or more & came away having seen her for the last time at 6.08. Dinner at 6.10... Mr Duncan [came] ... coffin was soldered up & put into the drawing room where I went to see it at 9.

Anne then received a letter from Revd Musgrave, regretting that he could not come to Halifax for the funeral: it clashed with the Bible Society Anniversary, but one of his curates would attend. This was surely a snub to Shibden. However, Duncan the undertaker was much more respectful of Anne's loss.

MONDAY 17 *No kiss.* Thick foggy morning ... breakfast at 8¾ ... 1ˢᵗ time [wearing] my new pelisse... Mr Duncan brought me a 3 yards long broad crepe which he surely [i.e. carefully] put round me & tied in front... Off from the house at 9.54 – the funeral procession much the same as for my father...

Though Anne did not record it in detail, the funeral procession wound its way from Shibden slowly down New Bank to the Parish Church:

Desired Mr Jubb to sit with me at church, & we went into the Shibden family pew opposite the pulpit. Mr Jubb sat during the... part of the service read from the pulpit – I stood the whole time. Mr Steward [curate] did the duty very well – without any affectation, very simply & impressively – better pleased with his manner than with the vicar's...[37]

At the church door in 50 minutes, at 10.44. All ready – alighted immediately & (Mr Jubb & I) followed the corpse into the church. Mr Steward did the whole duty in 26 mins – I stood over the grave the whole time – saw the coffin lowered & took one last look before coming away. It was the same vault in which my father [lay] & I had seen my uncle laid in 1826. I saw no trace of my uncle's coffin, yet my aunt's seemed to sink deeper down...

Home in ¾ hour at 12... Thankful that this solemn melancholy ceremony was over – all went off well & without bustle.

And then suddenly, without a break, Anne resumed normal life at home:

Sat with A~ reading Mr Pinnock's [edition of] Goldsmith's Roman [history] & looking over the plan of old Rome. Sent for Mr Duncan at 2, just before he went away – desired him to tell Mr Steward that I was much pleased with his manner of doing the duty. I begged Mr Duncan to give him, with my compliments & thanks 2 sovereigns... Nothing had happened [about the funeral] that annoyed me but [i.e. except for] the York joiners sending up by John Booth to ask for beer. Mr Duncan thought it had been the workmen in general. I ... said no! There was not a man of our own people who would have done such a thing. Mr Duncan and all the people [were] gone at 2.05. The bearers and mutes returned with me, & had cold meat & negus [hot port] afterwards, as at my father's funeral...

Anne maintained her military efficiency and iron self-discipline: they would not see her cry.

I could have had tearful eyes, and wept to [in sight of] the people ... had I chosen to give way. But I calmed [myself] & turned my thoughts as well as I could and seemed undisturbed upon my countenance. But my poor aunt! She was very good to me. I hope I shall never be ungrateful to, or unmindful of, the memory of her, or of my uncle; & I shall shew my real affection & respect by endeavouring to do as I know they would best have liked. I will try to do as well as I can; & may Heaven assist & bless my endeavours!

Revealingly, the sincere gratitude Anne felt for her aunt and uncle did not extend to her father or her mother, never a happy couple.

A~ & I changed our dress. Poor A~! She has been all kindness & attention, & grieved for my aunt as if she had been her own. We walked in the walk from 2.55 for 1½ hours…

Acknowledging Ann's kindness seemed almost an afterthought, though 1½ hours was a long time for them to spend walking. Then it was back to estate business.

Left A~ in the house, & put on my tartan cloak over my pelisse (the evening becoming very damp & foggy) & staid out till 6. With Robert Mann + 3… Then to the Lodge to see poor William Pollard – poorly still. Dressed – dinner at 6.20, coffee upstairs – A~ read her French – I asleep a while on the sofa. Then from 7.45 to 8.35 wrote all the above of today – writing my journal always does me good.

Mr Jubb has been so attentive to my aunt, the thought struck me as I went to church to give him a piece of plate, a silver cup or something in testimony of my thanks. I am almost glad the vicar did not come over – now I owe him nothing…

Very fine autumn day F54° now at 9.40. A~ & I while out this afternoon talked of the probable expense of travelling etc. I said we would be off as soon as we could, but did not hint at any particular time. Said we would form no plans now, but to be at Rome next Easter, if we could. [I] sat calculating my income – making our rough rentals [list] etc till 10.10 pm. Then sat with A~ looking into Hallam, *History of the Middle Ages*, till after 11.

On such a significant day, Anne had written 1,300 words in her diary.[38] It was then back to business as usual, Anne musing with Holt about where the railway might be built, about sinking another coal pit and what her mining rivals were up to.

SATURDAY 22 Holt could not settle about the coal on Thursday – expects to meet all the parties on Monday or Tuesday about it. Told him to get 2 respectable people to go down & investigate the trespass of Mr Rawson & that of Hinscliffe at Walker Pit, & Sam Washington to lay down [i.e. record] the latter on the coal plan... Holt to get his coal steward Joseph Clayton and Cookson of Elland to go down Walker Pit & examine the trespass on Monday or Tuesday next or as soon as he can. Came in at 6 ... read Saturday's *Halifax Guardian*.

Anne had now stiffened her resolve against Rawson.

SUNDAY 23 *No kiss*... All (except the cook) went to church at Lightcliffe... Came up to A~ – found her at luncheon (a little rice broth) – she has, at Mr Jubb's & my request, taken to luncheons again for the last few days. [A~] *out of sorts about the dinner bell ringing because I thought it the kitchen maid's place to ring it for our dinner as well as the servants'. A~ thought the footman ought to ring for us. I let A~ come round again gradually as we walked. Always best to take little notice of her being out of sorts. Gave her about a glass & half of malmsey madeira on coming in & left her in good humour & lain down.*

So, Anne was more relaxed about servants' etiquette, while Ann was more formal. Anne felt she could 'manage' Ann well, perhaps helped by a glass or two.

Walked with A~ in the walk... Read a little of *The Alphabet of Electricity*... Letter to [the servants' agency]... I had determined to give up the thought of engaging a housekeeper at present... I will pay her ... [for] the housemaid & groom... Disappointed in the footman who is only very tolerable... A~ & I read aloud to each other the whole of the evening service.

MONDAY 24 *No kiss*... Sat with A~ about a ¼ hour... Had Cookson sewing up a large rent in my old pelisse & mending my gloves while I took hot port-wine & water. Had come in very much heated with pulling down the old garden wall... A~ rode to Cliff Hill...

Letter tonight ... from Marian, Market Weighton... 'I know yourself & likewise Miss Walker would feel the present change [i.e. aunt's death] very sensibly, & I should be very glad if you had done all you thought necessary... I wondered how things could be managed last Monday, and I am very sincerely glad all was so comfortable as I am sure it would be a great satisfaction to you.'

Poor Marian remained excluded.

TUESDAY 25 *No kiss...* Told [Mr Husband] my intention of making him house-steward & having him & his family in the house during my absence.

So, October ended with the last of the last generation buried with due ceremony in the family vault in the Parish Church. Along with their servants at Shibden, Anne and Ann were now on their own. Ann's own aunt was still alive and needed visiting, but Anne had European travels planned. So where was Anne's emotional compass? Did it lie with her marriage to Ann or with her 'friend of [her] youth'? Mariana's visit to Shibden would soon reveal this.

III

MARIANA LAWTON VISITS SHIBDEN

NOVEMBER–DECEMBER 1836

NOVEMBER 1836

Mariana remained confined in an unhappy marriage. Anne Lister had spent Christmas 1834 at the Lawtons' home, going on her own. She recorded how Mariana was *'in bed with me, rather in the pathetics – she cannot get over her love for me'*. And of course, since then Mariana had written the most loving letter from 'your friend of your youth and affection' after Anne's aunt died. So the visit of Mariana to Shibden, now home to both Anne and Ann, was freighted with emotional significance.

Meanwhile, Anne had received a tantalizing letter from Venice from Lady Stuart de Rothesay, her most sophisticated friend, offering condolences. In Europe, fear of cholera continued, but they hoped to go to Florence, believing it 'quite safe'. She added: 'the Rhine we did by steam', 'of Switzerland, we got what was to be had by post' and 'at Milan we had very agreeable town life'. How close a friend was Lady Stuart de Rothesay now? Her tone seemed a little arch, for she must have glimpsed Anne's financial limitations.[1]

At the same time, radical politics continued to foment unrest. Formed in June, a London Working Men's Association now published 'The Rotten House of Commons'. In Halifax, a Conservative dinner for the Hon. James Stuart Wortley MP was held, attended by John Waterhouse, Jeremiah Rawson, Robert Wainhouse and many other men Anne knew well. However, not only could she not vote for Wortley, it was also inconceivable for her to attend this all-male political space.[2]

Meanwhile, Anne wrote a heartfelt letter to Vere Cameron. Vere had heard only indirectly (via Lady Stuart) of Anne's aunt's death three weeks earlier; and now Anne wrote about the melancholy of her loss.[3]

TUESDAY 1 *No kiss*... Wrote 3 pages to Lady Vere Cameron. 'My dearest Vere... I now see how lonely I should have felt & should have been, but for my little friend who is all kindness & attention. To me, misery has no name so comprehensive as <u>loneliness</u>. Vere! I never think of you, I never think of her [your own aunt] whose dearest wish was your happiness, without being thankful for the widening circle of domestic comfort that surrounds you...[4] It will do me good to see you; and I feel as if my spirits would be lightened & my pen more amusing from the other side of the water. God bless you! Ever dearest Vere, very affectionately yours, Anne Lister'... Dinner at 6.55 – coffee upstairs... Letter ... from Mariana Lawton to say ... will be here on Thursday or Friday.

So, Anne presented Ann to Vere in the diminutive, 'my little friend'. Meanwhile, there remained more immediate things on her mind, working with Robert Mann and others on the estate. And she waited for the significant visitor:

FRIDAY 4 *No kiss*... Went to the Lodge to meet M~ [on] the mail [coach]. She not come – disappointed. Came in to tell A~, thought M~ might ... have alighted at Halifax & meant to come by chaise. Walked a little way down the New Bank to meet her – no M~. Came back to A~. Out again at 2. A~ afterwards rode to Cliff Hill...

Robert Mann ... came at 3.45 to say Mrs Lawton was at the Lodge – went there immediately. M~ a little nervous so [I] kept her outside looking about till after 5. Soon after, went with her to dress – at 6 left her to change my pelisse etc [which was] wet. Dinner at 6.45 – coffee upstairs, sat talking. Shewed the sketches of Lodges [that] Mr Harper drew ... till 11 – then shewed M~ the cellars & sat talking till after 12. Then wrote the above of today till 12.30... Sat (an hour) with M~ talking till 1.25, then stood talking in my dressing room to A~ some time.

So Mariana felt on edge, Anne adeptly putting her at ease. This was Mariana's first visit since Ann had moved in, and she was probably over-faced by Shibden's impressive embellishments. The diary confirms that Anne's focus remained Mariana: the intimacy of their conversations is clear.

SATURDAY 5 *No kiss*. Breakfast at 10, having sat ¼ hour with M~ who had not closed her eyes to sleep during the night & would breakfast in bed. A~ had Mr Horner about 10.30, & I went back to M~. About

11 she had got up & I sat with her till after 1 – had talked of A~, of housekeeping [i.e. servants], of alterations [at Shibden] etc. [She spoke] *of Willoughby Crewe & of* [Charles] *being likely for* [a] *long life.*[5] *I spoke quietly but highly of A~. No love-making to M~, but my manner very kind & affectionate. She makes no attempt beyond* [word missing?], *but I think would intrigue with me gladly* [against A~] *if I chose.*

Luncheon at 2 – sat with A~ & M~ till 3, when A~ rode to Cliff Hill, & M~ & I went out, but did not get much beyond the barn in consequence of a heavy shower.

M~ strongly advised me last night not to change the name from Shibden Hall to Shibden Castle. Mentioned Mr A~'s magnificent new house in the old style called 'castle' & which (in ridicule) the people called 'the castle in the field'.[6] Said I was struck by what she (M~) said, and would not change the name without well considering the matter. M~ much approved of my taking the name of <u>Mrs</u> Lister.[7] Did not like my plan of turning the barn into the coach house & driving through it to the house, but liked my name of <u>Keep</u> for the barn, when it was turned into coach house. Then, explaining to her my plan this afternoon, she came round to my opinion, & much approved of it. On coming in, sat some time talking in the drawing room. [Ann had returned], then the sound of my voice making A~ feel sleepy, made her lie down & left her at 4.50 & went out for an hour – to the rocks...[8]

Mariana obviously remained desperately fond of Anne, yet chided her for her social pretensions. Mariana's own social aspirations seemed rather bourgeois to Anne; her other correspondents were titled, and would scarcely blink at renaming their house 'Castle'. Meanwhile, Anne grew aware that Mariana's visit had distracted her from normal supervision of the men working at Shibden.

Paid Robert Schofield & Charles Howarth & John Booth – not having been out, except with M~, till after the men were gone away. Know not what has been done during today... The horses to be turned in tomorrow – the cows have been there for 2 or 3 days...

M~ had not slept, but I found her up at 6.30 – dinner at 6.45 – coffee upstairs at 8 – we sat long downstairs, talking over the dinner table. Read tonight's paper while A~ & M~ talked over school matters. From 9.50 to 10.15 I asleep on the sofa, then came to my study ... wrote all the above of today.

So, for 1¼ hours the three women enjoyed a relaxed dinner. Mariana and Ann bonded, discussing conventional female philanthropy,[9] while Anne kept herself up-to-date with political news. There is very little written in code, despite Mariana's being at Shibden, though Anne still started each day's entry with two words:

SUNDAY 6 *No kiss*... Sat with M~ & A~ till all off to church at 2... Then sat 40 mins with Mrs A. Walker at Cliff hill – very glad to see us. Then went to Crow Nest. A~ left some plans & I left one of the coal plans with Samuel Washington... He shewed us all over the house...

Surely they had managed to impress Mariana with Crow Nest's grandeur? Certainly, Willoughby Crewe was curious, probably out of genuine concern for Mariana.

M~ wrote to Mr W. Crewe – he had asked her to tell him what she thought of A~. Then at the dinner table, very merry. M~ had a good night last night, and was all the better for it this morning & in good spirits. Read tonight's paper.

It was unusual for the Shibden dinner table to be 'very merry'. Was it because Ann and Mariana shared their news of schools? Or because there was as yet so little sexual or emotional tension? Unusually, Ann now took the sexual initiative:

MONDAY 7 *A tolerable kiss last night – A~'s own bringing on*... Some time with M~ *pour faire sa toilette*. Breakfast at 9.50 to 11 – then sat with her & A~ upstairs. M~ & I went out at 12.40 to the rocks... Took M~ to the end of the walk & came into luncheon at 2. A~ rode to Cliff Hill at 3.

Having seen Crow Nest, it was now time for Mariana to be impressed by Shibden's garden design 'at the rocks'. Then they took a long walk round the lower estate, so Anne could show Mariana Listerwick:

M~ & I went out again to the Lodge – round by Godley & Lower Brea road to Mytholm & Hipperholm quarries... [With] Joseph Mann ... then to Listerwick pit...

It might feel cosy at Shibden, but Ann Walker's relatives still remained highly suspicious of Anne Lister's motives.

A good fire in the drawing room – went & sat cozying there till 6.30 – dressed – dinner at 7.10 – sat downstairs… Read Mrs Edwards' curious letter to A~ in York in February 1834, & Mrs Edwards' queer note last April told the sort of persecution poor [Ann] had been subject to.[10]

Much quiet conversation with M~ during the day. Shewed & explained my different works & alterations. [We] get on very comfortably – M~ really likes A~ & the liking is mutual… *M~ made me say this morning that I would always love her, M~, but no shew of anything lover-like on either side.*

So, two mature women who shared a long emotional and erotic history now found a fairly happy resolution with the lives each had chosen. Mariana remained formally married to Charles, Anne united with Ann. Yet was the past completely passed? No. Mariana pressured Anne to say that she would always love her, but just could not show it. And Mariana's presence at Shibden seemingly had an erotic effect on Ann.[11]

TUESDAY 8 *A tolerable kiss last night…* A few minutes with M~, then had Mr Husband who wanted to shew me the new banisters for the hall stairs. Breakfast at 9.50… Looked about the Conery Ing [i.e. meadow]– went up to Walker pit, some time there. Came in at 1.20. Mr Musgrave had just called & also Mr Jubb – the latter went into the housekeeper's room & A~ saw him. I remained with the vicar in the South parlour.

Revd Musgrave was certainly a significant visitor. He was not only vicar of the prosperous Halifax parish but had also married into the Waterhouses, a key elite 'Blue' family. His visit was a long one. First, he apologized for not officiating at Anne's aunt's funeral. Then out came the begging bowl, on this occasion to fund to the church organ alterations.

He hastened to tell me Mr William Rawson and Mr Waterhouse had each given £5.00. I said it was exactly the sum I had thought of giving, and said I had much pleasure in giving him 5 sovereigns I immediately took out of my purse. The vicar much obliged… The vicar had asked [for] A~'s subscription to the organ – I declined for her – said my subscription was in fact from us both – it was from the house – but on the thing being pressed, I offered to give another sovereign, 3 to be in A~'s name and 3 in my own… [We] always considered what either did as done by both.

Anne then adroitly talked up Ann's philanthropy at Lightcliffe. She also mentioned the Wesleyan Methodist Sunday School nearby at Pule Nick, which Musgrave dutifully offered to enquire about.[12] Anne was too important a patron to alienate.

> He stayed ¾ hour... I had been particularly civil, but rather grave and stately... On the vicar's going at 2.05 we all came down to luncheon – it had been ordered at 1.30 and Mr Husband had been waiting since 1.20 to go with me to Stump Cross Inn & to Hipperholme Lane Ends about the Travellers' Inn water. Took M~ with me, leaving A~ to ride to Cliff Hill...

As a visitor, Mariana had her own bedroom. Here the three women began to sit together:

> Came in at 5.30 – dressed then sat with M~ in her room & A~ came & sat with us there, first time – dinner at 6.40... Drank my coffee on coming upstairs again at 9.45 – then opened the box of mourning rings that came this morning... Chose the 7 rings wanted – 4 alike for A~ & her sister, & for myself & mine [i.e. Marian] & for M~, & different rings for Isabella Norcliffe & Mrs Veitch.[13] Then till 12 wrote all the above of today.

WEDNESDAY 9 *No kiss*... With M~. Had Samuel Washington – gave him the other (the clean) coal plan – he is measuring off this morning... Off in the brown carriage, A~, M~ & I at 11.40...

The visit was up to Mr Outram in Stainland, one of Ann's farthest-flung tenants. His attraction was that he had an alpaca mill, just the sort of small-scale industry that Anne liked. Alpaca was exotic, and the Outrams were country gentlemen who knew how to entertain visitors.

> M~ much pleased with the manufacture (from the wool of the alpaca lama). Had wine & bread & butter – a long while choosing shawls & a cloak that A~ & I are to give M~... Then Mr Outram's oldest son ... shewed us over the mill. The young man has studied chemistry a little & mechanics, in order to be his father's engineer for a new water-wheel.

Anne was always alert to absorb useful information. The 1833 Factory Act had limited children's labour to eight hours a day, though still allowing adults to work much longer. This triggered agitation for an eight-hour day for all. From the mill owners' perspective, this new Act was unwarranted state interference, and the Outrams did not hesitate to express their opposition.[14]

> Got a great deal of information from the 2 gentlemen respecting the Factory Act of parliament – they think parliament must repeal the act … limit the working [to] 11 hours a day, & leave them at liberty to employ such children & at such ages as they like…

Then, rather unusually, Anne swerved the conversation to her own industrial enterprises, picking the engineering brains of young Outram.

> Mentioned my waterwheel-erecting at Listerwick. Young Mr Outram observed … the slower the speed [of water], the greater the power – the longer the water dwells on the wheel-breast, the greater the force it has – the breast being broad gives great advantage. Mentioned my intended mill & having asked £20 per horse power on 15 horse power…

Some very technical discussion followed, calculating profit per year on 15 horsepower. Anne was obviously grateful for these knowledgeable insights.

> Told Messrs Outram I should be glad to see them [again] … shook hands… Thought I to myself, 'this is the best information I have ever obtained'. A~ tired, lay on the sofa in Mrs Outram's parlour till the carriage was ready. I gave senior Outram ½ sovereign for the workmen, and we were off at 4.25, having been there just 2¼ hours.
>
> Stopt a little while at Whitley's [bookshop] on our return… Home at 5.45 – dinner at 7 – coffee upstairs. A~ & M~ talked over school matters while I lay sleeping on the sofa till 11.30, then sat talking – ½ hour with M~ in her room till 12.30.[15] Talked over her money matters – she has the £200 she had meant for [her nephew] William Milne in the Brazilian funds which pay 6 per cent invested in his own name (in trust for her own use) with Mr Lawton's consent by her trustee Mr W Crewe.

So this married woman's access to certain funds was channelled through two men, her husband and her trustee. Mariana's finances were further complicated by a financial arrangement with Anne:

> Said I thought I had best pay her the balance of the account between herself & me. She thought so too, if it was no inconvenience to me.

'No! not at all' – & we are both pleased & satisfied that <u>the money should be paid to M~ now</u>. A~ & I both satisfied & glad of this arrangement. I advised M~ to pay for [her niece, nicknamed] Percy's education as she intended, but try to do it out of income & keep all principal for herself – not give any part of it away during her life – to which I think M~ agreed. Fine morning... Kind letter tonight from Lady Vere Cameron, Brafield House.

During Mariana's visit, calls were paid to Ann's relations living out beyond Sowerby, though oddly Ann did not join them.[16]

THURSDAY 10 *No kiss*... M~ & I off at 11.30 am in the yellow carriage to call on Mrs Henry Priestley – at Haugh End at 12.30 to 1.35. The Priestleys very glad to see us – M~ talked chiefly to Mrs H. Priestley & I to him about property ... to be sold by auction... Mrs H. Priestley had intended calling at Shibden Hall on Monday – inquires after A~, will now delay the visit.

This visit out to rural elite friends was a success, social snobbery prevailing. They then returned through Halifax, shopping at the draper's.

Nicholson's shop – a long while there – M~ bought serge & flannel, & 1 ¼ yards silk at 4/6, to line the [Outram's] cloak A~ & I are giving her. Drove to Suter's [chemist's] for gum mastic & spirit of wine for M~; & I had Mr Suter at the carriage door. [I] inquired about the Pule Nick intended Charity school – he said he did not know a great deal about it, but it would be a good thing. [He said] no politics allowed, much less radical ones. I said his sanction [i.e. approval] was enough to satisfy me, & paid him a handsome compliment on his speech at the dinner just given to Mr James Wortley [MP for Halifax].

So this is how it worked. *He* says 'no politics allowed, much less radical ones', knowing this was exactly what *she* wanted to hear. Anne might not have attended this 'men-only' political dinner, but she would have read about it in the paper. This brief conversation reminds us that, though it seldom surfaced yet in the diaries, the threat of local Methodism and early Chartism continued to bubble away. For Pule Nick was just walking distance from Shibden.

Got out at Miss Hebden's [dressmaker] for velvet for A~... Then drove to Northgate hotel – 40 mins there – Mr Husband had seen & followed us, and shewed us over the place. M~ thinks it will be a

5 Shibden Hall, 'Perspective View: Garden Front', John Harper, 1836

magnificent hotel – much pleased with the Casino – will mention it to the Copps at Leamington – likely people to get me a good tenant.

Other than Shibden itself, Northgate House was by far the grandest of Anne's properties. She had certainly managed to impress Mariana.

Home at 4.25 – were to have been back for luncheon at 2. M~ & A~ took luncheon at 4.25 & I sat with them...

Anne seldom did lunch, even with two intimate friends. Then they all set off to Lightcliffe:

Took George behind the carriage, & M~ & A~ & I off to the school at 5.30 – 40 mins there – M~ & A~ much interested. M~ surprised at the goodness of the house & schoolrooms & seemed pleased at the scale & manner of conducting the school. Then call on Mrs Ann Walker at Cliff Hill, and there 40 mins. Mrs A. Walker evidently taken by surprise, but very civil & glad to see us. Home at 7.10 – dinner... The plans of Shibden arrived this afternoon from Mr Harper ... he will be here most probably next Wednesday. M~ much pleased with the drawings & much interested in the plans – talked them over.

At Shibden, however, it was not all grand architectural designs. When their temporary cook proved wasteful, Anne grew unusually angry: her diary provides a rare glimpse of domestic kitchen activity:

> A~ going downstairs came back & took down M~ & me to see the pig-tub – shameful waste of good meat... From 1.35 to 2.35 I turned out the contents... Told M~ to send off the cook ... in the morning, & send for Oddy... Sat a little while with M~ in her room. Then stood reading in my dressing-room my kind letter from Lady Stuart, Whitehall – Captain Stuart just returned from Persia, so no rooms for A~ & me at Whitehall – full of regrets – perhaps it is well – some talking to A~... *On return from Halifax, found my cousin gently come.*

FRIDAY 11 *No kiss*... Sent off John Booth at 11.30 to dress at home [in coachman's livery] & then go to Halifax for a chaise to fetch Oddy... Then went to M~ & A~ & somehow began talking of the plan of the house. M~ joined [with] A~ against building the East tower – this led to a long discussion. I gave way – said their observations were good, & the East tower should be given [up]. Then they thought I gave up my own way [i.e. my idea] too hastily & had better think about it.

Significantly, this was the first time that Ann and Mariana joined together against Anne over a subject in which she had so much invested. Did this bode well?

> I said I saw the thing clearly & my mind was as satisfied as it could be... M~ went to her room, & A~ & I remained in the drawing room. I satisfied her that I was satisfied – & the East tower is given up now after the working plans are come! Then went to see M~, explained that I was really satisfied & had convinced A~ I was satisfied to give up the East tower.

But Mariana was not at all happy about this. She suddenly switched the conversation to 'news' (unexpected to Anne) about what Ann really wanted:

> M~ said we should not be [i.e. live] much here. She saw A~ would prefer a house in London – would be glad to get out of the way of her relatives, & it was foolish in me to lay out so much money here. Thinks A~ very sensible – satisfied to leave me to her etc.

Mariana was hitting Anne where she knew it would most hurt: at Shibden and Anne's dynastic identity. And was Mariana really 'satisfied' about this now? Then a new issue arose: Mariana did not have as much money as she thought.

Dinner at 6.45 to after 8 – then asleep on my chair over coffee upstairs. On rousing up about 9, looked over M~'s account – found the balance in her favour only £304.9.7 up to 31 December next, instead of £400 as M~ and I had talked [of] & as she evidently expected. She behaved very handsomely, sure I was right. I was sure too, but yet felt dissatisfied & uncomfortable on finding M~ less rich by a hundred pounds than she expected. Said I remembered talking of her having (in 1833) £500... She did pay (17 Sept, she said, 1833) £200 per Hammersley's [London bankers]. M~ went to her room at 12 & I went & sat a little with her. Then with A~. Uncomfortable; A~ would have me turn to my Journal of the time (vid. October 1833). I did do so, & found an extract from a letter of that date to M~ satisfactorily explaining the business.

Ann had reason to feel uncomfortable: it was becoming clear that Anne had been financially entwined with Mariana. At the same time, as Anne's footsteps sped from room to room upstairs, an unwelcome truth had dawned on Mariana. She had begun to panic, hurling long-ago resentments at Anne. She accused Anne of neglecting one of her nieces on a visit to London three years previously.[17]

SATURDAY 12 *No kiss...* Ready at 9.50 & went to M~ for a few minutes. Then went down to Mr Husband ... [&] York joiners... Then went to Mr S. Washington who had brought me back the coal plans... Breakfast at 10.15 – found M~ had come down ready for being off – she took leave of A~ about 11.15 and we set off. Looked about us a little at home, & then walked to the Lodge. There from 11.45 to 12.25 when the mail [coach] drove up. Duncan Milne [a relative] jumped off from the outside & handed M~ in (Robert the footman too in waiting) – and she was soon out of sight. I had just had time to shake hands with Duncan Milne & wish M~ goodbye. I think her visit has been a satisfactory one – she said so. *But I think she did not expect to find me so really satisfied & attached to A~. Or so proof against* [i.e. resistant to] *all M~'s blandishments. She has reminded me constantly & very much of Mrs Milne.*

Harriet Milne was, of course, Mariana's sister. She had married an army officer and, like Mariana, her marriage was unhappy. Indeed, Harriet's flirtations became York scandal. More broadly, Anne's relationship with Mariana was certainly cooling. So did Anne wish to put this world of high-society flirting behind her? With Anne now committed in marriage to Ann Walker, Mariana knew she had been edged out of the picture.

She would have intrigued if I would, but I have returned all her open-lipped kisses chastely – tho' kindly always saying 'Mary, thou art a great pet' [i.e. a favourite]. *No symptom of passion for her has escaped* [from] *me. In saying once that, if anything happened to A~, I should feel quite lost* [i.e. lonely] *& must have someone, M~ asked if I would take her. I got off & made no reply. I think she was often disappointed at my calmness. The fact is, I am not sorry she is gone. In speaking of our going to Lawton, M~ seemed uncertain whether Charles would be civil to A~. Hinting at her family, I said that would not do. M~ to let me know in some* [while if] *I but not A~* [would be welcome]. *Could* [not] *understand whether Charles would receive A~ well or not. If we go to Lawton in passing,* [I] *told M~ we would only stay 2 days – said lastly our going at all was uncertain.*[18]

After this fateful parting of old lovers, Anne immediately returned to supervising her estate improvements, her mining plans and calculating coal profits. In other words, Shibden reverted to normal.

On my return home at 12.35, Robert Mann waiting for me to shew me the dry wall groined arching [with] Mr Husband... Oddy returned yesterday afternoon & cooked for us today, 1st time, very well.

SUNDAY 13 *No kiss...* Asked A~ if she would dislike having a [horse] gin or small engine to pull the coal up ... in Godley Lane (the engine to be hid from the road)... To talk over again tonight.

FRIDAY 18. Harper ... *should want three thousand for Northgate & here, and a thousand for the mill – and, said I, a thousand for other things. And I will leave an order at the bank to honour your drafts to the amount of five thousand. He did not say much, but seemed evidently pleased and satisfied.*

Business dominated the rest of November, with her suspicions about Rawson continuing, along with considerable work at Listerwick and Northgate. Meanwhile, Anne drafted a letter to Lady Stuart, attempting political reassurance:

Shibden Hall, Monday 28 November 1836

Dearest Lady Stuart

I now find that, in spite of all exertion to settle matters as soon as possible, I shall not get off more than a day or two before Xmas. This makes me more anxious to hurry on to Paris, where I <u>must</u> stay at least a fortnight... My thoughts turn strongly towards Italy, Rome and Naples in particular, if cholera does not frighten me into another direction... There is a strange fascination in [travelling]. I shall be like a bird escaped from its cage, when I am again *en voyage*.

From all I hear, I hope Mr James Wortley has much improved his popularity among us. His promise to vote for the 10 hour bill seems to have given great satisfaction, and, though I have not thought much on the subject, I am well inclined to believe his view on it is the right one. Surely there is a strong conservative reaction starting up every-where; but our constituency does and will require much careful and skilful management. I do not, however, despair – far from it, the horizon seems clearing. We shall probably have Sir Robert Peel, and many others we wish for, back in office, before summer months return. Heaven grant it! Believe me, always, dearest Lady Stuart, very truly and affectionately yours,

A. Lister

You will remember having heard me say that, should I survive my aunt, I hoped my friends and all the world would allow me the brevet [i.e. raised to a higher rank]. I think <u>you</u> will not object to it when you see [me] grown gray with all the business etc, of the last two years.[19]

December 1836

In late 1836 Anne, having ignored Mariana's jibe, continued to embellish the Hall, notably with a discreet cellar passage, allowing servants to move unseen. And she focused on her extractive industries, both stone quarrying and coal. She also still planned European travel. Yet money constraints continued, her business correspondence highlighting how bad her immediate financial problems were.

SATURDAY 3 *No kiss… No cousin during last night, but found it come on dressing, but not much…*[1] [A~] had Mr Horner at 10. With Booth about the cellar passage. Ordered it to be 2 ft 6 inches wide … wide enough for housemaid to pass along in an evening, merely to keep her from passing along the gallery.

SUNDAY 4 *No kiss…* Sat with A~ looking over the maps of Holland & Germany… At the school in 17 mins at 2.10, I waited in the carriage while [A~] was ¼ hour hearing the girls say their psalms for Wharton's bibles.[2] Then at boys' school… Only just in time at church… I was latterly asleep half an hour at Cliff Hill – Mrs A Walker in good humour & spirits…

Returning home, she wrote a short letter to Mariana, who planned to pass near Shibden on her way back from York, staying overnight in Halifax. Her proximity could not be ignored.

MONDAY 5 *No kiss…* George Beech will come as assistant gardener & farming man – at 16/- per week – no drinking – nothing more – quite enough – to board & lodge at the gardener's but sleep here to take care of the house if necessary – said I would take him if his character answered [i.e. satisfied]…

Wild windy day… A~ … is writing <u>a long</u> letter of extracts from cashbooks etc … to her sister tonight. Siding in my study & punctuating A~'s <u>long</u> letter till 11.30 pm.

TUESDAY 6 *No kiss…* Came in at 5.30 … read my letter … from M~ … York. Mr Lawton too ill to move sooner, but had not been in any danger.[3] M~ too had been indisposed … ½ York in bed from illness. The Lawtons and Mrs Milne will sleep at Halifax tomorrow – & M~ begs me to order beds at the White Lion.[4]

WEDNESDAY 7 *No kiss…* A~ & I off at 10.45 in the yellow carriage. Stopt for a moment at Mr Parker's door … gave him the [Marsh] stone advertisement…[5] And at Mr Stansfield Rawson's, Gledholt near Huddersfield at 1.15 – all the ladies of the family at home (did not see Mr Rawson) at luncheon – very glad to see us – we [were] very civil – sat 2 hours, & off to Cliff Hill on our return at 3.15… Mrs A Walker surprised but glad to see us… Drove round by the lodge – found the Lawtons had passed at 4.30 or before.

Drove to the White Lion (Halifax), there at 6.15 and stayed till 9.15. Dinner ready – dined with them and had coffee immediately after dinner – all of us very kind and civil and agreeablizing. M~ took me upstairs ½ hour to tell me the York scandal… M~ and Mrs Henry Belcombe had come to high words about A~ and me – Mrs H. Belcombe's abuse had been more than M~ could bear. Isabella Norcliffe too had not spared us – I took it so quietly M~ seemed rather astonished… The 2 ladies also declared I had said I ordered my letters to be directed to 'The Honourable Miss Lister' – what nonsense! I told M~ it was all quite incorrect but it was not worth a thought. Thought I, 'What a set of people! The less we jostle each other the better.' *I thought Charles and M~ and Mr Milne vulgar, and had no real relish for the sort of play I was making to entertain – they all seemed merry. M~ could not get me to promise to go to Lawton. I liked not the clique…* People neither A~ nor I know or care about is *un peu trop forte…*

M~ asked me to say I loved her better than anyone in the world, but I fought [i.e. resisted] till at last she made me repeat the words after her. She must have seen however that the repetition was not worth much. Her loving kisses I did not return but took all quietly. Home at 9.45.

In other words, Anne had not changed her emotional priorities since Mariana's departure a month earlier. And Anne no longer needed to rely on the gossiping, bourgeois York set. Nowadays, her friends lived either in or near London or else in Scotland, if not both. She just needed a loan to tide her over financially:

THURSDAY 8 *No kiss…* Letter tonight from Messrs Gray [York lawyers] to say I might count upon the money in April, £7,000, but the Lady would make it £8,000 if I preferred it. Messrs Gray had said they thought £7,000 would suit me better… Asked what security I propose giving.[6]

Anne's 'security' would probably be the title deeds to certain of her tenanted properties. What would her Uncle James and other Shibden ancestors have thought of *that*? Yet with April four months away, how could she otherwise progress both her estate ambitions and her travel plans? At least she could talk to Holt about prices for her coal; but that entailed haggling about price.

FRIDAY 9 'Yes!' Said Holt, 'but it is different now – coal is an advancing article.' 'Oh! Oh!' thought I, 'Then Holt would bid me more than he has talked of'. 'But think of this', said I, 'that is, of my keeping the colliery in my own hands, at least for a while till sure what it is worth…

Said I, 'And you know very well that now I shall have a colliery of my own, I am not likely to agree [to your calculations].'

This was a good example of Anne remaining canny about mining prices, given that coal was 'an advancing article'! However, the arrival of another letter would soon set her back.

SATURDAY 10 *No kiss....* Then had Joseph Mann ... brought 13 bills to settle. Dinner at 7.20 – coffee upstairs – A~ read French & I the *Halifax Guardian* of this morning. A~ was to Cliff Hill this afternoon...

Letter tonight from Mr McKean, Yorkshire District Bank dated today: 'Madam, I beg to take the liberty of directing your attention to the balance [i.e. overdraft] of your account which appears to be increasingly considerably of late, without anything in the shape of a return [i.e. payment] being made... I have to request you will have the goodness to make something like a return, or reduce the amount of the balance... I remain, Madam, your most respectfully, Adam McKean, Manager.'[7]

A~ & I sat talking this over – I said, truly, I was glad it had come – it shews the weakness of the Bank – it shews that, contrary to what I was told on opening my account, I cannot go on drawing & leaving my account unsettled till spring. I was told I might draw to any amount – I said a credit of £7,000 or £8,000 would be enough – but that I would settle the account any time on a reasonable notice. McKean seemed to think little of this at the time. At the moment of 1st reading the letter, I thought of settling & closing my account as immediately as possible... I thought too of going to Briggs's bank... I feel sure necessity prompted the letter – it is very civilly written. My thought of leaving the bank is already growing fainter – perhaps by tomorrow morning I shall be satisfied to settle my account & trouble myself no further. I will stop all [expenditure] that can be stopped in the laying out way [i.e. laying out money]. This satisfied A~ who behaves beautifully...

As a member of the landed gentry, Anne naturally blamed the bank for her financial embarrassment. After all, they were merely commerce, while she had inherited Shibden's ancient acres. Mr McKean had to tread a fine line – between alienating a prestigious local client and running his bank professionally. However, Anne had rather boxed herself into a corner. She had left Rawsons' Bank; and after all the Briggs were leading Whigs.[8]

Meanwhile, Ann had received another impertinent letter, this time from one of the Sutherlands about a relative of theirs, Sir Alexander Mackenzie:

Had just written all the above of today at 11.30... Now at 11.45 pm, *proposed to A~ the following answer to Mrs Sutherland's letter. 'Madam, I am sorry to be reduced to the very disagreeable alternative of not answering your letter at all, or to informing you that I consider it an unjustifiable impertinence. I am, madam, your obedient servant – Ann Walker.*[9]

In this peremptory rebuttal, like that earlier of the lieutenant of the Dragoons, Anne made sure that Ann adopted the right commanding tone of rejection. It seemed the word was out in Sutherland circles that Ann was still an unmarried heiress. Little did these relatives know!

SUNDAY 11 *No kiss*... Then musing over my bank account & what to write to Messrs Gray. A~ & I alighted at the school at 2, 20 minutes there hearing the girls say their Psalms ... said very imperfectly... 20 minutes at the boys' school – the Psalms very well repeated... ½ hour at Cliff Hill – Mrs A. Walker in very good humour & spirits. Home in 25 minutes.

FRIDAY 16 *No kiss*... The cellar-passage was cut through yesterday into the west tower by noon today... *Then helped A~ with her letter ... & wrote & copied my own letter* ... to Messrs Gray, solicitors, York... One thousand [pounds] out of the seven [thousand] will be enough till the 30th April... Mr Watson to come over on Wednesday or Thursday next... 'I am gentlemen, your obedient servant.'

Certainly, negotiating such a large mortgage loan, especially ensuring £1,000 immediately, required the presence of their York lawyer.

Meanwhile, events both in Halifax and nationally meant Anne spent hours reading the papers; it is unclear exactly what gripped her attention, other than national politics shifting before her eyes,[10] and the enlarging of Halifax, making Northgate's strategic position even more significant.

SATURDAY 17 *No kiss*... Before & after dinner till 10.30 reading the Halifax paper of this morning & the London [paper] come tonight.

SUNDAY 18 *No kiss*... At my desk at 11.10. *Wrote copy of letter to Lady Stuart till* A~ came to me before 12... Mr Jubb called... Town's news – property getting up in value in the town – Northgate to be widened...

Said I was quite indifferent about it – but if the town wanted my field
… I would take it into consideration [illegible] now about the rail-road
coming.[11]

TUESDAY 20 *A pretty good kiss last night between one & two. A~ turned & said
she wanted petting – came to me & without a word we soon managed it tolerably…*
Wrote note to Messrs Parker & Adam … to beg they would inform
Mr Wainhouse his account should be settled on the 8th of next month.…

**Anne hoped to borrow £2,000 from Ann's aunt. However, probably easier
would be a £4,000 loan from someone outside the family.**

Meant to have gone to Cliff hill – *to ask Mrs A. Walker to lend me two thousand
till one May. Prevented by Mr Parker coming & keeping me talking…* I espied
Mr Parker peeping in upon us – asked him to come & see what we
had been doing… It appeared that Parker had … £4,000 lying in
the Bank – which could be had in the course of a week if terms could
be agreed, and I would give a mortgage. 4% might be thought too
little. Parker saw I would not give more… At last seemed that the
terms would be left to Parker & his co-trustee & that 4% might be
taken & the money would be 18 years before it would be wanted.…

**Even by Anne's standards, this was a highly complex financial transaction,
involving leading local industrialist Mr Wainhouse.**

I was determined not to get beyond my depth [financially]… *I thought to
myself, 'I will see how I can manage. Take the four thousand or not, as may be
most convenient.' Parker did not want me to pay off W*[ainhouse] *just* [yet]. *I
said, 'No, I might perhaps wait a year & see how I went on. But I should give up
as immediately as* possible, all jobs & work not absolutely necessary…[12]

**In all these highly complex transactions, who could Anne trust? Meanwhile,
Shepley Watson arrived from York.[13]**

FRIDAY 23 *No kiss…* With Mr Watson till breakfast… A~ went off to
the school… Had the kettle & hot wine & water for Watson. Long
talk… If I should want a thousand more, [he] thinks I can have it
from Mr Bairstow…

**James Bairstow, under-tenant at Water Lane mill, was a machine-maker who
also provided coal for Akroyd's large mill engine. As a small-scale entrepreneur
he saw that good money could be made in Halifax down by the canal.[14]**

Saturday 24 *No kiss... A~ & I sat talking. I mentioned republishing her will. It did not do at all. She had been vexed at my naming it yesterday before* [i.e. in front of] *Mr Watson – did not like to be hurried to sign it now – would consider about* [it]. [Was] *put out – I said I would say no more.*[15]

Meanwhile, Anne proceeded with mortgaging certain of her properties as security for the loan of £7,000 at 4% from the Misses Preston, daughters of an established local merchant.[16]

Watson advised me yesterday not [to] mortgage Lister Lane fields – for then I should be obliged to give up my Northgate title deeds... I to authorize the Misses Prestons to leave them [title deeds] in the hands of Messrs Gray... [Watson] wrote to Mr Gray last [night] about the £6,000... [Had] shewed Watson on the great plan the locality of the field – my farm of Little Marsh, & the locality of Mr Rawson's coal-pits.

Did Watson return to York feeling he now had a good grasp of the murky world of coal trespassing?

A & I ... off at 12.45 & walked to the school in ¾ hour. A~ went to distribute the clothing at both schools (boys & girls) – I stayed a few minutes to see the clothing to the latter – very nice – for about 80 girls. Walked leisurely back...

Said I thought it unnecessary for the 10 men who wanted something for rearing [i.e. building] the Hatter's Street new cottages to have a supper at 4/6 a head – a bad precedent – 3/- a piece to drink at the Black Horse quite enough....

The Manns had waited 1¼ hour before I had done the last account, & went down to them at 5.30 & talking & settling with them till dinner at 7. The Manns think a well (in the middle stable court) at Northgate would be 15 to 20 yards deep... The Manns would thoroughly repair A~'s Spa-house coal-pit ... for £10. They holed [i.e. sunk a shaft] about 4 pm today in driving (to shew Hinscliffe's trespass) at a point 62 yards north of the place where we 1st came to the coal from Walker pit...

So Anne's Christmas Eve was more about coal trespassing than celebration.

Dinner at 7 – coffee upstairs – hurried to leave the servants at liberty – they have a gala tonight – allowed [them] till 12 midnight. A~ read French – no newspaper tonight – the mail not arrived... Sat by A~ in the blue room & till 11.40 wrote the whole of [journal]...

Snowed more as A~ & I went to the school at 12.30 to 1.45... The coldest night we have had ever since A~ was here? Could not get A~ off to bed – sat till 1.10 & then I left her poring over her school accounts & promising to come directly.

Sunday 25 *No kiss.* A~ so tired last night I literally carried her to bed... At 12.30 read the prayers & one of Paley's sermons in ¼ hour. The London mail did not arrive till 10 past [mid]night – sent Frank this morning – letter from Messrs Gray... Mr Barstow has the sum which you want now ready in the Bank...[17]

Walking home from the school, Anne did rapid calculations about how much security five tenanted properties would raise.

All this occurred as I passed Listerwick on my return from the school... We not at church till 2.45... ½ hour at Cliff Hill – Mrs A Walker in good humour & spirits – glad to see us as always for the last year past. Home at 5.15 – very cold – a great deal of snow... Read the London paper that should have come last night ... dinner at 6.45 – coffee upstairs – A~ read French – I somewhat ½ asleep on the sofa, then till 11 ... calculating Robert's wages... 105 days at £21 per annum = £6.2.0... Letter to Messrs Gray ... note to M~ ... F25° now at midnight. *Found my cousin come gently on getting into bed.*

Christmas seemed to mean very little to Anne and Ann. It was the third they had spent together. On the first, in 1834, Anne had visited Mariana, leaving Ann at Shibden; their second seemed to have been low-key and now 1836 followed this pattern.
In the 1830s Christmas was still a rather rowdy celebration, with the Shibden servants allowed to enjoy their 'gala' until midnight. Carols were still more like traditional country folk songs, though all this was beginning to change. The festival had yet to be tidied up by the Victorians: they introduced Christmas trees, crackers and Father Christmas.[18]
What Anne did late on Christmas Day was revealing. She wrote to Mariana. Some of her letter concerned a servant, Robert, going from Shibden down to Lawton:

Shibden Hall – Sunday evening 25 December 1836.

My dearest Mary... He [Robert] is to be the bearer of this note. His wages with me is twenty guineas, and livery as customarily given. I hope he will suit you...

I told you, on Thursday, I could not get off before the 12th of next month. I hope we really shall be *en route* about that time – but do not positively believe it, till you hear from me again. Adney's [i.e Ann's] best love... Our kind regards to Mrs Milne – mine, if you please, to Mr Lawton, and 'ye complements of the season' to you all.

Ever, my dearest Mary, very sincerely & affectionately yours, A.L.[19]

This Christmas letter was partly conventional: exchange of a servant, news about travel plans. Then it strayed into deeper waters. Anne sent her regards, but not Ann's, to Mariana's husband Charles.

MONDAY 26 *No kiss.* Wild wintry morning... Joseph Mann ... [about] Hinscliffe's trespass at Walker Pit... Listerwick Pit [to be] bottomed by the end of August... Only 1 man in each head can work at a time – 1 man will do 1½ yards at a shift... Costs calculated...[20]

Sat talking to A~, then till 6 wrote all the above of today. *Twenty minutes washing good deal of cousin then.* Wrote to M~... We shall get off the 12th of next month if we can... A~ read her French & wrote to Miss Rawson... Wild wintry day.

[marginalia] all to be done & the Colliery regularly working next September 12th.

TUESDAY 27 *No kiss.* In bed an hour before A~ last night... Mr Husband ... said [of] Miss Walker ... [and] her jobs [that] he had his own way & could manage. I calmly but impressively took up this 'broad insinuation' and poor Husband felt probably that he had been foolish, the insinuation being unmerited and impertinent. He said he never had had ... so little power anywhere – in any job, as here... I quietly ... successfully combatted this... Poor fellow! He saw he was wrong...[21]

At 5 had Robert Mann – came about the well to be sunk, or reservoir, at A~'s Water Lane mill – must be 3 or 4 yards deep – will cost £10... Robert Mann would wait till summer. The job would then be done (working night & day) as it should be done in a week. A~ ordered R. Mann to explain all this to Barstow, the tenant...[22] This reservoir will certainly cut off [dry up?] in summer so long as the engine is going. The supply of water from the well Messrs Rawson & Co made, by magisterial fiat last spring, a public well. Will Mr Rawson set the old women of Caddy field to pull the mill down?

So, the Water Lane mill episode, about whether it was a public well and about the Caddy Field women, still festered. Then Anne talked of the Listerwick incline and its complex costs:

Then talking with R. Mann. about the Incline ... 6 ins per yard ... [rails] better for the boys (hurriers)... Banksman's house & smithy ... engine & engine-house... Pulleys for the chain of the Incline ...[23] the colliery will have cost me £5,000...

Letter this morning from Mr [Shepley] Watson, York, saying the money was ready to be paid at a day's notice – [he] should see Mr Barstow today & will then write to me ... re payment of the money... Till one, wrote A~'s journal of today.

So, Anne occasionally wrote Ann's journal for her. Extraordinary, as surely the diarist was she who held the pen! Meanwhile, Mr Harper arrived at Shibden.

WEDNESDAY 28 *No kiss*... Looked a little at the copies (Mr Harper had just given me) of the working plans of the Northgate hotel, & the 2 pretty drawings of Shibden as I was to find it on my return [from travelling]... Now the East tower is given up...[24]

THURSDAY 29 *No kiss*... Holt thinks ... the Listerwick colliery to be complete, & ready for bringing coal out at the Incline, by 1 October 1838 & the Christening to be on that day.[25] Holt ... said he could put 5 or 6 colliers in as soon as Listerwick pit was bottomed...

[About] Hinscliffe's trespass ... talked over sending for Mr James Norris [a leading Halifax lawyer] & employing him, if Hinscliffe would not settle the matter without [going to] law. Holt ... agreed at last it would be the best... Mr Parker was 'lost in coal'... Some villainy...

Samuel Washington [need] not to have anything to do with coal if Holt would bestir himself & manage it himself – if he could make it pay me, I would keep it in my own hands...

Obviously coal, 'an advancing article', was foxing all the traditional professionals in the Halifax area. It spelled money, but it lay deep in the dark underground.

Mr Harper ... sat with A~ & myself in the little (south) dining room after our dinner. Long talk about the colliery and about letting Northgate... I authorized him to let the hotel... Long talk about the expediency of taking Mr Carr [as tenant]. A~ thought <u>he</u> ought to pay £500 a year...

Mr Harper had heard rumours in York that Anne was entering into foolish speculations, both at Northgate and about mining. Eventually he was satisfied that this was merely York gossip.

[He was] not surprised to hear the ground to be taken for widening Northgate was to be £3 per yard – my property in Northgate would soon be very valuable... We roughly calculated that about £120 per annum might be made in ground rents. Then I had left the ground for the 3 shops & 1 house in Broad Street & the sheep croft.

Meanwhile, as the town grew in prosperity, the *Halifax Guardian* reported that Conservative interests aimed to stem Whiggish and especially Radical enthusiasm among working people through the formation of local Conservative Associations.[26]

Friday 30 *No kiss*... Read the 2 last newspapers... Note tonight from Mr Parker – wants 4½% & more land in the security. A~ spoke to her aunt this afternoon about [lending] money for me.

New Year's Eve was always a time when Anne reflected. In 1832 she wrote: 'How different my situation now and this time last year... Who will be the next tenant of my heart?' In 1835: 'Another year is gone! How altered my position since last year at this time! ... God be thanked!'[27] Now, in 1836, did she remain so optimistic? Her finances still on rather a knife edge, Anne wrote 3½ pages in her diary for 31 December.[28]

Saturday 31 *No kiss*... To Mr Parker's office – he received my navigation dividends... Then to ... Mr Waterhouse's counting house to receive A~'s navigation dividends, taking a note from her authorising Mr Waterhouse to pay them to me. The 2 sons there – about ¼ hour talking about the navigation and railroads. Nobody but Mr James Norris for the railroad from Halifax through Bradford to Leeds – it was likely to fall through. Asked what navigation shares were selling at – J Waterhouse junior said £410, the last sold for £417 – would not advise me to sell – I said I was in no hurry, but intended selling when I could get a fair price. Said Mr James Norris had 11 years ago offered me £500 per share – J Waterhouse said if he had bargained to have them at that price 5 or 6 years hence, it might do very well.[29] The Manchester and Leeds railroad shares still at a premium of £5 but were at par a few weeks ago – the committee had to apply to parliament again. – J Waterhouse gave me a Lithographed plan of the [rail] line under the present act – many deviations proposed.

Anne clearly continued to align herself with canal traditionalists like the Waterhouses, rather than with James Norris and his belief in the new-fangled

railway. Afterwards, she trusted that her landed gentry credentials would smooth her tricky discussion with her Halifax bank manager.

Then to the bank – saw MacKean – explained that I really must have a banker upon whom I could draw [money]... In future my income would pass more regularly through my county banker [i.e. York] ... I can settle all by the end of April, but I must be able to draw in the meantime. I should like to be able to leave home – but if there be anything difficult or disagreeable, I will not run away, but stay to face it out. I might be able to pay something to lessen my balance before the end of April, but dare not speak with certainty before the end of April. Mr Harper would want an order for £6,000 but he would not want more than £1,000 (and that not all at once) before the end of April...

I read tonight's London paper – then till 11.45 wrote the whole of today... *Mrs Ann Walker said not a word this afternoon about lending me money, and A~ says I am not to say anything without [i.e. unless] Mrs A Walker mentions it again to A~, so that I have now no hope from this quarter.* F25° now at midnight.

Anne's immediate money problems would therefore not be helped by Cliff Hill. Ann would act as intermediary, so did that give her the upper hand with Anne? And, at her Halifax bank, Mr McKean was probably not taken in by her airy suggestion that 'I might be able to pay something...' Financially 1836 ended on a tricky note.

IV

MAINTAINING THE UPPER HAND: MONEY

JANUARY 1837

JANUARY 1837

As in so many heterosexual marriages, there were shared interests and activities – together with some continuing tensions, notably over managing the Shibden servants. More broadly, Anne always preferred to keep control of any situation. Yet could this be sustained when she remained in part financially dependent on Ann's family wealth?

Meanwhile, the political tensions that had bubbled in 1836 began to surface visibly again. With the introduction of the new Poor Law, the *Halifax Guardian* reported on the setting up of a Halifax Poor Law Union and electing Guardians of the Poor who would run the hated workhouses. Traditional communities resented such intrusion by central state administration.[1] Alongside, tensions grew between the Halifax Conservatives (with their celebratory dinner at the White Swan Inn) and certain Methodist chapels' Radical sympathies. Religion and politics, Anglicanism and Conservatism, all remained closely entwined.[2]

SUNDAY 1 *No kiss...* Read the *Halifax Guardian* of yesterday... A~ & I had the servants all assembled in the South parlour & read the prayers & one of Paley's sermons, very good, on new year's day... At Church at 2.25 ... Mr Fenton did all the duty... About 25 minutes at Cliff Hill – Mr Fenton arrived... The present [i.e. Whig] ministers wanted to make a radical bishop of Ripon – the archbishop of York said if they did, he would not give up [i.e. not contribute] his money. But if they would appoint ... our vicar, Mr Musgrave [a 'Blue'] ... he (the archbishop) would give up the money...

Sealed my letter to Messrs Gray, solicitors York ... beg them to let me know as immediately as possible if I could [have] fifteen thousands from the Misses Preston by the end of April...

Dinner at 6.30... A~ read her French, and afterwards read aloud from the London paper of tonight... Went to undress about 10.40 – about 11 heard a very strange noise of bustle & screaming in a confused undertone. Found Cookson & Oddy with A~ who had set her night-cap on fire, & thrown it blazing on the hearth-rug instead of, as she intended, into the fireplace. Everybody frightened but luckily no further harm done [other] than singeing a little of A~'s pretty flaxen hair – thankful that <u>she</u> was safe. Sat talking to near 12.

It seemingly took a dangerous fire for Anne to record Ann's 'pretty flaxen hair'. Next day, one of Anne's Northgate tenants arrived to discuss letting it as a hotel.

MONDAY 2 *No kiss...* Mr Greenwood arrived...[3] [I] had provisionally let it [i.e. Northgate] (to Thomas G[reenwood]) for £100... My uncle Joseph always said his house would one day be a school or an Inn – I chose the latter – did not like to let the whole place for less than 1/3rd of what I paid for one flat in Paris...[4]

Luckily for Anne, Mr Greenwood, a good source of town news, lent her a sympathetic ear:

Then talked over Mr Rawson & the coal-business – said I had been forced into opening the [Listerwick] colliery. [5] Greenwood said it was generally understood that Rawson had behaved very ill to me – mentioned the Water-lane mill business. Greenwood said Rawson had very often forgot [to behave like a magistrate], but never more than on that business – no justice in that – Rawson prejudged the case & behaved very ill...

[I said, to Greenwood] I must have more money between now and the end of April when I proposed clearing off everything [i.e. any debts]. From now to end of April, I should want £1,000 on the Northgate account – and perhaps £300 (not more than £400) on the colliery account. I could do with increasing my balance [to] £1,500 from now to the end of April... I said I could get £6,000, [not] mentioned from whom... I preferred having fifteen thousands in one sum at the end of April... Greenwood thought all this very reasonable...

Greenwood advised my not giving notice to pay in the 5 thousand at present...

Anne's confiding so intimately in Greenwood probably suggests more her financial desperation, rather than any close relationship.[6]

Letter from Lady Stuart... The Stuarts de Rothesays gone to Rome – if I make haste I shall find them [there] & they will be glad to see me... Matty Pollard ... drank tea in the housekeeper's room this evening to celebrate the new year

So, by New Year 1837, the disjunct could not be starker between, on the one hand, Anne's life as perceived by Lady Stuart (probably naïvely, rather than maliciously) and, on the other, her desperate short-term financial problems. Where should she turn to now?[7]

TUESDAY 3 *No kiss*... Read last night's London paper... Told Joseph [Mann] that if I did not clear £300 per acre by the coal, it would not pay me... Met the Vicar [Musgrave] & his 2 little boys coming along the Lodge road – apologize ... asked him in... I very civil...

Had Robert Mann in the upper Kitchen... [Long talk] about the colliery... Talked of Mr Rawson's colliery – his engine now pumps water 40 yards... The noise of the Engine & the 'sooing' of the water will prevent their [i.e. miners] being able to hear themselves speak – danger might come upon them unawares – they could <u>hear</u> nothing. In fact, Robert Mann evidently thinks <u>the job very dangerous</u>...[8] When the hard bed was loosed from before, we can tell what Rawson can or cannot have got...

Also visiting was her tenant Samuel Freeman, a loyal 'Blue' voter and stone merchant now grown prosperous, so an invaluable informant about stone quarrying and finances.

I would make up my mind whether to sell the stone or not – but the money would be useful to me now. Then talked of the Banks – he said our 2 ... two of the strongest in England... I hope poor Freeman has not been gulled by the Rawsons... [I said], 'Can you help me? I only want the help till 30th of April next – a thousand or two will do.' 'Yes!' said Freeman very handsomely, 'You shall have it – whichever sum you will – but I should give a week's notice to the Bank.' I said I was really much obliged. 'Of course, it would be at 5%.' 'Yes!

How?'… [I replied], 'Will you take bills at 3 or 4 months on the Yorkshire District Bank?' 'Yes!' … R[awson Bank] to pay Freeman's account in the District Bank, & the District Bank to credit me. Freeman did not wish Rawson to know anything about it. If he (Freeman) did a kindness, he did not wish it to be known. But perhaps I should name it… Freeman will call again in about a week – we shook hands – and I told him he had obliged me very much. Then came up to A~ & told her what had passed – sat talking…

When it came to money, the tables were now turned. Freeman, one of her tenants (albeit a prosperous one), could lend Anne Lister up to £2,000! And they ended by shaking hands. So were her immediate financial problems now solved?

Parker had this morning … [seen] Mr Jeremiah Rawson [who wanted] to know if I was disposed to sell him any coal! Parker answered he would communicate to me the application; 'He talked of a lease of 21 years!!!' A~ & I astonished – probably Mr Parker himself was not prepared for such an application from such a quarter.

After all, the effigy-burning tale was still just a year ago.

Note from Mr MacKean with my banking book. Balance against me [overdraft] £2,369.9.8, about £230 more than I expected or made out! … 'Perfectly agreeable to enter into agreement proposed … £3,000 to be paid for our credit at York…'

However, Anne preferred to enter into a local arrangement.

WEDNESDAY 4 *No kiss…* Snow a good deal gone… Wrote out Rent audit… Went down to S. Washington at 10.35 – settling with him about the rent day etc till 11.15. He thought £100 for Lower Brea too much… S. Washington to consider about [it]…

Then James Holt came, and a detailed colliery conversation followed. The Rawsons had to pull some of their coal out at a very inconveniently isolated pit up at Marsh:

Mentioned Mr Jeremiah Rawson's application for the coal. Rawson can't now get more than 2 acres per annum, because obliged to pull all up at the Marsh pit… They can't get 28 yards down with their present engine. What an outlay [i.e. expense]! Rawson says the coal does not pay him now. How can it pay him hereafter? Nothing, no coal for him to buy but of [i.e. except from] me or Mr Walker Priestley, 40 or 50 D.W, which Holt can get at ½ the expense [than] Rawson can…[9] Rawson's colliery can't last many years – must now turn off half his colliers – can't employ more than 10 or 12… Told Holt, if I did not clear £300 per acre, I should be forced into letting my colliery. Holt all in good spirits – said it would pay that – coal would keep up – my coal would always average 10d per load… All above £300 per acre would be benefit to pay me for my trouble in keeping the colliery in my own hands…

Small-scale rural industrialization now seemed unstoppable. When Anne met Freeman later, she learned that he was 'turning a corn mill of his into a worsted mill – would cost him £2,000'.[10]

Meanwhile, it was Shibden's rent day, with Washington busy collecting tenants' rents:

Upstairs at Stag's Head & sent for Aquilla Green…[11] [He] can keep on both mills, this here & the mill at Halifax… Had Sam Washington who paid me the rents he had received this morning at the Stag's Head… To see Thomas Greenwood, not the best farmer. 'No!' said S. Washington, evidently agreeing…

Reading the architectural magazine that came tonight… Letter from Mr [Shepley] Watson – the Misses Preston would be glad to accommodate me. They would hear from Mr Parker! Getting them a security for £8,000… Sat up with A~ talking.

All this high finance, involving both local and York lawyers, meant things seemed to be looking up for Anne – thanks to the Misses Preston of Halifax, plus Wainhouse's long-term loan. Thus on Saturday 7th, Anne went to the bank and got '£50 in notes'.[12]

SUNDAY 8 Left A~ at Cliff hill to stay till Wednesday. Wrote note to Robert Parker Esq, the Square, enclosing check for £154.5.6d dated tomorrow, to be paid to Mr Wainhouse, Washer Lane [Halifax] in full of interest up to 8th inst… Letter from Messrs Gray – Mr [Shepley] Watson will be here on the Manchester mail [coach] on Tuesday morning.

MONDAY 9 A~ at Cliff hill… Went down to Joseph Mann … examining Holt's coal-account & Joseph Mann's… Received from him for coal sold from 3 July to 31 December inclusive … 385 loads £13.4.2. total coal got… George returned from Shibden Mill with A~'s rents, £515.13.6…

Clearly, Ann Walker's income still far outweighed Anne's.

Short note to A~, Cliff Hill… Mr Watson's being here tomorrow morning… A~ to come home – leave at Cliff Hill what she would want there, & return for a night, after Mr Watson was gone. What orders to be given tonight about the room preparing & when George to go for A~…?[13]

[Mr Freeman] had brought £1,000 from Rawsons, Briggs & the Huddersfield Joint Stock Bank, of which last Freeman a proprietor. They all thought he had taken the money out to pay wages. Would see about another thousand pounds for me next week… £1,000 for 112 days at 5% = £15.6.10. Gave Mr Freeman a check … dated Halifax 1 May 1837 … on demand … £1,015.6.10…

I am much obliged to Mr Freeman. He can get to know what the stone … sold for… Freeman says … Little Marsh land is the best bit of stone I have… All banks alike – all at times call their money in when people least prepared to pay it. 'Mr John Rawson soft when stood up to.' Freeman thinks Mr Stansfield [Rawson] by far the best of them – he (Stansfield Rawson) much respected at Huddersfield…[14]

George brought me note & parcel from A~. George to be at Old Washington's for A~ at 3.30 tomorrow.[15] Very nice note from the dear Little-one… Wrote 4 pages … to A~ for John to take to little John tonight to take to A~ at Cliff hill tomorrow. *Bavardage amical* [i.e. gossip?] – some of the latter part in French – *Je suis bien triste* etc… Wrote … to Lady Vere Cameron – very kind letter.

TUESDAY 10 A~ at Cliff hill… Counting over my money – *took one hundred pounds from A~'s Shibden mill rents to pay Duncan's [undertaker] bill … for my aunt's funeral.*[16] *And took Mr Freeman's thousand to the bank. Off to Halifax at 11, down the Old Bank to the bank.* Paid in £1,100…

So what was going on? The funeral bill seems long unpaid, suggesting Anne's straitened finances and her dependence on Freeman's loan. Yet imagine walking down Old Bank into Halifax carrying £1,000!

A~ returned at 5 with a bad cold... Letter ... to the Lady Vere Cameron ... very kind letter – she is mixed up in my remembrance with many associations that I value highly – 'I cannot forget; & to be forgotten would give me nameless pain'... Will be off if possible before the end of the month... Had Mr Watson in the little dining room (South parlour)... Had hot wine & water & biscuits, & Mr Watson sat till 11 – the payments of interest, A~'s & mine, to be 15 January & 15 July...

Letter tonight ... from M~ Lawton to say Robert [footman] would probably be in Halifax tomorrow ... could not do at Lawton – hardly sense to take care of himself – will pass through Halifax on his way to Sheffield.[17]

WEDNESDAY 11 *No kiss*... Had widow Hall from Little Marsh... She gave me back the old lease from my uncle Joseph Lister – & wanted to beg something [i.e. payment] for the manure & the few set-stones. Both of right [are] mine... Gave her a glass of port wine & biscuits... 10 mins with S Washington – he values the Godley 4 cottages at £150 – to get them for me, quietly if he can – it will save me building new ones for the [Listerwick] Colliery [workers]...

2 girls, one a Miss Farrer (niece to Miss Hebden of Slack) would like to go to Paris to be a governess – very sorry I could be of no assistance to her – what a silly girl to come to me, a perfect stranger ... on such an errand. With A~ till 1.30...

Anne often showed her gentry hauteur when faced with such requests. Meanwhile, it was naturally appropriate for Anne to benefit from Ann Walker's larger rentals, yet for such transactions to be recorded in code.

To Cliff Hill... Home at 5. A~ tired – almost knocked up... A~ went down to Mr S Washington about 7.30 & received her Halifax rents that he had collected today. *About two hundred & eighty pounds, being about eighty pounds unpaid.* I sat reading... Then sat talking to A~ till 10.20 pm... A~ had letter tonight from Miss Rawson.[18]

THURSDAY 12 *No kiss*... Reading the newspaper... [A~] going ... to Cliff Hill to stay there till Sunday... *She gave me this morning one hundred & sixty [pounds] to pay Duncan etc – & gave me another parcel afterwards. As I supposed fifty, but I find it one hundred & twenty five, or in all £285.* A~ off on her pony to Halifax about 11.

Such financial generosity might be part of any conventional marriage. Ann had effectively given Anne all her Halifax rents to help pay her aunt's funeral costs. Indeed, Anne still remained partly financially dependent on Ann. Yet she always tried to retain some financial independence – just in case. There were, after all, no legal or financial provisions laid down for a lesbian marriage.

Much of the diary now just detailed estate business. However, political tensions began to escalate further. The *Halifax Guardian* reported that the Assistant Poor Law Commissioner had arrived, making preliminary enquiries about Halifax Poor Law Union. Then the local election of Guardians of the Poor for Halifax was announced; alongside, there was a banquet in Glasgow, celebrating the installation of Sir Robert Peel. And with Peel came recognition of the urgency of drumming up more 'Blue' votes – and hence the need to form local Conservative Associations.[19] After all, another General Election might soon loom.

On 17 January Anne received a letter from Vere Cameron, addressed to 'Mrs Lister':

My dear Miss Lister… Now must I really call you and introduce you as Madame? It will be quite unnatural to do so. I can quite understand that epithet being useful abroad, but in your own country the change will make more talk than it is worth…

Do not let any consideration connected with your little friend (is not her name Miss Walker) deprive me of the long looked for pleasure of your company, because I can lodge her perfectly well, and do not think of fobbing me off with one night…

Ever affectionately yours, Vere Cameron.[20]

Vere was practised at writing arch letters that could make Anne feel uncomfortable.

SATURDAY 21 *No kiss… A~ found her cousin come the first thing this morning…*
Mark Town signed his agreement for Wakefield gate field & part of Long field, & the 2 Manns witnessed it. [21] Told him he had no vote – I would not make him one [vote], because I could not do with my tenants voting against me, & he was under some obligation to vote with his Whig master, Mr Jonathan Akroyd. Said … I would see about doing up the old cottage adjoining his house … if it cost much, he (Mark Town) must pay something…

So Mark Town was employed at Akroyd's worsted Bowling Dyke Mills.[22] He was unlucky to be caught between his Tory landowner and Whig employer.

Was this Anne at her most politically ruthless? She would not 'make him' a vote since he worked for a Whig Methodist manufacturer.

Glanced over this morning's *Halifax Guardian* and read the London *Morning Herald* received tonight – confidence at last happily returning in the money market.

SUNDAY 22 *No kiss...* Church... Cliff Hill... Wrote to Lady Stuart... Dinner at 6.35 – <u>tea</u> (the Halifax coffee so bad)... Letter from John Lister's sister – brother is ill ... she asks for loan!

MONDAY 23 *No kiss...* Charles Howarth was at Little Marsh yesterday – a gate 10 feet wide wanted to be made for the quarry – 6 gates made, 6 more to be made... A~ very poorly ... full of cold.

TUESDAY 24 *No kiss.* A~ took 2 teaspoons of Epsom salts... Tea again instead of Halifax bad coffee... Little Marsh farm [new lease].[23]

THURSDAY 26 *She came to me & we had a good kiss last night.* Fine dullish morning...
   Letter this morning from M~ Lawton, enclosed in a parcel containing ... bandages for Buffler's [horse] sprained fetlock... Letter tonight from some man in Warley hearing that I wanted a female infant to bring up & offering me one 1½ year old!

Warley, just the other side of Halifax, was near enough to know of two 'single' women landowners living together at Shibden. Was this a genuine 'child sale' or at least the possible adoption of a luckless orphan child? Or was Anne being joshed again?[24]

SATURDAY 28 *She came to me & we had a good kiss last night...* Letter to John Lister, London. Also to Lady Vere Cameron & Lady Stuart de Rothesay, parcel to Lady Stuart, Whitehall... Dinner at 6.45 – coffee (arrived this morning from York) ... & afterwards sat reading aloud to A~ till 10... *Geological Sketches* by Maria Hack. A~ bought the little work some time ago, & seemed interested, I reading what was worth reading and leaving out the nonsense...

Maria Hack's *Geological Sketches and Glimpses of the Ancient Earth* (1832), including fascinating drawings of ancient elk skeletons, popularized geology for children. Back at Shibden, the farm animals were less exotic:

Wheatley the veterinary surgeon came again this morning, but I would not trouble myself to see him or the horse, the latter going on well... The dunghill partly removed today... Then undressed, then stood reading tonight's papers.

TUESDAY 31 *No kiss*... A~ rode off to the school... I sat in the north parlour planning the outbuildings, stables etc till 3. Then had the sexton (Issac Ingham) who brought me the rent of the pew [of] late Mrs Briggs, now Miss Patchett...[25] Some time afterwards had James Hartley, my Hipperholme quarrier... Wrote 3 pages of letter to Lady Stuart ... and to Lady Harriet de Hagemann...[26] Asleep on the sofa till 10. This sitting in the house 2 days together does not suit me... Afterwards read tonight's paper.

So January ended with most of Anne's financial anxieties solved; though it was not yet clear how these loans might affect the balance of her relationship with Ann Walker. However, recently sexual activity was initiated more by Ann than Anne.

V

READING AROUND THE WORLD: ORIGINS

FEBRUARY–MARCH 1837

FEBRUARY 1837

Party politics now permeated everyday life, even the renting of church pews. Indeed, some men, shortly to emerge as local Chartists, began to voice their utter hatred of a corrupt, undemocratic political system.

On an even wider world stage, young Charles Darwin had returned in October 1836 from his voyage on the *Beagle*. He brought exciting new evidence of the earth's history and met Lyell himself. In January he read a paper to the Geological Society of London, noting coastal uplift in Chile, finding shingle terraces and seashells high up.[1] He began to be feted and was elected to Fellowship of the Society. Yet how much could Anne Lister, a woman in distant Yorkshire, know of Darwin, let alone participate in this hugely exciting intellectual ferment?

Meanwhile, Anne remained immersed in her business concerns.

WEDNESDAY 1 Holt said we should have 20 colliers – could not reckon on a collier to get more than 22 corves a day working 8 hours… Holt to get an estimate of the Incline…

Long talk of … Mr Gilmore's pamphlet advising letting all our pews by auction to pay for the expense of the church. Even Mr Jonathan Akroyd, leader of the Whigs, says he will not support the scheme – it is unjust – only a few Radicals taken with it.[2]

Alongside, Anne still desperately needed immediate financial help:

Greenwood will consult his colleague whether they can advance me a thousand … before 1 May – said I wanted a thousand to send to Hammersleys…

Mr Husband came for the payment of some bills of A~'s... Speaking of the 4 shops adjoining the Northgate hotel, Husband thought they could be built for £400 apiece – but advised waiting a year when labour etc would be cheaper.

Now, a new tenant, Mr Womersley at Little Marsh, spelled a political opportunity:

THURSDAY 2 *No kiss*... Had Womersley... He was to go & sign his lease of the farm, Little Marsh, & S. Washington would give him possession. [I] hoped he would stay there [for] his life, and give me a quiet vote. 'Yes!' He thought between [his rent on] farm & quarry, he should have [i.e. qualify for] a vote & would give it to me...

However, with no Secret Ballot Act yet, there was scarce such a thing as a 'quiet vote'. Womersley obviously hoped the Whigs and Radicals would not notice his name on the *Poll Book* recording how he had voted.

From 10 to 11.45 read tonight's paper of [the] King's speech & the speeches in the two houses [of Parliament] – the address moved & passed without disappointment.[3]

Anne, like the rest of the country, was following national politics with increasingly keen interest, taking nearly two hours to read the newspaper.

FRIDAY 3 *No kiss*... A~ & I off in the carriage to Stainland etc at 10.55. Left at Whitley's [bookseller] to be bound the whole of the *Morning Herald* newspapers of the last year. Took Tombleson's *Upper & Lower Rhine* (2 volumes, 30/-) in the carriage to look at. Waited (in the carriage) at Nicholson's door [draper], reading, 25 minutes, while A~ made purchases.

Shopping offered a very visible distinction between male and female spheres: reading about exploration set against purchasing drapery. However, family visits were made together, first in Halifax then out past Sowerby:

Stopt at the door *en passant* at Haugh End to inquire after [the Priestleys] & left our card (Mrs Lister & Miss Walker) for Mr & Mrs Henry Priestley – both had been very ill – now out of danger. Then called on Mr & Miss Priestley (Thorpe)...

Once again, the social route to visiting Ann's extended family, entwined through intermarriages, was clear. From Sowerby and the Ryburn valley they took a sharp left turn steeply uphill and descended into the valley by Barkisland to see Ann's rural tenants (see Map II). On this trip, they happily mixed pleasure with business: out in the remote countryside, Anne helped Ann negotiate with Outram.

Up Ripponden Bank & through Barkisland to Charles Law's to see his new barn... At Mr Outram's at 4.50 to 5.25 to see about the mill goit. Outram wants to buy 200 yards of ground of A~... offered the rate of £100 per acre. I said that was 5d a yard – he should give A~ 6d per yard, & she consented to let him have 200 yards at this price, & he is to let her have a right of road [i.e. passage] into the Ing [i.e. meadow] & pay ... the same rent as now. Going to light the mill with oxy-hydro gas (same proportions of oxygen & hydrogen as form water).

SATURDAY 4 *No kiss*... A~ tired out & out of sorts... Off to the school between 10 & 11...

Anne then had a visit from Wortley's committee chair, expert at drumming up 'Blue' votes. Given the controversial new Poor Law, electing local Guardians to administer it became increasingly important:

Mr Holroyde came at 12 (senior) ... to solicit A~'s & my votes to appoint Guardians of the Poor. Mr Holroyde junior wishing to be the clerk – said I would consider about it & would inform A~, but did not give much encouragement about our votes at all.[4]

Wheatley the horse doctor came... Dinner at 6.45. A~ tired – she had walked home by herself, unknown to me till her arrival... *At dinner, opened Mr MacKean's note received yesterday – to say they could not advance me any more money. A~ inquired what then note was. I said: from MacKean. He was to send back the irregular checks. I would not tell A~ more. Annoyed – but I am better now.*

Two points are immediately clear: Anne's financial embarrassment continued, and this humiliation had to be kept from Ann who would probably be vexed, wondering where all the money had gone!

Asleep or lolling on the sofa while A~ read her French... Read the whole of the *Halifax Guardian* of today & skimmed over the London paper. The pressure on the money market as bad or worse than ever.

She would read about a local ratepayers' meeting to call for Guardians. The nomination of Jonathan Akroyd was shouted down with cries of 'The greatest tyrant in town' and 'An enemy of the 10 Hour Bill'. The Bill was also denounced by two emerging Chartists, the meeting ending in disorder.[5]

SUNDAY 5 No kiss. Fine frosty morning, F31° at 9. *Up to pot & quarter-hour on it. A long large motion...* Breakfast... *Then three-quarters hour on the pot in my dressing room – reading, the* [Epsom?] *salts working every now & then.*[6]
　Sat with A~ & had a basin of broth, & reading *Gentleman's Magazine* till [we] went to church... I afterwards sat reading till A~ returned... Read ... Lyell's *Geology* volume 3.

Interestingly, Anne had bought Lyell's third volume back in 1834: she liked to keep bang up-to-date intellectually. Yet as a woman, Anne was excluded both from universities and learned societies.[7]

MONDAY 6 *No kiss...* To Mr Parker's office – saw Mr Adam respecting voting for Guardians of the Poor... Mr Adam to come at 5 this afternoon about the voting. It ought not to be a party question... *Mr Parker to get me a thousand* [pounds] *of Mr Wainhouse by next Monday.* Then went to the bank ... he [McKean] very civil...[8]
　Came in at 5.35 to Mr Adam – A~ & I appointed him proxy to give our votes for the 5 Conservative named Guardians who will vote for Mr Holroyde as their clerk – giving the description of the property for which we voted in [the townships of] Halifax, Northowram & Hipperholme-cum-Brighouse (& I in addition to these, for Southowram for property & as resident ratepayer) – took us till after 6.

Anne and Ann as landowners had a Poor Law vote, and their interest had to be represented. However, elections were often rowdy, so they used a male proxy. Interestingly, Ann could vote in three townships, and Anne in four. Thus landed gentry women could exert some local political power.

Jack Green helping to get coals in this afternoon – Frank carting them from Walker Pit... [Read] the first 22 pages, volume iii Lyell's *Geology*.

TUESDAY 7 *No kiss.* I in bed an hour before A~ last night & nearly as long the night before...[9] At the top of the house, Booth & his men taking the slates off the present water-closet to make a lead gutter up against the [west] tower...
　Went to Cliff Hill for A~. Sat 35 minutes with Mrs A. Walker – very civil & glad to see me & in good spirits...[10] Met S Washington, told

him about his being proxy for our votes for the Guardians of the Poor – walked leisurely home.[11] A~ had been all the day … at the school…

Note from Mr Parker to say the £1,000 ready any time – but if not wanted this week, Mr Parker proposes Wednesday next week for the payment if that will suit me.

WEDNESDAY 8 *No kiss*… A~ wrote for me tonight to Messrs Parker & Adam: Mrs Lister much obliged … next Wednesday would do very well. I should be in town & would call at the office between 11 & 12.

THURSDAY 9 *No kiss*… Down the new bank to Northgate to meet Mr Husband – took him with me to … Water Lane mill – the foundry there a very slightly done-up building…

Sat a few mins with (old) Mr & Mrs Wainhouse.[12] Then to Roper's shop about fireplace for the north parlour… Then to Nicholson's – a few minutes at Whiteley's…

Had the collector, Mr Jeremiah Best, this afternoon & paid him [the] poor & constable rate for Northowram [township] up to 1 April next… Read … vol 3, Lyall's *Geology*, & then read … the debates in tonight's paper.

FRIDAY 10 *No kiss*… After 11 Mr Higham's clerk brought a paper for me to sign (as occupier of Hipperholme woods) resident – to vote for Mr Higham as Guardian of the Poor. [13] Both A~ & I signed, each of us occupying woods or something in the township…

Again, the new was entering the traditional world. The national government had determined that local Poor Law Guardians would be elected, but this was organized through ancient townships and with 'land ownership' still important.

SUNDAY 12 *No kiss*. A~ up early & breakfasted & was off to the school at 8.30… Off to the school & there at 2.15 – took up A~… Waited some time in church… Drove to Cliff Hill – sat an hour with Mrs A Walker before A~ came… Home at 5.50. Looking into Letter drawer in our bedroom – dinner at 6.40 – coffee – read a little of tonight's paper.

MONDAY 13 *No kiss*. 20 mins putting on A~'s gaiters – she breakfasted, off to the school… Came in at 6 – A~ not returned – set off to meet her & came up with her at Charles Howarth's – sadly tired.

The walk to Lightcliffe might look short, but it sloped down from Shibden to Red Beck, then rose steeply up to Hipperholme before flattening out.

TUESDAY 14 *No kiss...* Mr Harper dissatisfied with the joiners' work at Northgate – will speak to Mr Parker tonight... Kind letter ... from Lady Stuart, Whitehall.

So, while Anne was busy with estate business and immersed in geology, did she notice Ann's apparent tardiness to join her in bed? What might Ann have been not saying while Anne's finances were so fraught?

WEDNESDAY 15 *No kiss.* A~ not in bed last night till 2.30 – had breakfast & was off to the school this morning...

Down Old Bank to Mr Parker's... Gave Mr Parker a note of hand for the money... 'Received of Mr Parker one thousand pounds which I engage to repay on the 1ˢᵗ of May next with interest ... at 5%. A Lister.' And desired him to pay it into the Yorkshire District Bank this afternoon. Then to the bank – told Mr McKean [that] Mr Parker would pay £1,000 in on my account this afternoon, & I begged to draw up to this amount. 'Oh! Yes! Certainly' was Mr McKean's answer...[14]

A~ sadly out of sorts at having waited so long for dinner – I had no idea it was so late – had never heard the dinner bell – neither of us uttered during dinner... Looked over the paper – things seem beginning to improve in London.

THURSDAY 16 *No kiss – but A~ right again – she said she had heard me get into bed. Yes. And she began moaning & wanting notice & pity – but I pretended to be asleep...* A little while with A~, off on her pony about 8.30, to ride as far as [Hipperholme]... Out at 10 with Joseph Mann at Pump to see about the setting out of Listerwick Pit – had John Oates with us...

Sat reading Murray's *Encyclopedia of Geology* & the newspaper...[15] High boisterous wind ... hear the water falling from the rocks very distinctly.

SATURDAY 18 *No kiss...* A~ had been at the school all day – several talks with Mr Hutchinson. A~ would give him six weeks [notice] ... and if he could not do better ... he would then be at liberty, & A~ would provide herself with another master. Poor A~! What trouble & anxiety!

SUNDAY 19 *No kiss...* Rainy windy boisterous day... Took up A~ at the school, & at church at 2.30... Too rainy & stormy to call at Cliff Hill. Home at 4.25... Reading botany of Denmark, Norway & Sweden, Murray's *Encyclopedia of Geology.*

TUESDAY 21 No kiss... Sat musing & planning – *bedroom in west tower for A~ & myself & dressing room.*[16] A heavy shower... *Then writing copy of letter to Mr Harper...*

Why were these entries written in code? Perhaps Anne had not discussed this plan with Ann, or was it because of the extra expenditure?

I read partly aloud the <u>pith</u> of tonight's paper ... and a little aloud out of the *Encyclopedia of Geology.* Then at 10 went to my study.

Now married for three years, Anne, like many a busy intellectual spouse, sometimes seemed to prefer to spend her evenings absorbed in the latest geology books. Was this more interesting than playing backgammon with Ann; and if so, what did that imply for their marriage? Yet, when danger loomed, Anne's bravery was invaluable.

FRIDAY 24 *No kiss...* High wind all last night. Just as A~ was getting into bed at one, heard a loud knock. Called up John Booth, who went out & found his pistol. This roused me up, A~ fancying she had seen a light in the saddle room. Put on my dressing gown & pelisse & stockings (had slept in flannel drawers & socks all the winter) & went all over the house, all over the cellars, leaving John with A~ in the hall. Found the drawing room window-shutters unclosed & the door unlocked – & the buttery door into the kitchen unfastened. Got into bed again about 1.30. Rained early this morning & high wind...

Then had Taylor the tinner in the storeroom ... had him to do the cowslip wine cellar cupboard... Dinner at 6.40 – coffee – read the newspaper *and corrected A~'s letter to her sister about selling building ground at Golcar.*[17]

Winter weather could be perilously wuthering up near the Pennines, and Shibden was certainly exposed to such dangers. Indeed, Anne, despite her flannel nightwear, caught a cold and had to stay in bed.

SATURDAY 25 *No kiss...* A~ off on her pony about 11, to the school & Cliff Hill... [A~] wanted me to lie in bed till her return – tired of bed. Up at 12.40 ... out at 1.35 ... Robert Mann + 2... Dinner at

6.30... Then sat reading the *Halifax Guardian* of this morning & the London paper of tonight till 10.30.

Despite Ann's kindliness, Anne's poor health persisted.

SUNDAY 26 *No kiss*. My cold very bad – hardly any voice at all – breakfast in bed (a tea-cake & a large basin of hot tea) which threw me into a perspiration... A~ went to church at 3 – & back at 4.45 – very good & attentive – I lay in bed the whole day ... sat up in A~'s flannel dressing-gown & my great coat over all – glad to get back into bed – felt tired.

MONDAY 27 *No kiss*. Breakfast in bed – better this morning – could speak tolerably... Atlas to look at in bed, & thus amused myself, she sitting by me... Mr Jubb came & sat with us till 3... Said I should take my glass of wine... Finished my letter to M~ ... saying I had been 2 days in bed with a bad cold.

TUESDAY 28 *She came to me & good & short kiss last night...* [A~] went to Cliff Hill... I sat reading till 12.40 *Foreign Quarterly* ... good article on 'the foreign policy & internal administration of Austria' ... 'No spot in Europe so remarkable for natural varieties, nor any so little travelled, as the chain extending ... through Croatia & Hungary'... Railway from Vienna into Gallicia ... & to Trieste...

Sat 1/2 hour with A~. Ate a biscuit or 2... Coffee a little after 8 – from 9 to 10 played backgammon – A~'s thought – we played 3 hits and she won them all. Very kind letter tonight ... from Lady Harriet de Hagemann (Copenhagen) ... gave my letter to Miss Ferral – and they talked me over. Begs me to write & say when I am going & where – all [i.e. everything] about myself is interesting to Lady Harriet de Hagemann...

Found A~ gone to bed – she had complained of being much tired while playing backgammon. She had hurried into bed – could not bear to sit up any longer – would take a glass of wine which I gave her & left her about 10.30. Then about ½ hour skimming over tonight's paper. I fear poor A~ is beginning in the influenza – I have dreaded it for some time past.

So, February ended on a diminuendo, winter illness affecting them both. Alongside, Anne's elite Copenhagen friends 'talked me over', undoubtedly

gossiping about how Anne lived her life at Shibden now. When Ann suggested backgammon she was again victorious. After the period of discord, they had returned to enjoying shared activities in the evening. So how would their marriage unfold? Would European travel to exotic places such as Gallicia and Hungary provide an answer?

MARCH 1837

Anne remained a voracious reader, devouring everything that kept her informed about changes in the wider world. However, reading being predominantly a solitary occupation, it could involve penalties in any relationship.

WEDNESDAY 1 *No kiss.* A~ better this morning… Went to the top of the west tower… Sat reading till 10 the *Encyclopaedia of Geology* & tonight's London paper.

THURSDAY 2 *No kiss.*… Mr George Robinson came… What did George Robinson bid me for Lower Brea? Answer: '£20 a year more than the present rent.' 'Does that', said I, 'mean £80 a year for Lower Brea?' 'No! £70 for Lower Brea.' I said I should not take that, I had made up my mind, I would not take less than £80 for Lower Brea… George Robinson asked when he should come again. I said when it suited him, but he must have made up his mind. I said if we [had not] agreed, he would have the notices to quit as usual. 'No!' He would have no more of those. 'Very well then', said I, 'you will quit. You do not like being on lease & therefore you shall be under regular notice from year to year, or we shall not agree. What', said I, 'is to become of me if you should be a bankrupt.' … Memo: that the agreement passes through Mr Parker… Rent of Lower Brea £80. Notice to quit every year served by Mr Parker.

George Robinson was an unusual tenant: he lived in a substantial farmhouse, Lower Brea, and ran a sizeable mill; yet he was not a good businessman. An annual lease gave the landowner considerable power, with a notice to quit being a tenant's worst nightmare. For readers, Anne's diary is so detailed here that it is like having a recorder catching the harsh conversation between landowner and tenant.

Then Anne saw Holt about an engine for getting coal out at Listerwick via an opening into Godley Lane. Here is clear evidence that through Holt Anne employed boys as hurriers, dragging the loaded corves attached by a short chain to their waists in her Listerwick mine:

6 A hurrier pulling a loaded corve of coal, Halifax area, *Children's Employment in Mines*, 1842 Report

One boy would hang on the corves [i.e. small wheeled trucks] at both places [i.e. at mine and exit] and one would hand them on to get up to the staith [i.e. exit point], & one man to take care of the engine...[1] Holt to see engine-makers... Then a little talk about politics – Holt will not give a yellow [i.e. Whig] vote the next time.[2]

Dinner at 7.35 – coffee at 8.30 – read tonight's paper. From 10 to 12 had Oddy helping me to [move] out of the library passage, & put into the great oak chest in the upper kitchen, all the books of the two first (on history & biography) compartments, counting from my study door to the stove. Catalogued about 2/3 of the 1st compartment.

So Anne was not only her own archivist, but also her own librarian.[3] Such meticulous sorting was extremely time-consuming, and in a marriage this could have repercussions:

A~ out of sorts. Never right since just before getting into bed last night. She gave me an impatient answer & I did not speak afterwards. I fancied her right again this morning, but no. Wrong at dinner – so I said very little. Read aloud a little of the newspaper – but it would not do, & I took no notice. What a temper! A~ in bed by 10.30.

Friday 3 *No kiss. All fair this morning. I spoke as usual but not much. No tenderness on either side.* Ready & out at 8...

Could Anne imagine what it would have been like had it been *she* who had moved to Crow Nest rather than vice versa, so having to watch Ann sorting all her Walker possessions?

On the top of the west tower, top-room floor finished at 3 pm yesterday – with the joiners & the mason in my study... More shelves to be put in the [anteroom cupboard] to hold papers & pamphlets...

Anne then discussed with Joseph Mann, James Holt and Holt the engineer where the coal staith should be, each having a different opinion:

I set the thing out myself – walked over the line I wished it to go in – & everybody satisfied that my plan was really the best...

Anne was used to getting her own way, though we seldom hear what the men she employed said behind her back.

The engine (6 horse-power) would require 300 gallons of water per hour. Left the two Holts & Joseph Mann on the ground – & walked down the New Bank to the Library... Stood (2 hours) reading the *Foreign Quarterly* ... & the *Foreign Review*... Never looked off my book – but heard the voice of Mr Samuel Waterhouse junior who of course, seeing me so intently engaged, never attempted speaking to me.[4]

Went to the bank in passing & got £100 in their notes. Returned up the Old Bank & back at 4... Sent ... the masons from their drinking to my study chimney...

Dinner at 6.45 – coffee at 8 – read the newspaper [pithy] bits aloud. *A~ quite talkative at dinner & afterwards. I talked only civilly enough. She was eloquent against Cookson whom she wished me to send off if she complained to me. I waved this [away] but without saying anything annoying to A~. I shall not give in about Cookson for a trifle – tho' I see A~ is nearly bent upon getting rid of her. A~ will be like her mother, ordering & fussing about – & I shall [have] my work set to keep well-bred servants. But I will try to keep A~ in better order for the future. I will be a little more particular in keeping up my own dignity before [i.e. in front of] her. I see I must not give up [i.e. give in] to her too much.*

SATURDAY 4 *No kiss – but might have had one if I liked, for she came fondling – but though I spoke in as kind as usual tone, I was in no humour for more.*

High wind – rain & boisterous stormy morning... *I talked a little at breakfast. A~ queer but evidently wishing to get right? All against Cookson & in the mind to give her warning. Terrible. I said the chances were she would not get a better* [servant]...

So, while this was ostensibly just one further row about servants, was it more about Anne keeping up her dignity in front of Ann and maintaining the upper hand?

Sauntered about while the men dined. Met Miss Patchett at the entrance gates, who had been calling upon me for a subscription to the erection of a Church Sunday School. Very civil to her – but thought Mr Hope, the incumbent of the church, ought not to throw upon her, Miss Patchett of Law hill, the trouble of going about to get subscriptions. [He] should write or explain himself, his views of what amount was wanted etc...

What this conversation reveals is that, while it was fine for Ann to 'have' a school, it was less acceptable for Miss Patchett to go round soliciting donations. Better to leave that up to the minister.[5]

Note tonight from the Halifax Literary & Philosophical Society, a paper to be read on Monday on the sources of rivers.

Anne was keenly aware of the excitement currently pulsing through the geological world. Did she feel that the research on offer locally was somewhat mundane?

SUNDAY 5 *A pretty good kiss last night – I, finding A~ quite in the humour, awakened up for her. A~ not in bed till 1.30 or later... Writing till near 2 – rough copy of letter to Lady Vere* Cameron. Off to the school at 2 for A~. Mr Wilkinson did all the duty... Then an hour at Cliff Hill – Mr Samuel Washington there... Dinner at 6.40 – coffee.

However, in bed all was not well between Anne and Ann:

MONDAY 6 *No kiss. A trial, for she came to me & in the midst* [of it] *said she could not bear it.* Fine morning...

Had Joseph Mann, who brought me a very fine specimen of [left blank], from 85 yards deep in Walker pit – these fossils only found in the [coal?] called the whites...

So, coalmining was not only lucrative. Discoveries of fossils meant that it could also be at the forefront of the newest geological research.[6]

> Dinner at 6.50 – coffee – A~ read her French. I read attentively the long & very interesting article … on steam navigation to India… A ship-canal from Suez direct north to the Pelusium on the Mediterranean, 100 miles, through a series of lagoons.

No one could accuse Anne of not being at the cutting edge of global exploration![7]

Meanwhile, back at Shibden:

TUESDAY 7 *No kiss. She fondled me & came to me, but I would not try again last night.* Very fine morning…

Then with Robert Mann + 3… *A~ wrong again at breakfast because I had not told Cookson to look after (stir up* [i.e. poke] *now & then) my fire in the north parlour. What a temper A~ has. But I will master it some way or other or give up altogether. For* [i.e. in] *about eighteen months to come, I shall have only about four or five hundred a year to spend, allowing five to keep up Shibden. Then I shall have about eleven hundred, & afterwards as much more as the* [Listerwick] *colliery will make…*

So, was the row over Cookson merely the trigger? Anne's calculations about their relationship seem predominantly financial.[8]

> Finished my … very kind letter to Lady Vere Cameron – still tethered by the leg – can't get off before May… She will not run off to the Highlands without telling me… 'I often think of your singing, & hope little Vere will emulate mamma… I shall think of you at Rome…' Ask if Vere is interested in the question of steam navigation to India… 'I shall be off sometime & will tell you when as soon as I know. Keep me in mind, & believe me, always very faithfully & very affectionately yours, A.L.'

If Anne were to give up Ann and if Mariana was too middle class for her tastes now, would she turn again to Vere? It was certainly a very affectionate letter.

WEDNESDAY 8 *No kiss.* Ready in an hour. A~ off to Cliff Hill… Had Cookson in my study & library passage to dust all the books left…

From the Stump Cross [Inn] walked by Mytholm quarry to the
school [at Lightcliffe]. A~ not there – found her at Crow Nest –
surprised to see me... Walked about the gardens at Crow Nest (1st
time, I think, in my life) – said how I would cut the ivy (in lancet [i.e.
pointed] gothic-shaped windows) about the terrace ... & advised a
few more large young ... trees being removed... Then ... to Cliff
Hill – advised where to put an elm & beech removed... Went in to
pay devoirs [i.e, respects] to Mrs Ann Walker (always glad to see me
nowadays) for 5 minutes & then off home across the fields...

**Anne offered Ann considerable advice about planting trees, seemingly unso-
licited. And how extraordinary that this was the first time Anne had walked
around the Crow Nest gardens! Surely, even just out of curiosity, she would
have wanted to have had a look – especially during the last five years; or was
is it all too nouveau riche for her tastes?**

Kind letter from Lady Vere Cameron, Brafield House – after the 29th
inst, can receive me at Brafield House... They are expecting Miss
Cameron on the 14th '& she is a person who you will find very superior
in many respects to the generality of women'.

**Was Vere encouraging Anne to show an interest in her sister-in-law? Certainly,
Anne jotted down: 'The aristocracy of rank is by the law of man & I respect
it – the aristocracy of mind is by the grace of God & I revere it.'9**

THURSDAY 9 *No kiss. Found my cousin just appearing hardly discernible.* A~ in
bed ½ hour before me last [night]... A~ rode off to Cliff Hill... Had
Holt the engineer with his plan of the engine & Joseph Mann with
him... Mr & Mrs & Miss Edwards called & left their card about 3.

FRIDAY 10. *No kiss. Washing after much cousin.* Finish cold windy morning...
A~ off to Willow Field (Mrs Dyson) at 2, though it had begun to rain.
I then washed my cousin then.

Anne was always reticent about menstruating, preferring to hide all signs.

SUNDAY 12 *No kiss. Very little washing...* A~ up about 6 & off to the school
about 8.45.10

TUESDAY 14. *No kiss...* A~ would like to be [away] from home at Easter
– mentioned it tonight – agreed to go to Bolton Abbey next week.

Bolton Abbey in beautiful Wharfedale lay just twenty miles north of Halifax.
Ann seemed to find travel (and even the mere thought of it) sexually stimulating.
Did she share Anne's passionate thirst for new adventure, or was it just the
chance of getting away from Shibden?

WEDNESDAY 15 *A goodish one last night. She came fondling. Said in the midst I*
had never tired her so little. She had been out of sorts the latter part of dinner. I
took no notice at all – read aloud parts of the paper – just as if all was right.
And she came round. What a temper. I must keep her <u>*sufficiently*</u> *at* [a] *distance*
– have her [kept] *in order – and perhaps I shall manage her. I get out of her*
way now when she is wrong, if I can. If not, I give up all conversation, and am
grave & silent – but perfectly civil & shew no want of temper on my own part…

Anne's diary entry suggests that their relationship had now deteriorated. Was
Ann investing so much energy in her Lightcliffe school because things at home
were now growing so extremely difficult?

Gave A~ last [night] 3 admission ticket to the [Literary and Philosophical Society] museum for old Mr Washington & for Mr & Mrs S
Washington, & 2 this morning for Oddy & Cookson.

The Halifax Museum had become a 'go to' cultural destination for their land
steward, his family and Shibden servants.

THURSDAY 16 *A long, pretty good one last night, she coming to me.* Breakfast
with A~ at 8.30, at which hour F35°, fine morning – cold. Sat in the
little parlour reading the last *Foreign Quarterly* on the steam navigation
to India till after 10. A~ had Mr Horner…

So, their recent quarrel seems now to have blown over – for a while?

Coffee at 8.30 – read the newspaper & the first 20 or 30 pages Captain
[Basil] Hall's *Schloss Hainfeld* till 11.40.[11] Fine day. I was just ready to
get into bed at 12.20 when A~ came to say she was sure she had
heard someone attempt to open the gallery door into the little ante-room
and would have me go downstairs & look about. I went unwillingly
with a pistol in one hand and a candle in the other – not at all believing
this was anybody. But if there was, they must be thieves, a thought
that had not, till I named it, entered A~'s head. I would not go into
the cellars because I had caught my last (& late) <u>very bad</u> cold that
way. But looked into the north parlour & about, & not saw nor heard
anything.

FRIDAY 17 *No kiss.* John called us at 5.40 saying there was somebody in the house. A~ jumped up, so did I... They had come in at the north parlour window, and nothing seemed to be gone not even the plate. I got into bed again & lay very quietly, leaving A~ to inquire & tell me the news. She persists in the belief that they were in the house when she called me to look about, & [they] had remained in all night. Not a noise was heard till John heard something & got up about 5.15 or before – just before which Cookson awoke hearing them trying to unscrew the lock of her [bed]room-door. She called out to know if it was John who was there & this perhaps frightened them away. My feeling was shame that people could have got in, and thus had their full swing [i.e. freedom] in the house without our hearing. Yet nothing seemed disturbed, except my writing box moved off the table in the north parlour ... & the padlock of the great oak chest in the upper kitchen forced open.

Anne had courageously defended Shibden with her pistol. Revealingly, she felt shame that thieves had broken into her ancestral home.

SUNDAY 19 *No kiss. A~ wrong about my not at once giving George the handkerchief she had got & hemmed for George, instead of the one the thieves took. George was gone to bed. I told A~ she should give the thing herself – it was not like [i.e. right for] me to do it. What a temper she has, but I will master it – or give up altogether by & by. One good thing is that I gradually care less & less & about it...*

So, one consequence of the theft was an argument about the most trivial aspect of servant-management etiquette. Yet at least Anne, careful with her words (even in code), did not write 'care less & less about *her*'.

Church... Left A~ at the school... Finished my letter to Isabella Norcliffe [on the death of her mother]... 'There is an indescribable sacredness in the remembrance of her who has borne us through our first development into being – we cannot look into ourselves, we cannot contemplate the wondrous scheme of living entirely without recurring to the hallowed thought of her who, the chosen instrument of heaven, breathed into us the breath of life... Miss Walker's kind regards & condolence to yourself & to Charlotte... When you do write, may I hope that you will allow, and remember my succession to the brevet [i.e. higher rank] vacant by the death of my excellent aunt… Believe me, my dearest Isabella, always very affectionately & faithfully yours, A.L.'[12]

MONDAY 20 *No kiss*… Arranging my books in the new portable library in the drawing room… The masons had laughed the men into having drinkings again – said they were slaves – had Booth in about it, but desired him not to take any notice of it…[13] A~ did not return from Cliff Hill till after 6 – making alternations there… *A~ not at all right at what I said about her new lodge – she is very touchy now about what she does… Poor A~.*

TUESDAY 21 *No kiss*… Joseph Mann … Robert's 3 men … drinkings began again this afternoon…

> **[marginalia]** *A~ wrong, wants to get rid of Cookson & I will not hear of it.*

WEDNESDAY 22 *No kiss*… Very nice letter … from Lady Vere Cameron – Lady Stuart has let her house to Lord Lothian from 24 April… [Vere] goes to Achnacary in July. If she gives me any commissions to do in Paris, it will be to buy cheap books for furniture [i.e. book-shelves?] rather than use. Vere in mourning for Mr Cameron's aunt, Lady Abercrombie, who died at Edinburgh.

This was surely a not untypical Vere letter, with more news about her aristocratic relatives than interest in Anne at Shibden.

Then at last, Anne and Ann set off in the yellow carriage on their Dales trip. Their first stop was Skipton and the castle of celebrated Lady Anne Clifford. On their return, they stopped at Keighley:

MONDAY 27 *Long but good one last night*… [Off] at 9.35… Then the road pretty good to Keighley at 10.50… Went immediately to the Mechanics' Institute Mr Horner had mentioned… A new building for the same purpose wanted at Halifax. Mr Horner asked A~ to speak to me about ground for it…[14]

Keighley, a similar-sized town to Halifax near the Brontës' village of Haworth, had obviously impressed Anne. Could Halifax emulate Keighley?[15]

To Aked's the bookseller in Low Street to get the catalogue of the books at the Mechanics' Institute. A~ bought a little book, easy lessons in Mechanics, & I bought the Spirit of Etiquette by Lady de S-, printed this year, London. Read it afterwards in the carriage – evidently written by a gentlewoman – *de bon ton*... Off from Keighley at 12.20. Snow as we neared Illingworth Moor... Talked of riding to Keighley ... a wild rough country, interesting for contrast's sake & its nearness to our borough of Halifax, now <u>brightening</u> into the <u>polish</u> of a large smoke-canopied commercial town.

Home at 2.20 – a gentleman's carriage just turning out of our gate (towards Hipperholme) as we drove down upon it. Mr & Mrs Stansfield Rawson & the Misses Rawsons – *quel domage?* Mr Rawson has more architectural knowledge & taste than anyone hereabouts – better that he should look about [Shibden] amid fine weather & less discord [i.e. building work?].[16]

Put away my things... Changed my dress, back into my pelisse of cloth, & boots of cow-hide & hat of beaver, and off with A~ to the school & Cliff Hill at 2.50...[17] Looked into the *Morning Herald*... Surely Lord Palmerstone, & his coadjutors [i.e. supporters] & their politics will be beaten, by & by!

Palmerston was, of course, still Foreign Secretary. Anne hoped the Tories would soon defeat these Whig politicians. However, in Halifax and elsewhere, it was the anti-Poor Law protests that made headlines. Meanwhile, travel always seemed to heighten Ann's desire for Anne.[18]

THURSDAY 28 *Long tolerable one last night. A~ quite affectionate. Says the change of air & Brodies' plaster have done her good. She was very irritable before, she says – & has said several times – says she will have no more mysteries [i.e. secrets] – & seems intending to be good tempered & as she ought to be. Tho' she says nothing, I think she is sensible of my having always kept my temper.*

So, if Ann behaved 'as she ought to be', did this mean that she would 'consider herself as ... being under no authority but mine', as agreed three years earlier?[19] Anne then sent off a letter to John Harper in York:

Mention the chance of [my] being applied to for ground for a building for the Mechanics' Institute – not anxious to trust unconditionally to any committee the architectural credit of buildings to be erected on my own ground; should therefore like to have Mr Harper's idea of a building suited to the purpose required (lecture room, library, chemical laboratory, living rooms for curator) to be done for about £12,000, in good keeping with the casino...

To present-day readers, a 'Mechanics' Institute' seems to occupy a different social and cultural space from a 'casino'. One suggests self-education (and possibly even radical ideas), the other, gambling large sums of money. But 'casino' in the 1830s just meant a public room for entertainment.[20]

Ordered of Mr Oldfield, 4 dozen marsala as before – 3 dozen good sherry & 5 dozen good port ready for immediate drinking – to be paid for on receiving the wine… A~ began this evening to use the North parlour as her sitting room & we had coffee there.

So, expensive fortified wines could now be ordered in sizeable quantities at Shibden.

THURSDAY 30 *No kiss. I see A~'s irritability is returning, but she behaves as well as she can. Poor thing, we must be off as soon as we can…*
Breakfast at 9.30, having seen Mr Horner while he was with A~. He mentioned the Mechanics' Institute – but on my asking if I was to consider what he said as official, he answered 'No!' But it was said [i.e. publicly] he was in the habit of coming here & therefore they wished him to inquire if I should object to let them have ground [i.e. land for building].[21] I said I would consider about it. I was anxious for the spread of genuine knowledge, but would not inflict upon the town a building in bad architectural taste. I should wish to see & be satisfied with the plan of any building before its being built on my ground [i.e. Northgate]. I did not always admire the taste of committees. I would consider the thing – & asked what was wanted – a library, museum & school room, reading rooms, chemical laboratory… I asked him to give me a sketch of his own idea of what he himself should like – and I would tell him what I thought. I mentioned the building at Keighley as a faulty piece of architectural taste… He mentioned wanting a chemical laboratory under the building. 'That', I said,' would not be wise – it would put them at the mercy of any tyro [i.e. novice] to blow them up or not.' He wanted the lecture room to hold 600 people! Said they had 2,000 books – those, I said, would be easily placed.

Anne did not link a Mechanics' Institute's 'genuine knowledge' with the dangerous Radical ideas of certain Methodist chapels. For her, 'the spread of genuine knowledge' was often scientific. Yet perhaps when Harper suggested 600 people, Anne began to get a sobering glimpse of 'the mob'?

Breakfast at 9.30, sat till near 12 thinking over & sketching in pencil a rough idea of a building according to the wishes, rather perhaps than to the means, of the [Mechanics'] Institution. But Horner had said they had observed that they should be obliged to have a handsome building if it was near the hotel. The building in progress at Bradford, it is supposed will be done for £2,000...

Anne genuinely wanted the Institute to glorify her town. But was she, unusually for her, being politically naïve? Her diary recorded how she regularly read the weekly *Halifax Guardian,* which reported at length on 'New Poor Law Act: Public Meeting in Halifax'.[22] This meeting would have been in the Old Assembly Rooms, but that proved too small for the swelling crowd, so it adjourned to the new Market Place. Speakers on 'Poor Law tyranny' included Ben Rushton, a handloom weaver soon to emerge as a Halifax Chartist, and none other than factory reformer Richard Oastler himself.[23] There was also a wider picture of political protest across Yorkshire, with the first London Working Men's Association missionaries sent out to 'the provinces'. Indeed, popular Radicalism was unstoppable. Did Anne still think Tory landowners like herself could control the spread of 'genuine knowledge' by focusing on chemistry rather than politics?

Mr Samuel Bates came about 2 & brought his father's ... plans of the Listerwick mill...[24] Mr Edwards of Pye Nest has a mill at Ripponden [with a] water wheel... Wished me to ride over to see a new corn-mill at Hebden Bridge... Mr Henry Priestley going to build a mill in Cragg valley – 60 foot of fall [of water] ... had had Messrs Bates to level & value for him.

[marginalia] Listerwick pit to be begun sinking tomorrow.

So even Ann's relative, trusted Henry Priestley, was now expanding water-powered industry out into the steep Cragg Vale; here the water rushed swiftly down into the River Calder. Still, at least it was industry-in-the-country rather than Halifax's steam-driven mills which, being coal-powered, needed to be by the canal.[25]

FRIDAY 31 *No kiss*... A~ poorly... Off to Halifax ... to the bank... [Mr McKean] asked if it was true that Mr Carr was to have [Northgate]. 'No!' ... Mr McKean said he had not capital... I was given to understand more [people] were against than for. My object was to please the town... McKean advised advertising in the *North Briton Advertiser* published in Edinburgh – no politics... *Manchester Guardian* (politics blue), *Liverpool Mercury,* yellow – *Leeds Mercury* ditto – I mentioned the London *Morning Herald* & *Times* should be added.

This is a useful summary of the politics of various newspapers of the day. Anne's bank manager advised her to advertise in them all.

From the bank to Whiteley's – two Petitions on the table to the Houses of Lords & Commons, <u>against</u> the abolition of church rates, signed by the blue <u>heads</u> of the town, signatures 59. Mr Parker came in – asked if he had come to sign it – he said he had been asked at the bank (his bank, Rawson's), but answered he would leave it to the wisdom of Parliament to decide. He would not however refuse my asking, and signed it! Are his political sentiments so wavering or so weakly conservative?

Parker was, of course, a cautious lawyer. Yet even he could not afford to offend Anne Lister, inheritor of Shibden's ancient acres. The issue of abolishing church rates might seem a side issue by 1837, but the Anglican rallying cry of the 'Church in danger' seems to have endured.

Bought books from Whitley's... Returned up Old Bank. Overtook Mark Hepworth bringing stuff [probably stone] from Northgate to the front of Shibden Hall – asked him to sign the petition – and to ask Hardcastle, & any of the tenants he might or could conveniently see before tomorrow night when the petition is to be sent off. Home at 4.40. Sat reading a few of the first pages of Higgins on the Earth.[26]

So Shibden tenants were not only pressurized to vote 'Blue' at elections, but also to support Anne's current cause, church finances.[27]

Came in just after A~ returned from Cliff Hill... Dressed – dinner at 7 – coffee. Came upstairs to my study at 9.30 – reading Higgins ½ hour... Then went down to A~ in the North parlour & *sat hearing what she had written to her sister, & writing a completely new rough copy... Little Mary & Hannah [Sutherlands' servant] coming here. Said we would take care of them from Liverpool.[28] Avoided promising to go for them ourselves. Begged [Ann] to say nothing, to make no comment on what she had written about the [Crow Nest] Lodge – as she knew I was against it.*

In Ann's correspondence with her sister, Anne was now effectively holding the pen – helping her maintain the upper hand.
More broadly, by March 1837, with outcry against the hated Poor Law reaching a crescendo, how much longer could 'Blues' such as Anne hold out against political radicalism now widening into the Chartist movement?

VI

MAINTAINING THE UPPER HAND – STILL

APRIL–MAY 1837

APRIL 1837

At Shibden, March had ended with Anne's 'holding the pen' for Ann's letter to her sister. And, with Poor Law protests, was the country gearing up for a new General Election?

SATURDAY 1 Till 12, firing off my pistols – had John up to put in a new flint, & see what was the matter with the percussion pistol – the powder damp – dried it – surely all is right now.

After suspected intrusions by thieves, Anne needed her pistols in good working order.

SUNDAY 2 *Longish not very good one last night…* A~ off to the school 20 minutes ago – walked – hard frost last night – too slippery for the ponies. Breakfast … sat reading. the *Gentleman's Magazine* of last month – very interesting articles – on the Phoenicians descent of the Celts & Pelasgians…

Off to church at 2.10… ¾ hour at Cliff Hill. A~ had Sam Washington there who brought her the plan of the coal got by Illingworth as measured in the [pit] bottom by Holt at Shugden Head…[1] Sat reading in the blue room the Architectural magazine… Dinner at 6.35 – coffee. Read tonight's London paper, *Morning Herald*.

MONDAY 3 *Pretty good one last night.* Much snow… *Found cousin come gently & had all to prepare which had made me so long in dressing.* Breakfast at 9.45 with A~… Wrote to Lady Vere Cameron:

Shibden Hall. Monday 3 Ap. 1837

It was very good of you, my dearest Vere, to write to me so soon. I do not know what you could have done more charitable. All constraint is uncomfortable; and I begin to feel poor dear Shibden [as] a sort [of] exile... I shall not say much about the disappointment of not seeing you at Brafield, and [Lady Stuart] in London, because I am too much disappointed to talk about it. I never expected, I never thought of all this. How could I calculate that everything would take more than twice the length of time said to be enough? 'What works must be going at Shibden!' It is not the magnitude of these which is *dans le gêne* [i.e. inconvenient], but the difficulty of calculating exactly upon saying anything in these times. The whole of our social system has been strangely altered of late years. The operative classes are so often co-operative [i.e. organized] at radical meetings and beer-shops, that no one can tell what quantity of work will be done within any limited time. Add to this the twelve hundred miles of railroad to be made; and it will be well if we can get workmen to keep up our houses in comfortable repair. But surely you will <u>sometime</u> come and see me here, and I shall sometime see you at Achnacary! ... I shall be delighted at your giving me any commission to do in Paris, or elsewhere.[2]

TUESDAY 4 *No kiss*.... Breakfast at 9.10... Walked [down to Halifax,] forward to Northgate – looked about there – the top court-yard will be large enough... Then to Whitley's – ordered ... *hints on buying a horse, & bought flannel & riband at Foster's for cousin.*[3]

Back home, Anne had a long discussion with John Oates about an engine for her coal mine. Best to read about such challenges too:

THURSDAY 6 *No kiss*... Reading Lardnor on Steam Engines...[4] Off with A~ to Cliff Hill at 1.50 – A~ poorly & could not walk well... *A~ had been out of sorts at my not approving her* [Crow Nest] *lodge plan & this perhaps made all the poorliness. She could not bear to walk on going out of the house, cried & I took her & sat with her ten minutes in the necessary* [i.e. privy] *till she was rather better –* then A~ & I sauntered about. My eye that got lashed in planting the thorns yesterday afternoon, very painful.

FRIDAY 7 In bed all the day.[5] Found A~ had sent for Mr Jubb who came about 11.30 & ordered 6 leeches to be put on just under my eye (the right) – would send [for] the leech-woman... Mrs Wright put on 6 leeches at 3 pm, all off in ¾ hour. Kept on the bleeding with hot flannels & little poultices for about an hour after ... Mr Jubb's opiate lotion did good. Mrs Wright calculates 1 leech (with a good bleeding afterwards) to 1/3 of an ounce of blood.

SATURDAY 8 In bed all the day, did not sleep much, but my eye much better... Mr Jubb came about 11 – forced the eye open. *Could not sleep for A~'s snoring...*

MONDAY 10 *Could not sleep for A's snoring all night – determined to sleep in the kitchen chamber...* Breakfast at 12. A~ got the kitchen chamber ready for me to sleep in tonight – told Mr Jubb I had been so disturbed by the horses in the stable, [I] could not sleep last night or the night before.[6]

TUESDAY 11 Slept last night in the kitchen chamber & slept very well. 1st time of sleeping alone since A~ has been here. Poor dear A~! Very lonely to be without her.

So, this separate bedroom which Ann had got ready did not seem adversely to affect their relationship. Interestingly, none of this was written in code.

WEDNESDAY 12 Good night... We breakfasted in the blue room... Mentioned to Mr Jubb the Mechanics' Institute, & the new building they proposed erecting. Mr Jubb ... said he could not be more [opposed] than I was; but Mechanics' Institutes did & would now exist – best therefore for sensible people to join & influence them, rather than hang aloof & leave them to worse guidance...

Sat with A~ at her luncheon till near 2, soon after which Messrs Washington & Haigh came to get A~ to join the opposition of the bill in Parliament respecting the mill-reservoirs – to object to the high price to be paid per [vertical] foot for the gallons water of 2 reservoirs, the water to be 35/- per annum per foot of fall... The Haighs (A~'s Honley mill) will have 20 foot of fall – but they have a 14-years lease from A~ at a very low rent, and so A~ very wisely left them to oppose the bill themselves, or not as they thought best – she not choosing to have anything to do with it...

By 1837, with steam-powered mills multiplying, this seemed a somewhat anachronistic bill.[7]

Kind letter tonight from Lady Stuart, Whitehall, begging me to write…
Hourly expecting Lord Stuart de Rothesay… *Just went to A~'s door to
listen if she was asleep. She called to me, got into bed, she inclined & half-hour
with her & had a pretty good kiss & then went to my own bed.*

**So, the marriage was working well in bed, the new arrangement seeming
fairly mutual.**

FRIDAY 14 *Meant to have slept with her last night. Had a goodish kiss – she
inclined & was dropping asleep when she snored so I could not sleep. Got up &
went to my own bed at twelve & a half & was just comfortable when I thought
I heard her at my door. Jumped up & asked who was there. No answer – stood
with my father's pistols in my hand till I was cold. Then thought A~ would be
frightened if she woke & found me gone, so crept back to her – but no sleep – she
snored so. At three therefore went back to the kitchen chamber & slept without
waking till eight.*

**Meanwhile, Ann's snoring remaining a problem, 'my own bed' was now
definitely in the kitchen chamber.**

A~ came to me at 8.30 & sat by me for ¼ hour – she had never
awoke last night… A~ had letter tonight from her sister – Little Mary
& Hannah [servant] to come early next month. Letter tonight from
Messrs Gray – in daily expectation of receiving the money.

SATURDAY 15 *A good one – staid with her – till she began to snore at one &
twenty five minutes…* Had Cookson to help me down [into cellar] with
it, unpacked & put away, the wine received in 3 hampers from York…
5 dozen port, 3 dozen sherry & 4 dozen marsala…

Off to Halifax at 11.30 – down the Old Bank to the bank… Got
£100 in cash, & left £2 with Mr McKean for the poor distressed
starving Highlanders – a general national subscription for them…
Home about 1.30… Fired off the pistols & reloaded.

SUNDAY 16 Slept in the kitchen chamber (as since the 11th), my eye so
much worse last night… A~ back [from church] at 5… A~ dined at
6.30 & I had tea & teacake at 7. Had just before dinner shewn A~
my purchase at Whitley's yesterday, Russell's *Jerusalem*, she as much
pleased with the work as I, & before & after dinner read aloud 2 or
3 hours…[8] I never got up at all today – in much perspiration in the

evening after tea & this did me good. *Between six & seven incurred a cross thinking, as usual on these occasions, of M~ &* mused over the names of Adam & Eve...

Even now, six months after Mariana's visit, it was still not a clean break. Was Anne thinking of her mainly in the past or into the future too? A combination of reading *Jerusalem* plus thinking of Mariana had a powerful effect on Anne:

Ham the son of Noah ... *uncovered his father's nakedness... To cover one's nakedness generally means to copulate, or the act itself.* Eve became the mother of all living [beings]... *Penis from 'pen', high erect pennine alps high ditto. Was the groove a hollow or flutin, the sacred yoni of Eve or female privy part?[9]* ... Dr Adam Clark fancies that the serpent was in the form of a monkey ourang-outang – he must have beguiled Eve, for Adam & she had dominion over all the beasts of the field.[10] *They had been longer* [i.e. earlier] *created & had been procreated. The beast might make Eve understand the use of the penis – or she might* [let] *him copulate, & ask Adam to try – & then seeing that they were naked (& they eating an apple) may be but a manner of expressing their having copulated. The context hints this. The woman was immediately sentenced to conceive in sorrow. Apples have always been symbolic. 'Are your apples ripe? Are they fit for fucking?'[11]*

So, Anne combined thinking about Mariana with reading cutting-edge biblical commentary. It was a powerful mix. She understandably remained perplexed about exactly what happened in the Garden of Eden. Here surely is a memorable example of how an intellectually and sexually adventurous woman who was also a socially conservative Anglican remained caught between two opposing worlds: theology and new 'origins' science.

MONDAY 17 Took my draught [i.e. medicine] at 7 am – much better this morning... A~ read to me (Russell's *Jerusalem*, very interesting), & sat with me reading or sewing the whole morning.

TUESDAY 18 *Incurred last night thinking of M~ & the etymologies.*[12] Slept in the kitchen chamber, as since the 11th – good night – my eye feels tender...

Then Anne, as few others could, flicked her mind from the Garden of Eden back to estate business, discussing coalmining prospects with John Oates and Holt, and exactly where the incline would go.

Holt seemed altogether well satisfied – sure the coal will pay. He had told me Mr Akroyd had told him I should lose £10,000 by the Northgate hotel. I said the coal must make it [i.e. the loss] up...[13] Dinner at 7 – tea – A~ read aloud the newspaper & my letters... Letter tonight from M~, Leamington, asking advice [about her projected school]...

WEDNESDAY 19 Slept in kitchen chamber... Dinner at 6.50 – tea. A~ ... very poorly – indigestion... Called Cookson who got her undressed as quick as possible & I carried her to bed – gave her a glass of <u>hot</u> very weak madeira & water, & got her feet into warm water at 11.20... Left her about 12, then looked into the newspaper, & sat reading till 12.35 – just opened A~'s door & listened for a minute or 3 – she seemed nicely asleep.

THURSDAY 20 Slept in Kitchen Chamber... A~ much better. *Her cousin come...* F41° ... cast off this morning my woollen socks (worn under my black worsted stockings) and one double black silk handkerchief from round my throat – now wearing ... 2 thicknesses of coarse flannel.

Even in late April, Shibden weather could be bitterly cold.

Went into the hall cellar for wine... Mr Harper [came] about 2 ... gave me a rough draft of advertisement of the [Northgate] hotel – I thought it could not be improved... Harper at last agreed for the advertisement to appear immediately – we mentioned the following newspapers – London *Times, Morning Herald,* ditto *Post,* & *Examiner,* Edinburgh *North Briton Advertiser* – 1 Glasgow paper, 1 Manchester.

Harper had had no time to think of the Mechanics' Institute... The Mechanics' Institute at York ... could not pay the salaries now – wanted to bring in the subscribers (Harper gave £50) as answerable for these [expenses], but Halifax resisted. Said I should merely say in answer that I should not like to run any risk of the building being appropriated to any people that I might not like, in case of failure of the Institute; & if this matter could not be settled to my satisfaction, I should decline selling or letting any part of my ground for the projected building.

[marginalia] 1 Liverpool, 1 Leeds, 2 Halifax, *Galignani* [Messenger].[14]

Anne knew exactly which people she 'might not like' and had the power to pick and choose, while still wishing to be a local benefactor.

FRIDAY 21 A~ came to awake me at 4 – the dog barked – it was the chimney sweep come.

SATURDAY 22 Slept in the kitchen chamber as since the 11th inst… Had Holt the engineer … with another estimate of the steam engine…

Wrote 2 hurried pages to M~ … grieved not to have been able to write sooner… Would give her books the best security here I could during my absence … considering that I should probably be so much absent. Advised her calling a meeting of the subscribers to her projected School of Industry at Leamington, stating her case, & taking the opinion of the subscribers as to what to do. When not independent, prudent to avoid as much as possible all unnecessary responsibility. Sent off George … with my letter to Mrs Lawton, Claremont House, Leamington.

Female philanthropy was expanding. Yet was Mariana's ambition similar to Ann's with her Lightcliffe school: good intentions, yet no management training? This stood in contrast to Anne – who read, who knew, and who exercised real authority.

SUNDAY 23 Slept in the kitchen chamber… Sat talking to A~ till after 11… A~ & I off to church … & Cliff Hill… A~ had observed some time ago that the wine went fast – measured the height in the decanter of the contents … left by A~ at luncheon. The key is always kept by George or Oddy – the former has had no opportunity of drinking wine this afternoon. Oddy was left at home. Query: had she the key of the cupboard or not? We found more than a full glass of wine had gone…

Yet surely it was Anne and especially Ann who were the regular heavy drinkers?

Dinner at 6.45 – tea in the north parlour & read the newspaper there till 10, A~ asleep on the hearth rug, her … hair has been re-curled – very bad.

MONDAY 24 Slept in kitchen chamber… Went out to the Stump Cross Inn… Returned by Lower Brear, & saw Mr George Robinson standing at his door. [I] said he had never come to settle with me about the rent. 'No!' he said he thought it was settled – 'he must fall into [i.e. in with] my will'. As I had told him my ultimatum, I merely said 'very well'. He then said he wanted £40 laying out in raising his currying [i.e. leather-dressing] shop... I said, as for that, that did not make much difference – but I neither said I would nor would not do it.

Anne had about three dozen tenants. George Robinson might have been one of the larger ones, but he was hardly a good businessman. Aquilla Green of Mytholm was a smaller tenant yet entertained industrial ambitions.

TUESDAY 25 Slept in kitchen chamber... Home about 1 – found A~ at luncheon – she made me take a warm jelly – sat with her till 2... To Mytholm ... met Aquilla Green about 6.30 & stood talking about an hour... I thought the mill would neither answer to Aquilla Green nor to me, and I was in the mind to give it up... I had had lesson enough from people in higher rank than Aquilla Green (meaning Mr Rawson)... He said if I put up a steam engine ... he would pay more [rent]... He thought of its being a provisions for himself and his family – the rent was a very good one. I advised his building a mill at Bailey Hall... 'Well!' he (Aquilla Green) would wait to see the wheel going, & if it was then proved there would not be water enough for 20 horse-power, he would give it up.

As a small tenant, Aquilla Green had the cards stacked against him, made more complex by Bailey Hall being owned by Ann Walker. On top of which, with an election looming, party politics came to the fore again.

WEDNESDAY 26[15] Fine morning... Had Mr Mercer (Robert) [glazier] re Northgate... Off with A~ (both walked) to Halifax at 11.30... If there should be an election now, [Mercer] thinks we could not bring in [i.e. elect] Mr Wortley. Mercer is a staunch blue...

With women now formally edged out of politics, Anne and Ann were reduced to gleaning election intelligence from their glazier.

Off with A~ at 11.30 down the Old Bank, left her at Whitley's, and went to Mr Parker's office – 20 mins there with Mr Adam. Explained about Aquilla Green... Adam asked if I had got his letter respecting the Bailey Hall land. No! Would call for it.

Lawyers had ways of protecting landed clients such as Anne from vexatious liabilities. Aquilla Green's ambitions were, however, very small beer compared to Anne's crucial finances:

Asked Adam if, supposing the remittances did not arrive in time for Monday, my deferring the payment of the one thousand till the end of the week could be managed. 'Yes!' As soon as I got the money, Parker & Adam would be glad of the £500 advanced to Nelson.[16] *Parker & Adam, one thousand overdrawn at the bank.* 'Yes!' They shall have the £500 immediately that I can pay it, also the funeral [costs] & the bills due from A~ & myself for law expenses.

Adam was being exceedingly helpful to Anne about her cash-flow problems. A highly reputable law firm disliked being overdrawn: Anne was playing a complex high-wire game!

Then to the Bank – said I expected the fifteen thousand, or at least 7 or 8 thousand, would be paid into their branch bank at York on Saturday, but I was not yet advised of it. I would let Mr MacKean know the moment I heard of it. If I heard in time, a draft for £1,016+ would be presented for payment on Monday. If not, I would take some steps about it so as to prevent its presentation till the money was paid in on my account. But I had just given a check to Mercer the glazier for £80 which I should be obliged the bank to pay on Monday... 'Oh! Yes!' Said Mr Davison [assistant bank manager], McKean [away] from home...

Then went for A~... Found her at Nicholson's – some time there – Mrs Waterhouse came up & spoke to us – Mrs Rawson of Stoney Royde quite well again – I might see her any time from 10.30 to 1.30. Mrs Waterhouse talked of calling at Shibden Hall soon.

Given the looming election, 'Blue' families needed to stand ever closer together.

Thursday 27 *Found my cousin just come gently on getting into bed last night. Washing stocking this morning... Went in to A~ & Mr Horner – said I* had considered about the Mechanics' Institute... There was difficulty about salaries & expenses. Indeed, my present feeling was rather inclined to letting building leases [rather] than selling the ground... Mr Horner not gone – but nothing more said about the Mechanics' Institute...

Anne and Horner differed about Mechanics' Institutes. For Horner, who probably believed in adult education, it would also be a prestigious architectural commission. However, Anne feared that popular education might lead to more political trouble.

A~ came for me about 1 – sat with her luncheon & took a glass of melted jelly... Parcel from Whitley's containing Buckland's Bridgewater treatise on geology & mineralogy...[17] Wrote ... to the Honorable Lady Stuart, Richmond Park, under cover to the Lord James Stuart, Whitehall Place, London... *Had written rough copy – but easily & well-written letter...*

Shibden Hall. Thursday 27 April 1837

Dearest Lady Stuart

It really puts me in a fever to think your last and very kind letter reached me a fortnight ago, and I have not yet been able to write... I was unluckily confined to my bed by an accident ... which produced so much inflammation in my right eye, that I was obliged to have leeches applied, and be regularly laid up... I begin to be so sick of all my business concerns from the trammels [i.e. restrictions] of which I cannot yet escape, that, as I told Vere, it is charity to remind me that there is anybody so good as [to] think of, and care for, me. I never dreampt of tying myself down here as I have done. But things are clearing a little, and though I dare not think of setting off next month or even early in June, I do confidently hope to see you *en passant* during the summer, and Vere, too, for I trust she will still be with you when I leave here...

When are we to have a change of Ministers? I hope there will not be another general election soon; if there be, I shall have a thousand fears for Mr. James Wortley [MP] – these are queer times. I am very much tired of my confinement here, and sure that you and Vere can do no greater charity than write to me. Adieu, dearest Lady Stuart, and believe me always very truly and very affectionately yours,

A. Lister[18]

They will think me low? No! I am not that – but feverishly inclined, & feeling that I should be thankful to be off in comfort...

However, at present the only way Anne could be 'off in comfort' was with the aid of Ann's money.

Had just written so far at 6. A~ returned from Halifax this afternoon, and in returning sent George in with letter from Messrs Gray. Mr Watson will be here on Saturday with £8,000 at least – if not in money, in a bill at a short date [i.e. soon], of which the Misses Preston will allow the discretion.

At long last, Anne would receive the £15,000 from the Misses Preston she had planned for![19]

FRIDAY 28 Slept in kitchen chamber... Ready at 7.50 ... *changed paper & washed a little*. Off to Halifax ... to the bank – mentioned the contents of Mr Gray's letter of yesterday – should be at Halifax tomorrow – mentioned the bills to be paid on Monday... Then sat 25 mins with Mrs Rawson of Stoney Royd – Mr & Mrs Stansfield [Rawson] came in as I was going out – Mr S. Rawson walked with me to the end of Stoney Royde carriage road. Returned by Bailey Hall & up the Old Bank & home before 2...[20]

Dressed – dinner at 7. Mr Samuel Gray [landscape gardener] announced at 7.15... A~ went off before 10. I sat talking with Mr Gray about Russia till 10.30, then ordered him wine & water. Looked about the hall with him ... & came upstairs a little before 11 – sat with A~ at her bedside ¼ hour or more.

SATURDAY 29 Slept in kitchen chamber as since the 11th. No Mr Watson, as expected by the night mail. Sent down last night to tell somebody to sit up for him... In the cellar – and looking for wine account and dawdling in my study... Breakfast at 9.30. *Poor A~; if I say much* [she] *turns poorly ... nothing comfortable.*

Mr Watson came before 10 – shewn into the blue room – went to him at 10.30 – the reading of the mortgage deed took above ½ hour. A~ came in about the middle of it – 5 skins – I had signed it and she signed as a witness at 11.45. £8,000 paid today in a bill at 14 days... *I mentioned to A~ yesterday the re-publishing* [of] *her will – I saw she did not like the subject, yet supposed she would do it, as I told her we should have no other opportunity. On getting out the will just now she said in her queer ungracious way she should not do it this morning. I think I shall be foolish to ask her again. What is her idea? Is she afraid? It is time for me to be careful.*

The deed is dated 15th January last, and makes the interest payable at 4% (£15,000) 15 July and 15 January – signed a power authorising Messrs Gray to keep my title deeds at the office, and acquitting the Misses Jane and Ann Preston of all responsibility about them...

Went to A~ and Mr Watson – he and Mr Gray had luncheon at 2. *I mentioned the will; A~ explained she did not like being bound to live here, I explained no time* [was] *specified, a mere form* [i.e. formality]. *Only bound* [i.e. obliged] *to have fires kept* [alight] *and windows open and taxes paid. A~ satisfied and the will republished. All right...* Mr Shepley Watson wrote the memorial and he and Mr Samuel Gray ... and our groom George Wood witnessed the republication.

What a lot could happen in a day. £8,000 paid to Anne, with a mortgage deed that took over 30 minutes to read. Financial freedom for Anne at last! Yet alongside was Ann's reluctance to republish her will, mainly about being 'bound to live here', that is, at Shibden, and maintain the Hall. However, Anne seemed to have the upper hand with Ann now.

I off to Halifax at 3.15 ... to the bank... Got £100 in cash – and all my checks to be paid on Monday in anything required. Called at Whitleys, ordered Marshall's interest tables, and brought the *Quarterly Review*. Back soon after 4 ... sat a little with A~ who did not stir out today. At 5 had the 2 Manns and Charles Howarth – settled with them. Dressed – dinner at 7 – coffee – left Mr Gray. A~ and I came upstairs at 10.20.

SUNDAY 30 Slept in kitchen chamber... A~ off to the school at 9... Took Mr Gray in the carriage & off to church at 2.10... Out with Mr Gray till after 6... A~ came upstairs a little before 10 and I at 10... *Then went to A~, gone to her room – crying and all wrong. All the three* [servants] *(Oddy, George and Cookson) impertinent. The latter the worst. A~'s health could not stand it. I must choose between her and Cookson, whom, A~ said, had said I would turn away etc. I never uttered for half an hour, then said 'Turn them all away', and quietly talked to that purpose, said what I could unoffensively for Cookson. That I wished A~ had someone in view* [i.e. in mind], *but she must please herself. It is indeed melancholy. We shall soon not be able to get, and if we do get, shall never keep, a good servant.*

Though they had recently been getting on so well, late April saw one of their worst rows. So what had changed the dynamics of their relationship? Ostensibly it was about servants, notably Cookson. But had Ann now got a sense that, financially at least, Anne need not depend on her any more? Primarily, it was about money, with lawyers appearing at Shibden and, after much legal formality, Anne now having cash in hand. At a deeper level, however, it was probably also about Anne's prioritizing Shibden over Ann.

These were 'queer times' indeed.

May 1837

With its flurry of lawyers and bankers, April had ended on a dramatic note for Anne. The downside was arguments with Ann, ostensibly about servants (notably Cookson). Meanwhile, landscape gardener Samuel Gray remained at Shibden, setting out a laundry court and Dutch haybarn. And Anne, with scarcely a pause, swerved from major domestic crises to banking business down in Halifax.

MONDAY 1 Out about with Mr Gray till breakfast at 9.30... Came in with him (he to luncheon) at 2 or after. *A little while again with A~.* *What a temper! She now throws the Cookson business all on me, and repeated the alternative of my choosing between saying how ill I had behaved* [and] *saying I would not turn Cookson away. I said, as last night, I had not said exactly that. However I, with perfect temper, told A~ to do as she liked; but I thought, as I had done before, it would be foolish to do so on the present grounds. A~ had pothered and cried and dressed herself. I told her Cookson would not understand all this etc – till A~ told me she was too ill to bear more lecturing and I walked off...*

 To Mr Parker's office... Gave Mr Adam a check (no 107), payable to Robert Parker Esquire on order for five hundred pounds, in account of the moneys Parker & Adam had paid for me to Messrs Nelson [glazier] in account of Northgate; and gave another check (no 108) payable to Robert Parker Esquire for £1,011.12.0, being principle & interest at 5% on the £1,000 from Mr (William) Wainhouse...[1] Adam said Mr William Wainhouse had overdrawn himself on his bank. I waited a minute or two, then said I should be glad to pay Mr Wainhouse another thousand if that suited him... And he [Parker] & Adam would let him, Wainhouse, know...

Anne was being very courteous to Wainhouse, who had been so helpful to her.[2]

Out with Mr Gray till 6.45 planting out thorns... Dinner at 7.10 ... poor Mr Gray has very little in him, and A~ thinks him very finicking – but his taste, landscape gardening taste, is certainly good. He would not however get work on very fast without some helpmeet.

TUESDAY 2 Fine morning... Trees planted... Dinner at 7. A~ did not come for some time, then seemed tired & went upstairs again in less than ½ hour... I went upstairs at 10.30 & found her on the sofa,

looking tired – she said she was very poorly – but did not want me
– begged me to leave her quiet. Finding I could be of no use, went
to my room to prepare for bed. Hearing A~ going to her room (in
about 10 minutes, not more) – went to the door – but locked & no
possibility of admission… *A~'s illness a regular bad temper for I know not
what.*

**A locked bedroom door carried enormous significance.[3] Did Ann feel that
everything was done to suit Shibden, yet it was she who had been uprooted
from her family home? And financially it was Anne who had the upper hand
now.**

Had Mawson just before dinner, anxious to begin making the Lodge
road, as agreed. Hardcastle [tenant] returned in the afternoon …
<u>very</u> drunk.

WEDNESDAY 3 Very fine morning… 8.40 when A~ came to me – better,
but poorly with indigestion… She rode off to Cliff Hill…
    Coffee at 8.30. A~ better than last night but came upstairs about
9.30. *Went to bed at ten & three-quarters. She would have been fondling* [me],
but I was too sleepy & tired. However, I soon [found] *sleep impossible. She
moaned – called me up before twelve for a little water. But on her being asleep
& snoring, I left her at twelve & forty minutes – & went to my own bed.* Very
fine day.

**All the while, Anne was busy with Samuel Gray, working in the Hall and
down at the meer.**

THURSDAY 4 At my desk at 7.55… A~ had Mr Horner… Mr Gray
converted (or nearly so) to my plan of a little staircase across (west
side) to my uncle's room.
    Coffee at 9. A~ & I came upstairs at 10.30. She had letter this
evening from her sister – little Mary & Mrs Sutherland's housekeeper
(Hannah) to be at Leeds on Tuesday next. A~ to bring them from
there to Cliff Hill, & stay there with them till this day [next] week.
A~ had letter also from Mr Jonathan Gray – Mr William Priestley
can be compelled to pay Mrs Ann Walker 4% on the money left by
her sister. A~ & I sat up talking till 12.20.

**As well they might talk! Aunt Ann's sister was Elizabeth Walker, wife of John
Priestley, William Priestley's parents.**

FRIDAY 5 Slept in kitchen chamber… *A~ came to me at seven & lay on my bed talking till eight…* With A~ till 2.40 when she rode to Cliff Hill.

Anne then spent the rest of the day at Listerwick and planting bushes. However, trouble brewed.

FRIDAY 12 *A~ wrong evidently – as Mr Gray would easily see. What temper she has. Luckily I do not trouble myself much about it. We may travel together for a while – but how can I ever do with her in society? A vulgar pride is at the bottom of it. The beautifying of poor old Shibden may eclipse Cliff Hill. She is jealous of her authority, or rather of an importance which she knows not how to support. I must do the best I can. Query: if her aunt dies, will she not be got rid of?* Breakfast in about ½ hour…

This is certainly a fairly brutal coded passage, though arguably a candid one. It reads as if Ann meant almost nothing to Anne; and that Shibden and the Lister dynasty held more importance for her than Ann herself. The query about Aunt Walker's death presumably meant that the Sutherlands would 'get rid' of her up to northern Scotland.

WEDNESDAY 17 Mr Wainhouse begs I will pay the money or not, as may suit me 'as is most agreeable', very civil…

Coffee at 9… A~ came upstairs a little before 10 & I before 10 struck. ¼ hour with her in her room. *Low, cried – of no use her having workmen if she was not at Cliff Hill to look after* [i.e. supervise] *them. Then* [I said] *I would have her go & stay as long as suited her. She would have nothing to do with Cookson. Very well, look out for another* [servant], *but* [I] *advised getting a better* [one] *before she parted with Cookson. Poor A~. What a miserable temper.* Very fine day… Sat in my study reading.

Meanwhile, George Robinson remained a troublesome tenant:

THURSDAY 18 Out at 7.45… Met Mrs Robinson in the road – longish talk about their advanced rent – said I would not … give way about the notices to quit. Mrs Robinson said her husband would never sign the lease I proposed. [I] said I did not wish him to sign it – had no thought of making him the offer again. Had he signed it, I should have thought it right to be very liberal – as it was, whenever he left the place, he would just get what the law would give him – & said I would not lay out a sixpence.

Walked into the garden to talk, for Mrs Robinson did not wish to be overheard. Told me how well they were now doing. She had just bought a hundred pounds worth of leather & paid for it too – said they were very high rented. I answered that I really did not think so... However, she [was] gradually mollified – hoped she should not offend me etc, & we parted very good friends. But I fear there is something wrong – I fear it from her great boasting of sincerity. Sauntered back by the walk.

This was a civil yet tight-fisted argument with a tenant's wife, Anne not giving an inch.

FRIDAY 19 Fine morning... Cookson wanted to see me – her sister dead very suddenly – Cookson in great trouble. Gave her leave to go home this afternoon, to be back this day-week – & gave her six sovereigns in a/c of wages... *A~ slept with me in the kitchen chamber, first time – in very good humour.*

Unusually, Anne then repeated herself in her next coded entry, perhaps because she was so pleased at restoring her relationship with Ann.

SATURDAY 20 *A~ slept with me – in very good humour...* Came for A~ to walk with her to Cliff Hill... Soon turned back, A~ so weak & tired – put her to bed (to lie down) & got her a glass of madeira & a biscuit... A~'s birthday today – her 34th – thought of it at dinner, but of course in silence while Mr Gray was with us.[4] *Went to her on getting into bed – she not loth.*

SUNDAY 21. *With A~ last night till one & a quarter, & had a good kiss & a slumber afterwards...* Had told A~ as we walked along this morning, I thought we should stay over [for] the rent day. Out till after 2 – *then washed & dressed for cousin (found him gently come) & church.*[5] Off to church at 2.45... Heard the girls say their catechism... Sat 25 minutes at Cliff Hill – Mrs A Walker glad to see us...

Tonight's paper mentioned the arrival of Lady Stuart de Rothesay & Miss Stuart in Paris from Italy. Letter tonight from Messrs Gray; they disappointed at the non-payment of the money, but would take care it should be paid into the [Yorkshire] District Bank on the 27th – £7,000...[6] Found A~ asleep in bed at 10.20. Fine day.

MONDAY 22 A~ had been sitting on my bedside ½ hour – ready at 8.45.[7]

TUESDAY 23 Had A~ a little while at 7… Off in the carriage with A~ about 10.45 – left her at Whitehall [Hipperholme], she going forwards to Leeds to bring back little Mary, & I returned with Robert Mann + 5 to get up [the] great holly in Charles Howarth's little field… With Gray this morning & afternoon planning the opening of the Lodge gates by machinery underground communicating with the room upstairs at the Lodge…[8] Made coffee at 9 – skimmed over the London paper. The *Halifax Guardian* came tonight – first time, I think, on a Tuesday.

Had Anne been less preoccupied with Ann and with estate business, she would have noted a news item headlined 'Great Meeting of the West-Riding' at Peep Green, with radicals including Feargus O'Connor speaking.[9]

Note from A~ … said she had sent my watch by George – George knows nothing about it… Can it be lost? Is it possible? Poor Sibbella! My heart aches at the mere thought of such a loss… Mr Gray to [be] here again … next month. *Terms ten guineas a week.*[10]

WEDNESDAY 24 Fine morning… Off to Halifax … at the Bank at 12.30 – told Mr Davidson that nearly £7,000 would be paid into the branch bank at York on the 27th inst, & that I should give Mr Parker a check for £1,000+ on the 31st… Then a moment at Mr Parker's office door – all shut up in honour of the Princess Victoria's birthday – almost all the shops … shut up on [for] the same occasion.[11] Then called and saw Thomas Greenwood … looks very ill … poor fellow!

Anne then strode at an impressively fast pace:

Off to Crow Nest. By the walk & Lower Brea road & there in 35 minutes at 4.35. A~ gave me my [Sibella] McLean watch. She & Mr Gray & co busy moving the great variegated holly from under the Counting-house window at Crow Nest.[12] When all was safe, just walked with A~ to the door at Cliff Hill (she much tired – little Mary too wild for her, alarms her); & left her there & set off back with Mr Gray at 6.35…

Dinner at 8.15 to 9.30… Had Mr Gray upstairs… Gray likes the blue room – would do the tent room in the same way… Told him to make enquiries about the painter … who painted the glass windows in the great baronial hall at Arundel castle… I should not like to be detained [at Shibden] beyond July – sat downstairs talking about the Northgate hotel… Gray of the opinion I had best furnish the hotel, at least a certain portion of the rooms, but particularly the Casino & do it well & find good wines etc… Will do anything he can to help me – will talk it over with Mr Harper when he sees him.

So Anne still entertained grand baronial ideas about Shibden.

THURSDAY 25 Fine morning… With Charles Howarth & Booth, chalking out the floor of the new coach-house… About 5 or after, Messrs Holt of the Travellers' Inn [Hipperholme] & Waddington, deputy constable, came wanting to speak to me – to know if I had seen any men fighting at Holt's [inn] door last Sunday week? 'No! … had never seen any such thing – but would turn to my rough book.' Brought Holt & Waddington to the Hall – they had beer – turning to my Journal & read the principal occurrences of the day in question, from which it was evident that I had seen no fight. No! … Waddington thought nobody so particular [i.e. meticulous] as I was. Poor fellow! Such a thing as a journal was quite foreign to him. He seemed quite astonished when I calmly said I could tell what I had said and done for the last 21 years past quite as well as for last Sunday but one…

Anne's writing a detailed daily diary now became local public knowledge.

Found little John Booth helping his father to milk – told, <u>reminded</u>, John how often I had said I would not have little John employed here without my orders… Poor John! I said if his children were here, why should not Frank's be here too…[13]

The 2 carriages put into the new coach-house tonight, 1st time – the east doors put up this afternoon… Letter tonight from Mrs Cookson – her mother <u>very ill</u> – begs to stay with her a few days longer… From 9.45 to 10.20, read Higgins on the Earth.

FRIDAY 26 Slept in the kitchen chamber. Fine morning… A~ returned at 6 – I came in at 6.30. Mrs Ann Walker fast declining. A~ thinks she will not live over August – has given up all thought of going abroad & leaving her. 'Well!' said I, 'how lucky then that we have been hitherto detained.' Poor Mrs Ann Walker – condoled [i.e. grieved] with A~, very sorry. Dinner at 7 – sat talking in her room till 11.30. *Then undressed & went to bed to A~.*

SATURDAY 27 Fine morning. *Good kiss last night – staid with A~ till one &*
a half...

Anne then talked with Holt about coal at Northowram further up Shibden valley:

> I asked Holt if he meant to bid. 'No!' ... I said it would be foolish to
> let Stocks get it for next to nothing... Holt said the coal was of no
> value to him – he had no privileges – owned it was worth money to
> me. I said we would talk it over – but bade him not [to] say anything
> about it. I thought Stocks <u>tottering</u>... I must think about this North-
> owram coal. Holt says there is no occasion to sell low bed coal at less
> than 9d at Listerwick pit – seems to think trade will get up again, &
> appeared in good spirits. Said there was no colliery to pay much but
> this here [i.e. Listerwick]. Rawson all in trouble... Stocks's coal almost
> done...

**Radical firebrand Michael Stocks was not only a fierce political opponent but
also a coal rival. No wonder Anne was rather secretive about mining: it was
still possible for this very small-scale local coal industry to be very profitable.**[14]

Little Mary & Mrs Sutherland's housekeeper, Mrs Hannah Heap,
came between 11 & 12 to stay a few hours by way of introduction.
A~ gave me £50 just after Holt went, to help settle with the Manns
this evening, instead of sending [it] to the bank. Then with A~ &
little Mary at their luncheon – out with them at 1.15... Saw A~ &
little Mary & Hannah off in the market cart to Cliff Hill (Frank drove)
about 5.30.

SUNDAY 28 Very fine morning... Been reading Africa, Edinburgh Cabinet
Library... Off to church at 2... Drove to Cliff Hill. Found A~ & little
Mary setting off in Mrs A Walker's carriage. Saw Mrs A. Walker for
a minute & then drove off – in church 2 or 3 minutes before A~ &
her little niece. All sat in our pew... A minute or 2 at the school – then
to Cliff Hill...

Letter tonight from Messrs Gray to say the money ... would be
paid into the Yorkshire District Bank at York to be placed [in]to my
account yesterday...[15] 'Yes!' *Now let me turn carefully to my accounts &*
mind [i.e. take care] *what I am about.* [To] *finish jobbing* [i.e. estate jobs]
as soon as possible.

TUESDAY 30 *Incurred a cross last night thinking of M~, lightly as usual...* Sat reading till 9.15 Loudon's Encyclopedia of Agriculture article... Mr Harper came at 2.30. Out with A~ at the Lodge while he had luncheon. Then with him till near 4 & from 5 to 6 in the laundry & about... Cookson returned a little before 8. Off with A~ at 8.20 & walked with her in an hour to the last stile in the Crow Nest fields. Returned in 28 [minutes] & came in at 9.40, very hot – heated with my walk.

May ended with Mr Harper informing Anne of a promising tenant for the Northgate Hotel: 'I thought it lucky, if true.' And she also realized 'what a talk in the country my colliery has made'.[16]

More generally, had Anne succeeded in 'maintaining the upper hand? Financially, yes. She was no longer so dependent on Ann. The loan from Mr Wainhouse, and more recently the mortgaging of some properties to the Misses Preston, had given her real financial confidence. All she needed now was to '*mind what I am about*'. Meanwhile, her sexual relationship with Ann ('*had a good kiss*' and '*she not loth*') was very amicable. Yet Anne ended May with the coded words, '*incurred a cross last night thinking of M~*'. How would Anne and Ann's marriage pan out?

VII

GETTING BOTH WORTLEYS ELECTED
TO PARLIAMENT

JUNE–AUGUST 1837

JUNE 1837

Anne now felt financially secure. Yet could Ann Walker feel really happy living at Shibden?

THURSDAY 1 *Incurred a cross about two last night thinking lightly of M~.* Fine morning... *Then turned back to go to the water closet – rather loose-ish* [motion]. Was it the cowslip wine of last night?...

Then down the Old Bank to the Bank ... they had received the advice of the money, £6,851.13.6, being paid by Mr Gray into their branch bank at York. Got £50 in cash... Went to Whitley's ... ordered Nicholson's Builder's Guide ... & bought 2 little shilling pamphlets on etiquette. Then to Mr Parker's office...

Anne's wonderful combination of reading spanned both highly practical guides and small reminders on the finer points of etiquette.

Anne and Parker talked about Northgate. Occupying a prime site in Halifax, it represented not only urban social status but also potentially lucrative business.

[He] seemed to quite agree with me that the Northgate hotel should be advertised without loss of time. Said I would write to Mr Harper for this purpose... Said I [to myself] as I walked up Old Bank... 'Perhaps the hotel may pay me fairly after all.'

FRIDAY 2 Had Shaw the plasterer & paid him £50 in a/c of the plastering at Northgate. [Said] I was glad he had got the job … & [I had] been the best friend he had – hoped he would give & get us a good blue vote or two. 'Yes! That he would.'[1]

This illustrated the electoral significance of her hotel. If Shaw employed assistant plasterers, he could possibly get her other Blue votes. Then Anne turned to engaging a new servant who had been recommended.

John Burton – good character – hired the young man (Qt 16) at £16 per annum, including washing [i.e. he to pay for his own washing]. One dress [suit], one under[dress] & fustian dress & one hat per annum. John had £10 a year with Mr Fenton, & was washed for in the house… John to turn the washing machine – to take charge of the ponies or work under the gardener in my absence, as I may think best. To wear powder when out of livery – I to find the powder or allow him a guinea a year…

This set out starkly how a 16-year-old boy was hired. The livery and powdering were almost as significant as his meagre wage.[2]

Wrote rough drafts – fluently & to my mind [satisfactorily], *of the letter to Lady Stuart & … letter (long note) to Lady Harriet* [de Hagemann].[3]
Left my study at 3.45 and went out… Dinner at 6.40 – coffee … sat talking. Note from the Philosophical Society – a paper will be read next Monday entitled 'Halifax during the 17th century'.

The Listers were one of the few local families who could effortlessly trace their ancestry back to the seventeenth century.[4] Yet Anne would not attend; and it was unthinkable for a woman, however well qualified, to read a paper in public.

Note also from Mr Parker … [about] the Northgate hotel. *Read A~ my letters over.* A~ would like to see the schools in Berlin now, after reading Mr George Coombe's work on Education.

SATURDAY 3 Joseph Mann came for a hundred bricks to build the Listerwick pit cabin and set the bellows… Then had Rawson (William), plasterer for Stump Cross Inn – did the work as well as he could – it just paid him journeymen's wages – & he made a good workmanlike job of it. Lives in one of A~'s Hatter's Street cottages … pays £6 a

157

year & taxes. Has no vote, but would do his best to influence other people to vote Blue if he had a vote.

Meanwhile, Anne spent considerable amounts of money, paying joiners at Stump Cross Inn, continuing work at Northgate, and of course Listerwick.

Sunday 4 Very fine morning... *Tidying the blue room – putting A~'s things in her own sitting room (the north parlour) & dressing room till near one...*

Perhaps Ann now had her own sitting room in an attempt to enhance her sense of belonging at Shibden.

Wrote to Lady Harriet de Hagemann... Church... Called & sat 25 minutes at Cliff Hill – brought back A~ & little Mary & Mrs Sutherland's housekeeper, Mrs Hannah Heap, to stay a fortnight... At 8.15 walked with A~ & little Mary in the walk till 9 – then out ¼ hour by myself. Then coffee, A~ sent little Mary to bed at 9.40 & she (A~) & I then slept about ½ hour & came upstairs.

Anne now commanded building work at Shibden on a stupendous scale, which included building the terrace walls (see Figure 5).

Monday 5 Slept in Kitchen Chamber... Had Cowper, the bricklayer... I would try to be ready for beginning the walling – Cowper thinks 250 bricks would be a good load for a one-horse cart, & it would go four times a day from Swan Banks to Coney Garden. Mr Harper calculated I should want about 30,000 bricks – 4 times per day at 250 = 1,000 per day. But I think they would go 5 times a day?

Swan Banks brickworks was down in Halifax by the canal, Coney Garden was above Shibden Hall, and Old Bank was an incredibly steep hill for a lone horse to pull up a cartload of 250 bricks.[5] However, the scale of Anne's estate improvements demanded this, giving a vivid example of her driving a hard bargain.
She then wrote to Vere:

'If we live, I hope we shall spend a few quiet days together somewhere or other, by & by. I would rather it was here than anywhere, not meaning by this any disparagement of Achnacarry whose beauties I remember with a clearness that astonishes me... Are you at Achnacarry or where? At all rates, you have always your own place in my remembrance & regard. God bless you! Again affectionately yours, A. Lister'[6]

What does this loving letter to an old flame say about her relationship with Ann now?

Mr Jubb called at 1.20 & staid 55 minutes... A~ told him about her aunt, was failing fast – did not think she could get over the winter – we should be detained at home on this account. Mr Jubb to call as a friend on Wednesday...

Came upstairs & read over my letters ... to the Lady Vere Cameron ... & to the Lady Harriet de Hagemann, all under cover ... to the Honourable Lady Stuart, Richmond Park... Then sleepy – *& locked myself up in my room & slept half an hour in my chair, & then got out of the drawing room window to avoid little* [Mary]. *She caught me however, but I think I was in the garden first...*

Could Anne's slightly undignified exit by a window have appeared as all good family fun?

Mr Charles Norris came to me in the Lodge road – gave me his card in a forward familiar sort of manner. Came to ask A~'s & my vote for his getting his brother, Mr William Norris, a place as clerk to the Navigation Company. Said A~ & I were interested for his family, but we would consider about our votes – would not at present pledge ourselves.

Even the canal company clerkship was now political. With King William IV seriously ill and unlikely to recover, his death would trigger a General Election.[7]

Dinner at 7.10 – coffee – Little Mary went to bed a minute or 2 before 9. A~ slept on the sofa – I read ... Mr George Combe on Popular Education. Came upstairs at 10.20.

TUESDAY 6 Very fine morning... A~ came & brought little Mary for a little while... *Romp with little Mary who will soon, I think, like my society as well as A~'s. The latter in bad sorts today. But I now take little or no notice of her illness when it is of temper rather than health.* A~ called at ... Cliff Hill this afternoon – thought her aunt very poorly.

WEDNESDAY 7. Heard little Mary a Latin lesson – then out all the morning... Could not get into my study all the day – shut up to keep as much as possible the dust out, while Blythe & his 3 men took down the library passage ceiling.

Off to Halifax about 12.45 ... to the bank... Got a hundred pounds in cash. Then bought stuff for 2 black petticoats at Nicholson's... Returned up the Old Bank, some time in the house. A~ getting the camp bed George slept in (from the red room) into the blue room for me – the Kitchen Chamber too hot...

Dinner at 7.40. A~ out of sorts – I sighed over it in silence. Little Mary & I had coffee by ourselves. Poor child! How innocent, how buoyant her spirits.[8] Sent her to bed at 9.45 – & then came upstairs myself... *The child said A~ was not* tired *in this way at Cliff Hill. The whole house*[hold] *& Hannah too will see how it is. What a goose A~ is – & what a temper. Mercy upon us. What steady comfort can I have – what will be the end of it?*

Out of the mouths of babes and sucklings came a clear statement from Mary: Ann was fine when at her family home, but not when she was at Shibden. 'Home' had acquired contested meanings for her now.[9]

THURSDAY 8 Slept in the blue room 1ˢᵗ time last night... *Thinking of spending next winter at Naples with A~ or not. Musing about letting her slip off – or doing it myself. What real comfort shall I ever have in her?*

This is a woefully heartfelt lament. Anne appears not to see Ann's point of view, that Ann had given up her home and was helping fund Anne's ambitions for Shibden and for travel. Naples was about as sunnily far south as Anne could venture; though, of course, it was where Ann's brother John had died on his honeymoon just seven years earlier.[10]

Dinner at 7.05, coffee at 8 – little Mary at romps [i.e. play] & went to bed at 8.45. Then skimmed over the newspaper. Letter ... franked by Lord James Stuart from Lady Stuart, Richmond Park... At accounts till 12.05.

So, with Anne 'at accounts' well into the night, her relationship with Ann seemingly remained cool.

Friday 9 Fine but dull morning... A little while with A~... So tired & sick (bilious), sent A~ off to bed – in the red room (my aunt's room), a little while before the joiners came back from dinner – they had pulled all the ceiling down. Much pleased to see the span of the roof laid bare – thought of throwing the ceiling up to the top with framing in the hall – will consider about it...

From the meer to Mytholm on my way to Hipperholm quarry – met Joseph Mann there... He thinks £50 per D.W. for Dove House (both [coal]beds included) enough. 'Yes!' [I] said...[11]

Dressed – dinner at 7.10 – coffee about 8.15 – read the newspaper. Little Mary went to bed at 10, & A~ & I came upstairs at 10.15 & sat a little in my room (the blue room). Then till 10.45 wrote the whole of today.

Anne ended the day again recording, not what she and Ann had talked about, but Shibden business.

SATURDAY 10 The York joiners at my uncle's room... Went down to the meer at 11 – Robert + 6... Rain sent all to dinner a little before 12 – I took shelter in the hut & slept the hour the men were away...[12]

Had the 2 Manns at 6.30 to 7. Dressed – dinner at 7.20 – coffee. A~ read me a little of the paper – came upstairs at 10.20... Then sat up till 2, reading & cutting [pages] open Tredgold on Carpentry...

Anne had spent nearly *three hours* reading about carpentry! And the next day before breakfast:

SUNDAY 11 Had A~ a few minutes at 8.30 before she set off to walk to church. Sat reading ... a critique, very favourable, of Ranke's *Popes of Rome*, Berlin 1836... Then a little while dusting in my study when Greenwood (Thomas) came... Talked about [Northgate]... I was not in despair about getting a [hotel] tenant – should have plenty of applications – the only thing was to choose the right one...

A~ thought me late & was waiting at Hinscliffe's opposite the Crow Nest gates.[13] Mr Wilkinson did all the duty... Found Mr Rawdon Briggs at Cliff Hill – 1½ hours there...

Rawdon Briggs's visit to Cliff Hill was rather extraordinary, given that he was the leading local Whig. Also, Briggs was a Unitarian not an Anglican, as well as being the main rival to Rawsons' bank. So there was every reason for maintaining social distance. However, Ann's aunt undoubtedly owned canal shares, and Briggs's visit was a courtesy call. Little could he have imagined that Anne Lister would roll up! And Anne had every reason to distrust him.[14] However, he seemed to bring useful information, and was well able to talk plausibly about very large sums of money:

Mr Briggs spoke much on the subject of the navigation – receipts up to last Saturday for the year, £66,000 – dividends at 18% = £30,000...

The treasurer (Mr Waterhouse) has lately had as much as £32,000 in his hands... No better investment – agrees with me the railroad will not hurt the canal – the former will never pay. Mentioned to Stephenson a better [rail] line, but he would not listen to it, <u>his theory being to follow the water</u> (the courses of the rivers).[15] Mr Charles Norris not a fit person to succeed his brother – best to have somebody out of the business who would give his whole time to the navigation concerns. Salary = £400 a year. Mr Norris gives a clerk who keeps the books £100 a year (& therefore has a sinecure of the rest). His canvass [of votes] a private one... Said A~ & I were not pledged (said to ourselves as we came home, we should vote against him), but his canvass, private or not, was so active, I thought he would get the promise of the votes of the general subscribers. I had at first told Mr Briggs I should sell my stock as soon as I could do it well, but of course, had no thought of attempting it now.

Was Anne for once being rather gullible? Surely Briggs, a shrewd businessman, knew full well that the railway would soon pay?[16] Perhaps his game was to make certain that Anne, Ann and her elderly aunt did not sell their canal shares.

MONDAY 12 Fine morning... ½ hour with A~ & ate 4 oranges... Had Joseph Mann a few minutes – who brought his coal-book & paid me for the last few loads got in... Dressed – dinner at 7.10 to 8, & then came away before having had the finger glasses, & slept on the sofa...[17] At 9.30 had Cookson up to cut my short black hair, a great relief...[18] A~ sat with me until about 10.30 while I ate 5 oranges and she one. Then wrote all the above of today *and had A~ ten minutes – she tired. Her being tired is terrible enough to put anyone in the vapours. It was this* [that] *sent me off after dinner, just to get rid of her – for tho' I was sleepy after my dinner and cider, an agreeable companion was all I wanted. Poor A~, this she can never be.*

[marginalia] Mr James Norris called today, & saw A~ who positively refused pledging herself respecting the navigation clerk to succeed Mr (William) Norris.

TUESDAY 13. Fine morning. A~ came and sat with me while I dressed. *I said laughingly, 'Perhaps I may go to Leipsig Fair, whether you will bundle off* [i.e. pack for the journey] *or not.' She gave no answer, and I spoke no more.* Out – at the mere... Musing there till came in to breakfast at *9. Sent for A~. She did not speak, nor did I, except to say civilly, 'Half a cup,* *if you please*', *having myself poured out the first* [cup]. *And on coming away, I said 'I am going* [out], *Little One.' Still she did not speak.* Out again about 9.45…

Frank and Zebedee carting bricks from Swan Banks for the garden wall… Then came upstairs and till now (1.30) making memoranda and writing all the above of today. *Have not gone near A~, nor seen her. What a temper she has. This would be miserable work* [if it were] *to last forever. How and when will it end? I care less and less.* We owe two great duties to society, to be useful, and to be agreeable – and we more especially owe these duties to those upon whom our welfare most immediately depends…

Although not written in code, Anne was reflecting that Ann seemingly fulfilled neither of these 'two great duties'.

Reading till A~ came to me & staid till 3 – long talk about George & Susan. Oddy spoke to A~, but did not wish to be brought in [to the dispute] – thought Susan not to blame. *Eh bien!* Observed to A~ that I knew of no way of managing the matter well without Mrs Oddy consenting to be informant openly. *A~ seemed not to coincide in* [i.e. with] *my opinion. I quietly told* [A~] *to do as seemed best to* [i.e. for] *herself. She left me, rang the* [dinner] *bell, & is perhaps saying as I proposed. How ungracious she is.*[19]

Mr Jubb called this morning – thinks Mrs [i.e. aunt] Walker better… Dressed – dinner at 7.10 – coffee at 8 – played with little Mary. A~ took her to bed at 8.45, and I went into the drawing room & at my books (arrangement of) till 9.25. Then blow up with George … his for <u>ever talking</u> (he talks on all occasions if spoken to) always annoys me. *My cousin came gently just before dinner.*

WEDNESDAY 14 <u>Very fine</u> morning… Putting plate [i.e. china] chest into business room (late upper-buttery)… Note to Mr MacKean, Yorkshire District Bank, Halifax, for £50 for myself…

Anne was so well organized and focused on estate work as to have her own 'business room'.

The tower roof wood-work up today… Dinner at 7.20. A~ had a bad headache & I slept in my chair till roused up to speak to speak to Matthew Booth, shoemaker – came about grass in Walsh land… Very civil to Matthew – had him in & he had beer – will not vote again for the Whigs.[20] Coffee at 9.40 – sat reading last night's & tonight's papers… A~ wrote note for me tonight for … Mr S Washington… *I say little but am perfectly civil – take no particular notice of A~. All wrong yet* [i.e. still]. *She is a dull companion & I get tired.*

So, perhaps the nub was that the more Anne became organized at Shibden and could finance her own plans, the more she saw Ann merely as 'a dull companion'.

THURSDAY 15 *A~ wrong as ever, and I think more and seriously of being off. Came to my room about ten and a half … then sat musing and looking at road map of France. To spend next winter cheaply and improvingly at Montpellier? Looking to my accounts – settle all and be off as soon as I can. Be perfectly civil and properly attentive to A~, and she will do the rest to help on our quiet parting. It is a mesalliance* [i.e. unhappy marriage] *to me. The sooner I am quietly rid of her the better. I wish it was over. At this moment, I am pothered and feverish. Mais tout se passera…* Wrote the above of today till 11.45 – and then ate ½ dozen oranges… [Wrote] to John Waterhouse Esq, Well-head, compliments & enclosing a ten pound [note], being my subscription towards the expense incurred by the Registration committee…

With the King ailing and an election therefore imminent, the formal process of registering men who would vote Blue became increasingly urgent.

Brought down my business letter book till [up to] this time… *Read, to turn my mind from this miserable business about* [A~]. *I wish it was over. I see it will pother me more than it ought. But I will take it as well as I can. I feel as* [if] *my hand was trembling, though 'tis not in reality. She is gone, I suppose, to Cliff Hill. She has not attempted coming near me, nor have I troubled her since eight – when she seemed queer. Mrs Hannah Heap must see that all is not right & so must everyone in the house. Nobody here will be sorry? With more effort, I might have gone on till little Mary was gone? It fidgets me. Would that it were over. I must exert myself, settle my affairs & be quietly off.* Washed. Out again…

Dinner at 7.15 – told A~ Robert [Mann] had seen Mr Harper pass [on mail coach to York], but she making no answer, any further attempt at conversation was let alone… I went into the hall, then stood musing about the ceiling in my uncle's room till saw A~ pass to bed about 9.30… Note from Mr Waterhouse this evening, respectful compliments & thanks for the £10. Very fine day. *How foolish A~ is.*

Susan waited & must have noticed her not answering me at dinner. Little Mary did not come in at all.

[marginalia] *I saw A~ crying after dinner before leaving the dining room – but I did not seem to notice it. What a temper!*

Anne often describes Ann's unhappiness as 'temper', apparently not seeing how miserable Ann now felt about Shibden not being her own 'home'. Meanwhile, Anne continued to beautify her grounds, adding hints of Scottish picturesque.[21]

FRIDAY 16 Had John Booth & the gin horse (from 3 pm) carting [metal] scraplings to the glen bridge. Frank & Zebedee carting bricks from Swan Banks to the Coney garden... Dinner at 7.15 – coffee at 8.15 – hide-&-seek with little Mary till 9.30. Then read the paper – the King not expected to continue long. *A~ came round – her headache not being noticed, she was as cheerful for her as ever – and I, tho' grave, talked enough, though with measure.*

Mr John Priestley & Mrs Priestley & the 2 Miss (Mill House) Rawsons called about 3 pm & sat about ½ hour with A~.[22] Luckily I was out... *So A~ is getting right again. But I must be off some time – I must be prepared for it...*

Was Anne glad to have missed this visit from Ann's relatives because of Ann's grumpiness, or because she was so busy with estate work?

Ate 5 oranges just before getting into bed, and 9 between 1 & 2 today, & 9 last night just before getting into bed.[23]

SATURDAY 17 Dullish rather hazy morning... Note from Mr Waterhouse requesting me to send back the Registration subscription list, it being the only one the Committee had. Sent it back by the [Waterhouse] servant with civil note – very sorry to have given Mr Waterhouse the trouble of sending for it...

A~ wanted me, so a little while with her. She wanted the original saddle-room cupboard to be moved (from the house-keeper's room) into the saddle-room for George to put his clothes in & make way for John Burton the footman coming tonight (arrived this evening about eight...). Mr Jubb came at 2.15 to take out a front loose tooth for little Mary ... thinking, of course, the child sadly spoilt. He had been at Cliff Hill – thought Mrs Ann Walker much better for the quinine he is giving her. I hoped we could get off to the continent for 3 or 4 months by the end of next month...

The King better. A~ read me the [news] bulletin... Came upstairs at 10.35, and A~ sat with me twice about ½ hour & ate a couple of oranges while I ate 4.

SUNDAY 18 A~ came in, ready for church at 8.30... Breakfast at 10.10... George drove the gray [horse] in the market cart & the 3 women servants to church, first time... [I] took little Mary at 1.20. The market cart was just behind me, but I had just turned the corner into the is-to-be laundry court when I heard all was not right – alighted found the gray had jibbed [i.e. halted] – kicked & broke the shafts of the market cart, & upset it & all the women. All much frightened – nobody hurt but Mrs Heap who had hurt her wrist – she looked pale & sick ... a little brandy & bandaged it comfortably up... Susan had torn her gown so much could not go to church. Took Cookson inside, & Sarah with John Burton the footman who came last night, & off to church about 1.35...

Wilful horses could be dangerous. However, Anne was always able to deal with minor crises.

Mrs A Walker said she was better... I had told Mrs A Walker I should like A~ to get [off] from home for a little while, but that if Mrs A Walker was not better – or if she wished us not to go, we should not go. Sent A~ back alone to read her aunt Mrs Sutherland's letter... Mrs Heap's arm broken ... she seemed low & was in tears... Grieved about poor Mrs Heap...

Wrote all ... of today till 10.30, having in the meantime hunted out Joseph Booth's black coat & waistcoat ... all which luckily fit John Burton as well as if they had been made for him.

Into these domestic scenes, national politics began to intrude further:

MONDAY 19 Stood above an hour talking to Hilton about politics[24] – he will now give a blue vote – came to ask me to let him the Northgate ground for the fair. 'No!' said I had had a great many applications but had refused them all...

A~ & I off in the yellow carriage to make calls at 12... [First to Halifax] then to Pye Nest ... Mrs Francis Waterhouse & Mr Charles

Edwards and Mrs Dyson sitting at luncheon with Mrs Edwards... I felt *de trop* – but passed it off. The party went away & left Mrs Edwards & Mrs Dyson, who took us into the garden & hothouses. Mrs Edwards explained & apologized for not having called sooner after my aunt's death.[25] At Pye Nest from 1.15 to 2.05.

This was a socially complex visit to Ann's relatives. Was Anne experiencing exclusion from the extended Walker family? Afterwards, once the carriage had passed Sowerby, their calls grew more relaxed:

Then to Haugh End and sat with Mrs Henry Priestley – found her pretty well, but nervous at first on seeing us for the first time since her husband's death.[26] Then to Thorpe & sat with Miss Priestley... To Mill House & sat with Mrs William Henry Rawson (all the rest out) from 3.35 to 4.[27] Then to Heath [Halifax] & there with Miss Wilkinson... We then walked to Nicholson's shop, & I left A~ and little Mary there and went to Whitley's. Looked at books for little Mary...

Then home at 7.10, found Mr [Samuel] Gray returned. Went into the cellar – got out wine & put into the little ante-cellar 3 port, 3 sherry, 6 marsala, & ½ sherry & ½ marsala mixed... A~ came upstairs at 9.30 with little Mary & did not return. On coming upstairs at 10.15 found her asleep on the bed (dressed) lying down by Mary, also asleep... 5 minutes in the kitchen watering [i.e. putting] the fire out.

What a long day! Had Ann fallen asleep from exhaustion or from marsala at dinner?

TUESDAY 20 A few moments with A~... Getting wine out of the cupboard in A~'s store-room & arranging it (putting it in sawdust) in the hall cellar...[28] Dinner at 7.35 – Mr Gray & I out in front of the house till 9 – then coffee. Looked over the London & Halifax papers – no chance for the King lasting long. A~ went to bed ½ hour before me – a few minutes with her – wrote the last 8 lines till now 11.25.

At such moments political news moved swiftly, even among passers-by.

WEDNESDAY 21 Very fine morning... Met Wormersley going to Halifax & walked with him down Whiskam road. At the end of it, met Mr

Kitchingman who said the King died yesterday morning at 3am –
long talk about politics. Went to Matthew Booth's to enquire about
the masons that had built his houses for him. Hoped he would vote
right this time – he said he would talk to me about that another
time.

**So overnight, the death of William IV triggered election fever. He might have
been one of the least honourable monarchs, regularly lampooned by the press,
but his death had huge significance politically.**

FRIDAY 23 Very fine morning... Crowther the librarian called this
afternoon & brought me 4 volumes Maurice's *Indian Antiquities*.[29]

**This seemed a personal service on the part of the Halifax Literary and Philo-
sophical Society's librarian, bringing rare volumes to Shibden, and presumably
climbing up Old Bank!**
Meanwhile, estate work continued intensively:

SATURDAY 24 Lay on the bed from 6.10 to 7.20 – awoke at 4.30 – should
have got up had I [not] recollected at the moment that Robert Mann
& co meant to come at 5 am & stay till 1 to make up the day, so as
to have the afternoon for the fair...[30] Out at the pools till 11... Mr
Gray & I to be at the meer very early on Monday...
    A~ came to me a little before two to say the [canal] *dividends not paid today.
So I must go to Halifax, mentioning a little tour abroad. She cried – should not
like to go on account of her aunt –* [but] *should not like to be left. Unhappy to
confine me – thought me very impatient to be off.* [She] *said I had better give her
back her promise, & she would do as well as she could for (& by) herself – much
obliged for all I had done for her. I said very little in answer & that very calmly
& kindly.* [Said] *she ought to speak candidly & never leave me without an answer
at all – I was only anxious to know what her wishes really were. She left me ...
& I wrote* all the above of today till 2.10 & read... Maurice's *Indian
Antiquities* vol 1, read this work about 20 years ago with great interest
& much interested now. *I must think what to do about A~. I shall have
plenty more opportunities of being off.*

**Anne's 'union' with Ann now appeared near breaking point. Yet unlike Ann,
who cried, Anne kept her cool, seeming to prioritize travel ('being off') rather
than mending the bond in the 'promise'. And then, impeccably intellectual,
Anne turned her attention to Indian antiquities. And also, as a businesswoman,
to her bank account:**

Off down the Old Bank to the bank at 2.20 – got £70. Then some while at Walton's (the sadler's) & paid my bill. He thinks Mr [James Stuart] Wortley will come in [i.e. be re-elected for Halifax].

[marginalia] A~ gone to bed. Read the paper – came upstairs at 10.30... *In walking & musing, thought of staying quietly [here] till about next February & then being off abroad, with or without A~.*

Yet despite the coolness between Anne and Ann, they enjoyed a royal ceremony:

TUESDAY 27 Very fine morning... A~ took little Mary in the carriage to Halifax to see the procession & hear the proclamation of Queen Victoria... Then went down to the meer – Mr Gray there... About the meer drift mouth, where the intended boat-house is to be...

Off with A~ at 3 & took little Mary to [Hipperholme]... Went with A~ as far as Lidgate, then got out & walked to Hilltop, today being a remarkable day (the proclamation of Queen Victoria) & the [Shibden] Lodge road passable (the first coat of rubble just laid upon it), we drove along it – the first time of any gentleman's carriage having passed along it – very pretty drive...

Three points stand out. Ann went back to Lidgate. Seeing her old home, what did she feel? Once again, we do not hear her voice. Second, Victoria's proclamation was accompanied by high hopes for the young queen. Finally, and with due ceremony, they drove their carriage along the Lodge road for the first time.

Then home by Mytholm & Lower Brea wood & the walk. There just before the men went away at 6 – stood loitering about there with Mr Gray, & with him at the pools till surprised to find it 7.50. Dinner at 8. A~ behaved very well about it. Tea – she went to bed about 9.30 & I came upstairs soon after – the currant wine has made me <u>sleepy</u>. Threw myself on the bed & slept to 12.30. Then till 1 wrote all the above of today... Till 2.15, eating ½ dozen oranges & read today's *Halifax Guardian*.

Tuesday's *Guardian* had its front page black-lined to mark the King's death.

THURSDAY 29 Very fine morning – looking over the rent list Samuel Washington left with A~ for me... Out all the day, chiefly at the pools with Robert Mann & co, at the meer with Mr Gray... Mawson's 5 men building foundation walls of boat-house...

Dinner at 7.10 – afterwards with little Mary & Mr Gray at the Meer till came in at 9.15. A~ had made coffee but would not take any. *She seemed in right humour at first but soon fell off . She had lost the storeroom key that afternoon & got my key, & I had joked a little about [her] scolding me for taking it away too soon. Did this annoy her, it being at coffee, before* [i.e. in front of] *Mr Gray?*

Housekeeping responsibilities lent significance to keys. As well as Ann's sensitivity to Anne's scolding 'jokes', she also felt powerless in front of a witness.

Sat downstairs reading the paper, and my letter that came tonight from Mr N Alexander [Halifax lawyer] 'for Partner & self', offering me Mr Rawson's 'colliery & concerns at Swan Banks' at a fair price 'which he thinks himself called upon, both as a neighbour & a gentleman to offer' to me!!!

Anne did not often use treble exclamation marks, but this proposal certainly merited them! Was it a genuine offer or a hoax? Why would Rawson want to sell to a rival? And was the 'partner' reference yet another public embarrassment, like the earlier mock marriage announcement and effigy-burning story? There seemed little reason for Anne to take this offer seriously.[31]

Came to my room & found on my desk a note from A~, *as follows: 'Little one is very much obliged to you for all you have done for it. But it will be still more obliged if you will give it back its promise & let it go away from here, Shibden Hall, June twenty nineth.' I cannot say I am either much surprised or annoyed. She would not go abroad now on account of her aunt. How cunning she is. I have long suspected she meditated [about] getting off as well as she could. What will become of her? Marian [was] always warning [me] so to manage that I could do without A~. Perhaps nobody will be surprised at her going. How nicely she lets me get rid of her. What shall I do? Write to her sister? I must be off abroad, or stay as I sometime thought of, till February. How calmly I feel now that she herself has decided the matter. Is she quite herself?* Wrote all the above of today till 12.20.

The relationship had deteriorated yet further. It seems extraordinary that Ann refers to herself as 'Little One' and even as 'it'. How much had she accepted her inferior status, or was she exposing this power inequality to Anne? Ann suggested that she was not free to leave Shibden until Anne gave

'it back its promise'. This is surely one of the more shocking passages in the diaries, even for loyal fans. However, Anne's mind partly moved on to other business.

FRIDAY 30 Very fine morning. Had written rough draft of answer to Messrs Alexander last night. *Wrote ditto to Mrs Sutherland this morning & stood musing on both letters, but with satisfaction.* Squeezed into my toothpaste & drank off the juice of 3 oranges – the first time of taking them in this way. The weather hot … & feverish – *mais avec le temps tout s'arrange…* ¼ hour at breakfast [with A~] before Mr Gray [came]. *Began gravely with the assurance that A~ should have no trouble with me. She had only to do as she liked. She began crying. I changed my manner – said all this was ridiculous. She wanted a good whipping & I got* [to] *be right. I told her I must buy a rod, & in truth I must not indulge her too much. Said I should take her by Hull to Rotterdam (& Paris) the end of next month & she made no objection.* Out again…

Are 'she wanted a good whipping' and 'I must buy a rod' blatant examples of Anne's coercive behaviour? Yet Anne's stylish travel plans were only really feasible because of Ann's income.

A~ & I & little Mary & Mr Gray went to the meer at 8.30 for about an hour. Mr Gray towed little Mary the whole length of the water on a raft formed of the 2 large timbers… Came in at 9.45 – coffee – read the paper. A~ & I came up to bed at 10.35.

So June ended on a note of calm, domestic normality: towing a child along the meer. Yet just a few hours earlier a harsh conversation had reached a crescendo. How much had little Mary and Mr Gray actually witnessed of these marital tensions? And how were they apparently able to blow over so rapidly?

JULY 1837

William IV's death triggered a General Election. Locally, the Whigs were buoyant and the Radicals increasingly vociferous, so the Tories had to make votes wherever they could. However, in early July, Anne Lister, always an astute entrepreneur, remained preoccupied with her estate; and in Shibden Hall itself, not far below the surface of domestic normality, emotional turmoil continued.

SUNDAY 2 Off in the carriage (took Mr Gray & little Mary) to church at 2.45… Mr Bellamy preached 35 minutes from Roman viii 6 – the carnal mind is death, the spiritual mind is peace.[1] Then called & sat about ½ hour at Cliff Hill… Dinner at 7 – sat reading the paper at the dining table… I came upstairs – A~ sat with me & curled her hair & did not leave me till 10.25.

MONDAY 3 A~'s tenant Francis Carter of Hatter's Fold came to pay A~ a quarter's rent (30/-)… *Then went to A~, found her lying down. All right at breakfast – [I] did not know anything was the matter. Just asked if I should take the rent for her or if she would go down herself. She began crying. Mr Samuel Washington ought to settle these things. She was quite tired of paying him & having all to do herself. No, I was not to take the rent: she would send George. The man ought [to] give three months' notice or pay three months' rent.[2] She would send him to Mr Parker. I said I thought this would be more than it was worth. She had better take the rent & have done with the man. She cried, the more I said she was very foolish to cry about [it], she answered she would try to do for herself. We had not been happy of late – wished I would let her go away. I calmly replied I would not make her unhappy – she should do as she liked. Little Mary came in. I sent her down, then said, 'Well, my love, I shall give you a kiss' (did so) '& go out'. Which I did immediately – & saw her no more till dinner, when all passed tolerably. Went to the mere afterwards & on returning found coffee made, but A~ was gone to bed. Found her door fast [i.e. locked] on my coming upstairs. Well, now surely I shall get rid of her…*

Could it get any worse? It was almost as if Ann felt detained against her will at Shibden. Anne gave her a kiss, yet Ann ensured that her bedroom door was 'fast'.[3]

Meanwhile, Anne got on with business as usual. As well as Northgate, much concerned the Rawsons' offer of Swan Bank colliery. Holt was decidedly unenthusiastic, though he acknowledged it was well positioned:

Holt would not work Swan Bank colliery if it was given to him – it would not pay its way – but [a coal pit at] the bottom of the [South-owram] bank would be worth a thousand pounds to me… Said he should have to see Mr Jeremiah Rawson on Thursday. Told him to say … that the Swan Bank colliery could be of no use to me… Holt said if I could get this low bed loose [coal] & staith at the bottom of the bank, I could put in 15 or 20 colliers in 2 months from this time… Told Holt to do his best on Thursday & let me know…[4]

Then with Messrs Harper & Gray – stood out talking of the [Northgate] hotel etc – to send for Mr Parker tomorrow – <u>he</u> to let the hotel – [he] might otherwise feel neglected & not do his best for me in the business.[5] The advertisement to be out immediately... Harper thinks I shall have great many applications...

Out from 8.45 to 9.45 – at the meer with Mr Gray – coffee. A~ gone to bed – her door locked on my coming upstairs at 10.35...[6] *I shall indeed* [pray] *that heaven prospers me if I can make a reasonable agreement with Mr Rawson for his low bed loose* [coal]. *This will loose* [i.e. free] *me, so that I can do without A~'s help. What will become of her! But God be thanked for all his mercies...*

Perhaps surprisingly, Anne thanked God in her entrepreneurial dealings with the Rawsons, aiming to be free of Ann's 'help'. Yet the Rawsons were, of course, relatives of Ann's cousin Mary.

Writing out memoranda etc till 12.40. Then looking over rental till 1.15 – no! 1.30, *seeing what income I have without Northgate* [hotel] *or coal. I reckon profit from land in my own hands, at one hundred and twenty. I have about two thousand a year – & say interest & expenses, eleven hundred, then I have nine hundred a year to spend.*

TUESDAY 4 Fine morning... Breakfast with A~ before Mr Gray came. *Asked how she was – middling. I calmly said she could not be going on this way. I was very sorry – only wished her happiness – would not wish her to stay here if she thought she could be happier anywhere* [else]. *But it was a serious thing – in leaving here, she left independence & I thought almost every comfort. She cried but did not speak. As she had evidently done her breakfast, I begged she would not stay unless she liked it, & she was just gone before Mr Gray came.*

Perhaps Anne was being particularly disingenuous here. After all, Ann had had considerable 'independence' at Lidgate and certainly 'every comfort', albeit lonely, celibate comfort.
 Then, without a pause for breath, Anne returned to business. For a landscape gardener, Gray seemed to cast his skills net wide

Sat talking with Mr Gray about furnishing the hotel – he very knowing about beds & furniture in general – particularly about feathers ... feathers should be well stored ... or apt to smell putrid... Had Holt in the little room with the great [coal] plan before us... Talked over Mr Rawson's low bed sough or loose, & staith at the bottom of

[Southowram] Bank. Holt would rather give him a thousand pounds than miss it…

In other words, Holt seemed to have come round to this dubious offer.[7]

Went down to A~. She said she had written to her sister – & after telling [me] *the contents, gave me the copy of her letter to read. Little Mary & Hannah to go next Friday week. A~ said she had asked* [her sister] *for Crow Nest.[8] Thought of going to Scotland* [i.e. with them] *for three weeks & asked me to let George go with her as far as Edinburgh. She should order furniture in Leeds in going – at Kendells. 'Of course', I thought, '*[it's]* all arranged.' 'Well, then', said I, 'it is done. I can only hope you will be happy.' I supposed there was an explanation to her sister, & said 'I'm glad you have written, for if you had not I should* [have]. *I am satisfied this is the best way you could have managed the matter.' I was not a little surprised to find the letter so expressed that Mrs Sutherland would suppose A~ wanted part of Crow Nest for some friend – no hint at her going to Scotland. Nothing that was at* [all] *explanatory or that could not easily be got over. It might have been done to try* [i.e. test] *me. I saw this & laughed in* [i.e. up] *my sleeve but said nothing – & went to Mr Harper…*

So Ann planned to go to Scotland for three weeks, and had asked her sister about living at Crow Nest.[9] Perhaps Ann felt all over the place. She just knew she wanted to leave Shibden Hall, even if she did now know where 'home' was.

Went back to A~ … in the north parlour & sat with her till she rode off to Cliff Hill about 3.20. *Began by hoping her going to Scotland would do her good –* [yet] *she did not know that she should go. Said I had always thought she had better not go there without me – & that she had better make a very different journey & go with me to Rotterdam etc. I quizzed her a little & I think she was not sorry to get right* [with me] *again. When she said we had been unhappy of late, 'No', said I, 'not "we". I know nothing about it, & you have been more unhappy in your stomach than in your heart.'* Told A~ I had asked Mr Jubb (who called about 2.15) what he thought would be good for her…

Dinner at 6.15 – Mr Harper dined with us, he having to stay till 8 to meet Mr Parker, requesting advertising & letting the Northgate hotel. Sat at table about 1½ hour… Mr Parker came at 8 – left him with Mr Harper. Then had all gone into tea & coffee at 8.30. A~ had talked more than usual at dinner – joined in the conversation *con spirito*, & ditto at tea…[10] [Hotel] to be advertised immediately, in the *London Times* and *Morning Herald*, two Halifax papers, *Leeds Mercury*,

Liverpool ditto, *Manchester Guardian, Yorkshire Gazette* & *Edinburgh North British Advertiser* = 9 papers. Mr Harper said he had told Mr Parker what it should be let for to remunerate me (which seemed to be £450)...

A complex financial discussion ensued between Harper and Parker about the rent to be paid for Northgate. With Gray also present, it was eventually put to a vote, that is, five votes. Anne and Ann had equal voting rights with the three men. Eventually the rent was decided, on a five-year lease, with a Northgate clerk-of-works (a Mr Blyth) appointed.

A very full day, a bizarre mix of Ann's emotional turmoil and Anne's astute business dealings.

WEDNESDAY 5 ¼ hour with A~ till Mr Horner came about 10.30 & A~ set out sketching & colouring portrait of the house. Out till 11.15 – then ¼ hour in my study & off to the rent day... Met Samuel Washington – went together & at the Stag's Head at 11.45. And all received & paid & settled & I came away at 1.15 – everybody paid in full...[11] Home by 2 – with A~. Tied up £600, & at 2.45 down the Old Bank & lodged the sum in the Yorkshire District Bank, & left my banking book to be settled – Mr McKean as usual very civil...

Anne had marched fearlessly down Old Bank, carrying £600 in notes and coins.

Down Broad Street to the Northgate hotel – Blythe there in his new capacity of clerk of the works, & Mr Husband too...[12] He is to be at Northgate to teach Blythe! 'Very well', said I, 'but not longer than Wednesday.' Went all over the house with Blythe – terrible joiners' work – bad plastering i.e. crocked corners...

Here was Anne, confident in her own realm: strong, powerful, decisive – and now possessing money.

4 or 5 minutes at Mr Parker's office... Returned up the Old Bank. (A~'s cottage in Hatter's Street was really empty – found so this morning by Mr Parker & the constable)...

So not only did Ann Walker's Halifax properties cause endless problems (Water Lane mill), but some were also down-at-heel (Hatter's Street). What a contrast with the elegant grandeur of the Northgate Hotel!

Dinner at 7.10. A~ very sleepy, made coffee & then we both came to my room, & she on the sofa & I on the bed slept till 10.45. Then I had a couple of oranges & then a little cowslip wine with A~, & Cookson put her to bed, & I sat up writing out rough bank accounts of today till 12.10.

Thursday 6 Went with Mr Gray in the garden about the hot-houses – he shewed me pencil sketches of elevation ... told the gardener to set them out for me to see.[13] In the garden till came in with Mercer the glazier at 11.45 – & gave him a check for £50 in account of Northgate – 'dare not try for 2 conservative members this time'...

So now the General Election was on everyone's lips.

Took Charles Howath to the lodge – a man easing himself quite composedly behind the ash-place – the fellow sat quietly, in spite of us – this irritated me.[14] I called to Charles to take him & find out who he was... Charles made no effort [to follow him], & I told him I should not perhaps trouble him again... He saw I was very much annoyed. On returning, I offered Mawson's 4 or 5 rubble-breakers a shilling a piece for finding out & convicting anybody committing any nuisance at the Lodge...

Perhaps there were limits to what might be asked of a tenant? Unskilled labourers, with less dignity to stand on, would accept the landowner's shilling.

Before dinner had had Charles Howarth for money – gave him £5 in a/c but would not ask him in or give him beer. Said he had never annoyed me so much in his life. *Asked Mr Gray both at dinner & coffee if he thought it possible that Charles did not see the man. He smiled but gave no answer. It might be a good joke to him, but it was a bad one to me. If he begins to screen* [i.e. protect] *any other of the workmen, it is a bad look out.*

Mr Gray, discreet professional, knew when to keep his mouth shut.

Friday 7 Fine morning... Off to Halifax at 11.05 – down the Old Bank to Mr Parker's office... Parker thinks not much can be done with trespassers ... as at the Lodge yesterday... Said I should cover the place with papers [i.e. notices] against nuisance committing. Parker thought it the best plan to horsewhip the offenders.[15]

[I] mentioned in a whisper the contents of the letters from Messrs Alexander respecting the Swan Bank colliery – he looked astonished. Mentioned what I had written in answer, but said the low bed sough would be worth a thousand to me – I would give £500 down – would not bid more because the sough of no use to anybody but myself.[16] Asked if Parker could help me – he thought I could manage the Rawsons better than he could – but thinks I must put the matter into his hands at last [i.e. eventually]. Said I doubted that Holt would be able to manage it.

Parker was clearly reluctant to get drawn into an Anne Lister quarrel.

Then to the bank… Mr McKean thinks times rather better. Then to Greenwood's… [He] thought I should be satisfied with £300 a year for the [Northgate] hotel… Greenwood would engage to find wood and joiners … and do them as cheap as possible.[17] Said I should do nothing till the hotel was done with [i.e. completed]… £8,000 laid out, £2,000 I could have had for ground & £100 rent of the old house & land – could not well bind myself to take £300 a year for 5 years…

A minute or 2 at Whitley's ordering 25 printed papers [i.e. notices] 'Commit no nuisance', and bought 2 padlocks with 4 Keys (all the same) at Roper's. Returned slowly up the Old Bank & back between 1 & 2. Some time with A~… Then called down to Mr Holt – had spoken to Mr Jeremiah Rawson about the Bank Bottom coal-loose – and he told Holt he would see him again on Monday and say more on the subject [then]. Holt agrees with me they will higgle [i.e. haggle] and would rather not have anything to do with them unless it can be very well managed…

Then out till 7 – went into the cellar – 1 (bottle of) port – dinner at 7.15 – coffee at 9. A~ and I came upstairs at 10.30… *My cousin coming very gently on getting up … but did not put on linen or anything till the yarn stocking at night on going to bed.*

SATURDAY 8 Fine morning… Tete-a-tete with A~ ¼ hour… Then A~ had Bairstow [a Water Lane mill tenant] and paid him £63.3.10 for work done at his mill. *I had provided, & let her have, sixty pounds towards the bill.* Bairstow objected to sign his lease because it gave [him] no power to let off [i.e. sub-let]; and he wanted to let off a room for worsted frames. Times so bad, or [he] should not have thought of it.

I said A~ would willingly to take back [the] lease & mill, too, if he liked. But no! that was not the thing desired – they (Bairstow, Tetley and Cunliffe) had laid out a great deal of money. However, A~, if the thing [was] properly explained, said she might give consent in writing to under-let, and then all would be right. Long talk afterwards [with A~]...

I think Bairstow was persuaded not to split his vote, but to give a plumper for Wood – (not vote for Protheroe the radical candidate at all) – and perhaps he could persuade Tetley to do the same. Cunliffe <u>was</u> a radical, but is rather changing...[18]

So these negotiations over sub-letting Water Lane mill hinged in part on the tenants' voting intentions. Party politics had now risen to fever pitch. Tuesday's *Halifax Guardian* announced the election, with the Hon. John Stuart Wortley standing in the West Riding county constituency for the Conservatives (as the Tories were now known).

Yet it was of course in the Halifax constituency, after the controversial 1835 'window-breaking election', where fighting was fiercest. Here, James Stuart Wortley faced both Charles Wood, MP, an elite Whig politician with a national profile, and Radical candidate Edward Protheroe.[19] In 1835 Protheroe had lost to Wortley by a single vote. Dubious Tory tactics had not been forgotten; Protheroe was now gathering popular support locally. Chartist Ben Wilson later recalled how 'A song entitled "Protheroe is the Man" was ... played by all the bands in the district and nearly every boy you met whistling was almost sure to be whistling the tune.'[20]

Anne and Ann might not qualify as voters, but they nevertheless immediately leapt into vigorous political action. Ann Walker was the more uncompromising. Owning multiple small properties in the town centre, she 'had' more voters than Anne Lister. And whereas in the sprawling West Riding constituency they were political minnows (compared with the Whig grandees of Leeds and beyond), in Halifax every vote counted and they had considerable influence.

A~ had had Mr Sam Washington, and had told him of her canvassing Mallinson etc, and said she would quit him and every other tenant who voted for Protheroe.[21] Then [I] sat with A~ till 2.10. Had had note about 11 am from Mr James Norris respecting canvassing my tenants for the county for Mr (John) Stuart Wortley...[22]

[A~] rode off to Cliff Hill at 3.40. *Then washed and out again...* Dinner at 7.40 – asleep on the sofa in A~'s sitting room (north parlour) – coffee – we both came upstairs at 10.30. *Very good friends now.* Mr Jubb's blue pill & effervescing draught (during this week) have done A~ good.

Any rift in Anne and Ann's relationship had now healed (and perhaps not just due to Jubb's medical prescription). Identifying a common enemy helped the two women to become good friends again. Anne and Ann were now bound tightly together by their unflinching opposition to Protheroe and anyone who had the temerity to vote for him. Their relationship now seemed more balanced, even if Ann still got irked about the servants.

MONDAY 10 Walked with A~ & little Mary as far as the turnpike on the way to the school. *A~ rather out of sorts at first to find I did not approve her letting Cookson go with Mrs Heap to drink tea with some people at Halifax. Got A~ tolerably right again before leaving her. How will all this end? Can I really get on forever with A~? I cannot yet believe it...*[23]

Had Mrs Cookson to bring in my gloves she had mended. Told her I was sorry at the idea of her making acquaintances in Halifax unnecessary – she behaved very well about it and said she could explain it to Mrs Heap & would excuse herself from drinking tea at Halifax this evening. She would be glad of £5 – paid her £10 that is her year's wages in full ... = £16 per annum.

TUESDAY 11 Very fine morning... A~ had her tenant Ogden who promised to give a vote for Mr James Wortley...[24] Came in at 7 – then in the cellar, 1 port, 1 marsala – dinner at 7.15... Mr Adam came about 8.20 ... about electioneering purposes – to help us make more votes and tell us how things went on. He brought the subscription book towards Mr Wortley's election expense – only 2 names down: Messrs Waterhouse and Rawson (Christopher) for £40 each. I put down my name for £20. Mr Adam seemed to place the book towards A~, but I thought she ought not to be asked. I gave £50 before – £20 is enough to give now...

So Anne, though without a vote herself, remained a key Conservative donor in Halifax. Mr Adam had thought Ann Walker was worth a try too.

A~ & I returned to the dining room about 8.45. Asked if she would really go abroad for 3 months. She thought she could not leave home for more than a month – could not [go] for longer during Mrs A Walker's life.[25] I said this seemed a great confinement which <u>might</u> last for some years. A~ always thinks her aunt cannot or will not continue long. She owns the confinement is very great – and the obligation of going [to Cliff Hill] every day often irksome, but she thinks she ought to keep it up. I said I did not think the obligation quite so necessary as she did, but really I did not know what to say about it...

Was Anne being disingenuous? When it was her aunt nearing death, she had wanted to stay close by. Meanwhile, Mr Adam was good for political gossip:

Mr Adam thought Mr Protheroe likely to turn out [i.e. defeat] Mr Wood – but impossible to tell till the last moment – promised to let us know how things went on.

WEDNESDAY 12 Told Holt I had well considered the business – sure no agreements could be confidently be made with Mr [Jeremiah] Rawson, and desired Holt ... to say that he, Holt, had mentioned the thing to me and I had said I would have nothing to do with it, but would abide by my answer to Messrs Alexander. If Mr Rawson chose to make me any definite proposal, he might do so – but I would offer nothing...

About 2, John Booth came to tell [me] Mrs Henry Priestley & Miss Larkham had called – very civil to them – Mrs H Priestley asked if anything remained of the hall.[26] Shewed them over the house and cellars – they had walked from the Lodge... Asked Mrs H Priestley to come and spend a day with us – she will come next Saturday – both A~ and I very civil...

Mrs Priestley was special. She was not only related to Ann Walker but also had a link via Mariana to Anne Lister; and Henry Priestley had died only a month earlier. Still, an invitation to spend a whole day at Shibden was rare!

A~ sent for us to witness the signing of Bairstow's lease of Water Lane mill. Messrs Bairstow, Tetley and Cunliffe came... I had told Cunliffe, the radical, he ought to give us a split vote for Wortley, and the others should plump for Wood.[27] But finding Bairstow awkward about signing, I quietly said A~ did not care whether he signed or not, and I wanted her to go out & she had best leave them. So out we all went for ½ hour, at the end of which time George came to say ... that they would sign, on which we (A~ & I & Mr Gray) went to them in the Upper Kitchen at 9.40, and Mr Gray and I witnessed their all signing the lease, and I witnessed A~'s signing the copy of the lease written by herself, which Bairstow and co took away with them...

Was a lease-signing ever so entangled with electoral politics?

About 3.10 came a man from Mr John Dearden junior, the chairman of the [Conservative] County [i.e. West Riding] Election Committee, with the subscription book, to defray the election expense of Mr John Stuart Wortley. Too much to pay expense of the 2 brothers, borough & county. 4 names down: Messrs John Dearden, Waterhouse, Rawson (Christopher) & Holmes for £20 each.[28] I put my name down for £10.

Paying for one brother was acceptable, but two did seem expensive. Also, Anne probably grasped how slim was the chance of getting a Conservative, however well-connected, elected in the Whig-dominated county.

FRIDAY 14 At hay barn. Ordered the 3 masons & 4 lads from there up to the house (to come at noon) to finish the West tower rigging... A~ had Samuel Washington & I saw him. 43 D.W.+ of mowing this year, mowing & hay-making & stacking ... at 13/- per DW...
  Came in about 1 – some time with A~ who gave me a hundred pounds, £64.10.0 to pay Mr Gray... [Down to] the Bank ... gave them the fifty pounds Bank of England note I had just received from A~, & took out (brought away with me) £100 in their notes & check for £136.7.2 payable in York to Jonathan Gray Esq. £64.10.0 for A~ and the rest for myself up to tomorrow. Returned up Old Bank.

Life at Shibden remained a mix of the utterly traditional (hay-making), plus the brand new (the West tower was the first major extension at Shibden). Alongside ran complex financial interactions within their marriage.

SATURDAY 15 With Robert Mann + 3... John & Robert's son James gone to hear Mr [James] Wortley speak at the Piece Hall... [A~] had note tonight from Mr Adam ... saying so many voters declined giving any answer [on their voting intention], it would be impossible to know the result of the election till it was over.

SUNDAY 16 A~ off to the school (walked)... [I] staid talking to Mr Gray about the [Northgate] hotel and [Shibden] terraces... Off (took Little Mary & Mr Gray inside and Cookson outside) to church at 2.25... Called and staid 55 minutes at Cliff Hill – Mrs A Walker in good looks and spirits... Some time at Crow Nest examining the pillars ... to be covered with ivy...

Dinner at 7.15 in 1¼ hour – tea. A~ came upstairs at 9.30 & I at 10 – skimmed over the paper… [A~] *evidently low & not knowing what to write to her sister – I talked quietly and kindly. In substance, she might leave me if she thought it best – but appearances should be considered, and she had best stay till I went abroad. However, I think she considered to stay. At least she seems so inclined for the present – & I wrote her a copy of letter to her sister to go tomorrow.* Little Mary & Hannah to be off from Leeds next Friday evening, & in Edinburgh at Saturday evening…

Anne deftly placed the decision on to Ann and what 'she thought it best'. Yet, as so often with Anne, 'appearances should be considered', that is, the public face presented to the outside world. And Anne was still helping Ann hold the pen.

A~ would have written several days [ago] but waited for Mr Jubb's opinion as to Hannah's being fit for the journey… *'We are very much obliged to you for your kindness about Crow Nest. Mrs Lister desired me to give her kind regards and say that she had been at my elbow when I wrote. I should have explained to you then our little plan for the convenience of looking after my aunt, but you shall hear of all this when I write again. Little Mary is very well and Hannah's arm going on as well as one can desire. Believe me etc.' A~* seemed pleased to be got out of this scrape so nicely. I think she does not want them to guess the truth.

Anne had helped Ann 'out of this scrape'. However, 'the convenience of looking after my aunt' seems purposely obscure.

MONDAY 17 My letter to Lady Vere Cameron, kind chit-chat. 'If, my dearest Vere, I ever have a day of rest, it is Sunday… [I] think & believe we shall meet again if we live. I shall be at liberty again <u>some time</u>… The truth is, I am in any element but my own, and I shall get out of it as soon as I can… I now <u>hope</u> that I can get off for the winter… But who can count upon the morrow? … I do hope to be in Paris, though perhaps merely *en passant*, before the end of November… I feel at this moment as if I could not possibly bring myself to spend next winter here. I am heartily sick of a longer abiding in my present position without some break. We are all bustle within and without, county and borough. It is quite terrible – a company of police and military sent to Huddersfield to enforce the Poor Law. Two-thirds of the population, out of work, vow vengeance against it. Mr Cameron was paid for his wool only just in time. The quiet days of old have "parted never to return". Ever very affectionately yours, Anne Lister.'

This rather artful letter, with its emotional undertones and Ann invisibilized, ended on a note of brutal honesty about their shared political anxieties, here expressed in one of Anne's most memorable lines.[29]

'Tis now 8.30... [A~] *has written to her sister what I wrote for her last night...* A~ off to Stainland at 10.30 – to James Schofield to say if he did not pay up his arrears, he would have a notice to quit... About 11 am came Mr James Mallinson – with 5 country newspapers from the office of Messrs Parker and Adam – containing the advertisement of the Northgate hotel...[30] A long while with Mr Gray ... in the West tower top room, planning book cases... What a self-satisfied ignoramus Mr Husband is!

Tuesday's *Halifax Guardian* headlined the dissolution of Parliament, together with Hon. John Stuart Wortley's visit to Halifax.[31] There was no time to waste. The local Conservative organizer for the West Riding, Mr Craven, a solicitor, began rounding up voters.

TUESDAY 18 Letter ... from Mr Craven about county voters. Gave it to A~ to see after [i.e. to check on] her tenant, John Pearson.

THURSDAY 20 Had Abraham Hemingway who came to explain about his vote. A blue at heart, but if he gave a blue vote (for Mr the honourable John Stuart Wortley), Mr Holland would take away the road for which he pays 6/- per annum...[32] And Abraham brings all his ... tillage that way, so could not do without the right of cart road... Had the large [estate] plan down to see how I could manage about the road...

Here was one of Anne's more substantial tenants holding a rational discussion with her about his access route and voting. She fully understood his dilemma.

Met Holt ... he saw Mr Jeremiah Rawson yesterday – on mentioning the Bank-bottom coal-sough (loose) and staith, Jeremiah Rawson said it was worth 2 or 3 thousand pounds. 'Then', said Holt, 'I have done. I wanted to have begged you a little for it – now I shall <u>never</u> try to beg for anything from you for it', and Holt came away. 'Well!' said I, 'You know I told you how it would be – I will have nothing to do with them... But', said I, 'when they see the platform begin & a good start made, then they will be at you again. Then do you laugh & tell them [Rawsons] they are too late. I will have nothing to do with them.' Holt says, 'As soon as we have begun at the low end (Listerwick), we can set 10 or 12 colliers at work'...[33]

Here was the coal rivalry with the Rawsons at its fiercest. Anne was confident that strategically she had the upper hand, and they would be beaten by her, for locally 10–12 miners was big business. Anne immediately got to work with her pit-sinking plans: she knew her colliers could dig *down*, but the Rawsons down at Swan Bank (plus a small isolated pit up at Marsh) had a much harder challenge. It was a dark, satanic, underground game.

[I] asked [Holt] if my coal at Listerwick would not be worth more than his at the top of the hill (very near Law Hill...).[34] 'No!' He thought not... Then [I] astonished him by asking suddenly... 'Why can we not <u>oust</u> Mr Rawson [and] make a cut across & join their colliery to mine, bring your coal out my way?'

This was surely Anne catching Holt unawares, asking him to be as deviously ambitious towards the Rawsons as she was.

'Very well', said I ... 'make the colliery pay <u>me</u> & <u>I</u> shall be satisfied.' Holt said 'Jerry (Mr Jeremiah Rawson) had told him he had heard he (Holt) had bought my coal.' Holt [had] said, 'No! No price had been asked or offered.' 'Well! Should I work it myself?' 'Why', Holt [had] said, 'She says, if other people can make coal pay, she has the same chance they have.' 'Oh!' said Jeremiah Rawson, & as if enlightened and dropped the subject. Holt says he can get to know all about how Rawson is going on, from his (Rawson's) colliers. It was perhaps about 1.30 when Holt went away – to be here at 12 noon on Saturday & let me know... 10–12 colliers at Listerwick will pay something handsome...

The industrial rivalry with the Rawsons remained bitter, made worse by their being Ann Walker's relatives. Anne's diary caught the nuances of conversations between Holt and herself, along with Holt's memory of what 'Jerry' had said to him. It was almost like having a tape recorder trained on Shibden.

Sat with A~ in the little dining room talking over what Holt had told me etc. Then ... mused over my colliery concerns. I better & better understand the value of them. I must look into what Holt let fall [i.e. let slip] about the extent of my loose...

It seems telling that, in the middle of a ferociously fought election, Anne still devoted time and energy to sticking a dagger into the Rawsons. Party politics was important, but industrial competition probably more so.

Dinner at 7.10 – coffee at 8.45 – played a game of chess with little Mary – who hardly, not quite, knows the moves... Skimming over the paper. A~ & I came upstairs together at 10.30 – she ½ hour in my room. [She was] at Cliff Hill this afternoon about 5 – finding the Mill House Miss Rawsons there, would not go in.

'The Mill House Miss Rawsons' were daughters of W. H. Rawson, who had married Ann's cousin. He, of course, was the brother of Christopher and Jeremiah Rawson, all suspicious of the Shibden relationship. So it was all rather too close for comfort. We can imagine Ann arriving at Cliff Hill's imposing entrance, only to recognize the carriage standing at the door and immediately turn tail.

FRIDAY 21 Fine morning F57½°... Mr Jubb came to [see] Mrs Hannah Heap's arm... He told us Mr Charles Norris was elected clerk to the navigation in the place of his brother, Mr William Norris. Had got such a number of proxies [i.e. proxy votes], nobody could oppose him. No fit opponent offered himself but Mr Garlick, a quondam [i.e. former] book-seller in the town & very respectable – he at once gave up all opposition. Mr Charles Norris should be a good man of business – salary £400 per annum...

The Norris brothers were past masters at arranging matters to their own satisfaction.[35]

Mr Harper came about 11.30... [Said] I hoped to be off abroad in November, sooner or later – at any rate, to be off before Xmas... [A~] got off to Leeds in the carriage, taking with her on their way home again Little Mary & Mrs Heap... A~ came back at 9.45. Tea & coffee – skimmed over the newspaper. A~ & I came upstairs at 11... The remainder of my hay about (not quite) put into [hay]cocks & left safe for stacking tomorrow. *Saw A~ was low & went to sleep with her & she thanked me.*

SATURDAY 22 *Slept with A~, the first time since the eleventh of last April. She seemed pleased at my doing so. Said I was tired & she ought to make haste to sleep. So no effort at tenderness made or expected, & all was right, but tho' I lay*

185

quiet & did not speak, I did not sleep till late, *about two, & then slept soundly.* Fine morning...

A~ had Mr Sam Washington soon after 10... Told him to see about the Halifax fields – I wanted to make a vote or two – & mentioned my intention of building two ten or twelve pound houses at Northgate – thought of a butcher & a blacksmith...[36] Then had A~ ¼ hour till 1.15. Had Mark Hepworth [tenant]... [A~] off to Cliff Hill at 3.30... Coffee at 9.30. Skimming over the papers, A~ & I came upstairs at 10.30.

Anne 'had' Ann, almost as if she was one of her tenants! It had been another exhausting day.

SUNDAY 23 *Slept with A~ second night, but too tired for tenderness...* Off with A~ to church...

Polling in Halifax borough was on Wednesday 26 July, in the county some weeks later. So all eyes were on Halifax: a couple of votes could make or break the election. The exact boundaries between the Halifax and county constituencies were crucial. Anne's diary now has a plethora of small tenants' names.[37] Hinton, one of Ann's tenants, was keen to present himself as Mr Fix-it for the Blues:

Had A~'s Hatter's Street tenant Hinton till 2.30 – about A~'s tenants, John Mallinson, Hartley & Standeven – [asked] if A~ would be contented to let them split their vote. 'No!' Would say no more to the 1st or 2nd & the latter could not vote. Might Hartley stay if he gave a split [vote]? 'No! Let [him] give a plumper for Wortley & then talk about staying.' Hinton said he could get 20 votes for £100. Then [I] said, 'Tell some of our [Blue] Committee – I think there are 20 blues who would be glad of the votes.'

This vividly documents how Ann Walker, though voteless herself, exerted relentless political pressure on her small, town-centre tenants. However, '20 votes for £100' sounds a bit of a fetch![38]

Then till 6.30 wrote ... to Lady Stuart. Easy chit-chat – she is right – I should not be well without travelling. 'My mind is so bent upon it, I feel as if it would fidget me into a fever if I was to abide another unbroken 12 month in one stay [i.e. place]... Here I am & here I must be till near the end of the year. Surely I shall then see you, if I survive all my disappointments... Do not quite forget me... Should have written last Sunday but fancied we might know better how we [i.e. Blues] stood if we waited a few days. For the [West Riding] County, we hope Mr Wortley is sure [of election]. For the borough, we must wait the event. I remember telling you about 12 months ago, there were great fears for Mr James Wortley [MP]. Opinion has made a great turn in his favour since then; but still, I believe … the fight will be a very close one; & if we do gain the day, it may be a second time by a majority of one [i.e. a single vote]. The conservative interest has not yet had time to grow to its full strength… I can improve my own interest very materially in the course of 2 or 3 years. We had a few rotten boroughs before the Reform Act – there will now be more & more, & we shall all be rotten ere long. The united Whigs & Radicals are buying up all the votes they can – they may outwit us – the whole thing depends upon [voter] management. But the weight of property in the borough is decidedly conservative. It is very feverish work. Always dearest Lady Stuart, very truly & very affectionately yours, Anne Lister'

This is a fairly characteristic letter to Anne's elite correspondents. She offered good cheer for James Stuart Wortley's chances of holding Halifax, yet implied that Whigs and Radicals were 'buying up all the votes', and it was 'very feverish work'.

Dinner at 7.10, coffee at 8.10… To 11, digesting A~'s letter to Mr [Jonathan] Gray respecting Mrs Ann Walker's life interest in £4,000 left to her by her sister… *Wrote rough draft of a new letter.*[39]

MONDAY 24 To Cliff Hill… [Mr Gray] staked out the intended new approach road … nearly opposite the church, & thence a nice winding [drive] to the house. We all went into luncheon at 12… Dinner at 7.10 – so bad a cold had come on since morning, came upstairs & went to bed on leaving the dining room. A~ with me while I undressed & then left me – I slept in the blue room.[40]

TUESDAY 25 Fine morning. Hinton here soon after 8 … wanted so particularly to see me, that I got up (my cold very bad) & was dressed & downstairs in 35 minutes. Haley … has a vote for the borough – to get it if possible. [I] said I would do what I could – Hinton to see him first… Then had Hinton again – [I] sent him to Empsall the butcher, & Holt the engineer, to see if James Holt had a vote for the borough…

Then had Matthew Booth – he and his wife very civil – he shewed me a printed circular he had had from the chairman of Mr Wortley's committee.[41] Matthew had told, & would tell, nobody but me – but he should go at 9 am tomorrow & vote for Protheroe & Wortley. I told him we were very much obliged – he would do us no good – but he would do us no harm.

So this would be 'a quiet vote' before polling grew rowdy. However, by splitting his vote between Wortley and Protheroe, the effect was neutral. 'Mr Fix-it', on the other hand, merely wanted to oblige:

Hinton had been waiting for me a little farther on in the road. He said Mr Protheroe would be at the head of the poll – splits [i.e. split votes] must be for Wortley & Protheroe. Had seen Empsall & Holt [engineer] (James Holt had no vote for the borough) & each would give a split [vote]. I to get Haley if possible. Home at 6…

Then had Haley, an Irishman … a Roman Catholic. He was very well inclined to vote for me – 'would as soon oblige me as anyone – so sorry – but durst not'. 'Why?' 'For fear of the public – the priest had not absolutely asked <u>him</u> for his vote – nor [had] anybody else.' It seemed <u>he</u> had not promised it – but they had called & told his wife he was to vote for Protheroe & Wood. I told him to go to Hinton tonight at the Orange Tree [pub] in Winding Lane – which he said he would do, but I have no hope of his vote. Went into the cellar for port…

'They' had told Haley to vote for the Radical and Whig candidates, a reminder of how greatly Irish issues surfaced in elections. With Haley's fear of 'public' shame, Anne must have sensed the 'Blues' losing their grip in Halifax.[42] Meanwhile, the *Halifax Guardian* loyally headlined its appeal to 'Conservative Electors' to 'Vote Early. Very Early!' and tracked Mr Wortley's progress.[43]

Read the paper while Mr Gray had coffee… My cold very bad but better than last night. A~ would like a little tour on horseback – mentioned Whalley [in rural Lancashire].

WEDNESDAY 26 Slept in the blue room. A~ called me at 7.30, but got into bed again after opening the door & fell asleep. Fine morning. *A~ came & staid & dressed me.* Breakfast at 9.30… Robert Mann + 7 levelling the terrace walks… Had brought the state of the poll at noon:

Protheroe: 400

Wood: 392

Wortley: 264

This latest election news was eagerly awaited at Shibden, However, after all their political string-pulling, Anne and Ann were aghast at the result.

Went into A~ soon after 2 & sat with her till 3. Mr Wortley's being so far behind incomprehensible. A~ & I very sorry – but never despair – we will manage better in future? A~ will have a vote from Throp or quit him.[44]

Two things are striking. First, Anne and Ann spent an hour lamenting the election result. They could not understand it: not just Wortley losing, but his losing so ignominiously. They lived high up, cut off from radical feeling down in Halifax.

Second, who *was* Edward Protheroe? He had links with Halifax, his mother being John Waterhouse's daughter. A Whig MP for Bristol 1831–32, he spoke in the Commons in favour of the abolition of slavery.[45] When he tried his hand at Halifax in 1835, he lost by one vote, triggering window-breaking protests.

THURSDAY 27 Mr Gray got his luncheon, & he & I off … to Northgate… Consulted Gray about [neighbouring] Anne Street – how to make it neat & inexpensive – think of putting my colliery people there, Holt as agent, the 2 Manns as bottom [coal] steward & banksman, & the book-keeper, blacksmith & carpenter as voters for the borough…

No worry that it would be a long walk for them up Old Bank and along to Listerwick. All that mattered was that Anne got half-a-dozen voters shoe-horned into Halifax.

A~ had a letter from her sister tonight – thanks for our kindness to little Mary & Mrs Heap. Whitley & Booth [bookseller] sent up the state of the poll at Leeds on closing at 4 pm today… Leeds like Halifax has thrown out the Conservative & has two Radicals to our 1 Whig & 1 Radical…

With A~ from 10.20 to 11, she in bed & taking tea – I took a cup with her – then undressed & looking over & adding up checks [i.e. cheques] paid & cash received at the bank since the rent day – looking into accounts till 1.25. *I am determined to wind up* [i.e. reduce] *my expenses as soon as I can.*

Friday 28 Slept in the blue room... Dinner at 7.10. A~ & I came upstairs from the dining room – she had Cookson & undressed & went regularly [i.e. as normally] to bed, & I sat in the great chair by her, & slept till 10.20 & from then to 12.30 read the newspaper... Note (brought to me in the garden this afternoon) from Mr James Norris, requesting me to canvass Messrs Stephen, John, & James Nelson, master builders.[46]

The Halifax *Poll Book* now recorded that 970 electors had voted: 496 for Protheroe, 487 for Wood and just 308 for Wortley.[47] The Whig grandees had no need to trouble themselves with a 'mock marriage' announcement as after the 1835 election. But for Anne and Ann, this contest had been disastrous. However, the larger West Riding election was still to play for. So, there was not a moment to lose in canvassing all their tenants with county votes.

Sunday 30 Fine morning, slept in blue room... Very sick ... huddled myself into bed – still retching.

Monday 31 A~ came to me before 8 & sent for Mr Jubb who was here by 9 – said I had a great deal of fever, & begged me to lie in bed all the day... A~ sat with me the whole day... Had veal broth about 1.30 & 5pm...[48] A~ went to undress & I got up at 10 to tidy my bed & room & fold up my clothes & slept pretty well afterwards.

Ann was very attentive to the ailing Anne, surely what a good marriage is partly about. They were closely united in sickness and in politics, sharing a deep fury at Protheroe's success. So after the Halifax election's bitter disappointment, were 'the quiet days of old parted never to return', as Anne had recently written to Vere?

August 1837

Electing its two MPs for the West Riding triggered high emotions across the county. Ten miles north of Halifax, Haworth was the home of the Brontës. Here, on the 'Blue' platform, Branwell Brontë and his father were drowned out by a 'hullaballoo'. In Wakefield on the other side of Halifax, there was a riot, with two people killed before the cavalry arrived.[1] In Halifax, politics had moved out to the countryside by Shibden and Lightcliffe: for Anne and

Ann, that meant paying a visit to their rural tenants. And repercussions from the Halifax election still rumbled.

Tuesday 1 Late this morning, but free from headache... This afternoon had Mr Crapper, the rope-maker, & paid him a small bill for rope (8 June last) – he is a staunch active blue – wanted to see A~. Mallinson of the Black Horse [inn] had said A~ had told him if he would not vote for Wortley she would quit him. And Crapper had betted 3 sovereigns to one that A~ had not said any such thing. 'No! I believed she had not.' She had called to remind him of his promise not to vote at all... He said he must look to his customers, & I (said A~) 'must look to my tenants' & rode off – but she had not quitted him. He is not under notice to quit whatever he may be, & if (as Crapper said) he (Mallinson) had plumped for Protheroe, he had broken his promise given some time ago to A~, & I believed she would quit him.[2] Crapper asked if A~ would send him a note. 'No!' I said she would not write about it, but if Crapper chose to come & bring Mallinson & any respectable person (Mr Adam, if he would come), I dared say A~ would have no objection to repeating before them what had passed...

This complex post-election tale shows the formal limits of a landowner's power to threaten tenants with notice to quit. They could say things, but would not write them down; so it remained 'he said, she said' rumours.[3]

A long extract from the *Halifax Guardian* of the account of the yellow [i.e. Whig] riot yesterday at Wakefield – all the fault of the yellows in beginning it. Read almost the whole of it aloud, till feeling my throat uncomfortable, I was obliged to get A to help me out – came upstairs at 9.35.

Wednesday 2 Wrote & sent off by John Booth note to Messrs Parker & Adam ... to ask them to send a note to quit to Mr John Dennison who took the 2 fields in Hopwood Lane [on Halifax outskirts]...[4] Then sat with A~ a little while in the north parlour...

However, political attention had pivoted sharply eastwards, to Anne and Ann's rural tenants voting in the county. Once again, the diary pages are littered with the names of their small tenants.

Thursday 3 Slept in blue room... Note from Mr Parker ... about the votes of Charles Howarth, George Naylor & Henry Dodgson – if he should send to [i.e. for] them – wrote back in pencil 'Yes! They have promised'… Out a little while in the garden – a man came to me there at 4 to say George Naylor & Dodgson shuffling?[5]

Then, without a pause, Anne walked briskly up the steep Pump Lane (see Map I). At the top, she turned left down Dark Lane to Upper Place farm:

Off immediately to George Naylor's… Talked some time to his wife – she said he should vote. [I] explained that I understood his farm to be at £50 & he had paid that once – it was well worth it. I had shewn favour to him but did not intend losing a vote…

Wives, controlling the domestic doorstep, played a key role in elections, ensuring that husbands did not wander off. Naylor had no vote in 1835, but now he qualified as his rent had reached £50. It was then just a short walk further down to Lower Place farm:

To Dodgson's – the wife evidently bad to manage – Dodgson wished not to vote at all. Explained that I would not neutralize my estate – would rather he voted for the yellow than not at all. I would do as fairly as I could to everybody, but I meant to have all my tenants vote my way. Stood talking ¾ hour, chiefly to the wife.[6]

Then just below Lower Place:

Saw a yellow handkerchief out at Dumb Mill cottages. Said it seemed disrespectful to <u>me</u> who was known to be so blue. I did not ask them for blue [handkerchief], but hoped they would not put up yellow. 3 or 4 women came – very civil – very sorry – it was a boy who had just put it up at the top of the chimney – it should be taken down again… ¼ hour with Aquilla [Green]'s wife – he would have voted for us, but through some mistake could not vote.[7]

Home in 5 or 6 minutes – washed hands, & going to dinner at 7.15 when Mr Barber came about George Naylor & Dodgson – said I had been to them to myself – <u>hoped</u> they would both vote for us. [8] Poor Mr Barber had <u>dined</u> with 20 at the [White] Swan – agreed we had been beaten in the borough for want of looking after [the blue interest]. Very hearty in the cause, & shook hands with me <u>very cordially</u> 3 or 4 times on finding me so staunch [a Blue].

In other words, the Halifax election could have been won with more 'looking after'. The West Riding 'Blues' must be more effective towards their tenants![9]

Dinner at about 7.25 – just going in to coffee when Messrs Schofield
& Henry Flatter came[10] – with a note from Mr Dearden about George
Robinson & two of A~'s Shibden [Mill] tenants (Bottomleys). Stood
talking at the door till my head felt cold – then a few minutes in the
upper kitchen. Schofield would answer for [i.e. organize in?] the county
(in future) & I for the borough – so all in good spirits. But Mr Wortley
above 30 [votes] behind-hand tonight...[11]

A~ got back two minutes before 6 – her pony fell in going (in the
3-cornered piece of Crow Nest carriage road!) & cut its knee – not
the least hurt... Coffee about 9 or after. A~ came up to bed about
10? I meant to have gone to her tonight, but found the door fast [i.e.
locked] on my coming upstairs at 11.30. I had stayed downstairs
skimming over the paper for 5 or 6 minutes.

**Meanwhile, attention had to be paid to Ann's tenants, the Bottomleys with
their traditional mill up Shibden valley.**

FRIDAY 4 Off with A~ at 7.50 to her tenants Bottomley at Shibden Mill
to canvass the votes of the 2 sons – the oldest [gone] from home.
Saw [younger son] George – he would not vote at all – a simple
looking young man, but said it in a way that shewed he was not [to]
be persuaded by A~. His mother evidently for his not giving A~ his
vote – said what could they do – they had their trade to consider. A~
said not much, but that she thought her tenants ought to vote on her
side, which would otherwise not be represented at all. The young man
looked sullen. I said, 'Well! You have refused your landlady the only
favour she has ever asked. I hope you will not have an opportunity
of refusing her many more favours.' He answered, 'I hope not.' 'Very
well', said I, 'when you have a favour to ask, what will you expect?'
I heard no answer, & A~ & I wished [them] good morning & came
away, she determined to quit the people – and I quite agreeing she
was right...

**Ann had become as intransigent a landowner as Anne. But to what effect?
Anne now relied on a local fixer called Mawson:**

George Robinson gone off with James Norris to vote. Had sent Mawson
off as I set off with A~. Then at 10.25, just as I was setting off with
Mawson, came Messrs Barber junior of Southowram & George Naylor
& went down to them... I considered George Naylor as a bona fide

tenant at £50 per annum – & he paid me 30/- in full of that rent for the last year...[12]

George Naylor ... talked over his neighbour Dodgson – George Naylor said he would have voted for us but for his wife. Said I was very sorry – that I was determined to have all my tenants vote for my side of the question, & those who could not make up their minds so to do must provide themselves with favours elsewhere.[13]

This was almost as direct a threat as a notice to quit.

George Naylor to try Dodgson again and Mr Barber to go for Abraham Hemingway. Then went into Mr George Robinson who had been waiting some time – very civil – mentioned my having omitted sending him a notice to quit – found he had given [us] his vote very willingly...

Robinson definitely wanted to ingratiate himself, as did Ann's Stainland tenants:

Just going out when A~ came to say Mr Outram [senior] was here, & she had got a note to ask her to go to William Hirst (Moor Mires) & she was going. Mr Outram had promised her his vote – I advised A~'s having a chaise to follow her to bring back William Hirst... Folded the [note], adding 'a chaise to be sent for Miss Walker to William Hirst's'... John [Booth], on presenting the note, saw the fly with William Wilkinson sent off immediately, and I returned to Mr Outram & sat with him...

This herculean effort to get right-thinking voters to the polls meant a thunder of horses' hooves out into the countryside around Halifax.

On reaching my own back Lodge gate found Messrs Barber & Hemingway looking for me. Told Hemingway to give us his vote. I would not be humbugged by [anyone]...

The West Riding polling day was hugely hectic for 'Blue' landowners like Anne and Ann. Ann Walker had started her day very early at Shibden Mill and ended up in far-flung Stainland. Anne Lister had an easier task: she could walk round her estate to visit the tenants she needed to persuade.

Came in to A~. She had dexterously put her tenant (William Hirst) into the fly, in the faces of ... [a] yellow, & saw driver drive off at a famous rate.[14] She called at Cliff Hill in returning – Mrs Ann Walker seemed pleased at the adventure & dexterous management...

This confirmed that Ann's behaviour had the backing of her family.

Dinner at 7.10 – coffee – skimmed over the newspaper – after all our exertions, close of the poll at Halifax at 4 pm:
[Lord] Morpeth 1,275. [Sir George] Strickland 1,245 [Hon. John Stuart] Wortley 629! A~ & I came upstairs at 9.30.

After so much exertion, another bitterly disappointing result! Tenants such as George Robinson and William Hirst had voted for Wortley, but they were drowned out by Whig voters. Lord Melbourne's Whig government continued in power. The 'Blues' had been trounced: Branwell Brontë's effigy was carried through Haworth and then burned. Yet at Shibden, the two women were once again bound together yet more intimately by a shared common enemy.

SATURDAY 5 *Slept with A~...*[15] Breakfast (A~ sat by me) at 10. Mr Sam Washington had brought her some rents & me my accounts... Mr Jubb came soon after & sat with us at breakfast. A~ told the story of canvassing William Hirst of Moor Miers. I said we must not be beaten again – must manage better. I thought of sending for Messrs John Dearden junior, chairman of Mr John Wortley's County Committee, & Mr John Edwards Dyson, chairman of Mr James Wortley's borough committee of the Conservative Association, & Mr Adam & Mr Jubb himself, to talk over my plan for the better management of voters. Mr Jubb not to breathe [a word] about what I had said – should send for them for 12 at noon on Monday, & Jubb to be here at that hour...

'Better management of voters' remained the battle cry. Though voteless, Anne nevertheless planned to 'send for' the men who could fix things. Certainly, there was a dramatic growth of local Conservative constituency associations, particularly around urban areas where the traditional culture of political deference was weakening.[16] But would these local leaders obey her summons?

Down the Old Bank to Halifax – ¼ hour at Mr Parker's office – mentioned the tap [room at Northgate]. 'Yes!' he thought it might be well to let it. [I] asked Mr Adam to come up some evening & talk over election matters. Saw from his inquiring look at Parker to see how *he* took it, that Parker would not like Adam to supplant him here. Thought I, 'Adam may come when he likes. I will not send for him or Mr Dearden junior – Mr J. E. Dearden will be enough.' Then to bank & got £50 in their own notes...

Kind letter tonight ... from Lady Stuart, the Lodge, Richmond Park.[17]

So, for Anne and her diary, the West Riding election was now past. Anne never dwelt long on lost battles. Instead, her mind turned to business, particularly Northgate, calculating the cost of furnishing the hotel. She also planned a market nearby, and she still hoped to house 'my colliery people' there. And she continued to play her cards close to her chest on all these developments.

SUNDAY 6 A~ off while I was asleep. Breakfast at 10 with Mr Gray... Then with A~ [bad cold] at her bedside while she had tea ... then read the paper.

Politics might not be on Anne's side. Yet as a businesswoman, little could stop her.

TUESDAY 8 *Slept with A~...* Mr Harper came ... approved of my plan of a low colonnade of shops in front of the hotel, to screen off the market – 40 yards of frontage towards the hotel = 7 shops ... 3 public houses... 'Oh! Oh!' thought I, 'if I waited quietly, I shall perhaps make my way well enough'...

Dinner at 7.20, A~ out of sorts, went to bed immediately... Still no letter for her from Mr Gray respecting Mrs Ann Walker's money concern with Mr William Priestley. I sat calculating... *Mentioned at dinner what Harper said about [William] Priestley – & I think this set A~ wrong. She grew speechless ever after, & I found her crying but speechless still in her room. What a tiresome temper!*

Ann and Anne both distrusted William Priestley; it was family inheritance, rather than Anne herself, that had set Ann's teeth on edge:

WEDNESDAY 9 *Slept with A~. Came to me of getting into [bed] – said she was naughty & was all right [now], but I could not get her to tell what had been the matter...* A~ sat with me till after 10, when Mr Samuel Washington came for the day to make up her rent book & accounts, & having done [these] before 5 pm, did up my rent book & accounts... With Robert Mann + 7 at the terrace wall-race low end for little tower staircase down into the field...

John Harper's plans had evolved since his 1836 drawings. This staircase offered a conveniently hidden exit from the terrace for workmen. Meanwhile, she discussed with Harper who might become her Northgate hotel tenant. Anne certainly remained in serious expansionist business mode, combining this with politics, thanks to a master joiner called Hainsworth.[18]

Hainsworth came ... mentioned the market... Said I had my own plans but would oblige the town if I could. Told Hainsworth to get me 2 tenants for my 2 [Halifax] fields – 2 votes. A~ & I were determined to have voters – would not rest until we had about 50. Hainsworth much pleased, entering upon a long recital of our praises at the Conservative Association, now consisting [of] 600 members. Wanted a room for general meetings that would hold some thousand people...

Two local women landowners praised at a meeting from which they were effectively excluded! Yet it must have grated with Anne that she now had to pick up political intelligence from a joiner.

Dinner at 7.40 – coffee. A~ very agreeable & sat long at table & afterwards at coffee, till we both came upstairs together at 10.05 & she sat with me in the blue room 20 mins or more – then wrote all the above of today.

THURSDAY 10 A~ had Mr Horner – breakfast at 9.05 with Mr Gray & sat talking till 10 about the Russian railroad to Moscow from St Petersburg...

However, the inheritance feud with William Priestley still rumbled on:

If William Priestley did not pay the money, Messrs Gray would threaten him with a Chancery suit. Brought the letter in to A~, sat talking it over till near 1 – agreed that Mrs A. Walker had better write her own instructions to Messrs Gray... *I wrote A~ copy of what her aunt should write...*

A~ & I set off to walk to Cliff hill... In returning, a little while at the Listerwick engine pit & wheel-race... All should be ready for Joseph Mann's going on with the engine pit... Came in at 7.10. *A~ wanted me. Her aunt had written the letter A~ had written, copy of letter to Messr Gray. I wrote her another shorter letter for herself which she copied & sent.* Dinner at 7.25.

So Ann's aunt was in agreement with Anne: rather than William Priestley, it was Ann who would gain after her aunt's death.[19] However, this inheritance dispute now entered the bedroom:

Friday 11 *Last night she had pain in her stomach. Gave her a tablespoonful of sheer brandy – she turned to me & had a goodish kiss. I heard her crying afterwards. I feigned sleep & talked – said distinctly 'the receipt you see is of no use to him'. (Mr William Priestley against her aunt). This caught her attention & I think helped to stop the hysteric tears & she fell asleep...*

Mr Hainsworth came about 9 this morning ... sat talking politics. Hainsworth all for my [Conservative] Association system – he himself can influence, can count upon 20 votes. Mr Holroyd the attorney their present active secretary to the Conservative Association of which Mr John Edwards is chairman. All applications to be made to, & information given to, Mr Holroyde – but Hainsworth himself could give [me] a great deal of information. He & Messrs J R Dearden & Mr Holroyde [would] be glad to come here & talk things over. Said I should be glad to see them...

Never mind that there had now been *three* General Elections – in 1832, 1835 and 1837 – from which women had been explicitly excluded. The key local Conservative men would 'be glad to come here' to discuss Anne's system.

Hainsworth asked if I had many applications for the hotel... I said it was not yet exactly settled. I thought however it would not stand long empty after it was finished – but it was so planned that it would easily turn into shops & private dwellings – something must pay. Said I had begun my platform & hoped to have my [Listerwick] colliery complete in 2 years – should loose [i.e. release] 112 acres of coal of my own.

Anne, always canny, recognized in Hainsworth a good source of Halifax gossip. She talked up her commercial plans in town and industrial strategy at Shibden, knowing he would disseminate this information. However, would Anne's planned 'Blue' meeting at Shibden actually happen?

Saturday 12 *Slept with A~...* Thunder shower ... a perfect river running through the entrance passage from court to garden, rain pouring in... [Letter] to the (London) application for the hotel... 'The hotel new & not quite finished – I am in treaty [i.e. negotiating] for nine old-established coaches – not only a good opening for wine & spirit trade, but the best cellars for the purpose (built expressly for the purpose) for part of the building. The success of the undertaking depends upon the capital at command, & the exertion of the individual. The hotel has every modern convenience in superior style, & a Casino is a splendid room, capable of dining 300 persons...

Dinner at 7.40 – coffee – skimmed the newspaper. A~ & I came upstairs at 10.15... Then undressed ... & sat undressed in my study from 11 to 11.45 writing all ... of today.

Anne remained an astute promoter of her hotel's unique potential.

MONDAY 14 *She began the thing last night & seemed having too good a kiss to bear. I therefore left her & she moaned & fidgeted half the night after, & got up (this morning) out of sorts – temper, I think, alas – what queer discomfort-making person...*

Holt the engineer came... Glad he had given us a vote – if he voted altogether against us, I should not have thought more of him or his estimates... Down the Old Bank ... went to the bank ... check (as usual) for £600 to be paid to Messrs Hammersley & co bankers, London... Then to Whitley's ... [bought] *Poll Book* & Mudie's *Popular Mathematics*.[20] And at Mr Parker's office again ... read him copy of what I wrote to Mr Hodgson [London] on Saturday about the hotel. 'Nothing', said Parker, 'could be better... The hotel ... would be a good speculation. Would make my other property adjoining much more valuable.' I hope the hotel will turn out well, & if the coal does too, I shall be thankful – I do not despair. Just mentioned Holt's offer to Mr Jeremiah Rawson to buy the low bed sough, & J. Rawson laughing & saying it was worth thousands... I did not consider Rawson's coal worth anything...

Came in at 7.15, A~ having returned from Crow Nest 5 minutes before – very much tired *but right as to temper* – dinner at 7.35... Came up with A~ at 9 – put her to bed, had Cookson to help... Sat reading Mudie's *Popular Mathematics* ... and Clarke's *Innkeeper's Guide* etc.[21]

TUESDAY 15 *A~ poorly but in* [good] *sorts...* Mr Gray gave me drawing of gallery adjoining west tower... *Then half-hour writing part of rough draft of letter to Lady Stuart*[22] ... in answer to hers received Sat 5th inst... Sure of her being amused & happy now while she has dear Vere:

'How it would delight me to be able to pop in[to] you for a few hours! But I dare not think of it – I have so tied myself that I cannot move for the present. Yet surely the time will come – I live in hope, or I should not live at all... Only do not quite forget me, is all I ask... Our young Queen seems to acquit herself marvellously well. What a pity we have not been able to send her a greater majority of Conservatives! Our party seemed to count upon success for the county. The borough, I myself had little hope of – our exertions were too late; and, as I thought & said long ago, our opposition was not sufficiently well organized for the struggle we must all have known awaited us. The populace, not the property, of our borough is represented – but this cannot last for ever. What is become of Lady Stuart de Rothesay? If she is within easy reach of a couple of brace of moor-game, may I ask you to be so good as [to] forward them, keeping the other 3 brace for yourself... I feel for all who have workmen about their own especial home. It is fifty to sixty ties of this sort that bind me here so fast... My love to Vere, & believe me, dearest Lady Stuart, very truly & very affectionately yours, A Lister'.

Anne is adept in carefully crafting her letter to bury bad political news among chat about moor-game and workmen. Lady Stuart must not think Anne's own political influence was waning. However, any optimism that the influence of 'the populace cannot last for ever' was misguided. The *Halifax Guardian* reported 'Mr O'Connor at Halifax', at which meeting Feargus O'Connor announced his plans for a radical Chartist newspaper.[23] Could it get any worse?

Went to the Terrace tower, Nelson's 2 masons and 4 labourers gone – inquired – Robert Mann thankful they had all got off before I came – all quite drunk – had been drinking a footing all afternoon... Say I thought of summoning the men before the magistrates for drunkenness & making them pay the penalty...

Letter, franked by Lord Stuart de Rothesay, containing kind full ½-sheet from Lady Stuart & ditto from Lady Vere Cameron, Richmond Park... Saw John Booth pack (in the 2 hampers ... 2 brace of moor-game, fine birds), 5 brace of moor-game for ... Lady Stuart ... and 5 birds (...for the Duffins ... & for Isabella Norcliffe)... Frank to take both hampers to coach office before 7 tomorrow ... coach to London & ... coach ... to York...

This palaver, pre-refrigeration, was how fresh game reached distant cities.

Then wrote ... to Isabella Norcliffe... 'My dearest Isabella – you have long since infected me with the bad example as to letter-writing, or rather its almost utter neglect... If I had leisure, I ought to write, & would write to Mrs Duffin... with a brace of the moor-game I have this morning directed to you... I shall send a hamper by the earliest through-coach [to York] tomorrow morning, and my note by the morning mail... The moon shines brightly in at the blue room window, & reproaches me with all the litter [i.e. paper] scattered in every direction. Have you done [up] your own house? I am [as] far as ever from having [any]where to lay <u>my things</u> in mine. From workmen at my own especial home, Good Lord deliver me for evermore! ... I am completely tethered [here]. If you <u>can</u> write, let me hear from you – if not, never mind... Miss Walker is fast asleep in bed. My love to Charlotte, & believe me, my dearest Isabella, very affectionately & very faithfully yours, A. Lister'.

An extremely warm letter, again with moor-game obscuring so much, and probably telling Isabella less than she knew already about Anne's relationship with Ann, only mentioned at the end and then by surname.

WEDNESDAY 16 *Slept with A~ who is less out of health than temper...* Went into the cellar – took the first bottle of marsala ... that arrived last night from Mr Farrer's, Halifax – fiery stuff. Sat a little while with A~... *A~ would seem ill or out of sorts to Mr Gray. She talked a little lastly* [i.e. finally] *to him, but came up to bed from the dining room at eight & three quarters. I followed & asked what was the matter. I saw all was terribly wrong. She said she should be much obliged to me to let her go. I said quietly, she should do as she liked – but on calmly pressing to know what was the matter, she said 'what might be a provocation to one might be none to another'. I should break her heart. I could get no explanation, but she was unhappy. I waited a little while & [was] really moved to tears. She said she had not the gift of the gab as I did. I said that [if] she was unhappy I regretted very deeply, but I was quite innocent of knowing how that could be from any fault of mine. But perhaps she would rather that I wished her goodnight. She turned & wished me good night, & we saluted* [probably: kissed]. *I said in tears, 'I should give her very little trouble', & came away...*

This was an unusually emotional scene, for Anne was rarely 'moved to tears'. Could their relationship plunge any lower?

What shall I do? Surely the business with A~ draws to a close? What can I do with her? Better she should go? Anything would be better than this perpetual worry.

I am better for having written the above. A thousand things come into my head. But I will go to bed – I shall be calmer in the morning. No, I am calm enough. But I shall feel less worried. Shall I be off as immediately as I can? ... Sat reading the Saturday paper till 10.25.

Anne was in unusually deep despair, her head plagued by uncontrollable thoughts. Then, true to form, she turned to the newspaper.

THURSDAY 17 *Slept in blue room – my mind seems comfortably made up. A~ has been preparing Crow Nest & has wanted to be away from here for long* [time]. *How lucky I have not introduced her to anyone! The sooner she goes the better.*[24]

Anne was now decisive. Her killer phrase regarded how how lucky it was that she had not introduced Ann to anyone who mattered in high society.

Went down to A~ ... staid ½ hour with her. *Talk over last night. Why did she not come to me this morning? She did not know whether I should be glad to see her or not. Very sorry. I said the worst of it was – she shook my confidence so terribly. Yes, she knew that must be. I said others could be made unhappy as well as herself. I said this would not do. She must make up her mind to go or stay – but she ought to go properly* [i.e. decisively]. *I said I really could not stand this. I would do anything I could for her – except one thing. Did she know what that was? 'No.' I said no more. But the one thing I kept to myself was – that if she left me, I would not take her back again. I said she would be dull at Crow Nest by herself. I could get off abroad in six weeks, I thought. However, it seems to me she is sorry this morning & has no present intention to leave me. Steven* [Dr Belcombe] *was right – that I should have a great deal of trouble with her. 'Well, I shall suit myself. I can have excuse enough for being off any time – & letting her do her own way. But while she is with me, I must hold the rein tighter.'*

Anne defensively closes the door on any reconciliation; yet this is followed by her thinking 'I must hold the rein tighter', as if Ann were a horse.[25]

Wrote the last 15 lines in ¼ hour till 9.50, when A~ came up to say she had made my tea. She sat with me at breakfast... [I] came in at one & sat at luncheon with A~ & Mr Gray... A~ rode as far as Hipperholme quarry & I walked by the side... She then dismounted & we walked into the village of Hipperholme...

Ann owned considerable property here. The licensee of Hipperholme's Hare and Hounds pub had significant political influence. One particular local man

'ought not to have a licence' – but was promised one 'if he would vote for the Yellows'. Indeed, daily life was politicized, even the remotest countryside out at Coley:[26]

A~ & I then walked forward to [Coley]... Sometime in the church – very pretty church ... really does credit to Mr Bradley the architect...[27] The monument to the late Michael Stocks ... who was for several years a Fitzwilliam trading justice [i.e. radical magistrate], making about £2,000 a year; but ousted at last for some disgraceful business... A man whose litigious cleverness many feared ... and whose very name was a by-word of reproach! 'Hum!' said I 2 or 3 times as I read over this <u>monumental insult</u> ... said 'is not this very like a pack of [lies]?'... Then by Priestley Green direct to the Crow Nest gates & Cliff Hill...

Anne hated Michael Stocks. A landowner who also mined coal on his land, he had stood – unsuccessfully – as the Radical candidate for Halifax in the 1832 election. This remained a sore point, for the Radical candidate, Edward Protheroe, had just robbed Wortley of his Halifax seat. However, would Anne have worked up such a political rant against Stocks had it not been for the emotional stress of the night before?[28]

Mrs A Walker looked pale & infirm but seemed glad to see us... A~ seemed less tired after her walk (during dinner & afterwards) than she has been for long – coffee. Came upstairs at 9.30, A~ went to her [room?], I had Mr Gray in the tower, determining & planning about wainscotting the tower passage till near 10. Then a little while with A~ & skimmed over the paper.

Indeed, after the searing row, their country walk (and perhaps also a political rant) seemed to have done the two women a lot of good. There was an affectionate reconciliation:

FRIDAY 18 *Slept with A~. Good kiss, she saying it did not tire her all...* Mercer the glazier came at 10.20 ... talked of doing the tower windows... Hour in the cellar mixing sherry & Farrer's marsala, ½ & ½... A~ came upstairs... *Mixed three-quarters Farrer's marsala with one quarter of wine & A~ liked it very much.*

SATURDAY 19 *Slept with A~. She lay down naked after washing & staid with me, I grubbling her...*[29] At 10.45 went to Braithwaite, the blacksmith Mr

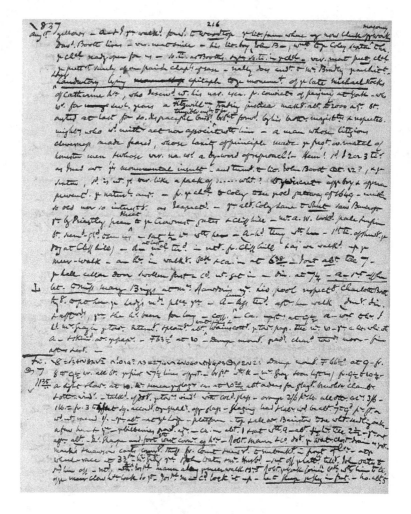

7 Anne Lister diary page, 17 August 1837

Husband employed for Northgate hotel work… Found the man was a radical … so casually asked which way his political opinion leaned.

August closed tranquilly, Anne and Ann seemingly living in married harmony. However, Anne soon had other thoughts in her mind.

MONDAY 28 *Slept with A~...* Came in to breakfast at 10.40... Out again at 11.15 *having first come upstairs for a few minutes & said my prayers with tears of gratitude trickling down – & then wrote in pencil on a loose bit of paper: 'I think perpetually of A~'s leaving me & wish it more & more. How merciful Providence has been to me! Given her to me to spirit me up in the beginning & now takes her away just when I see that she could not make me happy'...*

A~ came upstairs at 9.40 & I a few minutes after... The model of Switzerland ... placed as before on the large oak table. I intend my portable bookcase & books to remain where they are till my room in the west tower is ready for them... Sat 1/2 hour with [A~], partly at her bedside. *Saying after dinner that Parker would want [to see] Sam Washington about [evicting her tenant] Standeven. Put her out of sorts. But I gave her cherry brandy for poorliness – & took no notice of the temper. Mr Gray must see how the matter stands.*[30]

It was less than a fortnight since their last reconciliation, but there seems little personal optimism between them now. As Anne saw it, with Ann now wanting to leave her, Providence was surely very merciful.

August ended with neither Wortley elected to Parliament. However, the *Halifax Guardian* printed the exhortation of Conservative leader Sir Robert Peel to 'Register! Register! Register!' The paper added helpfully: 'Register, register all good votes. Object, object to all bad ones. With proper care, the [West] Riding is secure; and the Boroughs of Halifax, Bradford and Huddersfield may be recovered.'[31] But this was surely wild political optimism.

VIII

Two Fortunes are Better than One

September–October 1837

September 1837

In 1834 Anne had suggested to her Norcliffe friends that 'two fortunes are better than one'.[1] Now she confided optimistically to her diary that 'I could get off abroad in six weeks' – on her own. However, this was not to be. Her estate improvements tethered her to Shibden. It was to Northgate and coalmining that Anne now looked for her financial future. Yet the challenge of funding these still loomed.

TUESDAY 5 *A goodish kiss last night… Took* [A~] *to the new upstairs water-closet & she used it, first time – staid with her there.* Then out at 9… saw Messrs Thomas Greenwood & Little (china & pot seller) walking up the field… Mr Little had come about the cattle market. Shewed him Mr Harper's drawing & ground plan… Poor man! I think he felt ill at ease. *I talked very little for* me *& was I satisfied at having done so. I will talk less & less – leave the people to talk more. I think I will not shew Mr Harper's drawing in future – the exchange etc will only frighten them – about the value I set on the ground.*

FRIDAY 8 Supposing that the colliery did not pay me sufficiently… Sat up looking over [my] banking book & writing out list of checks since 6 July last, till 12.15. *I have only three thousand one hundred & ninety two pounds left in the bank (balance).*

Meanwhile, Sunday visits after church to Aunt Ann now took on a darker turn. For William Priestley could not ignore these regular calls at Cliff Hill: he had been cut out of the Walker family circle. Just as they sat down for dessert at Cliff Hill, a letter arrived from Jonathan Gray casting gloom on their chances in court with Mr Priestley.

Sunday 10 Mr William Priestley would have a plausible plea in his defence – he had partly managed his aunt's affairs & been favoured till now that she was under hostile influence.[2] She must own herself incapable or inexperienced in business, & her state of mind now & for some years must be ascertained. And if A~ should go abroad while the suit was pending, Mr William Priestley might get Mrs A Walker to quash it [i.e. his claim], but A~ & Messrs Gray would be in an awkward predicament. <u>True</u>. A~ out of spirits about it. I said I thought it all right. A~ might be glad of Mr Gray's letter. Mrs A Walker had best ask William Priestley's answer, whether he would pay the money or not. If he would – very well. If he would not, she had only to deduct it from his share under her will, or cut him out altogether... Yet A~ seems out of heart about it. *She said she never thought of going abroad while a* [law] *suit was pending. I merely said there was never any likelihood of a suit. 'But', thought I, 'I would not be tied down by any such suit. We have gone on very well together of late. She feels that I am of use to her just now, but I have no confidence in her <u>devotion to me</u> simply for my own sake – &* [she] *may want to stay at home when I want to be abroad.'*

Of course, William and Eliza Priestley's suspicions about Anne's designs on Ann dated right back to 1832.[3] Now, with Ann having lived at Shibden for three years, these suspicions had morphed into bitter litigious squabbles. And now Anne had an additional layer of suspicion: that Ann valued her merely as being 'of use to her just now' (i.e. offering legal advice about the inheritance rift with the Priestleys). Ann's aunt was indeed wealthy, living alone at Cliff Hill with six servants.[4]

Monday 11 I had Holt & Joseph Mann ... came to say the water was so low, the [water]wheel went so slowly, it could not keep the engine-pit dry. They must begin sinking Listerwick pit & have the gin going tomorrow. Very well – be it so... [A~] brought back the letter to Messrs Gray, solicitors, York ... signed by Mrs A. Walker... Sat by A~'s bedside from 10.35 to 11.15 talking – *she in good sorts.*

Wednesday 13 Robert Mann thinks [my] coal ... will average 10d per load ... A good collier will get 25 loads a day... Might set on 5 or 6 colliers in the hard bed – 'yes!' For I shall then get up to Mr Rawson['s mine] & prevent his stealing...

207

Dinner at 7.15 – tea – York coffee not arrived – Halifax coffee not good. A~ & I came upstairs at 9.25. *Ten minutes with her at the water closet...* Tea between 8 & 9 & read the paper. Had Crowther the librarian just before dinner.

THURSDAY 14 Much rain in the night... A~ had Mr Horner till 10.30 – then with her emptying the new china closet for about ½ hour....

Anne had a letter from Mariana asking for advice about schools in Germany.[5] Her reply was classically artful, helpfully advising about German education, yet patronizing about Mariana sacrificing her 'good looks' to her school scheme. And the triangular relationship had scarcely shifted since Mariana's visit: Anne remained far closer to Ann than to Mariana.

Robert [Mann]'s men barrowing soil against the flower garden wall... Joseph Mann sinking Listerwick pit, & one man sinking vent-pit [for ventilation].

It sounds as if the garden in front of Shibden was almost completed, and Listerwick now making real progress.[6]

TUESDAY 19 *A~ quite wrong, would not speak... I made an effort to get her to speak. Asked what was the matter. Said I ... wanted comfort – she ought to give it. Her not speaking was not kind. All in vain, so I came to my room. What comfort shall I ever have in her? My affairs are bad enough, but I will look thoroughly into them. Pray to God for help & comfort, such as no human being an offer. And then when I have got all straight, I will be off to Montpellier?* From 8 to 9 in my study, looking over & arranging bills, letters etc...

Anne was in despair over Ann's not speaking. All Anne had left was to 'pray to God for help', since people had let her down. However, their relationship soon thawed, thanks to a common enemy.

Came in at 5.50 – dressed. A~ came to tell me about Mr W. Priestley's having arrived at Cliff Hill just after she came away – asked for a bed there & stayed all night, & got Mrs A Walker to sign a revocation of the instructions she had sent to Messrs Gray, & an order to return all the letters that had passed on the subject (Mr W. Priestley's into the bargain) to her through him! *A~ had written a rigmarole* [i.e. rambling reply] – *wrote her another shorter notice on the thing & to inform him his letters were now in her possession.*

Why had William Priestley been so impetuous that he wanted to stay overnight with his aunt, a neighbour? Once again, Anne brought her cool legal mind into this bitter inheritance feud. Elderly Aunt Walker could undoubtedly have done without these wrangles. She certainly had far greater affection for her niece Ann than for her bullying nephew William. In this rectangular rift, was it time for Anne to tighten her control?

Wednesday 20 *A~ quite right this morning, but I am determined to lead her on a tighter rein...* Breakfast with A~ & Mr Gray at 9 in about ½ hour, then with A~ till after 10. *Writing copy of letter to Mr Gray* [lawyer] *for Miss A Walker to sign, desiring Mr* [Shepley] *Watson to come over immediately. To be at Cliff Hill at ten on Friday morning by chaise from Leeds. Mr W Priestley to be cut out by codicil on A~'s return this evening. Her aunt had signed the letter & seemed quite pleased to do what she said would so vex Mr W Priestley...*

A~ returned very soon after 6 and we talked till 7 – she sent off tonight her letter to Mr Gray signed by Mrs A. Walker desiring Mr Watson to come over... Mrs A. Walker much vexed at what she had done – thought Mr W Priestley had behaved very shabbily, to give her no time for considering – but he would not let her leave him that night till she had signed the paper which he had brought ready written! Poor Mrs A Walker wished she had sent for A~. Dinner at 7 – coffee, read the newspaper.

[marginalia] A~ had letter tonight from Captain Sutherland announcing the birth of a little girl on Sunday 17th inst.

Thursday 21 Fine morning. Had A~ ¼ hour – she had just written to Captain Sutherland ... congratulating him on his little girl on Sunday. A~ mentioned Mr W Priestley's having been over on Tuesday night, & would not leave poor Mrs A Walker till he had frightened her into signing a paper brought with him ready written, revoking the instructions she had given Mr Gray respecting the annuity; A– observing that perhaps in the end he might find 'honesty the best policy'...

Skimming over *Popular Mathematics*... About 10.30 came Mr Craven – I had sent for him yesterday... Consulted him about trespassers... No law against people wandering about the grounds... Then long talk on politics – the system of Conservative Unions etc. Explained my ideas for the subject as to finances & securing votes & property. Mentioned the case of Charles Howarth – pays just £50 & lets off a couple of cottages but farm worth £70 per annum. Mentioned my 2 Halifax fields. *That A~ would quit Mallinson & Hartley.* Mr Craven seemed to think about what I had proposed – said he should be glad to call again & I said I should be glad to see him – he staid till after 11.

Mr Craven obviously could not openly disagree with a landowner like Anne Lister, so he just politely equivocated.[7]

FRIDAY 22 Fine autumn morning… A~ off on her pony to Cliff Hill… Mrs A. Walker sent us a couple of chickens this afternoon & some plums & greengages…

Such gifts were obviously in appreciation of Ann and Anne's support in her hour of need against William Priestley.

Mr Watson had arrived at ten and a half in a gig – alone & off back again about three, all being done as I had suggested to A~. The codicil made cutting [out] Mr W. Priestley, and Watson took away with him all the three wills & codicil & all. All had gone off at Cliff Hill much to the satisfaction of Mrs A. Walker & A~, the former admirably ready & knowing what she was about, clear-headed & sound of memory as A~ or I could have been. Her disapprobation of W. Priestley's conduct strongly marked. Dinner at 7.20 – coffee, read the paper.

SATURDAY 30 Fine but dullish morning… We lay awake till after 12 last night, talking of one thing or another. *I told* [her] *if she would keep me, that is the household, taxes servants' wages & all, so as to leave my own income clear, I could do very well. She seemed not averse. I asked* [her] *to consider what she would like to be spent – for we might spend just what she could spare out of her income – a thousand a year would do. And I repeated all this this morning.*

So September ended with Aunt Ann having trounced William Priestley, and with Ann's financial future surely even more assured. Was Ann really not averse to the arrangement Anne suggested, seemingly so much to Anne's advantage?

William and Eliza were most definitely among the most pointed critics of Anne Lister's unorthodox relationship up at Shibden. But there were others. Two years earlier, at the 1835 election, the West Riding Whigs had outed Anne and Ann with the 'mock marriage' announcement.[8] **Then in 1836, the effigy-burning tale dramatically illustrated Christopher Rawson's industrial rivalry with them.**[9] **However, this inheritance row was much closer to home, indeed actually inside Cliff Hill itself.**

But there was nothing these male critics could do about their suspicions that Anne was using Walker wealth to fund Northgate, Listerwick mine and Shibden improvements. In the face of this, both Christopher Rawson and William Priestley seemed to have forfeited their dignity. Clever Anne Lister, who could well have been a lawyer, had succeeded again!

October 1837

Anne now set out to explore at the very top of the Shibden estate and beyond, touching Rawson's land (see Map I). Yet it was probably not just idle curiosity that took her up there.

Thursday 5 *Pretty good kiss last night.* Fine morning… Off to Barrowclough [Lane]… From Little Marsh (the new barn ½ up) at 12.35 – to Law Hill [in Southowram] – looking about me from the field above the house there – very fine view. Then across Mr Rawson's fields to his quarries, gazing & sauntering…[1] Back to Little Marsh & home by Pump at 2.

Friday 6 Much rain in the night… Had Mr Jackson from Duncan the tailor with patterns of cloth for groom & for George – ordered to be 4 guineas + breeches strapping. Clothes to be sent home on Wednesday night, & cloth of the same piece to be kept for footman's dress & undress suit. Breakfast, A~ sat by me…

There were few better indicators of social rank than the livery of groom and footman – to be seen, admired and noted.

Saturday 7 *A~ had not long since had Cookson* [to help her undress] *when I went to bed last night, but was not asleep. Not quite in good sorts. For I had just after dinner said something about … if she had had more disappointments, when she said she had had a great many. And on my saying I had not disappointed her – it seemed that I had. She was right on waking this morning. But on my gently wanting to know how I had disappointed her, she got wrong-ish again. And [I] left the breakfast table before Mr Gray & when she had only poured me out one cup of tea. And tho' all passed off tolerably when I saw her afterwards, yet my own feeling was uncomfortable & I mused of getting rid of her.*

How different the tone of this conversation from that just a week earlier, about Ann bearing the household expenses.

WEDNESDAY 11 Fine morning... *I with her at the water closet – she is now in very good sorts.* Till 10.55 wrote all the above of today,

THURSDAY 12 A~ had Mr Horner at 10... Had Mr Parker about the hotel... Asked if he knew whether Miss Marian was likely to settle at Halifax or not – he thought not – the reports had died away...

Anne had to ask her lawyer for news about her sister, her only surviving relative. Anne presumably now had an extra level of concern: Marian might have taken William Priestley's side against Anne and Ann.

Shewed [Mr Jubb] Mr Harper's bird's-eye view of the Northgate ground laid out for [the] Exchange & Cattle market. Jubb admired the drawing... John Booth brewed today – 1ˢᵗ time in the new bre-whouse... The York joiners took down the hatchment to the memory of my aunt this afternoon – and A~ & I went out of mourning...[2]

Dinner at 7.20 – coffee– asleep – read the paper... Then upstairs at 10.20 – ½ hour with her talking over household expenses etc. [I] thought our whole establishment here would be kept up for a thousand a year as it is at present – or rather, including footman & groom & gardener, under-gardener & John Booth & 1 farming man, & Oddy & Cookson & housemaid & kitchen-maid – 3 saddle horses & 2 farm horses & our gin-horse, and one cow...

Here, then, was the full complement of servants by autumn 1837: four female servants and six male. How magnificent Shibden had grown since Anne's 1832 return. However, this came at a considerable cost. Anne's hopes now focused on Northgate, and on Listerwick pit to start producing coal, hopefully in seven months.

Holt much approved my plan of turning Listerwick pit into [an] engine pit & sinking an air pit [i.e. vent shaft] next [to] the road... A 4-horse[-power] engine ... & we may be getting coal by the 1ˢᵗ of May [1838] or before... Holt thinks there is no doubt I can clear 4d per load. Therefore, if there be only 4 loads per square yard, I shall clear £320 x 2 = £640 per annum...

Anne always liked to persuade her agents to her opinion, especially in the dirty business of coalmining.

Glad he [Holt] had come over to my opinion at last... 'Very well,' said I, 'only give me what I ought to have, & I shall have no objection.

The principal collieries will then [be] in your hands & Stocks & mine;[3] & there is enough to do for us all, & we can keep the prices as they should be – only we can agree to behave fairly & honourably.' Thought I, as I mused about it this afternoon, 'I see how it is – a 14 horse-power engine in Lower Place Park field would pump for us all[4] – but they shall pay for it fairly…'

It seems that Anne now understood that whichever coal owner controlled the horsepower could control the price of coal. And that she was well positioned compared to the Rawsons down at Swan Bank.

She came to me just as I was beginning this [page] & sat about ½ hour. Then afterwards till 12¼ wrote thus far… Sat up looking at the large [coal] plan…

Anne then replied at length to a letter Vere had written from Achnacarry:

Shibden Hall. Thursday evening. 12 October 1837

My dearest Vere,

… I had no idea of your going northwards quite so soon… It was very good of you to write amid all your hurry at Whitehall – a letter, too, which pleased me more than any you ever write me before… I wish I heard from you much oftener. What most prevents? Your 'large small family', or my not-<u>single</u> potherations? Your letters always enliven and do me good. They interest me more that I think you are aware. The very circumstances or your going to settle at Achnacary seems to interest me more than if you were going to settle anywhere else. Railroads and steam bring us near; and I do not despair of seeing you by and by. Perhaps by the time you have set you house in order, I may be at liberty; and you will make no stranger of <u>me</u>. If it were possible, I should be off to Paris before Xmas, but I have not hope of it… I must wait patiently yet a little while – the fact is, I have been terribly disappointed in more things than one. But I never whisper a complaint even in my own ears. If I <u>have</u> been, in some sort, taken in, I am at least determined to work myself out again. Life is exertion, and wholesome stimulus might be wanting, if all went well with us too easily. 'For human weal Heaven husbands all events.' I never cease to acknowledge this with thankfulness; and, tho' my soul had not much kindred [spirits] here, it never dwells upon the want, nor loses for five minutes its natural elasticity of spirit...

Thank you for all your news... When did you hear from Copenhagen? Do give my love to Lady Harriet... But I may reappear, and at Copenhagen too, one of these days. I shall not, however, stir from here, or do anything material, without your hearing of it from myself. I am sure to write to you oftener, the moment I have anything interesting to communicate, but, at present, my whole cranium full of ideas is not worth a farthing. Do pray write and tell me all about yourself and your large small family, as soon as you have time to spare, remembering always that few if any are more truly interested in yourself, and all concerning you, than yours very affectionately.

(A.L.)[5]

This is a particularly elegant and affectionate letter, written with more warmth than in the discussion of German schooling with Mariana, and making no explicit reference to Ann.

Meanwhile, Shibden's extravagant expenditure continued, including expensive bottles of wine:

Friday 13 Wrote for a footman who thoroughly understands his business [i.e. duties] – and ... being about 30 years of age... Off with A~ to Halifax at 11 (walked)... I went to the Bank & got one hundred pounds. Ordered at Whitley's Adcock's *Engineers' Almanac*... Then up the Old Bank (A~ much tired) & back at 2... Dinner at 7.10 – coffee – read the paper. A~ & I came upstairs at 9.20 & lay slumbering on the bed in our room ½ hour... Read Collieries & Coal trade ¼ hour.

Then Samuel Sowden called, the tenant who had caused her particular political trouble before, talking of tenants 'turning off the landlords'.[6] Sowden now seemed more compliant, even voting for Wortley in the West Riding election. Together they had a practical discussion:

Saturday 14 Mr Sowden came about his rent... And it ended by Mr Sowden's [saying] 'he must fall into my will' and he agreed to pay £83 per annum. Talked of Walterclough Mill...[7] Said I thought of having a mill of 20 frames – could his sons afford to pay £19 per frame at Listerwick? ...

Reckoned up the time Mr Gray has been here ... 17 weeks at ten pounds [a week] = one hundred & seventy... Out with Mr Gray & Booth & Robert Mann – the arched top stone over the flower garden cistern put up this afternoon... Paid Mr Gray ... £170 in one hundred, one fifty & two tens Bank of England [notes]. Gray had talked at dinner of popping over from Leeds some Sunday to see what we were about. I very gently & civilly set this aside by saying I ... would not begin again till next spring or summer...

Joseph Mann said they could pull over 10 colliers very well at Listerwick pit, and 10 colliers ought to get 2 acres of coal and more – but did not think we could sell so much – but we could sell one acre or more. At the accounts till 1.30. *I have still twelve hundred & fifty in the bank.*

Anne now found herself rather near the financial edge, postponing further work and fretting about the likely returns from coal.

MONDAY 16 With Robert Mann, to set all five platform carts to bring soil to the garden... The road so terrible along the laundry court wall, the poor <u>weak</u> horses could not get their one-horse carts without a chain-horse. Robert would rather they went back to their own job & so would I...

Engineer Holt had waited for me some time at Northgate – he had brought 2 plans of worsted mills... 20 frames on the ground floor, & the 2 storeys above for wool-sorting, reeling etc... 'But', said I, 'with this additional accommodation should not I have £20 per frame?' ... The mill will cost every farthing of £900. Holt will do the shafting & gearing for £150...

However, Anne did not have a spare £900.

Home from Northgate about 4.30... Had Joseph Mann out of doors... Listerwick pit 5 yards deep in water – Holt to come tomorrow... Dressed – dinner at 7.05 to 8 – coffee. A~ read French, the 1st time these 17 weeks, ever since Mr Gray returned.

THURSDAY 19 Fine frosty morning... Wrote to Mrs Thompson, Register Office ... York... 'Mrs Lister thought the footman mentioned ... might be likely to suit her (Mrs Lister) but she would not give more than twenty pounds & livery the first year nor more than 20 guineas afterwards, & would enquire particularly as to he being sober & trustworthy & thoroughly understanding the place & business of footman...' John Booth & Abraham went (about 5 pm) with 2 one-horse carts & brought from Halifax the 5 hampers of wine from Mr Oldfield's, York…

Even if the poor horses came up New Bank rather than the steeper Old Bank, it was still a mighty pull to haul the heavy hampers up to Shibden.

Dinner at 7 – coffee. A~ read French, [I] finished my Michelet's *Synchronic Tables of Modern History* & [she] began her own little precis of modern history by the same clever author … [I] read the paper.

The women of Shibden remained intellectually curious and engaged.

FRIDAY 20 Soft damp morning… Came in at 6.30 – the idea of making (driving) a new road from the house to the [kitchen] garden struck me this afternoon – to come out under the great ash tree just on the other side of the road. If this could be pretty easily done, it would rid me of all the pother about Gray & his pools – & getting the road past them <u>somehow</u>…

This was the track that would later tunnel under the upper road, linking the garden in Conery down to the elegant terraces in front of Shibden.[8]

A~ received tonight from Whitley & Booth's 2 volumes (*Modern History*) & J Brunton's *Compendium of Mechanics* – both of us taken up with our books – then coffee. A~ read French & I the newspaper & at Brunton again while A~ sat up cutting out [cloth] for her school till 11.20.

This presents a good example of an evening in a companionate marriage. Yet Anne had been so busy with estate business that this was the first time in ten days that she had written more than a few words in code:

SATURDAY 21 Out till breakfast with A~ at 9. *On going to bed last night, A~ seemed not against going to Paris for a month after Christmas, but had asked where the money was to come from. Saying I hoped soon to have done with workmen – adding something insignificant, I scarce know what, about the alterations. She did not speak. 'What', said I gently, 'have your nothing to say?' Answer: 'No, nothing.' I stood silent a minute or two – and then, without uttering, came to my room. On getting into bed, she was not asleep – but seemed so, and I took no notice, but fell asleep by & by.*

I saw all was not right at breakfast, but I talked (as nearly as possible) as usual. Out all the morning till about one & a half. Then came & sat a little with A~. Talked as far as I could as if nothing was the matter. Then came away to send John to the bank, and had Booth etc. And found A~ gone to Cliff Hill. How all this pothers me! I have several times laughed & said she must keep her pony, [but] must allow me a thousand a year for everything.[9] *She has never said she would. Says nothing on the subject. Is she afraid or tired of me or what? Why should I be so pothered? Can solitude or anything be worse? I have thought against & for Mr Parker as my steward & manager. Will he not be better than Washington? Who had best remain to [i.e. working for] A~. I feel in thraldom.*

What a silent yet seismic row. 'A thousand a year for everything', up to and including a footman. Indeed, Anne seemed to be planning her travels, apparently on her own. Then she carried on in her diary as if nothing much had happened:

Out all the morning... Aquilla Green passed by ... stood talking, it seemed an hour, in the road, about the mill – the wheel not answering etc... Told A. Green to get me a good tenant for 16 to 20 frames if he could – he said he knew many spinners & would mention the mill...

Found A~ gone before 3. Then till 3.45 wrote all the above of today. *I am better for writing my journal, though my feet are wet & I begin to feel their cold.* Life is exertion. *Deo volonte, the ship may [get] right again...*

Very unusually, Anne now wrote her journal in the afternoon, then added a philosophical thought. She had been greatly shaken by this silent quarrel.

Dinner at 7.05 in ½ hour – then coffee in the north parlour & sat reading *Travels in Spain & Portugal* till 9. Then came upstairs – fire in the blue room – read the newspaper – *and burnt several months' cousin papers till ten, then till eleven reading* Brunton's *Compendium of Mechanics...*

So Anne had had to postpone burning her sanitary 'papers' until the fire in late October (presumably storing them somewhere discreet during the summer). For womanly secrecy about this embarrassment, a fire upstairs would be private.

Letter tonight from Mrs Thompson... William Rennie ... will take the £20 for the first year, & never more than 20 guineas. Wrote to Lady Vere Cameron *till two.*

Again, this seems a sign of Anne's fragile response to the rift with Ann. It was rare for her to stay up writing a letter till 2 a.m., even to an intimate friend.

217

SUNDAY 22 Dressed – off to church at 3… In church before Mr Wilkinson began the sermon – preached … from Philippians ii 12 – to work out our salvation with fear & trembling.[10]

Although Wilkinson was probably not the most inspiring preacher, at moments of personal turmoil Anne grasped at religion for succour.

MONDAY 23 Breakfast at 9. *A~ not right, for she saw me silent, but she had seemed as if right in bed this morning, & [I] did not then find out that I should be grave – tho' what I did say & do was in the usual manner.*

Ann's being 'not right' surely stemmed from the vexed question of her paying for the upkeep of Shibden.[11]

A~ off (to Cliff hill) at 10… Asked Cookson after her mother, & if she would object to her going abroad… I said it would of course be a disappointment to me to suppose all ready [for travelling] & then for Cookson to leave me… Engineer Holt came this morning … about the 6 horsepower [engine] for Listerwick pit… Found collier Holt there with Joseph Mann – set out the site of engine house.

SUNDAY 29 Reading Maurice's *Indian Antiquities* … about two, *incurred a cross thinking of M~ from reading of phallic worship.*[12]

So October ended with her relationship with Ann still quavering. Were two fortunes better than one, or would Anne and Ann go their separate ways?

Meanwhile, on the final day of the month, Tuesday 31st, Anne, Ann and the servants all watched a Mrs Graham sailing in her balloon. She had ascended from the Piece Hall, and they saw her gliding over Hipperholme.[13]

That same day the *Halifax Guardian* published a letter from Richard Oastler addressed 'To the Hand-loom Weavers of the West Riding'. The government had appointed commissioners to enquire into the distress of these impoverished weavers, and Oastler urged them to 'call meetings in your villages and in your towns. Appoint committees … to visit from house to house, to obtain information… Give the commissioner an accurate statement of the actual sum you have received in wages.'[14] These enquiries would soon have far, far wider political repercussions.

IX

YORKSHIRE BUSINESSWOMAN, NORTHERN STAR

NOVEMBER–DECEMBER 1837

NOVEMBER 1837

Chartism began to flourish in the industrial heartlands of the West Riding: towns such as Halifax, Huddersfield and Bradford. Feargus O'Connor even planned to start a Radical newspaper, to be published in Leeds.[1]

However, Anne Lister, ever the canny businesswoman, had her mind on her industrial initiatives, notably making Listerwick profitable. Meanwhile, Anne and Ann planned their travels, including a visit to the ancient city of York, away from the smoky mills of the West Riding.

THURSDAY 2 Damp hazy morning... I said I should try the colliery under Holt's management, with Joseph Mann as bottom steward & Robert [Mann] as Banksman. Holt proposed having a book-keeper... I said, I meant the coal to pay ... & it [book-keeper] must wait accordingly...

Dinner at 7.15 – tea – then read the newspaper. A~ read her French – then we each wrote our journal.[2] Told her as I wrote it what had passed today with Holt – said I had not wanted to tell it before, for fear of the news being too good to be true... Read a little in Murray's *Encylopedia of Geology* on Indian botany.

FRIDAY 3 Opened the hamper of new marsala to get our bottle for dinner. A~ had letter from her sister – *it took me till near eleven writing copy of answer*... Left A~ downstairs just finishing her letter to her sister.[3]

SATURDAY 4 Fine morning... Sat with A~ at luncheon & afterwards in the north parlour till 3.15, when she went to dress for her ride to Cliff Hill & was off about 4.30. *Talked matters over. She did not like my having so much* [money] *on hand at once* [i.e. at any one time] *– and cried & I thought all was wrong. But I managed to turn the tide & set all right again. Talked of her allowing two thousand a year for travelling – & for the year's expenses. Talked of going to Naples the middle of January. She said we ought to be back in May, but I gently turned this off to summer past* [i.e. after summer?]

Visiting Naples, the city where Ann's brother John had died on his honeymoon seven years earlier, would certainly be expensive.[4]

Meanwhile, Anne grew increasingly frustrated with Ann's moods. She turned instead to drafting a letter of condolence, having just heard that Mariana's mother was seriously ill and likely to die:

Shibden Hall, Monday 6 November 1837.

I received your letter, my dearest Mary, last night... And I am sure you are well aware how sincerely I sympathize with you... Her course in this world may be run, & her spirit wafted to those regions of purer joy where the weary are at rest...

Mary! <u>She</u> is happy – 'tis those who stay behind to whom is left the scarf of sorrow – the desolate place in the heart that knoweth its own bitterness. The loss of a Mother can fall upon us but once... She in whose bosom we nestled first – whose heart first loved us, & loved us most unchangingly. She is thought of often, longer, & more tenderly than those can tell who never tried it...

Let me hear from you soon. I shall be anxious to know that you are all going on as well as can be expected under such melancholy circumstances. If you pass this way on your return, we shall hope to see you & do the best we can towards your <u>accommodation</u>... But we <u>can</u> muster 2 bedrooms, so that you may count upon 2 beds being filled as you please.

Adney joins me in love, & kind regards, & sincere condolences to you all...

The rather stilted letter tailed off without signature; and indeed it was never sent, for Mrs Belcombe did not die.[5] Instead, Anne turned her attention to finding a suitable tenant for her Stump Cross Inn; then:

MONDAY 13 A~ & I off to York at 3 by the fly. At Leeds in 2.05 hours – 10 minutes changing horses… Alighted at the George Inn at 8.15 – a great concert – the George Inn full – sat in the Great Room & had tea. Obliged to come over … to lodgings to sleep & breakfast.

SUNDAY 14 A~ busy writing her journal – left her & off to the Duffins in a fly [carriage]… Mr Marsh had passed through Halifax … much admired Northgate hotel. On returning, took up A~ & called at the Norcliffes' & sat with them 4.40 to 5…[6] Invited Isabella & Charlotte to Shibden, & told Norcliffe he was hardly to be forgiven for passing the [Shibden] Lodge the other day … but slept at the White Swan in Halifax. Home at 5.05 – sat talking in our bedroom… Had Mr Harper from 7 to 8 … [about] tenant for the hotel.[7]

Their York visit included sophisticated leisure activities: a visit to a wine cellar ('the wine nicely laid in sawdust') and Anne's having her hair dressed.

WEDNESDAY 15 Breakfast at 11.10 to 12. Then A~ & I out – called at Marsh's bookseller's shop. Then at Dr Belcombe's to enquire after Mrs Belcombe… Then walked into Micklegate to the Duffins' – gone out in the carriage… Left A~ sitting at the Duffins' ½ hour while [I] sat during this time with Mrs Anna & Miss Gage.[8]

Then they saw Mr Shepley Watson, Gray's solicitor:

FRIDAY 17 [A~] talked over her aunt's affairs about the annuity & will, and explained about Mr William Priestley… Tea on Mr Watson's going at 9.30. From 10.30 to 11.40, wrote out the whole of yesterday & today and while I wrote A~ wrote her journal.[9]

SATURDAY 18 A~ had breakfasted & was off to the will-office about 9.30. All things ready packed & myself at breakfast at 10.30 & sat reading Higgins's *Geology* till 12. *A~ went off, out of sorts – what for I know not – unless that I did not get up when she did this morning.* Out a minute after 12 – bought toothbrushes at Shackleton's. Then to the will-office – a minute or 2 with A~, and then [I] went to the Norcliffes' & sat with Charlotte & Isabella till 1. Then back to the Inn. A~ not returned – went again for her to the will-office, and after a minute or 2 left her, & returned to the Inn to pay & settle all…

A~ returned at 2 – and all being ready, we were off home at 2.05… At Leeds at 5.25 – five minutes changing horses – & home at 8. Tea & sat reading the last two *Morning Herald* newspapers till 10… Letter tonight from M~, Scarborough – her mother likely to recover… Letter also … from Lady de Stuart de Rothesay … & ditto from Lady Stuart.

A~ quite out of sorts – ever since she got up – all right last night. What a temper! Seeing her so wrong, I began to read on leaving York – and she read or seemed to sleep. And we neither of us spoke the whole way back. Except that I twice asked her in vain to have a little wine & biscuit as we got nearish to Leeds. Fine day – brought back in my purse £8.11.2 + some halfpence.

SUNDAY 19 So bilious could not raise my head from my pillow. A~ brought me a cup of tea & walked to Cliff Hill – off about 10.30… Returned … about 4.30, ten minutes before M~ and Mrs Milne went away. [They] had stopped their carriage in passing & walked from the Lodge here… M~ came up to my room about 2.30, sat a little while with me on my bedside, & roused me up. The surprise had relieved my headache – put on my great-coat over A~'s flannel dressing-gown, and went downstairs with M~ to Mrs Milne. Shewed them, at M~'s request, into the tower & over the house & into the turret, & along the turret passage, into the servants' hall. *Costumée* [i.e. dressed] as I was (M~ ran alone up the terrace steps, much admiring the terraces) – we then sat talking & had hot wine & water, & thus A~ found us. They were off about 4.45, M~ promising us a week's visit about a month hence. *This brought* [us] *to speaking & we were tolerably right.* I got up as I was – dinner at 6.30 & tea between 8 & 9 & then went upstairs & was in bed in 5 or 6 minutes.

MONDAY 20 Very fine, sunny, frosty morning… A~ off to Cliff hill about 11 on her pony… Came in at 12.45 & had a basin of veal broth. Then at 1.15 opened & read my letters, franked by Lord Stuart de Rothesay & received on Saturday – & sat down meaning to answer them, but felt disinclined. Felt that I had best not lean too long & intentedly over my desk – dawdled about over one thing or other – putting away journey [i.e. travel] things, looking over papers etc. A~ returned at 5 – sat a few minutes with her… *She not quite right, so came away – what a temper! How can I get on with her in comfort? I mentioned after dinner, having opened my letter from Lady* [Stuart de Rothesay] *& that the old one* [Lady Stuart] *would like me to go & see her – wished I could do so*

& get off a fortnight before our setting off from London. A~ thought I could do it – but I now saw the effect. She got out of sorts again… She feels that her society is not prized above mine, & here [Shibden] *is & will always be the sore. Well, I must make the best I can of it. But I think we cannot get on together for ever.*

Meanwhile, the Chartist newspaper, *The Northern Star*, began publication on 18 November. It gave coherence to Radical demands, offering weekly news of local political activities plus a declamatory letter by O'Connor. From Leeds, it was rushed across to Halifax, undoubtedly passing below Shibden at Stump Cross Inn. People waiting for its arrival lined the roadside.[10] The political zeitgeist was changing. However, Anne herself would scarcely notice any such excitement.

Tuesday 21 A~ & I sat down to breakfast about 11 *and made it up – she was sorry…* Had Messrs Shaw, plasterer, & his half-brother Picard, sadler, the latter for the Stump Cross Inn. All went on well – the man looked respectable… Tho' I had said I was not certain, but the Inn might be let … but I happened to say, I should want a blue vote, when I saw from his manner of waving [i.e. wavering] that the man was a radical – on which I said at once, I would not ask him, nor did I wish him to change his opinion, but that I should not let the place except to one of my own way of thinking – did not respect him less for not changing his opinion – but resolved not to let it except to one of my own party. Therefore Picard needed not trouble himself to make further enquiries about the Inn… I was not aware of Mr Picard's politics or should not have said a word.

Here was Anne Lister, even outside election times, at her most implacable: against having any tenant who was a Yellow (i.e. Whig) or, worse still, a Radical.

On my coming in immediately to follow two men who wanted A~, found it was Mr Lister the auctioneer & a Mr Holdsworth, who came to ask for the radical Hartley to [be able to] stay in his little shop at Halifax. [A~] declined seeing them…

So Ann was as intransigent as Anne about renewing leases.

Cookson asked me just before dinner if I would raise her wages – how much did she wish? Two guineas, I think she said – but I answered, 'You have now sixteen pounds. I will raise you to eighteen'.

Cookson had been in service at Shibden since the spring, and here Anne revealed herself as a fair employer.

WEDNESDAY 22 A~ & I lay talking this morning… Had the fire lighted in the blue room… Made out bank check account. *Have only two hundred & seventy* [pounds] *left.* Dinner at 7 – Edward [new footman] seems likely to do very well.

THURSDAY 23 *Washed out three cousin stockings used in York &* breakfast with A~… Then had A~ in the blue room, looking over Mr Nelson's plans & sections … of the Leeds & Manchester railroad – nothing worth A~'s copying…

There was much debate about the exact route that the Leeds–Manchester railway would take. The Pennines proved a major challenge, and the chances of its climbing up to Halifax high above the River Calder any time soon remained slim.

Then ruled out model of Letters Index, & general index for journal books [i.e. volumes], the ruling to be done in future by Messrs Whitley & Booth.[11] Then in my study reading Clark's *Cellarman* till 1.15 pm… Then went to the [Listerwick] iron pump-pipes going to Mytholm tomorrow… A~ read French then wrote to her sister while I read the newspaper.

FRIDAY 24 Came into A~ a little after one & sat with her talking till 2. *She gave me one hundred pounds to put into the bank till we wanted the money. I said I should like to put something in, even if I took it out again directly.*[12]

SATURDAY 25 Down the Old Bank to the bank – got fifty pounds in their notes, and left (paid in) one hundred pounds in Huddersfield & other county [i.e. West Riding] notes, *received from A~ yesterday… Dinner at 7.15… Came upstairs at 9.10… Then lay down & slumbered till eleven – wishing to then write to Lady Stuart, if I could. Then dawdled over my letter – written last Monday – till twelve.*

The visit to London and Lady Stuart had assumed huge significance for Anne. This was partly because it kept open an enticing social world, including Vere Cameron, Lady Stuart's great-niece. And also because the visit would be without Ann Walker.

SUNDAY 26 Got wine out of the cellar, 1 port, 1 marsala, & 1 claret to give to Rachel Sharpe, cook at Cliff Hill, for a sick relation…

From 11.30 to near 1 wrote … to Lady Stuart – a chit-chat [letter]… *From then to three & a quarter copied my letter to Lady Stuart.* At 3.15 to about 4, A~ & I read the evening prayers to our four women & two men [servants] in the little south parlour… Then sealed & sent off my letter to the honourable Lady Stuart… Dinner at 6.30… A~ read French & I (afterwards, bits aloud) the newspaper, long and interesting communication in favour of steam navigation to India…

Shibden Hall. Sunday 26 November 1837

I am delighted, my dearest Lady Stuart, to have heard from you, and so good an account, too, of yourself… What a happy family party you must have been at Highcliffe![13] And how magnificent the place! I should not know it again. What a suite of rooms! As for woods, and walks, and everything outside, I can easily imagine Lady Stuart [de Rothesay]'s taste would do all the most fastidious fancy could desire. As [a] landscape gardener, she is the very best amateur I ever saw – her judgement is that of an artist. I often think of many of her random observations, to which I am sure I myself owe more than to any other source of instruction on this subject. With her aid to show off his lordship's architectural genius, the place may well be magnificent. I should like very much to see it, and should it be two or three years before I am in that neighbourhood, the picturesque will have gained a great deal in that time.

What a pity you have all been hurried off so soon! If the real business of Parliament is to get on no better this session than the last, the good of meeting so early is not very obvious. However, we must go on hoping. Things can hardly be worse; and surely, therefore they will mend by and by. How admirably the Queen seems to acquit herself! It cannot be that she is radical or even much Whig, at heart. Times are still very bad, perhaps worse here than at this time last year, tho' people hope for a favourable change in the spring. But winter stares us in the face; and it is terrible to think how many of the poor are out of employ.

I am glad to hear of Lord Stuart's being in such high spirits, this seems as if things were looking better at headquarters. Perhaps I may by and by see *son excellence*, our young Queen's representative, at

Vienna. I long to be able to tell you my plans, tho' I hardly dare attempt it just yet.

But, dearest Lady Stuart ... I shall be delighted to hear of your being comfortably settled at Whitehall, and dear Vere's loss will not seem quite so heavy to you there where you have so many friends. I supposed she intends being confined at Achnacary – it is certainly a beautiful place, but I always wish it was more southwards; tho' as far as I am individually concerned, it really seems a mere step from here.[14] A five hours' drive is all the necessary posting (from here to Manchester) – railroad and steam will do all the rest.

But I hope to see you in London long before I see Vere at Achnacary. I do not, at present, know anything likely to prevent my being off from here by the end of January. I feel as if I should be like a bird escaped from its cage. Believe me always, dearest Lady Stuart, very truly and very affectionately yours,

A. Lister[15]

This letter vividly reveals Anne's frustrations at Shibden and her yearning for travel, especially to renew elite friendships.

Meanwhile, Anne had still not found anyone suitable for her strategically sited Stump Cross Inn. She had to be be selective, for the tenant would have a parliamentary vote – as did Anne's coal steward Holt. *He* was in a tricky position: at the 1837 West Riding election he had voted for the Whigs.[16]

MONDAY 27 [I] enquiring something about Holt's blue vote. He said he thought he should have nothing to do with voting. 'No! No!' said I, 'that won't do – you really must vote'. He had just come from Mr Akroyd – getting water for him.[17] *Eh! bien* – but Holt shall give me a vote, or give up his agency for my colliery.

TUESDAY 28 With Robert Mann & Benjamin paving at the rocks... Spoke [to a] carrier of Halifax, about the Stump Cross Inn – recommended, he said, by Greenwood (Thomas). [I] told the rent – inquired about a blue vote – had never interfered. [He] wished to have as little to do as possible with politics, but promised to give me his vote quietly...

Called in to Mr Jubb – he congratulated us on having let the Northgate hotel – it seems to be thought [so] in the town... Will drink tea with Mr & Mrs Crossland & settle about the hotel – to draw up instructions for the lease to be signed by Mr Crossland.[18]

WEDNESDAY 29 Mr Harper & I [had] long talk about the Northgate hotel, the mill etc – and speculation in general… Harper staid with Mr & Mrs Crossland from 6 to 11 pm before he could settle about the hotel [lease]… After a long talk, it seemed [in] Harper's opinion, it would be better to paint the casino as originally intended… Mr Crossland to take possession of the hotel on the 1st of January… It seems Mr Parker may think Mr Crossland would have done me a kindness to take the hotel on my terms – with rent or without![19]

November ended with political differences further sharpened. The new Halifax Conservative Association held its meeting at the White Lion Inn. Alongside, the *Halifax Guardian* headlined 'Owenism in Halifax', about 'a newly-designated society in this town, denominated "Socialists" who met in a room at the Union Cross Inn', inspired by Robert Owen of New Lanark.[20] Many Radicals drew inspiration from Owenist idealism. But this was not the Scotland that Anne Lister admired. Political lines were hardening almost to breaking point. When she accidentally visited 'our tinner, not knowing anything of his being an arrant Radical', she noted that had she known she would not have visited.[21]

DECEMBER 1837

The diary now flowed along almost as three parallel narratives. The first was Anne's relationship with Ann, and its ups and downs. The second was Anne as an energetic entrepreneur, battling the perilous Pennine weather. Third were her travel dreams, reflected in her impressively wide reading and in her letters to elite women friends, presenting her more public face.

SATURDAY 2 [A~] off to Cliff Hill at 3.40 – *she gave me twenty pounds*. Then out again with Joseph Mann waiting for me about platform walling & more stone for air-gate pit… Reading the newspapers & looking over Adcock's Engineers' pocket book that came last night.

MONDAY 4 A~ & I sat talking – had asked her at breakfast if she had paid Holt's bill for coal measuring at Shughead & Bouldshaw.[1] 'Yes!'… Mused over this. Then Holt is not over-abounding in money or in truth!… I will plan the colliery works myself… Tea between 8 and 9 – then A~ & I sat in the north parlour writing our journals.

WEDNESDAY 6 In the stables & about till near 6 – a little while with A~. *She gave me ten pounds towards bill for Northgate*. Some time in the wine cellar… Two swans first seen on the meer this morning, strayed from somewhere. *Cousin came gently about dinner time.*

THURSDAY 7 To the bank – left my banking book & got £50. Mr Davidson said the Directors would with pleasure advance me what I wanted (I had named a thousand).[2]

TUESDAY 19 Off to Halifax… Went into Birtwhistle's [booksellers] in passing & bought Walsh's *Journey from Constantinople to England*…[3] Then to the bank – got my banking book – saw McKean – he said they would willingly advance me a thousand. Mentioned my colliery account – McKean said he should be happy to do anything I wished – would keep an account for the colliery – it would be no trouble. Returned up the Old Bank… A~ returned from Cliff Hill at 5, just after the arrival of my cart from there with 16 fine trees for the terrace avenue.[4]

WEDNESDAY 20 Very rainy night & morning… About 1.45 John Booth came to say the water was running over the meer-embankment… Sam Booth brought word that Mawson was at the meer, & begged me to send all the men I could muster. Sent Sam, & Robert Sharpe the mason, & Gray the mason's labourer… Desired Sam to get all Joseph Mann's men. I staid … till about 2.45, then seeing a rush of water from under the rock bridge went first to the low fishpond across the road… The embankment … had burst & the water was flowed nearly down to the bottom of the meer-goit leading to the water wheel. The roots of the large oaks … were washed bare… The whole of the Ings [i.e. meadows] like a sea…

Jack Green & his father-in-law were staring in mute astonishment – and I said not much… A couple of the colliers were there – had narrowly escaped being drowned in the low mine – only just escaped the rush of water…[5] [I] stood musing over the scene of devastation… I never saw such a [flood] before.

Sam brought word this evening that Dumb Mill bridge [over Red Beck] was washed away, & much damage done at Halifax. Returned home very wet (rained incessantly all the day) about 4. Dressed – had Robert … putting up clothes-pegs in my drawing-room closet…

Did Anne ever wonder if she had over-reached herself in the Pennines with her landscaping and mining ambitions?

Cookson had 10 leeches this afternoon on her side, & Sarah the kitchen-maid 6 on her temples, & she & Susan the house-maid, very poorly this evening. Thoroughly rainy windy day & evening & wind whistling & very wet night.

THURSDAY 21 Mrs Cookson better tho' very weak, & George the groom must take medicine & be confined to the house tomorrow – what a sickly set!...

Dinner at 7.05 – tea at 8 – read almost all aloud to A~ several pages of Walsh's *Journey from Constantinople... A~ was ... wrong this evening – lay on the sofa crying – and would not read French, & came to bed. Was smiling before & at dinner – but annoyed I suppose at my reading the 'Journey from Constantinople'. What an uncertain, uncomfortable temper.*

Very nice letter tonight from Lady Vere Cameron ... Stirling [Scotland] – chiefly to announce her expected confinement in March – would like a boy.

Vere then went into elaborate detail about possible names and godparents.

FRIDAY 22 A~ & I lay talking this morning about Lady Vere Cameron etc, the proposed manner of naming the child gives me no pleasure... Dinner at 7 – tea at 8 – read the paper – then wrote the above of today till 10.15. A~ read her French in ¼ hour – came upstairs at 10.40... *Found A~ crying over her prayers* – gave A~ castor oil in brandy & water.

SATURDAY 23 Mr Jubb came about 12 to see Mrs Cookson, the 2 maids & George... *It is low fever as last winter – owing to the locality – so much wood or the water about. Should all live well. I am right to take brandy & water at night – a teaspoonful with three or four* [of] *water...* A~ off to Cliff hill... Part of the wall down near the rock bridge ... in consequence of the flood & the meer embankment bursting...[6]

Came in at 5 – dressed ... dinner at 7.10 in ½ hour – then came upstairs – wrote 1½ pages to Lady Vere Cameron:

Shibden Hall. Saturday evening, 23 December 1837

My dearest Vere,

... Your episode on the Americans delighted me... That species of pride inseparable from vulgarity is a nuisance against which one ought to recover damages. Heaven defend [us] from Mobocracy! Democracy is not the word – the demos of antiquity was respectable; and the Democrats of old Athens would have spurned their namesake of this present day.[7]

There is no longer any chance of my being off to Paris … on this side of Xmas… It is twenty years since we had anything like such a flood – the brook below the house rushed with such fury into my little meer… The torrent left behind a scene of Swiss desolation, and as it roared down the valley, tore up bridges, and drove the barges on the canal on to the high road … and report says, forty thousand pounds worth of damage done. This, and a stagnation in trade, and the excessive irritation occasioned by the New Poor Laws, are really terrible.

Monday evening. 25 December. I was interrupted even on Saturday. I am sick to death of business… I will escape the first moment I can. I have no time for reading, writing, or anything that pleases me. I live on remembrance of the past, and hope of the future; for the present wearies me. I fear there will be no getting off these three months – but I shall not stir without telling you…[8]

SUNDAY 24 Rainy night… Sat reading downstairs till 2.20 (& looking at maps) Walsh's *Journey from Constantinople*. Off to Cliff Hill at 2.30… Mrs A. Walker looking better… Mr Younger's curate, Mr Wood, did all the duty… Went into the cellar for marsala – dinner at 6.30… Came upstairs at 10.35 at which hour F50°. A~ came & sat by me, writing her journal till 12 while I read forwards of Walsh's *Journey*.

MONDAY 25 Xmas day – rainy night & morning … breakfast in 20 minutes… Then read … Walsh's *Journey* – & off to church… At the girls' school at 10.05… Mr Younger did all the duty … then had the sacrament = about ½ hour. Luckily Mr Younger, having a party at home, did not dine at Cliff Hill, so A~ & I returned together, & home at 2.10…

Christmas remained very low key.[9] And their disagreement about travelling was far from settled.

Sat with A~ near ½ hour at her luncheon – talked over going abroad the end of next month. 'Out, out of the question', said A~. To go for six months – then if to go for only 3 months, or she would not object to six weeks, why go in winter? Better wait till summer. I proposed going in April for the six months of fine weather. On combatting the impossibility of leaving Mrs A Walker, A~ mentioned her farms being out of repair ... in Stainland... I see how it is – I have told her now & often, she ought to throw off all thought of home concerns for a time. My warning voice is drowned – the truth is, few properties hereabouts of the magnitude of A~'s are altogether better managed than hers.[10] But a sad prepossession [i.e. prejudice] of the contrary takes hold of her mind. How sad! I see the thing in all its bearings – but what can I do? Nothing. *Let not want of energy creep over myself. A~'s mind will succumb. I must wind up my own affairs & be off. I thought of this yesterday – let the gardener manage all – and make what he can of the garden & land – & live in the house, I allowing him [money] for one strong woman servant to keep the house clean. Mr Parker to be steward? Or can I go on with Washington? Go next July or August & take only Oddy. Send the carriage back from Leeds to be taken care of at home. And Oddy & I embark at Hull for Rotterdam. Then get to Paris & then ... as circumstances may direct. Surely, at the worst, without hotel or colliery, I shall have five hundred a year clear after paying interest [on loans] & keeping up the place. And I could keep myself & Oddy on this till times mended. I cannot go on with poor A~. What will the Sutherlands do with her? How melancholy. But it is not my fault. I know not that I am to blame in any way.*

So 'our union', sanctified just three years earlier, was once again under threat.

Came upstairs about 2 & till 2.45 wrote all but the 2 first lines of today. Just sat down to finish my letter begun on Saturday to Lady Vere Cameron, when called down about 3 to Robert Mann... [He] thinks we shall be getting coal before midsummer.[11] Would drive two heads along Rawson's land within ten yards of my boundary, & then the trespass, if there be any, would be found, & I could come on [i.e. proceed] for damages on account of coal taken & water let loose upon me.

If this was correct and Rawson had (even indirectly) caused the horrendous flood at Shibden that endangered miners' lives, then it would indeed be a serious legal matter.

A~ came for me about her letter to her sister & [I] went to her about 4 & sat talking till near 6.

Initially the conversation was about the sisters' Crow Nest farms; then it reverted to travel plans and Ann's adamant 'out, out of the question':

Got upon the subject of going abroad – told A~ the consequences of too long potheration [i.e. fuss] might be more [serious] than she thought. The pain at the back of her neck not to be trifled with... I mentioned [her] first 'No!' that [it] would be summer. Then second ['No'] April next for going to Hull to embark there for Hamburg – thence to Berlin ... for six months. A~ said she knew where I meant to go: 'St Petersburg & Moscow.' 'Yes!' & we then sat talking it over, & I do hope we shall get off?...

[Read] Walsh's *Journey*. Dinner at 6.30, tea at 8. A~ read French – we looked a little at maps. A~ sat down & wrote to her sister. I read the paper (that should have come last night) till 9.25, then came upstairs. Wrote ½ page to Lady Vere Cameron. Then A~ came to me and sat with me till 11.45 – reading over her <u>long</u> letter to her sister.

So, as low-key (almost mundane!) a day as any other: business, letters. However, while the Christmas Day quarrel was seemingly smoothed over, on Boxing Day:

TUESDAY 26 Joseph Mann who came to pay his rent ... to pay me for 35 loads of coal at 7d [a load] got in driving Listerwick Low mine = £1.0.5... [Ordered] Kitchener's *Traveller's Oracle* – sat reading... *Theory of the Constitution* by J B Bernard Esq – very interesting – gives good promise of the rest.[12] *A~ came up & because I had got two of Melvile's sermons that she wanted, all wrong & went out in tears. What shall I do with her?...* Passed A~ in the stairs, just setting off for Cliff Hill,

WEDNESDAY 27 Wrote, altogether different from what I wrote on Saturday & Monday (A~ thought it vapourish [i.e. despondent]) to Lady Vere Cameron – certainly not vapourish. Kind affectionate easy chit-chat [letter] – beginning with the subject of the sponsorship [i.e. godparents]. 'There is no difficulty, my dearest Vere, in bespeaking my interest for a little Sibbella. The difficulty would be to persuade me, that such a <u>miss</u> was "a miss in every sense of the word"...[13] And it will give me great pleasure to congratulate you on ½ a dozen more such *chefs d'oevre* [i.e. masterpieces]... It will delight me to hear that she has given less trouble than any of the rest [of your children?].

Never fancy me gone till you have it from myself – Xmas is already past; & here I am business-bound as ever. I am sick almost to death of it… I told dear Lady Stuart, I hope to be off by the end of next month – *nous verrons*… "We cling to those & that to whom & which we have been accustomed". "Affections are stubborn things" – and where they root them deep, they root forever. *Vale valeque*, my dearest Vere – *Buona Notte*. Do you sing much now? or is your own voice hushed by sweetest harmony of Cherub-kind? Always affectionately yours, A.L.'

About small Sibella, Anne seemed to write rather convolutedly, perhaps 'vapourish', as Ann had suggested.[14]

Then in 20 minutes wrote 2½ pages of inquiry after M~. Thought she would have been here or written before this – had told her I should be anxious to hear of herself … afraid for her, her mother & Mrs Milne… Have had 4 servants ill – now better that if M~ comes tomorrow, we can give her welcome & cheer enough to keep body & soul together, & something to spare. Not to pother & write a long letter – a line or 2 will satisfy me, if conveying the intelligence of her being well. A~'s love. 'Believe me, always, my dearest Mary, very affectionately & expect[antly,] respectfully yours. A.L.'

This seemed a rather anxious letter to Mariana, as if she was feeling neglected.

A~ has had Booth after his seeing the Water Lane mill. Too much water in the brook now to judge exactly of the damage done – but nothing very serious…

A few minutes with A~, dressed while she sat by me in the blue room & read my letters… Sent off my letters to Lady Vere Cameron … & Mrs Lawton… Had Joseph Mann for ¾ hour … speaking of the railroad lengths … near Littleborough [i.e. crossing the Pennines] … the cost of the tunnel at ten hundred thousand pounds. 'Poh!' said I.[15]

Tea at 9 – A~ read her French. Note tonight from the Halifax Philosophical Society – a paper to be read 'on the Increase of Crime viewed in Connections with the Education of the People'. Read aloud to A~… Bernard on the Constitution.

Thursday 28 ¾ hour in the wood above the walk choosing out an oak & beech to complete the terrace planting… Came in at 5.35 – 25 minutes with A~. Dressed – read Bernard. In the cellar, one marsala – dinner at 7 – sat in the dining room reading [Bernard] aloud to A~. For an Elective Monarchy! Madness. Tea about 9. A~ read her French... [Note from] the clerk to the Halifax and Wakefield road – to say the trustees meant to apply for a new Act 'for enlarging the terms ... of the last Act'... [I must] look after [i.e. watch] this Bill. They will have my Whiskham road to Southowram, and will set up a toll-bar to catch my colliery.[16]

Sunday 31 Reading Pinnock's [edition of] Goldsmith's *History of Greece*... Off to church at 2.40 ... just finishing the Psalm as we got into our pew...[17] [Later, A~] & I read aloud between us ... a very sensible article in tonight's *Herald* on Bernard's work on the Constitution... 'Mr Bernard is a philosophical conservative.'

By the end of 1837 Anne still had unresolved estate issues, with no tenant yet secured for Stump Cross Inn, and with road reformers now threatening tolls that would eat into her coal profits. And, however widely she read, her travel plans remained in the air.

X

Reading around the World: Russia

January–February 1838

January 1838

Anne was increasingly reading right around the world, her imagination stretching far, far east. And 1838 was the year when her increasingly ambitious travel plans at last took real shape. It was also the year when Chartism fully established itself as a radical force.[1] However, New Year's Day 1838, unlike the start of Anne's other years, felt just like any other day.[2]

Monday 1 Fine morning. F43° at 8.40. A~ off to Cliff Hill soon after 9 – I looking over rough books, letters, Journal etc respecting A~'s bill… £83.4.4, thought this bill was paid in the deduction from the £7,000 paid to me the end of last May…[3]

 Down Old Bank … to the Bank… Times [are] mending, said Mr McKean… Then some time at Northgate with Greenwood – he would now advise letting the ground off at the fair!… Mr Crossland would be glad of it – he thought of calling it the Lister Arms! I begged Greenwood to explain my wish to have it called simply the Northgate Hotel kept by Mr Crossland.

Tuesday 2 Not perhaps more than £1,000 of damage done to the Navigation works by the flood – ordered luncheon… Mr Bull & his companion sat till 2! I wish it were possible to manage these matters in less time. It seem Bull dabbles in architecture – will shew me the plan of some houses he has planned for Mr James Norris … Elizabethan with modern comforts… Bull a member of the Engineering Society Institution in London.

Such professional societies did not, of course, admit women, undoubtedly adding to Anne's irritation with Mr Bull.

WEDNESDAY 3 *A~'s cousin came tonight...* A~ off to Cliff hill ... she rode Felix... I walked by her side as far as Mytholm... Came in to Sam Washington at 6, who paid me the rents he had received at the Stag's Head...

Anne's half-yearly rents totalled £795.4.0½d.[4]

Came upstairs at 10.50 – stood talking to A~ in the tent room. Letter tonight from M~ ... has been busy at Leamington giving up their house there – not to return – must be at Lawton in March – the alterations too expensive to allow much money for anywhere else – good account of herself & her mother.

THURSDAY 4 Very fine morning... Down the Old Bank ... to the Bank – paid in £500 in notes + £150 in gold... Left my banking book...

Then to Whitley's – some time there – saw Bernard on the table – said it was a mere pamphlet that I had sent for – mentioned to Booth that the book was not fit for everybody, & pointed to page 199: Elective Monarchy.[5] *Bought three little things on etiquette – four & sixpence ... & got a work on planting & a veterinary chart...*

Returned up Old Bank... Mr Carter rode up ... a meeting to be called next week at Lightcliffe to lay a church rate. Mr Holland & Mr Stocks will get up a violent opposition.[6] Mr Carter meant to have written to A~ to ask her interest in favour of the rate – hoped I would be so good as [to] name it [to her]. 'Yes!' But Waddington or someone had best write out a list of the ratepayers – why there were 200. But if A~ did not know them, she could not tell [them] what interest she might have. Waddington ... to bring the list here tomorrow night & have 2/6d...

So, given that the church rate was highly political, Ann Walker had influence as a major Lightcliffe landowner.[7]

Then stood talking to Joseph Mann till after 6... My calculations [at Listerwick]: 5 loads per yard at 9d per load. 'Yes!'... But at Walker pit only 4 loads per yard – the bed there only 15 inches thick...

Clearly, Listerwick would pay better than Walker pit, where coal seams were unprofitably narrow. Then a minor misunderstanding over a tenant's rent prompted Ann's tears again.

A little while with A~. Told her of Bottomley's coming this evening… [She] had not named the rent… I could not have done worse – a terrible interference tho' so innocent on my part. A~ burst into tears from vexation or poorliness or something – saying <u>she</u> had very little comfort. My expressions of sorrow availed not much, for I was always sorry & always did the same again. May I know better & do better in future!…[8]

Dinner at 7.05… Then told A~ about the Lightcliffe church rates etc, and she will exert herself on their behalf.

FRIDAY 5 Had Mr George Harper at the Back Lodge gates between 11 & 12 this morning – settled that he has the Stump Cross Inn – rent £130 – a blue vote, as mentioned before – & I told him this morning he should have a lease for three years…[9] G. Harper to come next Monday week to sign his lease…

It must have been a great relief to Anne that the inn was finally settled: Stump Cross was so strategically situated – and now with a tenant promising a Blue vote!

Finished reading last night's paper – went into the cellar – 1 marsala – dinner at 7.05. A~ poorly but better this morning. She had Bairstow this morning about the repairs to be done to the water-wheel [at Water Lane mill] – wanted to hurry A~ into doing them immediately… A~ read French – tea at 9…

Had Dodgson a little before 12 this morning – came to ask for an old door – told him about his wife's radicalism & how I grieved about it – but I could not keep a tenant who would not support me. He said his wife had changed her opinion a good deal since I saw her – he thought she did not want much convincing now. Said I had long thought of going to see her – he wished I would go.[10]

MONDAY 8 Had Samuel Washington to pay A~ her Shibden [Mill] rents. *Five hundred & three pounds, plus Charles Law [Stainland] has not paid.* S. Washington also paid me my cottage & pews rents.

TUESDAY 9 Hard frost… Dinner at 7.05. A~ read French – tea about 9 & sat talking till came upstairs at 11… *Talking this evening about my affairs – I must be helped, or run away somewhere – where I could live on three hundred* [pounds] *a year.* [Ann asked] *'What would it take to settle my affairs?' I answered, 'About a thousand pounds.' A~ cried & I almost* [did]. *At last, talked her into better heart. It seemed she would not leave me abroad – would bring me back.* [We] *would go away for four months. I estimated our travelling expenses at three guineas a day, including living and at five posts a day.*[11] *Said five hundred for four months, and a hundred of expenses for home servants left there* [i.e. at Shibden] *& taxes etc. Talked of Moscow.*

Was this when Ann really grasped Anne's financial dependency on her? And the ambitious travel plans that reading Walsh's *Journey from Constantinople* had triggered?

WEDNESDAY 10 Dinner in ½ hour, then sat at dessert about ¾ hour… With [A~] in the tent room till 12 struck… The servants had their Xmas party tonight – till 12… The women in the house & Matty Pollard – the two men in the house & Robert Norton, the York joiner, & John & Sam Booth & George Thomas, the farming man.

A servants' party at Shibden was quite rare.

Rang my bell, & told Oddy to remind the servants that 12 had struck and it was time to break up the party, 12 being the limit hour fixed. *A~ counting her Hipperholme rents – about four hundred & thirty pounds.* Snow showers during the day … fine moonlight night now at midnight.

THURSDAY 11 With [A~] *counting out her rents. Gave me five hundred to put into the bank – one hundred & sixty being her interest to Mr Gray, & the rest for my own to the Misses Preston etc. A~ … sent by George three hundred to Briggs' Bank & kept one hundred & forty six at home. She will have a rent day of sixty pounds more in a fortnight. This will make thirteen hundred of her receipts this Christmas, and she has Honley mill & Hinscliffe's coal besides…*

So, Ann Walker had received £1,300 receipts for Christmas rents, with more still to come. Here is very clear confirmation of the scale of Ann's rents compared to Anne's, plus the entwined complexity of their finances

Off to Halifax at 2 by the Lodge to the bank – left there my [bank] book, & as I thought, £500 – but on afterwards calling for my book,

Mr Davidson said £400 (and the one hundred tumbled out of my pelisse on dressing for dinner)...

This shows exactly where Anne kept large sums of cash secure when she intrepidly walked down into Halifax! In the library, she chose Captain Cochrane's *A Pedestrian Journey through Russia and Siberian Tartary: To the Frontiers of China.*[12] **It was** *the* **travel book that now gripped her imagination:**

¼ hour at the Library & chosen there 4 vols of Travels... Cochrane's *Pedestrian Tour in Russia* etc 2 vols, Tobin's journal written while with Sir H[umphry] Davy in his last illness & his death. Returned up the New Bank by the old [Godley] road to Listerwick about 3.30.

MONDAY 15[13] Fine clear frosty morning, <u>very</u> cold, F14° at 9 am... A little after 12 to near 2, wrote to Lady Stuart de Rothesay...

The letter explained why Anne's departure had been so delayed:

Shibden Hall. Mon. 15 January 1838

My dear Lady Stuart,

It is really very good of you ... to inquire so kindly after me in the midst of all my *contre-temps* and *desagrements*... The season became sickly, and we had four servants laid up; but I had no idea of being afterwards <u>home-bound</u> by the serious illness of both [my] architect and clerk-of-the-works... It would be too imprudent to go away till I myself have seen to the winding up of all outstanding accounts... I now fear it will be spring before I can count upon being free. I find that, upon a moderate computation, the most feasible projects cost twice the time and money they were estimated to cost, and that the first course we should all of us take with estimates, is to double them.

I am awakened, therefore, from the dream of spending next Easter at Rome. It would have delighted me to spend a few days *en passant* with [elderly] Lady Stuart; for life cannot last for ever here to her or to me – but my lot is cast for 8 or 10 weeks longer ... and I must make the best I can of it, remembering always that *comme on fait son lit, on se couche...*

The cold is intense here... Fahrenheit stood at 14° at midnight last night and at 9° this morning. It cannot be much worse in Canada, where nevertheless, I hope your nephew, Lord Alexander, will cover himself with laurels.[14] I wish we could send him a few recruits; the beer-shops might disgorge abundance, but military spirit is not the favourite spirit among our mechanics who love their pleasant home... How this will [be] in future, who can tell? Power looms supersede the hand-weaving parents, and now there is a piece of newly-invented [spinning] machinery in rapid progress which will [do] the work of the children.

Have you seen that book of Bernard's on the constitution? Not fit for every eye. On electing monarchy and state religion, he seems a visionary and a madman, but he is strong and clever against democracy. A person like Lady Stuart de Rothesay ... might read this book, cull out the good, and be interested and instructed...

Is it true that our radical ministers are such favourites at Court? (The Poor-law will oust them, if they do not take care. Baines, [Leeds] M.P. in his Coach Travels, harangues his *compagnons de voyage*, denying that this measure was Whig doing. No! it was all the Duke of Wellington and the Tories.) The people, the demos (not the rabble), is coming to its senses and will help the Queen to turn her servants out.

My love to Louisa and may our new year be one of good to us all. Believe me, my dear Lady Stuart, always very truly yours,

(A.L.)[15]

Inspired by her adventurously wide reading, Anne wrote like a captive lion pacing around its cage. And she chose to talk of Lord Alexander out in Canada rather than mention Ann Walker.

Then wrote & sent to William Gray junior esquire, Minster, York, order the Yorkshire District Bank for £460, being £160 from A~ to old Mr Gray & £300 to the Misses Preston... Joseph Mann ... brought me his calculations of what the coal probably makes = £378.2.6 net profit per acre. Dinner at 7.10 – & sat talking in the dining room till 9. Then A~ read her French... Joseph Mann thought the colliery would make £200 or more the 1st year – i.e. from midsummer next to midsummer 1839.

SATURDAY 20 Breakfast. *A~ out of sorts but I take no notice...* Joseph Mann told me that Mr Rawson had turned off Illingworth & the bottom-steward & all his family, that had been there so long – it was said, because the colliery made nothing [i.e. no profit]. But Joseph agreed there must surely be something else.

Did this mean that Anne had at last triumphed over the Rawsons in their coalmining rivalry? Had she really driven them out?[16]

SUNDAY 21. Sat reading over the breakfast table till about 12... *Travels in Norway, Sweden, Denmark, Hanover, Germany & the Netherlands* by William MacWilson, 1826... Then looked into vol 1, Granville's *Russia*. Off to church at 2 – a moment at Cliff Hill. A~ thought me very late ... the service had begun on our entering the church – Mr Wood did all the duty – preached very uninterestingly... Home at 4.30 – sat reading German grammar till dinner at 6.30 – read the newspaper.

MONDAY 22 The thaw has begun... [Out till] called in about 11 to Mr Parker... Gave Parker back the rough draft of the Northgate lease ... also Sam Washington's plan of the premises to be let at Northgate with the hotel... A~ had Sam Washington while I had Parker... Tea – read Captain Cochrane's *Journey* ... great praise of the Irtish river and of the beauty of the frontier between Russia & China at the head of the Irtish.[17]

TUESDAY 23 F32° at 9 am... Came in at 4.50... A~ read bits aloud from the *Halifax Guardian* – tea.

As Ann read aloud the Halifax newspaper, they learned that there had been a 'Meeting of the Radicals of Halifax' on Monday. The chair had proposed a resolution that Parliament be petitioned upon five key Radical demands: the secret ballot, universal suffrage, annual parliaments, equal representation and no property qualifications for MPs. Handloom weaver Ben Rushton argued that 'taxation without representation was no better than robbing a man on the highway'. After the resolution was passed, Rushton took the chair, and introduced discussion of the Poor Law, saying: 'He had now been a common labourer for thirty-three years ... and had the consolation of knowing he might retire into a Bastille and finish his existence upon fifteen halfpence a week.'[18] It was the harsh poverty of handloom weavers such as Rushton that the new Poor Law supposedly addressed.

Anne and Ann must have seen this report; but Anne's thoughts were elsewhere.

WEDNESDAY 24 Read & made little notes from *Journal of a Tour made in the years 1828–29*, through Styria, Carniola [i.e. Slovenia] & Italy, whilst accompanying Sir Humphry Davy, by J J Tobin, 1832. Interesting little volume – Sir Humphry Davy reached Geneva about noon 28 May & died a little after 2 am on the following day, 29 May 1829...[19]

This account sends a small shiver of anticipation down the reader's spine, knowing that Anne herself would also die unexpectedly while on exotic travels.

THURSDAY 25 *Found my cousin come ... had all to prepare...* Read vol 1, Cochrane's *Journey* – made several notes & look at maps...[20] *Washed.* Went out at 3 to the Lodge ... so slippery I had been obliged twice to sit down & slide over the ice... Read a little German... Cochrane's journey – made <u>no</u> notes tonight – fine frosty day.

FRIDAY 26 Snow during the night... Breakfast at 9.45 & till 10.55, A~ reading aloud the first few pages of Lardner's *Encyclopaedia History of Russia* ... very interesting. Sat in my room (from 11 till 12) reading German... Then a minute or 2 with A~ cutting out chemises for me etc... A little while in the cellar – got pint (the ½ of the bottle, lowest quality from York – the other ½ [had been] given to poor old [man] who died, starved to death of cold at the beginning of the storm.)... *Then washed...* A minute or 2 in the west tower – fire there 1st time in the old grate that was in my uncle's room, now the Oak room. I always think I shall manage getting to read German & to speak as much as will suffice... I began [learning it] in Copenhagen – I find it much easier now than I did then![21] Why? For I have done nothing at German since then till now.

Anne was absolutely determined to conquer this language before she travelled.

Thinking of late of going to Russia – via Hull, Hamburg, Berlin & the usual road to St Petersburg; or if no longer time required, perhaps by Copenhagen, Stockholm & Abo. From St Petersburg to Moscow & Kazan etc[22] – for this purpose, got Captain Cochrane's travels – and thought that a little German might serve us well... On Tuesday, I got out my Copenhagen <u>Danish, French, German & English</u> vocabulary & I have since looked into [it] night & morning while dressing, & mean to pay attention to it by bit & bit as I can. I have not much time to spare – but must do what I can to make my way...

Captain Cochrane was a hugely impressive walker and a truly compelling travel writer. Anne was now absolutely determined to get to Moscow and perhaps as far east as remote Kazan! (However, other than 'a little German might serve us well', there was scarce a reference to Ann nor to the cost of this exotic journey.) It was all about travel books and languages.

John Booth & George Thomas sweeping & shovelling away the snow so as to make a good track. Came in ... sat reading cursorily Granville's *Journey to St Petersburg*, vol 1.

SATURDAY 27 <u>Very</u> cold – breakfast at 9.15, & A~ read aloud several pages Lardner's *History* [of] *Russia* till after 10. Then in stables & farmyard... At road books – marking out distance to St Petersburg etc. Then in the cellar – 1 marsala... Had Booth (David) who had received drawings for the Casino from Mr Harper... Reading ... Granville's *Journey to Russia* till dinner at 7.10... Then calculating the value of a German mile in English yards – & dozing over the fire till 11.

SUNDAY 28 Off to church at 2... One of the horses had a shoe off – waited a few minutes till it was put on again – in the meanwhile, got the organist to play (lamely) the coronation anthem – home at 4.30... Read (partly aloud) the newspaper – & then, while A~ wrote her journal, read ... Charles Lardner's *History of Russia*.

MONDAY 29 In spite of the snow, A~ rode off to Heath [grammar school] before 12 & got back at 4 covered with snow – having had no success in persuading Miss Wilkinson of the expediency of her father having an under-graduate of the universities as usher & curate...[23] Can't find my rough book journal of 1830 when travelling with Lady Stuart de Rothesay. Are they in Paris? Surely they cannot be lost!

TUESDAY 30 Sun peeping out... A~ reading aloud Lardner's *Russia*. Then had Thomas Pearson, who came in after killing the pig... Some time at Listerwick pit – Robert Mann driving – 5 yards deep of water in the pit yesterday – had the gin-horse yesterday & got the pit cleaned so as to begin sinking again this morning... Tea in the dining room & I read aloud chapter 5 (very interesting) Lardner's *History of Russia*.

WEDNESDAY 31 *A~'s cousin came this morning...* I went into the farmyard & loitered about... Came in about 12.30 – then with A~. Then in the cellar, 1 marsala... I sat reading German till 3.30... Snowing again now... Turned to my rough book of 1834 & began trying a rough draft of travelling & other accounts from 1 January 1834. Dinner at 7.05 – read the paper... Tea ... A~ looking at genealogical tables & making notes from Lardner's *History to Russia*. Then read ... vol 2 Cochrane's *Journey* ... & came upstairs at 11.10.[24]

So, apart from some routine estate business, Anne remained unshakable in her passion for exotic travel. Yet had Ann Walker been completely won over to this major expenditure of both money and time? Ann was 'making notes from Lardner's *History of Russia*', which you would surely not do unless you planned to visit there.[25]

Meanwhile, the *Halifax Guardian* reported further signs of modernity: the Halifax Mechanics' Institute advertised lectures on chemistry; and a public meeting was held about a new branch railway coming up to Halifax, part of the Manchester and Leeds Railway.[26] However, Anne and Ann's thoughts were far, far away.

FEBRUARY 1838

February was the month when Anne's travel plans firmed up, inspired especially by Captain Cochrane's compelling *Pedestrian Journey*. Meanwhile back at Shibden, Listerwick pit progressed, despite the usual drainage and flooding problems. Given her plans, Anne wanted speed from her miners: so these were the driving years at her coal pits.

THURSDAY 1 A~ breakfasted at 8.30 … sat reading Lardner's Russia to me as I breakfasted… [Then] sat with A~ reading her geographical magazine article on Russia… Left A~ just beginning a letter to her sister.

FRIDAY 2 Sent note to Mr McKean, Yorkshire District Bank, Halifax, and enclosed check no 212 for £100 – gave John Booth too £25 to pay 4 bills. *A~ let me have thirty pounds for this purpose & fourteen six & pence last night which she enclosed for me to* [give to] *Mr Jubb…*

[Joseph Mann came about] Listerwick pit… Brought me 2 little nice-looking specimens of mid-band-coal… Joseph wants to see Holt… I said they must get on as fast as possible – and unless Holt hit upon a better plan, [he] must try with a hand pump to get the pit sunk as low as possible… Said everything must be got on with as quickly as possible – Joseph to inquire about the 6-horsepower engine that Holt & Thomas had to sell.

Meanwhile, Ann's charitable work at her school carried its own staffing problems:

SATURDAY 3 Fine morning… A~ read … Larder's Russian history… Then sometime with A~. Mr Hutchinson smokes in the school instead

of teaching & Mrs Hutchinson drinks... Then talking to Joseph Mann
till 6 ... Joseph says Holt lies too long in bed in a morning – not up
at 10 am yesterday...

From 6.15 to 7 walked up & down in the west tower – my study
that is-to-be. Robert & John (the two York joiners) got into the place
today, & got up one of the work tables ... & put up a small piece of
the framing for the book-shelves – surely there will be something to
be seen done next week. Dinner at 7.20 – sat reading a few pages of
vol 2 Cochrane's *Journey*.

**Anne then spent three hours 'inking over rough book accounts'. Travel excite-
ment could not, however, be suppressed, for the newspapers told of exciting
innovations:**

SUNDAY 4 Looking at maps & ... [*Morning*] *Herald* of Friday 2nd – the
steam navigation of the Danube will be open in the spring from Linz
to Odessa, Trebisond, Constantinople & Smyrna. The large steamer,
Stamboul, which is to ply between Constantinople & Smyrna will set
out on its first voyage on the 11th March...

Off to church at 2 ... at Cliff Hill in 20 mins... A~ waiting... 1
port, 1 marsala... A~ poorly tonight – bad headache.

MONDAY 5 Messrs George Harper & his 2 bondsmen, his brother & Mr
Bottomley came – referred them to Mr Parker where they would find
the [Stump Cross Inn] lease ready for signing... Said I generally kept
the leases – mentioned the term being of 3 years or 5, if they liked,
but Mr Bottomley seemed to prefer 3 – saying he would in that time
see whether the place suited him or not. I said it was [all the] same
to me, so long as I had a good blue vote.

FRIDAY 9 A~ overtook [me] a little way from Mytholm, & I walked
by her side as far as Listerwick pit... In the farmyard – John &
Sam Booth cleared out the hen-house... Came in about 6.15 – went
into the cellar – 1 marsala – at accounts till dinner at 7. A~ had
... further accounts of Mrs Hutchinson's drinking. *A~ got annoyed
because she thought me more annoyed* [about the Hutchinsons] *than she
liked – said crossly she would not give up the school. I had said, now & before,
I was afraid it would not work well at the present. However, I made no reply,
came upstairs for twenty minutes & we have neither of us said many words
since.*

While Anne controlled many initiatives, Ann's school was her main local philanthropic activity, so she set good store by it.

SATURDAY 10 Fine morning, hard frost... *A~ not right again, but I begin to take it very composedly & merely say nothing...* Then to Listerwick pit & there till after 5... Came in at 6.30 – ¼ hour in the West tower – dressed – dinner at 7.05 & sat reading German till came upstairs.

However, Anne's coded passage then told a very different story:

Plum pudding today. It struck me it was the tenth [of February], *the fourth anniversary of my* <u>connection</u> *– union? – with A~. She had remembered to order the pudding. Yet* [Little] *One made no allusion to the day. The thing struck me – 'How odd', said I to myself. It was only as I came in from my walk that I congratulated myself on her being away* [i.e. out of the house]. *Tis an incubus* [i.e. devilish nightmare] *taken off me. What a temper she has – yet the plum pudding* <u>softened me</u>. *As I came upstairs, I told Oddy to let us have a plum pudding tomorrow – & A~ shall have a bottle of malmsey madeira of which she is very fond.* Had just written the last 15 lines... Went into the cellars & got a bottle of Malmsey madeira for A~ tomorrow. Then sat reading the newspaper till 11.30.

So Anne only belatedly recalled that it was the fourth anniversary of their betrothal. [1] She tried to make amends but, perhaps so engrossed in her newspaper, it lacked real empathy

SUNDAY 11 Very fine morning... Off to church at 1.50 ... met Mr Wilkinson... The melancholy mortifying feeling that I was again too late... We were in our pew before the organ began playing... Home in ½ hour at 4.20... Went down to A~, laughing at the trick I had played [on] Edward last night – found the wine left outside his cellar-door, so locked it up in my cellar. Dinner at 6.30 – the plum-pudding & pint of malmsey madeira of which we drank & enjoyed the half. *All right – the wine excited A~ & I grubbled her well – her own bringing on, for I should not have been so inclined.*[2]

MONDAY 12 *Goodish one last night.* Fine morning... Finished Captain Cochrane's *Pedestrian Journey* vol 2, much interested. Then till 4.25 sat looking at maps (reading Murray's most excellent *Encyclopaedia of Geography* articles – Russian dominions & Tartary... Ran out at 4.35 to Listerwick pit – about ½ hour there...

In the west tower – dressed – read German till dinner 7.05 – sat over the fire talking. Speaking of Moscow, A~ said she should not like to be absent longer than 3 months. 'Then', said I, after thinking a minute or 2, 'there is an end of Moscow.' I asked if she would return with Cookson at the end of the 3 months from Hamburg, or I would see her to Hull. 'No!' A~ would rather not go at all. *Now came another silence. I read German & A~ settled accounts – & she was going off to bed when I asked for a kiss – & I began gently reasoning – quite useless. She said I should not like it if I was in her place. I tried to reason, again in vain. Followed her to her room. She said she fretted very much of late. She had done by herself [i.e lived on her own] – perhaps she had best do so again. I quietly said I was very sorry – I would not be the cause of her fretting. She had often before talked in this way – she had but to make whatever arrangement would suit her best. Poor thing – but I now take it very calmly. We shall see how it will end. I must determine & I must take the opportunity to be rid of he.*

The disjunct between reading about Tartary and Anne's relationship with Ann could scarcely be more acute.

TUESDAY 13 Sun peeping out. *A~ came, owned she had been naughty & gave me a kiss & was right. I reasoned a little – asked what was her bane [i.e woe]. She said 'temper'. I agreed & also shewed that the value of things depended on our belief in their permanence – & said that in talking of doing by herself, she played with edged [i.e. sharp] tools – and shook my confidence.* Went out about 10...

So this discussion now became less about Russian travel and more philosophical, about their different approaches to life.

¼ hour with A~. A little talk about our projected journey – nothing less than the summer should be taken. A~ should tell her aunt we thought of going to Germany, & should be away all the summer, all the fine weather. How will it end – *je n'en sais trop*. But under 6 months, there is an end of our going to Moscow – we could not be there [in] under one month at the quickest...

Came in at 6.05 – a few minutes with A~, and as long in the West tower – the shelves now put up from the west window to stairs. Dressed, dinner at 7.05 – went from the dinner table into the cellar for a bottle of old Madeira. Read aloud the London paper after tea, A~ read her French. Came upstairs at 10.50, at which hour F16°.

Friday 16. Went down to A~, breakfast at 9 – came upstairs at 10.30, *having written her copy of what she should write* [to] *her sister...*[3]

[In Halifax] went ... to Mr Parker's at 12.20 & stayed 50 minutes – signed & brought home with me the Stump Cross Inn lease to Mr George Harper... Parker then mentioned the Swan Banks colliery a complete failure – his authority so good (the crony of Jeremiah Rawson junior), did not doubt its authenticity. Mr Rawson had laid out thirty thousand pounds – and now gave up the colliery in disgust, & had given it to Jeremiah Rawson junior, to whom it would be a good thing if it made one per cent. Jeremiah Rawson junior tired of serving [i.e. selling coal to] little families & was trying to get the great consumers – Mr Edwards of Pye Nest etc. I said it would be well if the colliery did make 1 per cent – I doubted much that it would – more money must be laid out... Then asked Parker if he could get me £2,000 – 'Yes!' on landed security money that would not be called in...

After six years of mining rivalry, Anne must have felt jubilant at the utter failure of the Rawsons' colliery.[4]

Meanwhile, she wrote to elderly Lady Stuart:

Shibden Hall. Thursday 22 February 1838.

It seems to me, dearest Lady Stuart, a long time since I heard from you... I have very often thought of you since the beginning of this long, severe, and still continuing storm, and longed to know how you bore it: it is indeed very trying to everyone... But hope springs eternal, and with me too, in spite of all my disappointments.

One scheme has been swept away after another, yet still the mighty maze has never been without a plan. It is very good of you to be so interested about me. I only wish I had something to tell you that could amuse you. What will you say to my again thinking of Russia? You were against it whilst I had none but servants about me. Now that my little friend will occupy the then vacant carriage-corner, I should like to try what can be done in five or six months. Hammersley wrote me about a month ago that there were more demurs and difficulties at the Russian Embassy, than at any other. I think Lord Stuart would be so good as [to] vouch for our being <u>true</u> people. Conservatives at home – no meddlers in politics abroad – respecters of the powers that be, and quiet observers of prescribed rules. It would delight me to see you, and talk it over. My present thought is to go by steam from London to Hamburg, and thence make the best of our way onwards. As I cannot leave here before quite the end of next month, I should not care much about the sixty hours' sea voyage. The weather might be fine in April. My great anxiety is to get off – once *en route*, the rest would *s'arranger*. But do write to me, dearest Lady Stuart. I am anxious to hear a good account of you and everybody, and what good expectations are afloat in London. I have been struck of late by seeing Lord Stuart's name so often coupled with the Duke of Wellington's at this party and that...[5]

Indeed, eminent Lord Stuart could offer the key to entering Russia. Here Anne did make clear that she would be travelling with 'my little friend'. Yet again, Anne veiled her 'union' with Ann (not to mention her financial dependence). Rank must be preserved at all costs, so Ann was effectively marginalized. At Shibden, the two women usually knocked along well enough together; but their travel plans were not helped by continuing tensions, as Anne soon confided to her diary:

WEDNESDAY 28 A good deal of snow had fallen during the night... Stood ½ hour before dressing ... resolving to learn to write & read German writing as soon as I can. Then for a moment before breakfast, turned to Cochrane volume 1...

Breakfast at 9.20 in about ½ hour – then out in the stables... Parcel from Mr Bull containing his bill ... read over [it] in astonishment – £38.2.0!!!... I feel irritated to have been so taken in. Went in to A~. She thought the bill might be £20 – it seemed to us both a little like swindling? A~ owned she should feel as much annoyed and irritated as I did...

A~ poorly but more out-of-sorts – reading the lesson for the day, as I found her doing yesterday.[6] Is she going wrong again? I asked for a little comfort – a bit of petting – she began crying – I said she had no reason to fret – should not do so for me. Whatever [money] came to me, she was very well off. She could not be hurt [financially] – and she used to say she would keep me. 'Yes', she would keep me, but she could not keep the [Shibden] estate. I said quietly, 'the estate would keep itself'. But if she would make any proposal, I would come into it [i.e. go along with it] if I could. A little more passed in this strain, she not speaking. I got affected [i.e. it affected me] – said she would think of me some time & I then came away. I suppose the thing will blow over as usual. But had I not best get her to make some proposition that can be acted upon?

Ann obviously felt heavily burdened by Shibden's finances; meanwhile, Anne remained more cynical about the outcome of this dispute.

> Looking over the accounts ... till went down to A~ at her luncheon at 12.30 & sat with her till came upstairs at 2.20. From then till 4, at examination of my accounts of 1833 – *to see my real receipts & borrowings...* Then ½ hour with A~ ... dinner at 7.05. A~ read her French – tea – I read, partly aloud, newspaper. A~ wrote her journal.[7]

So February ended with their travel plans firmed up, and with Anne grown resigned to Ann's vacillating moods: her crying and then soon after 'all quite right' again. What did all this suggest about their marriage? That it would have been fine, had Anne not read Captain Cochrane's tantalizing travel books? Yet did they really have the time to visit Moscow and travel even further into Russia? And if they did not, where might they travel?

XI

How to Get Off – and Where To?

March–May 1838

March 1838

The pressure was now on: to get Listerwick working profitably so that within a month Anne and Ann could be off travelling.

FRIDAY 2 Robert Mann came to say ... about the engine made by Holt & Thomas & now on sale ... to pump the water & pull the coal. Then talked of the colliery... Ordered Robert some mutton & potatoes in the servants' hall...

Then walked forward with Robert Mann ... [he] thinks Listerwick will pay pretty well after all. Mr Rawson's colliery however ... could not go on long – & I should have a chance of buying the coal round about now at a reasonable price.[1] Rawson's colliery costs £20 a week in salaries & galloways [small horses] & engines, without reckoning anything for coals, getting & yarding [i.e. storage] & outlay... 'Suppose', said I ... 'If my coal should pay pretty well after all, I shall be thankful'...

To Mr Parker's, about ½ hour there... Parker to make further inquiries about the navigation stock – but I will not take under £420 per share...

Mrs A Walker not up when A~ arrived, had lain in bed waiting for Mr Jubb to examine her side – enlarged. Mr Jubb thinks her in a precarious state – [he] said a month ago we might go [i.e. travel] where we chose – would not say so now. Somehow, I despair of getting off on the 2nd of April.

So would their Russian travel be postponed? Ever optimistic, Anne continued her reading.

SATURDAY 3 Stood reading Cochrane's *Journey* and looking at maps till breakfast at 9.30 in about ½ hour. Then had Robert Mann – Holt will send me an estimate [for the engine]…

Meanwhile, Parker and Adam reported no difficulty in selling the navigation shares at £430.

[I] would not advise A~ to sell [her shares] under £450, but I thought she would be right to take this for all her 40 shares… I am for selling my shares now at £430, A~ so inclined also…

Owners of canal shares had to be canny. Industrial activity in Halifax remained buoyant, but the advance of the railway – so much more profitable – meant that the value of such shares would inevitably decline. Yet it was not advisable to look eager to sell, otherwise their value would fall further.

All the while, coalmining remained crucial, requiring lengthy conversations:

[Had] Joseph Mann … from 2.45 to near 5, settling & talking matters over – <u>he</u> agrees with me, it will be best to leave a good [underground] barrier against Mr Rawson… Told me Mr Holt's brother said Holt had neglected his own concerns as much as mine – he has £300 out in debts owing to him… Had the plan of the estate down respecting the barriers of coal to be left etc… Dinner at 7.15 – & sat reading Cochrane's *Journey*.

SUNDAY 4 Off to church at 1.40… No organist or singers – the organist has taken the organist's place at one of the Halifax Methodist chapels – could not get paid at Lightcliffe. The church rate meeting to be held at 3pm next Thursday…

This was a blow to the established church at Lightcliffe. It had lost its organist to the Methodists, who presumably, with larger congregations, could actually pay him!

Mrs A. Walker pretty well – I did not see her. ½ hour with A~ in our bedroom… Dinner at 6.30 – tea – read the newspaper… Kind letter tonight … from Lady Stuart de Rothesay… Hears I have had a considerable windfall! I wish I had. Came upstairs at 9.55 … rubbed A~'s back 20 minutes with spirit of wine & camphor as usual.

This rumour was presumably speculation about how Anne was funding her lavish plans, both on her estate and for travel. The Stuarts were probably not aware of Ann Walker's comparative wealth.

MONDAY 5 To Listerwick pit... Returned & home by the walk & found Holt [there] at 1 – & had him about an hour – said I had never been so annoyed as about the tubbing.[2] My sister too annoyed & inconvenienced at his not paying his rent...[3] Holt said (engineer) Holt had told him I had agreed for the steam engine – 'No!' said I, 'never did anything of the kind, as he (collier) Holt very well knew'... I was really sorry for him – he seemed at one time ... as if almost in tears. Poor fellow! My heart relented more than I chose to let appear...

Here Anne balanced sympathy for Holt with acting as an astute businesswoman: the latter won out.

Went [down] to see the new fish-market – 9 stalls – the 2 best let for £20 a year each... Then to Mr Parker's ... ordered the navigation shares (13 & a fraction) to be sold for £430 each – and returned up Old Bank... With Robert Mann ... till 7 – dressed... Dinner at 7.20 – tea. A~ read her French, [I] wrote the above of today...

Coal agreement ... as written from Holt's dictation. 'Joseph Mann & Co agree to take Listerwick pit, to sink to the soft bed coal, & the airgate pit ... for one hundred & sixty pounds. Coal head (a mine between the 2 pits) to be left 4 feet wide & 4 feet...'[4] In addition to the £160, the Manns to receive five shillings per score for every score of coal got out of the mine. Holt calculates there will be 12 corves per running yard ... =£52.10.od. The Manns [to] find everything but gin-horses. Joseph Mann to sell the coal on my account as well as he can – Holt averages it [at] 7d per load.

[marginalia] coal £52.10.od, getting £22.10.0, profit £30.0.0.

So Monday was a busy business day for Anne: Halifax, Holt, the Manns. All done at impatient speed, as if raring to set off on her travels. And Listerwick *had* to be profitable, unlike the isolated Walker pit.[5] Here, the steam engine for pumping and pulling out coal was crucial, despite arguments about costs and who would pay:

WEDNESDAY 7 Booth here – he gave me Garforth's estimate ... [for] the 6 horse-power engine... Breakfast at 9.15 – said [to A~] what Booth was come about & then joking said 'But I shall be kept.' 'Yes! But not your engineers.' Somehow a certain foolish *attendrissement* [i.e. softening] stole over me, & my words for the remainder of breakfast were few – *the tears starting. 'Well', said I, 'if the estate was sold perhaps A. B. (Mr Abbott) would make a bid – and perhaps I should bear the thing with as much composure as could be expected.' I should run away. Poor A~ was in good humour – there was no fault of hers. But how different she from me? At least I hope so. Her income, well managed, would easily set all right. But I cannot count upon anything. She has not heart to say, 'Well, never mind, we can manage.'*

Ann baulked at paying for Anne's mining engineers. This made Anne panic. Her reference to Mr Abbott making a bid seems to spring from nowhere; it perhaps drew on her fear that Marian, should she marry, might inherit Shibden.[6] Anne, however, could always find solace in her diary.

Took a few turns in front of the house... Crowther the librarian came with subscription list for a grand concert... Sent word down by Edward for Crowther to put down A~'s name & mine for one ticket each. Had A~ ten minutes – she is just gone now at 10.15 – writing my journal has done me good...

Sent for Holt... Stocks gives 4/6 a day for a one-horse cart, which goes twice a day & takes 16 loads to the Dyehouse in Washer Lane... However ... he [Stocks] is as stupid as a mule – his wife can do nothing with him – we both agreed she was far too good for him.

Stocks remained Anne's coal rival at the top of Shibden valley; carting his coal across to Halifax and down near Sowerby Bridge sounded totally uneconomic.[7]

FRIDAY 9 Tea & A~ read aloud Sir Robert Peel's <u>admirable</u> speech against the colonial policy of ministers.[8]

SATURDAY 10 Read Lardner's *Russia* vol 3 – but read disturbedly & uncomfortably, A~ came in & out – breakfast at 9.

SUNDAY 11 The ground white with a sprinkling of snow... Before & after breakfast making notes for Captain Cochrane's *Journey* vol 1, a <u>little</u> book intended for taking with me in travelling, meaning to be as little encumbered with books as possible. Dressed – off to church at 1.50...

Then 40 mins at Cliff Hill, & home about 5.30. Settled to go to call on the Stansfield Rawsons tomorrow near Huddersfield, & ordered horses to be here at 10.30 am. Wrote ... note to Messrs Parker... that I have no objection to selling the remainder of the [navigation] shares in 2 lots at the same price as those shares already sold... A~ wrote her journal & told the little domestic troubles of Cliff Hill – listened & consoled.

Stansfield Rawson might have been a brother of Anne's industrial rivals, Christopher and Jeremiah Rawson, but he and his family had three things in their favour. First, he was not directly involved in coalmining, so not an economic competitor. Second, he managed the Rawson bank's Huddersfield branch – a healthy distance away; and, though commercial, this was still a fairly respectable professional occupation. And third, his daughter Catherine was a very close friend of Ann Walker's. Or at least had been...

Monday 12 Change of dress from pelisse to *la robe* (to make calls) made me so long (1¾ hour) in dressing... Then had Mr Adam for a few minutes – signed away ... one share navigation stock £432 and 4 shares ditto at the same price £1,728 = £2,160 [minus] the broker's commission = £2,150 received this afternoon or tomorrow & paid into the Yorkshire District Bank... Told Mr Adam to sell the remaining stock (7 shares & about 1/5 share)...

Here was a useful little windfall: over £2,000 into Anne's bank account. Her planned trip to Europe looked increasingly promising, with Anne less heavily dependent on Ann to fund it.

Would today's calls be the last of the social visits to Ann's endless relatives for a while? Anne saw them as increasingly dreary: there was definitely no need to dawdle in Halifax. Rural Sowerby was better, but even so...

Off at 10.55 in the yellow carriage with A~ to make calls... Third [call,] Pye Nest at 11.40 to 12.02 – saw only Mrs Edwards ... she seemed pleased to see us & satisfied at our having called ... met Mr Edwards (at his own Lodge) returning from Halifax in his open carriage... Fifth, Mill House at 12.40 to 12.57. Mrs William Rawson & two daughters – vulgar exclamation of surprise on seeing us, but very civil. Sixth, Haugh End, Mrs Henry Priestley ... at 1.05 to 1.35. Mrs Henry Priestley very glad to see us and in good spirits at first, but ... they say she is low & nervous & not well.

Her husband had, of course, died fairly recently, and she was a long-standing friend of Anne's, and a relative of Ann. Yet:

She had the life of some Mrs Hawes on her table – an Evangelical unfit sort of book for Mrs Henry Priestley in her present state of mind – she will fall into 'a low way' if she does not take care. I advised her going to the Rhine this summer. 'Oh! No!' She must be staying – yet said, if she had a person like myself to go with, she should be glad to go, Poor soul! Can't Mrs Milne of M~ take her?[9]

Almost as bad as 'vulgar' was 'Evangelical', meaning the wrong side of the Church of England spectrum, too close to Methodism and distant from the Established Church of Revd Musgrave and Shibden.

Obviously Mrs Priestley looked up to Anne, perhaps hoping she might be a travel companion. Cosmopolitan Anne responded at her most resplendently patronizing.

Seventh ... at Thorpe at 1.45 & sat with Miss Priestley 9 minutes ... Off from Thorpe at 1.54, and eighth at Mr Stansfield Rawsons near Huddersfield at 3.18 & off from there at 5.15.[10] Mrs Rawson & two misses Rawsons (Catherine & Emma) – all very civil and all went well till Mr Rawson came in, perhaps about ½ hour before we came away.

This should have boded well, but:

As I have always considered him a man of taste & knowledge in architecture & a mild mannered agreeable person, I was glad of his coming in. He inquired how I got on with my alterations, & this led to his so disputing, disparaging, doubting, or what not, the antiquity of Shibden Hall (very unlikely, he said, that a small house like that should have the antiquity I supposed) that he evidently saw the conversation did not please me. In fact, I felt annoyed & offended at his manner – though I gently defended the antiquity of the present house as supported by internal testimony – the walls being a comparatively modern casing, the chimney being evidently put in after the original building of the wooden house etc, & the house evidently built before the use of chimneys known or put in practice here. Chimneys probably first used in the C14th... Mr Rawson then observed that there were papers of the house he lived in of 1393 (ninety something). 'Yes! But', said I, 'it is evidently this house was not then standing in anything like its present state – the style of the building is quite sufficient on that point.'

He said nothing – he was conscious the thing admitted not a question. (Did he come home from Halifax in a bad humour about something?)

On saying I had taken away the hall chamber, he proposed ornament & arched work for the ceiling, and seemed sure the hall <u>could not</u> look well without it – the beams would look awkward... But on my explaining the situation of the beams, he seemed better reconciled... I said the antiquity of the house was so far of moment [i.e. greatest importance] to me, that, but for that, I should have pulled it down at once. As it was, I merely wished to put things as nearly as possible as they used to be, not to make alterations. Additions were another matter & were done without any affectation of imitating the old style...

Mr & Mrs Rawson wondered at our sending our post-horses to the Inn & seemed to take it wrong... Mr & Mrs Rawson then pressed us to stay [for] dinner & pressed <u>disagreeably</u> much. In fact, poor A~ & I were delighted to get off at 5.15.

This was a serious row. Maybe Stansfield Rawson had come home in a bad humour. But it was also likely that he had talked to brothers Christopher and Jeremiah about the Swan Banks coal rivalry, so hearing of Anne Lister's seeming to triumph. Interestingly, he chose to quarrel about Shibden's architectural integrity and its claim to 'antiquity'.[11]

There were other layers too. Back in 1832, Anne had noted, 'Mrs Stansfield Rawson looked odd at finding me' with Ann Walker at Lidgate.[12] And Catherine may have talked to her parents once her close friend moved into Shibden, fuelling concern that Ann's wealth was being used to finance Anne's ambitions.

Back home from this complex round of social calls, Anne found relief in her colliery day book and accounts. Of these books, two would be kept by Joseph Mann, under coal steward, and one by his brother Robert, banksman.

Wednesday 14 With Robert Norton (York joiner) in the West tower till 12.30... My study in the West tower to be cupboarded... Then sorted out the *Morning Herald* from 19 August last...

To Listerwick ... & stood talking to Joseph Mann. Holt in the pit at the tubbing... Tomorrow to settle about the Engine, & coal sheds, & low mine etc.

Came in at 6.50, dressed – dinner at 7.15 – coffee for the first time I know not how long. Read the newspaper... A~ came to me about 10.50 – ¼ hour reading aloud to me her long letter to her sister & then sat adding more (& copying) till 11.45.

Thursday 15 Making extracts from Cochrane's *Journey* vol 1 till breakfast at 8.50... Went down to Holt (James) at 10 till 10.50... Mr Rawson has had some conversation with Stocks – Rawson said that his colliery had only cleared a hundred pounds last year...

Holt & George Naylor came to me at the Rock bridge – bad news – they were all in good spirits a couple of hours ago – but now the bottom plank but one of the tubbing was forced out of its place by the force of water, & all to undo again...

Had A~ a few minutes – then at *Collieries & the Coal Trade* till 4.35 ... reading respecting tubbing etc... Coffee, A~ read French – I read the newspaper. Left A~ cutting out frocks for the school.

With the Pennine rainfall exacerbating flooding problems, coalmining was never straightforward.

FRIDAY 16 To John Oates's & stood talking to him near an hour – his plan the best & least expensive ... it was all the pressure of the water... He thought £500 not too much for the total expense of 8 horse-power engine...

Called in about 3 to Thomas Greenwood [Park Farm] ... had accidentally met with Mr Rawson's old steward who had had the management of the pits 40 years, [was] turned off now, but the Rawsons allowed him something to live upon. He told Greenwood the colliery was paying fairly, but not too much – they could get coal for fifty years to come. I repeated what Rawson had said in the bank – that the colliery did not make him more than £100 last year. The old steward said it was the engine in the bottom that added most to the expense. Greenwood all for my getting coal as immediately as possible – 'Yes! But I must have an engine first. Should leave the colliery accounts to be kept by Mr Parker'... Came upstairs at 10.10... Making extracts from Cochrane's *Pedestrian Journey* vol 1. A~ came to me for a minute or 2 at 10.30.

With Anne's colliery plans almost ready, she could set off travelling soon – were it not for Ann's ailing aunt. Now help came from an unexpected quarter: Mary Priestley, W. H. Rawson's wife. It appeared that she was 'almost' brought up by Ann's parents, John and Mary Walker.

SATURDAY 17 Mr Jubb here perhaps about ½ hour – Mrs A Walker has got cold from going into the cellar, but 'is [doing] very nicely' – no organic disease. Mr Jubb thinks A~ & I may set off [soon]. I observed, before A~ came in, that she was not the only niece – and if anything did happen, A~ had done her best, & her own health required something. There was Mrs William Henry Rawson, who had been almost brought up at Crow Nest by her uncle & aunts, and she would be at hand.[13] Jubb quite agreed that we might get off – but advised A~'s not telling her aunt too long beforehand. He to write to us under cover to Messrs Hammersleys. Said we thought of the north of Germany – Leipsic fair – might be off in a fortnight – could be from Hamburg to Hull in 60 hours. Then sat with A~ at her luncheon… [A~] rode off in a snow shower to Cliff Hill.

How very convenient to 'find' a second niece, 'almost brought up at Crow Nest'. Mary Rawson could liberate Ann and Anne so they could set off on their European travels with scarce delay.[14] With a few final tweaks to her colliery plans, Anne was almost good to go, with only clothes to plan once coalmining was sorted.

Sunday 18 Susan had overslept herself & I was obliged to wait till she got out of my dressing room (blue room) and the fire did not burn – so lighted the one in the tent room (our bedroom)… Before & after breakfast, till 12.30, had Cookson, trying on all my gowns & fichus & settling about these things for the journey…[15] Off to church – took up A~ at Cliff hill – in ample time … ¾ hour at Cliff Hill – Mrs A Walker, in spite of her cold, looking very well & in good talking spirits. Home about 5.30 – stood talking to A~ in our bedroom till near 6 – half hour making extracts from Cochrane vol 1… Coffee – I read the newspaper and then left A~ writing her journal & came upstairs at 9.45.

Monday 19 Had Holt & Garforth at John Oates's settling about the engine till 8… John Oates to be consulted when necessary & to go down into the pit. I said he should go down & so would I and Holt too – we would all go. All passed off well – said I was much obliged to John Oates, but would say thank you again when we had tried the scheme & found it answered…[16]

Came in at 6.45 – went into the cellar – port marsala (& madeira to be opened in a day or 2) – dinner at 7.10… Packet this afternoon from Messrs Parker containing note saying … paid into the York District Bank at Leeds to my credit £2,155 for the five navigation shares sold … and that they expected the remainder of my shares will be sold this week – the parcel also containing the Northgate hotel lease to Mr Crossland[17] … and Thomas Greenwood's agreement for the Northgate land at £40 per annum…

So, largely thanks to selling her canal shares, Anne was finally getting her financial ducks in a row, just at the right time!

Sat looking over Journal of last year respecting A~'s Shugden Head coal – could find nothing – nor could A~, who sat with me looking over my journal & mending my stays till 11.40.

This seems a very affectionate domestic scene, Ann mending Anne's stays. Yet when they looked over Anne's diary together, it was surely just the handwritten pages that they read.[18]

TUESDAY 20 Plan of Charles Howarth's better than John Oates's… Poor Charles Howarth – he is a clever-headed, good-hearted man that can't be trusted.

WEDNESDAY 21 *A~ out of sorts – that is, out of temper, but I now care little about it & quietly leave her to herself.* A~ had Samuel Washington who brought my plan of the land for the colliery…

A little while with A~, *coming right again & quite so this evening.* Then in the farmyard… To Listerwick pit for a minute, then some time talking to John Oates – he is still for his own plan… [I] said Holt must come & speak to me.

THURSDAY 22 A good deal of snow in the night… Holt came – had seen John Oates – both agreed that Charles Howarth's plan would not do, on account of the puddling. Holt had thought of another plan which John Oates agreed would be best of all. 'Yes!' Told Holt to order it to be done…

A~ in trouble about the school – Mr Hutchinson had his nose broken (covered with sticking plaister) & said he had had a fit last night – what sort of a fit? Did the enemy enter in at the mouth? Very few scholars there today. I repeated to A~ (I had said so on her making up her mind to give him notice to quit) that were I in her place I should dismiss the school[master] before leaving home. What can girls profit from a drunken schoolmistress or the boys from a schoolmaster given to fits of whatever description? The school (or rather Mr & Mrs Hutchinson) are a sad disappointment to us.

Anne, ruthlessly rational, had a point. This school offered a contrast to Miss Patchett's in Southowram. Meanwhile, Anne continued making extracts

from Cochrane's *Pedestrian Journey*. This, with her colliery activity, kept her busy.

FRIDAY 23 A little small snow... Breakfast at 9.15 – almost immediately came Holt of the Travellers' Inn with the two petitions to Lords & Commons against beer-shops – I did not keep him waiting but signed both 'A. Lister'... A~ thought she needed not sign & I did not press it, therefore she did not sign...[19] *A~ in bad humour, I could not guess why – so took no notice – & never went near her. But she called me in on her return from Halifax..*

SATURDAY 24 A~ had S Washington – [I] had him with Holt a minute or 3 ... [about] the colliery plan... Sat with A~ at her luncheon & about an hour. *She attributed all her unhappiness in* [to] *Scotland & her sister's conduct* [i.e. response] *to my letter to her sister, saying A~ was not fit to live alone. She always thought it very hard – cried.* [I] *said she had had a glass &* [a] *half of madeira. I saw how it was – she will drink in the end, has too much today.*

So the culprit was partly madeira; and also Elizabeth Sutherland's correspondence with Anne, about Ann not being 'fit to live alone'.

SUNDAY 25 Reading *Encyclopedia of Geography* article, Tartary etc... In church 5 minutes before the service began – Mr Fenton ... preached 25 minutes from Hebrews xii 1, to bear all with patience – good sermon... [A~] had told me as we drove from Crow Nest that her aunt had asked her not to go abroad – that she (A~) might be at Cliff Hill while I was away. A~ had been disappointed & grieved – somehow I was taken quite by surprise. Yet though our journey that I, & I think A~ too, had set our heart on, must be given up, still it was no caprice of A~'s or mine; & I was at once resigned & reconciled. 'For human weal [i.e. happiness], heaven orders all events.' And I at once began to find out possible & probable advantages, & cheered up & reconciled... [A~] wanted me to go abroad without her, knowing that I really wanted to make a break here... How could I leave poor A~, at the very time she would want me most? Impossible. But said I would go & spend 2 or 3 weeks with Lady Stuart – this might save us all. Dinner at 6.35 – coffee – looked into the newspaper, but one subject engrossed us – sat talking till came upstairs at 10.20, at which hour F32° – very fine day. Then went to A~ & stood talking in our bedroom near ¼ hour.

Strangely, Anne could remain calm about this setback, as it emanated not from Ann but from her elderly aunt. This bound the two women closer together:

MONDAY 26 *Incurred a cross last night very quietly while A~ was snoring between one & two & awake till after the latter hour.* Fine morning... Told [George] of the change in our plans... Had Edward & told him the same ... then told Cookson. All evidently surprised & disappointed...

I set off at 3.30 to Hipperholme to meet A~... About 5 when I got to the school... Then walked with A~ to Cliff Hill & left her there at 5.35. I did not go in...

Dinner at 7.15 to after 8 – [A~ reported] Mrs A Walker looking remarkably well. A~ annoyed & I too at the ridiculousness of our journey being put off... Sat talking to A~ till came upstairs at 11, at which hour F37°. I got irritated about Mrs A Walker – only hoped that [she] would let us get off [soon] ... but doubted it. If it did not please Providence to take Mrs A Walker, A~ & I might remain these 10 years, too great a portion of my remaining life. A~ would sacrifice the better. Poor A~ hurt – thinking probably and apparently as I do – but durst not think so, and ... not my intention to hurt poor A~. Away with the subject – may I seldom mention or allude to Mrs A Walker in future!

Anne felt frustrated with Ann's aunt. Yet she was relatively powerless. Anne had been able effectively to banish her sister Marian, but no such solution offered itself for Aunt Walker.

TUESDAY 27 *A~'s cousin came...* Down the Old Bank to Mr Parker's ... [about] navigation shares – five sold & paid for – five more to be sold ... £432 per share ... to be paid to Messrs Parker & Adam. Asked if Mr Wainhouse would take a thousand or £1,500 – 'Yes!'[20] ... Returned up Old Bank... Went into the cellar and got 1 madeira... Read the *Halifax Guardian*.

WEDNESDAY 28 Fine morning... Mr Adam had been waiting some minutes – signed the transfers of five more navigation shares at £432... At Listerwick and in the garden – said the gardener might order one new melon frame to his own fancy & might have 4 men till the end of May...

Anne now felt sufficiently confident financially to expand her exotic garden ambitions.

Mr Harper had arrived ... settled all about the wainscotting of the tower & passages – to be done like the top of the stairs in my tower-study. All done at Northgate but the wall...

[marginalia] The gardener told me he & Sam & a lad at 10/- a week could manage the garden = 2 acres, and flower garden and walks and all.

Ann, however, saw this as pure extravagance; Anne then suffered from insomnia:

THURSDAY 29 Counted every clock [chime] last night from 12 to 3 inclusive, & did not even slumber to near 4 – the room hot, tho' I had partly taken off [i.e. damped] fire before getting into bed. *A~ wrong – I had mentioned after dinner what the gardener had said about two men & a boy, and added that if we had a gardener at Cliff Hill, it would cost us as much. I saw this was going wrong. So being sleepy, [I] leaned back in my chair & did sleep at last, but heard her sobbing aloud – soon after my eyes were closed & she hardly spoke when I went in to coffee. What a temper. Shall I escape this time or before getting abroad again?*

Wrote the above of this morning till 6.40 – then breakfast. *A~ terrible. Surely it will end in a parting this time!* Came upstairs soon after 9 – read last night's paper. Had Edward Chapman [footman]... He owned he could make more at the George Inn than his wages here... When A~ told me this morning, I asked if she would speak to him – or if I should tell him to stay – her answer took me by surprise. 'No!' she was quite indifferent about it, & seemed indifferent about everything here. I can't understand it. I asked if anything was the matter – if anyone had annoyed her – if she was well – no answer. How extraordinary – this will not do...

The exciting travel plans that had brought them together had been collapsed by Ann's aunt; and now Anne's extravagant plans for Shibden gardeners had made matters worse.

Came in about 12.30 to Mr Jubb who came to see if he could do anything for us before our setting off... I briefly explained the change of plans, adding I feared it was not for good – & that perhaps none of the parties would be really pleased by it. I feared it was not for A~'s good...

Mr Harper came… He did not wish to raise my expectations too much, but thought the Northgate hotel would be worth £700 per annum at the end of the 5 years… Harper valued … my present outlay at £8,000 and rent to be £1,200 (per annum) for the next 5 years. It is a terrible job – Harper owned that he should do as I did – not paint the Casino in the £200 way first intended. 'No! I had laid out enough', I said.

Out with Harper … asking him to draw me up his opinion of the antiquity of Shibden Hall – he says the hall is very old – before the Tudor time, for in that era the timber houses were sat on stone walling as a high as a man… Harper said he would give me an imaginary sketch of the hall as he supposed it was more anciently before the alterations of walling… Said I thought I could prove it to have been an inhabited house 4 centuries ago…

So the spat with Stansfield Rawson was not forgotten. To Anne, Shibden's claim to antiquity remained absolutely crucial.

Dinner at 7.10 – Edward gone – Susan waited – nor A~ nor I spoke, except to ask her what sort of pudding. I was sleepy after my restless night last night, & on leaving the dining room came upstairs to the blue room & lay down on the bed & slept comfortably till 10.25. *A~ terrible. I shall have a thousand pounds more to pay, I see, for Northgate. My thoughts during the day restless. I must be off as immediately as possible. This is no time for dawdling. I must lay out no more [money]… My thoughts turn to living quietly in or near Paris – the sooner I get rid of A~ the better. At all rates, she will not add much to my happiness. What a temper that has thus blighted all prospect of comfort with her!*

Friday 30 Very fine morning… Breakfast at 9 in about ¼ hour, then went upstairs & read last night's paper. *A~ still wrong, so I said nothing, but that she did not need [to] wait for me; & off she went, to my great relief.* Went out about 10.30…

Sauntered to the top of the hill & down the old Wakefield Road into Old Bank & thence to Mr Parker's… The last 5 navigation shares will probably be paid tomorrow; Parker had agreed to pay Mr Wainhouse on my account £1,500… Navigation share market was getting very dull…[21] I spoke of Northgate as a terrible job – I had always calculated a certain amount of loss, but this calculation would be doubled… Somehow his great care of the Crosslands in this business has not quite satisfied me – he owned today for the first time that they could hardly fail to make money.[22] I thought to myself as I returned up the Old Bank, 'If heaven spares the place & me, I will see what I can make of it at the 5 years end...'

Then at 5 at Listerwick pit & first time [I] went down. 1¼ hour in the bottom with George Naylor & Holmes[23] at the tubbing... Watched George Naylor solder in one of the bolts... Expensive & troublesome as this tubbing is, the water might be made very valuable.

Anne understood the mighty power of steam engines and their reliance upon water supply. On her first trip down into Listerwick, she stayed an impressive 75 minutes.

Came in at 6.55 – went into the cellar, 1 port, 1 marsala. *A~* [came]... *and she afterwards talked a little – & she was coming round. I have been graver ever since, but have talked & calculated for her about her farming & have perhaps seemed too good* [i.e. too helpful?]. *She cannot bear* [i.e. deserve?] *spoiling. However, I shall not forget this...* I am sadly bilious tonight... Talking & coffee.

Anne was calculating fairly regarding how much to help Ann with her estate farms.

SATURDAY 31 Sat with A~ ... read over her letter to her sister. *Got* [her] *quietly right again without any thinking been said about it.*[24] A~ off at 3.10... Some time at Listerwick ... stood talking to John Mann in the cabin... He fears the railroads will hurt the coal trade hereabouts...[25] Sat reading Rhind's *Elements of Geology* that came from Whitley's tonight... At accounts – I find I have already [spent] £8,000+ for Northgate... Terrible – I feel out of sorts with Mr Parker for turning all the custom of the county against me in letting it. Perhaps 'tis well. I think of getting all settled with him and having no account [i.e. dealings] at all with him. At last, I veer round to taking S Washington in preference to Parker... I feel tired, wearied, worn tonight – annoyed at my affairs... I seem not to myself to have less sense than the many – *au contraire*, and yet I have acted like a fool?

What a month March had been for Anne, especially the last few days. Her relationship with Ann was on-and-off; their travel plans put on hold; their destination uncertain. If Anne could get away, would it be on her own, with just a trip to London for a few weeks? In which case, goodbye Moscow!

April 1838

March had ended rather dismally for Anne. Her plans to 'get off' were desta-bilized, her relationship with Ann remained fragile. Could April make things better?

Sunday 1 A~'s messenger [came] with her letter to her sister, arrived about 9.30 – it took me 25 minutes to read and seal and send off the letter. F42° at 10 – stood looking into *Wanderings by the Loire* that came last night till breakfast about 11, and sat downstairs till 1.40 reading the first 80 pages Rhind's *Age of the Earth*, interesting little work...[1]

With Charles Darwin's revolutionary research still little known outside male scholarly circles, it still seemed possible to call a book on such a controversial topic a 'little work'.[2] Then without pause, Anne set off to church.

A godsend not to have to return to Cliff Hill after church... Home at 5.15 – sat about ½ hour with A~... Dinner at 6.30 and afterwards for about an hour making extracts from Cochrane's *Journey* vol 1 (Siberia).

For Anne, even just reading about exotic travel to remote places seemed more engaging than Ann's company. This did not make for the most joyful of birthday celebrations:

Tuesday 3 Fine cold morning, F31° at 7.05 and 39° at 9. *My forty-seventh birthday. A~ [all] right, but who can tell how long she may continue? My most joyless birthday...* Breakfast at 9 in about ½ hour.

Anne then turned her attention to stone quarrying, discussing it with a local dealer called Bentley. Industry needed coal, but of course little could be built without stone. Anne showed herself more intrepid than the stone dealer:

At Listerwick Pit soon after 3 – [I] went down for ¾ hour or 50 minutes. Bentley went away on my going into the pit – he durst not go down. Found John Oates in the bottom – the tubbing are but 4 planks in height – will be done on Thursday...

    Took Bentley to Sunwood quarry to value the Delf hill [stone] & give me his opinion what I had best do...[3] Asked Bentley what he would [charge to] manage the quarry for me for & keep the accounts, & sell what [stone] I did not want. He said he would go [to the quarry]

2 or 3 times a week, & manage all for 5/- a week. But he would [sub-] let the delving [i.e. digging] – he would find [a man] who would keep a daily account of what was got and what sold, who could do it for 6d a week extra... [I] said I would see Booth, & let Bentley know my determination [i.e. decision], but desired him to set a [stone-]dresser on immediately at Hipperholme quarry...

Dinner at 7.15 – asleep on the sofa – coffee at 10. Came upstairs at 10.15 and wrote all but the 2 first lines of today till 11.15.

So ended Anne's 'most joyless' birthday. She continued to record the most intimate details in code.

WEDNESDAY 4 *My cousin came very gently just before breakfast...* A~ off to Halifax before 11, *I pothering a pair of old stays – wish I could cut out my own corset.* Had begging letter from stage-players brought by some woman – told Oddy to send her away, saying I never attended to things of this sort from strangers and burnt the letter.

For Anne, kindness was something offered to friends and neighbours, servants or tenants, not to importuning strangers.

SATURDAY 7 Had note from Mr Parker per messenger enclosing the balance of my last sale of navigation shares, and the account of £1,500 paid to Mr Wainhouse... Came upstairs and looked over the packet from Mr Parker containing £215 in Bank of [England?] paper [i.e. notes], one fifty, one ten, the rest fives. £1,500 paid to Mr Wainhouse and £440 paid to Yorkshire District Bank at Leeds. *Put the balance into the pocket of my travelling bag...* Wrote note [thanking Parker] for note and packet...

With A~, walked by her side as far as Listerwick pit till 5.45. *I had rung for Oddy to take charge of my note. A~ came up as I was giving it to O~. Fancied I was saying I know not what, and I immediately afterwards found A~ in the north parlour in an agony of tears and suspicions. She said I should break her heart. 'Poor thing', thought I, as I staid to get her right – and lastly gave her a glass of madeira and a biscuit. What will be the end of it all? I will be off at least for a while as soon as I can.*

When it came to money, Anne appeared to trust her servants (here, Oddy) more than she trusted Ann. Yet money secrets could be the worst betrayal of a partnership. Ann appeared to feel marginalized at Shibden. No wonder she felt agonized about Anne's transactions.

Otherwise, Anne's home life continued as normal: she read a new edition of Bakewell's *Geology*[4] and she kept a careful eye on Listerwick costs. However, Ann's financial suspicions of Anne refused to fade away:

> Dinner at 7.05. *Unluckily, just before leaving the dining room,* [I] *laughed and said nobody flattered me so little or scolded me so much as she did. She said I had said enough ... and got wrong from that moment...* A~ went to bed at 10.10, leaving me to make coffee for myself – had two cups as usual and came upstairs at 10.25... *Went in to A~, found her in bed and Cookson curling her hair – asked if she would* [like] *some wine and hot water. 'No' was the answer in that well-known tone of temper I cannot now mistake. Surely it is impossible to get on with her. But I really take it calmly nowadays.* Sat reading ½ hour Bakewell's *Geology* till 11.05.

You knew where you were with geology (or at least you thought you did). And, of course, Anne's other consolation was correspondence with her women friends, including hints about far-flung travel:

TUESDAY 10 *Somehow, I think more of A~ than she deserves. I wish well rid of her.* Looking over Bakewell and De la Beche (Geology) till 9.[5] Then breakfast and sat downstairs talking till 10. Soon afterwards sat down at my desk and wrote ... to Lady Stuart de Rothesay:

My dear Lady Stuart

I really cannot imagine how more than a month has slipped away since your kind congratulations on my beginning to see my way out of England. I had arranged everything, and fixed the day, when a very unexpected circumstance, but not a <u>windfall</u>, upset all my Russian plans, and tied me down here for some time longer... However, I am fast recovering from my disappointment, and busy planning again... Perhaps I cannot be quite off till near Xmas; but I can be away [sooner] for a little while; and I have just written, and offered myself for two or three weeks to dear [elderly] Lady Stuart, promising her and myself to have nothing to do but sit and talk, and leaving her to name whatever time she likes best, after the end of this month. I shall send my carriage to the coach-maker, to have whatever done to it that may be necessary for a long journey; and my manservant shall return home. It was only yesterday I was able to decide on this...

I should like to know the real value of conservative triumphs...

Believe me, my dear Lady Stuart, very truly yours, A. Lister...[6]

Anne then wrote to Lady Vere Cameron in similar vein, adding 'give a kiss for me to little Sibella, and to little Louisa too'. As usual in these artful letters, there was no mention of Ann. Yet surely the 'very unexpected circumstance' undermining their travel plans had been triggered by Aunt Walker's poor health.

Copied my letter to Lady S de R. Then A~ came to me all in the dolefuls about a handkerchief frill. Tried to get her right. She [said she] *had been very hardly used twice, by me and now by her aunt. Never thought* [now] *of going to Cliff Hill as she had done – could not bear* [it].[7] *When she came here, thought of going abroad. And when I said I had offered her to go away to any friends or do anything I could, she said she did not like to go with* my *servants. I said she had the whole management* [of them]. *I said I had nobody to advise* [consult] *with –* [she] *might write to her sister. 'No, that would be very hard.' 'Well', said I, 'if I could but have my own way, I should not fear.' 'Indeed',* [she said] *but she did not like to be an automaton.*[8]

I was very calm and quiet – and said, by and by, she must forgive me if I did not forget the word 'automaton'. I *would not break her heart, nor use her hardly* [i.e. harshly], *nor make her an automaton. These things could be easily settled – but every sensible* [person] *kept up appearances as well as they could.*

She sat for all the while on my knee. I begrudged the time and said I must seal my letters and go out. She had before declined reading them. She now said, as [she] *had waited so long, she might as well read them. Her curiosity got the better* [of her]. *She made no remark nor did I. I hope I shall be rid of her by and by. Had I not better remain a little with Lady Stuart, if I can with any comfort? At least I had best not return to A~…*[9]

The repetition of the word 'automaton' is striking, as is Ann's sitting during this conversation on Anne's knee, usually a position of intimacy and trust.

I made my own coffee and sat reading the Halifax Guardian till 10.30… I looked very grave at dinner. A~ had a headache – temper-sick, so I let her go off to bed – & have taken no notice. I must be rid of her, be it as it may. Her bad temper, vulgar pride and littleness of mind – would be an insupportable drag upon me for the rest of my life.

Surely I shall get on some way. I dread the loneliness of it, but heaven will provide, even against this in some way. Had A~ been barely tolerable, I could have got on. Perhaps I am obliged to her aunt for making me this opportunity of getting off. Does A~ suspect my thought of not returning to her? Cunning & suspicious as she is, does she think that I hope not to trouble her long?

'Vulgar pride and littleness of mind' seemed very harsh words to use about your partner. Could there be any going back after this? Certainly, Anne seemed to cling to her hope of a London visit. She then immediately turned to colliery matters. It had been a long emotional day, which Anne ended by writing:

Has A~ thought much of losing the forget-me-not ring I gave her? Then read Bakewell's *Geology* for 10 minutes till 11.35.

WEDNESDAY 11 Talking to John Booth – to brew every 3 weeks, 46 gallons… Minute or 2 at Listerwick pit in returning, finding fault with John Mann's boy for beating Maynall, the gin horse, over the head.
　　Came in about 12.45 – sat with A~ at her luncheon – some talk… This led to the subject of her being ill etc, allusion to what she said yesterday, and my deep regret that it was so totally out of my power to be any use to her… A little explanation, calm and gentle on my part – no wish of mine to make automaton [of her]… Poor A~, who seldom stoops to reason, took refuge in her usual silence, and walked off to the north parlour – probably to waste her health & happiness in unnecessary tears. 'How melancholy!' I said in sorrow, 'that as it was so totally out of my power to do her any good – I was of no use. Perhaps I was better out of the way than in it.' Poor soul! She sees all through a false medium – she thinks herself ill-used! <u>What</u> can I do? Had just written so far at 1.50 – *heard her in her room and just went to say I had come to ask how she was. Poor thing, her temper had given way and all got right again! All this is tiresome wearying work to me. But my mind is made up. I will be the disaster or be off.*[10] *She promised to be a good Little One and do as I told her. Poor thing – she is little fit to be left to herself.* With A~ from 1.50 to 3.

'A good Little One' promising to 'do as I told her' surely sounds like a relationship with a very unequal dynamic. Perhaps such a dynamic was not unusual when there was a large age gap, one partner with so much more world experience than the other?

GOOD FRIDAY 13 Off to the church at 10.05… Drove to Cliff Hill – Mr Wilkinson arrived about 1.05 and in about 10 minutes administered the sacrament to Mrs Walker and A~ and myself. Then sat talking and eating his cake and wine till about 2.30. Then A~ and I walked about, looking at her new walk… Home about 3.15 – changed my pelisse, put on my old one & everyday dress… Booth came after 4…

Went with him to John Oates's and sat there talking over the [colliery] plans ... thinks the coal trade coming this way.

SATURDAY 14 Had stood before dressing, reading over the letter to Mrs Sutherland and making a little explanatory addition – and looking into the *Morning Heralds* for an article on the fine arts for A~ to see – Fuseli's lectures at the Royal Academy...[11]

Settled with the gardener... Letter tonight, franked by Lord Stuart, from Lady Stuart, Whitehall – will be very glad to see me at the Lodge [Richmond]... *No mention of length of time – perhaps I shall find a fortnight too long...*

Joseph [Mann] sinking (Listerwick pit) till 10 tonight ... has got to the second hard band [of coal], and not a drop of water – very good sign – we shall probably bottom the pit without difficulty. Supposing Halifax and its vicinity to maintain 20,000 room fires... Suppose ½ the quantity to be supplied by Wyke [Bradford], by canal and sundry places... Then 20 acres remain ... to be wrought by Rawson, Holt, Wilson, Stocks ... and myself. Rawson cannot do much more ... Holt and Stocks are distant from the town... It seems probable that I may be able to sell by and by, and when well established, 4 or 5 acres a year, or <u>perhaps</u> more if my coal is of as good quality as is expected.[12]

EASTER SUNDAY 15 Breakfast at 11.10 and sat downstairs reading the *Quarterly Review* till 1.50 – excellent article on animal magnetism, and another on Spanish banditti – very interesting. Off to church at 1.55... Having made our visit before church (Mrs A Walker well as usual), returned home direct... [A~] read her letter from her sister that came last night as we returned – Mrs Sutherland wrote very properly on the subject of Mrs A Walker's having so deranged [i.e. disrupted] our continental [travels], thinking it hard upon A~...

This sympathetic letter from Ann's sister would be the crucial trigger in reinvigorating their travel plans.

Sat talking in the dining room till 8.15. [I] proposed our going to Paris for 2 or 3 weeks, and then A~'s returning home and leaving me to pay my visit to Lady Stuart. A~ thinks Mrs A Walker poorly – really may suffer from the hot weather when it comes. It seemed to me we had better take [i.e. seize] the moment and be off for a little [while] without saying a word about it, and we should be more in the way [i.e accessible?] at Paris than in making (as we talked on

271

Saturday) a tour about the south-eastern coast or in Cornwall; A~ coming and joining me in London after my visit to Lady Stuart. A~ agreed – I proposed being off tomorrow fortnight, the 30th inst. Settled to be off about 2 pm on that day, not breathing a syllable about it to anyone but to Mr Jubb on the previous Sunday morning; to Mrs A Walker in the afternoon on returning from church and merely telling the servants to be ready and ordering the horses for London.

So at long last it was now settled: to set off unobtrusively for Paris in a fortnight.

MONDAY 16 Thinking of our journey – go by Ostende or Antwerp as the packets may suit [us] best ... from Antwerp to Paris by Brussels. Making extracts from Cochrane's *Pedestrian Journey* – Siberia – vol 1...

For the indefatigably adventurous Anne, Paris would have to suffice, rather than more ambitiously walking in Cochrane's eastward footsteps, as she so longed to do. She took consolation in a long colliery talk with the Manns in the Listerwick pit cabin.

A~ wrote to Miss Rawson, and Mr Buckle to send her the wills next week.

TUESDAY 17 Robert [Mann] is of John Oates's opinion as to the endless chain – and I should clear 4d a load. Dressed – dinner at 7.20 – coffee – read the newspaper... [David] Booth brought packet from Mr Harper ... asked if I would light the Casino with gas. 'No!'...

Long talk this afternoon as I returned from John Oates's with Mr Crapper who was returning from the great Conservative dinner (at 5 pm yesterday at Leeds, present 1,140 diners) – Lords Wharncliffe, Mexborough, Maidstone, Sir Francis Burdett etc. Crapper and about 30 from Halifax... Rubbed A~'s back with spirit of wine and camphor 20 minutes.

So it counted for naught how much land Anne owned, how vigorously she doorstepped her tenants at elections, or how much her coal could produce. Politics had become a male domain: women were totally excluded from attending the great Conservative dinners.[13]

WEDNESDAY 18 Stood reading ... then dressed... [A~] had David Booth – she doubts whether she is liable to make up the damage done by the flood at Water Lane mill – Booth's estimate of this work = £50.

THURSDAY 19 Fine morning... Sat reading *Quarterly Review* (July 1837), review of Laborde's *Arabia* till 10 – then out all the rest of the day... [A~] had been checking accounts... *I wrote her rough draft of her summary of the account and letter to Washington on returning him the account...*

Holt came before 12 and we stood talking till after 1 under two great yew trees. Listerwick pit bottomed early this morning – a specimen of the coal sent up before breakfast – of very excellent quality... determined to have an endless chain, with which determination Holt seemed quite satisfied... Holt said the main gates should be 4 foot high and 4 foot wide ... said he had no doubt the colliery would make a £1,000 a year but not at first...

Dressed – dinner at 7.20. A~ poorly – said she was tired – worn out – went to bed at 9 – I made coffee – sent her a cup after she was in bed – read the newspaper... From 10.40 to 11.15 sat reading the *Review* and the article on Laborde's *Journey through Arabia* etc. – very interesting.

FRIDAY 20 Some time talking to Joseph Mann between 1.00 and 2.00, and walked with him from the Hall to the pit. He begins work at 2 pm and works his shift till 10 pm. The coal is of excellent quality – but the bed is only 17 inches thick. But John Oates said it would average five loads to the yard, nine loads would weigh a ton.

SATURDAY 21 At 11.00 A~ and Hinchcliffe and David Booth and I all walked to Listerwick Pit and went down into it.[14] A~'s first time of ever going down into a pit. Christened the pit Listerwick Pit, I laughing and saying A~ was godmother, Hinchcliffe and Booth the two godfathers, and I [the] parson. A quarter of an hour at the bottom. A~ and I went down and came up together in a corve. She behaved very well, showed no fear, and seemed much interested. She and I each gave Joseph Mann a sovereign towards the christening fee for the men...

After all the long, hard work underground, this was indeed a triumph worth celebrating with due ceremony.

I sat with A~ at luncheon till after 1. *Writing her copy of letter to Mr William Grey to ask if she was liable to the repairs at Water Lane mill...* Took Robert [Mann] to look about at Sunwood quarry and Hipperholme quarry. *Told him I should be off next Monday or Tuesday – but he was not to name it to anybody*... Sat reading downstairs last *Quarterly Review* till 9.40, finished the article on the travels of Plato – sleepy.

Sunday 22 Off to Cliff Hill ... home at 5.15... Stood 20 minutes talking to A~ in our room. Mrs Walker seems to have a presentiment and fear of our going – had rather knocked herself up yesterday by going into the cellar – but seemed to me well as usual today. A~ determined we shall get off this time... A~ had letter from Mr Buckle with wills; left her writing her journal... Was looking over my writing case when A~ came up at 11 with terribly long frightening face, and 'What do you think!!!' Wondered what calamity had befallen us – a relief to me to hear that Cookson had had a letter tonight to say her mother was alarmingly ill – to go home tomorrow, little chance of going with us on Tuesday week. I immediately thought of taking Oddy and leaving Mrs Briggs here. A~ sat talking till near 12.

Monday 23 *A~'s cousin came tonight*... Mr Jubb to see A~'s face, and Mary, the little waiting maid, [and] footman. A few minutes with Mr Jubb – he will come again on Thursday morning – did not tell him of our intended journey...

Holt would have all one-horse carts... The coal to be sold at the pit at 9d per load – should be sold in Halifax at 1/-.Therefore, the more I can cart myself the better – the quality of Listerwick pit better than Lightcliffe, [so] that much [of my coal] will go Hipperholme way...[15]

Competition over quality and price was finely calibrated among local coal owners.

Stocks 'melancholy' – has only low bed loose that will last him about 3 years – and then [he] must set up an engine and lift his water 50 yards. Now all is to go right – Messrs Holt, Holmes and <u>self</u>! are to be all agreeable and reasonable. *Eh bien! Nous verrons*... Had Joseph Mann for near 2 hours, till 5.29 – talking all over...

A~ just returned and gone into her room – with her a minute or 2 – then out in the farmyard... Dinner at 7.10 – coffee – from 9.20 to 10.10 in the wine cellar – laying in sawdust the 4 dozen [bottles] sherry from York – and 11 bottles currant wine made by Cordingley, in the same compartment as A~'s 15 elder[flower], 16 raisin quarts and 11 ditto pints, and below close to the door left on entering, 22 red currant, 15 ditto and 13 orange – and on the opposite side 5 cider.

So Shibden now had an enviably full wine cellar! This domestic munificence seemed to augur well for Anne and Ann as, in the previous fortnight, a conjunction of separate events had combined to enhance their travel chances. On Sunday, Ann had joined Anne in being 'determined we shall get off this time'. Yet they still did not tell Mr Jubb of their intended journey. It was to be kept secret

So now, Anne's earlier impatience with Ann's 'littleness of mind', the quarrels and tears were all somehow forgotten. The final piece of the jigsaw puzzle was, of course, Mr Jubb's visit on Thursday:

THURSDAY 26 Had Mr Jubb between 11 and 12 – [we] mentioned our going on Tuesday – he recommended Carlsbad for baths (vapour baths) for A~. Too far off – I mentioned Aix en Savoie or en Provence, and she mentioned Baden Baden.[16] Jubb to call at 8 or before on Monday evening next…

The doctor's imprimatur further invigorated Anne and Ann's travel plans. For surely a visit to one of Europe's celebrated spas would be truly beneficial for Ann's health? However, if they were indeed to set off in just five days, their travel arrangements must be put into action fast. Anne as usual never wasted a minute.

Off to Halifax… A minute at Mr Parker's… Then to Whitley's – ordered 25 quills, 3 bottles of ink, and 12 small rough books… Left my banking book at the District Bank, and went to Mrs Briggs – asked her to come for a few weeks on Tuesday afternoon. 'Yes! With pleasure' – the market cart to go for her any time after 12 at noon.

Then Anne rapidly swept a final eye over Listerwick pit and the men (John Oates, Robert Mann and others) working on her estate.

FRIDAY 27 A~ had letter on Wednesday night from Mr William Gray – to say she was not bound to repair the damage done by the flood to Water Lane mill… Samuel Washington to inform the tenants on Saturday. Did not change my pelisse – dinner at 7.05 (went into the cellar – 1 sherry) – asleep sitting on the sofa while A~ and Mr Gray sat talking over plan of alterations at Cliff Hill…

In her last few days at Shibden, Anne maintained a frenzy of industrial activity, mainly over stone and coal, seeing the tenants concerned, paying bills and settling accounts.

SATURDAY 28 Sauntered home along the brook all the way by Dumb Mill bridge to Mytholm mill & home by Listerwick about 4.30. Found A~ dressing – ¼ hour with her – she rode off to Cliff Hill at 4.45 – had told Oddy of going with me to London – Oddy much pleased – promised to keep the secret till Monday. I not to go to church tomorrow, but stay at home and get ready...

It was 7 pm before I had despatched the letter to 'Messrs Hammersleys, Bankers, London', asking them to get my passport visaed, it being my intention to embark in London for Antwerp on tomorrow week and proceeding thence by Brussels to Paris, taking with me my niece, Miss Walker and two servants (Susan Oddy and George Wood). Letter also to 'Messrs Pearce and Baxter, Coachmakers, Longacre, London' ... also to 'Mrs Hawkins, 26 Devon Street, London', expect being in London on Thursday evening to dine – shall be glad if Mrs Hawkins can take me in for 2 or 3 days ... (myself, Miss Walker and 2 servants as usual).[17]

Significantly, Anne presented Ann here as her niece rather than companion.

SUNDAY 29 [Everything] all done up ready in my drawer with French money etc in A~'s chest in our room... About 3 began to prepare my linen etc for portmanteau. A~ back by 5 and staid with me an hour... Dinner at 6.30.

MONDAY 30 *Washing cousin stocking, though very little...* The ground white and snow falling... Had A~ and then Oddy ... chose out gowns for Oddy to take with her... Dinner at 7 – Mr Jubb came almost immediately. A~ with him for a few minutes – then had him in the dining room while we finished dinner. Sat talking after he left us till near 9... Gave Mr Jubb A~'s address, to the care of Messrs Hammersleys, Bankers, London – ended by agreeing that he need not write unless there was something particular to write about or unless there was anything we could do for him...

F35° now at 10 pm. From then to 3 in the morning, at the colliery accounts (finished them) and hunting over old account books for London and Paris addresses, and copying the last 4 letters into business letters book etc. A~ did not come upstairs until 2.30 – terrible work – not any packing done.[18] How shall we get off tomorrow I know not, considering all the business we have to do with Samuel Washington.

After this strange and difficult month plagued by so many quarrels and tears, their travel plans had rematerialized quite suddenly. And, thanks to Ann's poor health and conversation with Dr Jubb, their destination suddenly swivelled southwards, heading down through France to one of Europe's celebrated spas.

Yet there was still so much to do.

MAY 1838

With their departure imminent, there was a myriad of commands to be issued.

TUESDAY 1 A~ had Samuel Washington & I had Booth & Joseph Mann & sent them (while I breakfasted) to Listerwick to see about the engine chimney being carried up against John Oates's house end... I then had Samuel Washington & Booth & Holt till near one... Booth quite astonished at my going so suddenly. Gave him a check for £150 and left all the rest to him & Sam Washington...

S. Washington had dined in the housekeeper's room – not gone till about 3 pm – then sent John Booth to Halifax to pay bills... Note to Mr MacKean ... enclosing check for £60, & desiring twenty of this to be given to the bearer & the rest sent in the bag...[1]

We had hoped to get off at last this evening – talked it over – ordered dinner at 6 but not able to sit down to it till near 8! Put away newspapers etc, and packed by snatches – persistently interrupted from the time of sending John off at 4.30. Had Robert Mann with several bills at 6 – and George Naylor, carpenter and paid him for yesterday and today at the rough oak fancy railings along the Lodge road...

Went into the cellar ... a couple of hours before setting off & got 1 sherry, brought with us... Locked up the keys with several others, in the right-hand drawer of the oak painted chest standing in the library passage – and brought away 1 pint bottle malmsey madeira from the bureau in the blue room.

Dinner – coffee immediately... From about 9 to after 10, at accounts – then began to pack my imperial [i.e. travelling trunk].

Both Anne and Ann then stayed up all night packing, with Ann still working at her school accounts.[2] Then, at this momentous time, a new person entered their lives: Bluemantle, the official specializing in pedigrees, that is, family trees of the elite.

WEDNESDAY 2 A~ had done her [packing] and now sat working at, & finishing, her pedigree for Mr Harrison Bluemantle,[3] which took her till near 3 on Wednesday morning, & then afterwards sat at her school-accounts – so that we both sat up the whole night. I called John at 4, and desired him to call George & order horses to be here at 6.30, hoping to be off by 7 or soon afterwards.

Then at 4, looked into my Journals for the deaths to be entered in my pedigree by Mr Harrison...

My uncle Joseph Lister, obit a few minutes past one am, Saturday 8 November 1817.

My mother died at 2 am, Thursday 13 November 1817.

My aunt Lister, my uncle Joseph Lister's widow, died 9 pm, Monday 4 February 1822.

My uncle Lister (James Lister) my godfather and to whom I owe all I have, died Thursday 26 January 1826... At 1.05 pm, my uncle James Lister was first found by Cordingley about 9 am or soon after, lying dead on the floor of his bedroom ... the impression is still vivid in my mind.

My father Jeremy Lister died Sunday 3 April 1836 at 4.45 am, the anniversary of my birthday.

My aunt Anne Lister, my godmother, who also gave me all she had & loved me much, died as I stood quietly at her bedside, Monday 10 October 1836.

This lovingly tender moment underlines the huge significance Anne gave to her Lister ancestors. For Anne, dynastic continuity at Shibden counted for so much.

Breakfast at 7... Siding & dressing. Just saw Mrs Briggs for a minute or 2 & gave her some outdoor keys – & gave John Booth 3 ditto. Mrs

Briggs & her daughter arrived yesterday evening by the market cart which John took for them – to stay & take care of the house till our return. At last, all right (A~ busy to the last at her papers, books or 1 thing or other) and off at 10.05 am, taking with us Mrs Oddy & George (Wood, the groom), not having intimated to them or to anyone our intention of embarking in London for Antwerp & thence going by Brussels to Paris. Oddy delighted to be taken – George all on the alert & equally pleased. Put up for him (on the carriage seat under the cushions) the almost new undress black coat that was Joseph Booth's.[4]

It might seem odd that, while arrangements had been made earlier for Mrs Briggs and her daughter to look after Shibden, Mrs Oddy and George Wood were only now, almost as an afterthought, asked to leave home and accompany Anne and Ann to Europe.

Not a moment to write journal of yesterday (or this morning) during the whole 24 hours. But thankful to be off at any hour – never stirred out yesterday ... nor on Monday. Therefore saw the Lodge road railings the first time *en passant* this morning – grotesque [i.e. picturesque] & pretty. Mr Gray's taste <u>always</u> good?...

Horses from the Northgate hotel & Felix & his fellow horse took us by the Northowram road in 2.20 hours, in spite of ... [it] having rained more or less all the day.[5] Heavy shower just before our entering Doncaster at 3.50 pm...

Enter Bawtry [beyond Doncaster] at 5 pm – just as I finished writing (in the carriage) these memoranda in pencil... At Grantham at 10.50 & stopt for the night – tea – came upstairs at 11.50 – in bed at once.

THURSDAY 3 Good bed & comfortable room, & refreshed by our 2 or 3 hours sleep. Off from Grantham at 6.15 – and stopped at Stamford to breakfast at 9.20. Bell Inn – good breakfast – very nice chamber maid... Off again at 10.14... [Wrote to] Mrs Briggs at home ... & wrote to M~ & to Marian, and A~ wrote copy of letter to her sister. Today, as yesterday, we both slept a good deal...

However, when they arrived in London they found that Mrs Hawkins, apologizing very civilly, was unable to take them in.

[She] had taken us an apartment at Crawley's Hotel... Alighted at Crawley's, the so-called York Hotel, at 9.55. Very nice large sitting room *au premier* looking onto Albermarle Street & well furnished – a nice bedroom opening into small room with French bed serving for my dressing room. Oddy very fairly near – quite within reach – George, too, in the house – very well satisfied. Had written & ordered dinner – nothing appeared but soup – so had each a basin of it & had tea immediately afterwards – and went upstairs about 11.30.

It had been a hectic couple of days. However, by staying in Albermarle Street in Mayfair they were at one of London's most fashionable addresses. And, as had happened before, their sexual relationship warmed as they were now away from Shibden.

FRIDAY 4 *Good kiss last night.* Fine morning – waited for the hairdresser. A~ & I long in dressing & not downstairs till 11.20 – breakfast. Very nice clean (new) carriage & civil coachman & good horses from Pearce the coach-maker. Out about 12.30 – drove to 114 Park Street, Hutton tailor, & ordered groom's coat & waistcoat & pair of trowsers (all of mixed cloth) for George… Then drove about seeking Miss Lloyd (recommended by Mrs Lawton, whose name we never mentioned), dressmaker, Upper Brook Street – found her in Lower Brook Street, no 56. A~ took her a dress to make up – had her measurements taken. Perhaps Miss Lloyd may suit our purpose – hurried off. A~ to be at dentist, 42 Albermarle Street at 2 – took up Oddy & set down A~ & her a few minutes past 2.

With errands done, and Ann sitting captive in the dentist's chair, Anne was free to enter her own friendship circles. Luckily, all these social visits were nearby. Yet, as with the hotel, Anne had apparently not been expected on this particular day.[6]

I drove off to Whitehall – Lady Stuart gone. Then drove to 4 Carlton Terrace – admitted – found Lady Stuart de Rothesay & Louisa sitting with them. Surprised but glad to see me – soon went into luncheon & helped twice to vermicelli soup. Lady Eastnor & one of her younger daughters came in & then Mrs Dundas. Sat 1/2 hour very comfortably. Lady Stuart at East Combe… Lady Stuart de Rothesay wanted me to put off my journey for a fortnight or longer & go with Lady Stuart to the Lodge. Said I really could not do this – very sorry – too unwell to go to agreeablize.[7] Had thought of getting well & then trying to be agreeable. The Stuart de Rothesays have some thought of letting their house for the Coronation to Marshall Soult, in which case they will all go to the Lodge & there will be no room for me.[8] Said I would drive over to Eastcombe tomorrow.

From Lady Stuart de Rothesay's, drove to Lady Gordon's, 34 Hertford Street.[9] Found her & Georgina and Cosmo – and saw Alice, a fine girl aged 16, not to be introduced [into society] for one year more. I said I would by & by order a butt of sherry of [from] Cosmo, £80 per butt for the best – any colour I liked...

Sat about ½ hour with Lady Gordon – till Lady Charlotte Luscombe came in, which sent me off. Lady Gordon begged to see me on my return. She was laid up with cold & rheumatism... I joked her about having refused me – & she said, as if offhand enough to be unaware, 'Yes! & I have never repented it but once – that is, always.' Of this I took no notice, but by saying with a smile, 'I daresay we should have done very well together.'[10]

So Anne was living two London lives. The first involved travelling with Ann Walker of Crow Nest estate, redolent of Yorkshire bourgeoisie and new money. The second was with Lady Stuart's circle, including Lady Gordon, one of Anne's earlier flirtations. They were all titled, albeit minor aristocracy. During these social visits, it seems that Anne never mentioned Ann. Rather, she was in effect performing her correspondence with her own women friends, Ann left behind for the moment.[11]

Returned home direct from Hertford Street & took up [in the carriage] A~ about 4 & drove into the city. Called at Pearce's, Longacre 103. Then to 123 Fenchurch Street about [our] passage by the Princess Victoria packet to Antwerp. (All busy with the Coronation...) Took our places (berths) & got ready for embarking the carriage. Ourselves £2.2.0d each – carriage £5. Total including two servants = £12.14.0d of which paid £6. Bought biscuits at Lemann's [French baker's], Threadneedle Street, and thermometer at Bates, & A~ left her watch & I my [Sibella] McLean watch at Rundle's. Stopt a moment at Pearce's & bought hat for George... Home about 7.15 – dinner almost immediately – *potage à la Julienne* – pot of roast loin, spinach & potatoes & a pudding. Pint of madeira for A~ & bottle of Claret for myself, of which we respectively drank ½ – both slept till 10 soon after when we went upstairs to bed – ate oranges – and dawdled over getting into bed – *and had a pretty good kiss & then fell asleep.*

Meanwhile, London bustled with Queen Victoria's coronation.

SATURDAY 5 Fine morning ... hairdresser came about 9 – dressed A~; & then me, during which time A~ had Miss Lloyd the dressmaker – and adjusted the Imperials for going with the carriage to be embarked. Mr Harrison Bluemantle came at 11 & waited ten minutes or more, then staid ½ hour. Took away with him A~'s sketch of [her] pedigree which she had done very recently, & took my pedigree to enter the deaths.

Harrison Bluemantle was naturally a very useful fount of social gossip:

The Coronation to be on the 28th June – to cost about £40,000, as did the coronation of William IV. No procession – no place to arrange it in – would be 6,000 who would have the right to join it... The Queen could not sleep in the cloisters of Westminster Abbey, as did George IV, to be ready for next day. Could not undergo the fatigue of a banquet – about 12,000 peers – the length of the peeresses' robes [are] in proportion to their rank – a duchess's train 6 foot long on the ground.

Every peerage [had been] bought by interest of one sort or other. Lord Ashburton (Baring) bought up *The Times* newspaper, since which it is Conservative, and has made £10,000 a year more; realizes, after paying all expenses, £60,000 a year. The Whigs did not know the consequences of their own Reform Bill. Three parties now – Whigs, Tories and Radicals, any two of which joining, must [i.e. could] turn out the other. The present ministers will never resign. Bluemantle evidently a Whig, and soon saw we were on the other side...

Anne, aspiring to heraldic recognition, may have felt slightly out of her depth here. However, London also afforded her the opportunity of picking up useful ideas on interior design.

At 12.40 left A~ to write to her sister & I drove off to East Combe. Turned to the left just after passing over Blackheath – fine drive – the long line of Greenwich railroad arches had something of the look of an ancient aqueduct. At East Combe in 1¼ hours at 1.55.

Lady Stuart was much surprised, but very glad to see me ... looking much better than when I saw her last... Gave her my [Paris] address, no 27, rue St Victor – promised to write... I declined taking luncheon & also declined going upstairs. Glad I went [into] the room we were in, looked upon the distant Thames – a fine view – & had one window down to the ground (on the other side) opposite to the fireplace, & opening into a pretty flower-garden. The room book-shelved all round, about 6 foot high – the shelves thrown back so that the wall above (papered) was flush with the books on the shelves – all forming one line – no projection – the effect of this good & very comfortable. The drawing room at Shibden might be done in this way? Passed an hour with Lady Stuart – & returned in 1¼ hour & home at 4.30, having stopped a moment in passing at Hammersley's & brought my passport signed by the French ambassador.

Sent away the horses for an hour & George dined & then about 5.15 A~ drove off to no 5 Endsleigh Street to see Mrs Plowes – near an hour there – very glad to see her.[12] Pressed her but not disagreeably, talking [about] her plans, but quite satisfied when A~ said she really did not mean to tell them [our plans]; Miss Edwards of Pye Nest there.

Miss Edwards was, of course, related to Ann's late mother. Again, there were two fairly separate social circles here in London: Ann's West Riding family and Anne's minor aristocracy friends.

While A~ was away, I sat writing up my journal from the beginning of Tuesday, when about 6.30 Lady Stuart de Rothesay & Louisa were announced – very glad to see her – said it was very good of her to come. She brought me the directory of the hotel [that her friend] liked so much: Hotel Voltaire, Rue de Lille – also mentioned, should this be full, Hotel Mirabeau, Rue de la Paix. To write to them under cover to Lord Stuart de Rothesay through the Embassy – to send the packet to the embassy porter...

Connections like Lord Stuart de Rothesay were so helpful!

We cozying very comfortably when A~ returned & came in – taken by surprise to find the de Rothesays here. Introduced her – all went well – they did not stay more than a minute or 2 afterwards.

So finally, these two separate social worlds met, albeit extremely briefly. Only Ann's own diary would record her reaction to this surprise meeting.

Then dinner at 7.30. A person from Mr Pearce brought the bill (paid it) = £16.3.6 for what had been done to the carriage... And the rest expenses of carriage and horses and embarking the carriage... Hutton brought home George's clothes – Miss Lloyd sent A~'s gown & petticoat (waist trimmed)... Sent George to pay the bill.

A~ & I respectively finished one madeira & claret – had given them into charge of the waiter last night, & none of the wine seemed to have been taken. Sat talking some while – then at our writing – then tea between 10 & 11 & writing again... Then till 1.40 (sent Oddy to bed at 12) sat writing to M~, Marian, Mrs Briggs, & Mrs Bagnold – to be left in the letter box here tomorrow morning... A~ wrote to her aunt while I was writing – directed & sealed my letters – we did not go upstairs till 2 or after.

This flurry of letter writing offered a reminder of how adventurous crossing the Channel was at this time. Travel to Europe remained daring, even in the age of steam-powered ships.

SUNDAY 6 Had the hairdresser, Mr Faulkner, sent to A~ then myself & let him give Oddy a lesson on my head, as yesterday, how to do my hair. Packed – breakfast at 9.40. George put into the hotel letter box my letters – to Mrs Lawton, Lawton Hall; Miss Marian Lister, Market Weighton; Mrs Briggs, Shibden Hall; and Mrs Bagnold, Post Office, Halifax – paid all. Off from Crawley's hotel, Albemarle Street at 11.05...

At the Iron Wharf, Tower Stairs in ½ hour – lucky we had 25 mins to spare – too many things by half had been left out of the carriage yesterday – cloaks, bottles ... a terrible bundling into & out of the boat, charged 2/6 on account of a cwt of luggage, said the man...

The vessel was under way at 12 noon before George & I had got all arranged inside & outside the carriage. I had not a dry thread on before [i.e. after] all this was done. A~ & I sat a little while in the carriage – then on deck above an hour. Strong cold wind in our faces drove us into the carriage again. A~ hungry – had biscuits & wine & we both ate heartily of the remaining tongue we had brought from home & ate biscuits & I too (and A~ again) took a little madeira. We enjoyed our meal about 3.30... Afterwards went down into the cabin...

I paid the captain at his desk in the cabin the remainder of the packet passage – Princess Victoria, 140 horse-power – Captain Woodruff a gentlemanly enough sort of man – carriage £5, A~ and myself 2 guineas each, the servants £3.10 – £12.14.0. Then settled ourselves in the carriage – the wind very fresh. [The packet is] an

Antwerp-build vessel and our crew Belgian – speaking Flamand and German. I had had no idea of this – like best to trust to my own countrymen at sea. I breathed not [a word of] this, but it came across me often during the night as the vessel pitched & I was sick & feverish – held out till 7 pm when the strong wind & rough sea were more than my stomach could withstand.

Again, Anne's diary writing understandably runs from one day into the next.

MONDAY 7 And from 7 pm on Sunday to 10 am this morning, Monday, when we had got within an hour of landing, I was sick. I think I never slept more than a few minutes without being interrupted by the feeling, or the action, of sickness. A~ began about ½ hour or more after I did, but recovered by about midnight... The rough passage (everybody, passengers, on board sick but 2 men) had delayed... It was 11 before we let off steam (stopt) alongside the quay at Antwerp... A~ and I and Oddy came off with the 2 writing cases and A~'s journal and my travel bag.

Meanwhile George took charge of getting the luggage and carriage off the boat and back on to dry land. Now they could set off through France for Paris and beyond.

It was the right moment for them to leave Britain. The next day, on Tuesday 8th, the 'People's Charter' was published in London. Its 'Six Points' included voting by secret ballot, which would have undercut the power of landowners such as Anne and Ann to coerce their tenants at elections; and universal male suffrage, confirming their complete exclusion from parliamentary politics.[13]

Epilogue

They had at last 'got off'. Europe was their oyster! From Antwerp, they headed for that most enticing of destinations, Paris, taking in some sightseeing *en route*: visiting Waterloo and descending a coal mine near Liège. However, as they neared Paris, Anne found that Ann's health troubles resurfaced. On 27 May, after dinner when she and Oddy put Ann to bed, Anne confided in her diary: '*We had drunk our bottle from Moets; and A~ tipsyish without her knowing it; and I not inclined for writing. Mr Moet's champagne very good... Incurred a cross thinking of M~ sitting on chair in my dressing room.*' The next day, with champagne continuing, Ann's problems grew worse: '*A~'s face looks very red and bad. I often think of Doctor Belcombe's telling me I should have a deal of trouble with her.*'[1]

They arrived in Paris the following day. Ann's face was still blotched with a rash. They saw Dr Double: Anne had consulted him when she was in Paris earlier. He advised Anne to take Ann without delay directly to the far south-west of France. Here, in the Pyrenean foothills, at spas in St Sauveur and Barèges, Ann could take a course of health-restoring baths.

However, they only left Paris on 20 June, heading south-west to the spa towns on the slopes of the Pyrenees. This was a route that Anne had taken in 1830 with Lady Stuart de Rothesay. After various detours, on 9 July they eventually arrived at St Sauveur.[2] Here they stayed for a few weeks, seeing the medical director of the St Sauveur baths. He was most particular: 'Must have an order from him before A~ could have a bath at all – he read Dr Double's *ordonnance* – agreed with all, but the douche to be applied for 10 minutes every morning to A~'s face.' However, Anne confided in her diary: '*Poor A~ in better sorts, but no companion for me. I am always in the fear of getting her wrong. She cannot bear my opening a door or anything – 'tis miserable.*'[3] Anne then diverted herself, as was her habit and her joy, by standing undressed reading Charpentier on the geology of the Pyrenees.[4]

St Sauveur was a delightful spot to linger and explore Gavarnie and the beautiful foothills. However, Anne often wished to venture further than Ann. Indeed, by 19 July, Anne had become fascinated with Vignemale, the highest peak in the French Pyrenees. She was, after all, already an accomplished mountaineer.[5] Was Vignemale really inaccessible from this French side, or was there a way to the top? It was Charles, one of their two local guides, who helped Anne discover that the route to the summit had been found only the previous year. But would Ann Walker cope with these dizzying altitudes? After trying a smaller climb, it was clear that she was not up to it: on this practice descent the guides had to half-carry her down. Ann would stay behind.

By 4 August Anne had every detail of the Vignemale climb meticulously planned. On Monday 6th, she and her two guides would leave at 3 p.m., with Charles's brother-in-law coming back with Ann and the horses. Charles had crampons and an iron stick for Anne. Her own diary record of her clothing is often quoted:

I was dressed as I have been ever since my arrival ... flannel waistcoat and drawers ... chemise, stays, short cambric muslin under-petticoat ... over which striped jaconet waist[coat] with high collar and long sleeves – broad-hemmed 3 frilled muslin fichu, and over this double muslin handkerchief and double dark silk ditto; and then my black merinos dress lightly *outaté* and *doublé de persienne* ... and crossed over my chest, a light black China crape shawl. I had had ... tape loops put round the bottom of my dress and strings at the top; and just before setting off, had my dress tied up all round me just about or above the knee. I wore ... strong leather quarter-boot shoes with nails in (made here for the purpose) and black sateen gaiters.

What is strikingly clear is that, even when Anne was climbing the Pyrenees accompanied just by two local male guides, she wore female dress: there was little bending of gender rules even here.

So, as ever well-prepared for all eventualities, Anne took Charpentier's map of the Pyrenees plus her little notebook with her passport in it. 'Yet I was lightly equipped and my heart was light', she noted. Anne and the guides climbed high, spending the night in a small and rather crowded *cabane*. They set off again at 2.45 a.m.; two hours later they stopped for breakfast and the horses were sent back. Climbing higher, her crampons sometimes on, Anne and her guides reached the top at 1 p.m. Anne wrote their names and put the piece of paper in a bottle, and after an hour they began their descent. Once they reached the *cabane*, even Anne felt tired. The long climb down continued.

Conquering Vignemale was one of Anne Lister's most heroic achievements. Yet her diary entries as she reached the mighty mountain peak were so brief as to seem an anti-climax. Vivien Ingham, the pioneer authority on Anne in the Pyrenees, called them 'disappointingly terse'. Maybe reaching a mountain top after a demanding climb does not lend itself to much eloquent writing.

Anne and Ann met again down at Gavarnie. However, it was not all over yet. The Prince of Moscow claimed in *Galignani's Messenger*, the English newspaper published in France, that, accompanied by his brother, on 11 August *he* had made a successful ascent of Vignemale. One of the guides had not been honest. War was declared between Anne Lister and the Prince of Moscow. Anne got another more honest guide to sign a certificate stating that she had made the ascent to the summit four days earlier, on 7 August. Anne's note was also published in *Galignani's Messenger*.[6] The Prince of Moscow's competitiveness underlined how rare women mountaineers remained and how magnificent was Anne's achievement.

*

Magnificent indeed! 165 years later, in July 2003, having read much of the 1838 diary, I determined to tread in Anne Lister's footsteps, and to climb mighty Vignemale to its forbidding peak. With my partner, sister and brother-in-law (an experienced mountain climber), we set out, staying in the spa village of Luz-St-Sauveur. We stayed overnight in the mountain refuge, got up at 6 a.m., grabbed breakfast and set off at 7 a.m. By the time we reached the snow-covered glaciers, we had put on crampons and were roped up. At the windswept summit, there were panoramic views to admire. But there was little time. On our descent, we had to recross the glacier *before* the sun began to melt the crevasses hidden beneath the snow. With every hesitant and stumbling step, I felt growing admiration for Anne Lister. What an extraordinary woman, what an amazing achievement! I have never felt more in awe of her, nor held her in greater respect.[7]

*

Meanwhile, back in 1838, by mid-August the diary began to include more coded passages again, often Ann Walker's complaints about Anne's high-handedness in making travel arrangements.[8] On reflecting on her own achievements, she commented: 'I have made each ascent for my pleasure, not for éclat. What is éclat to me? What is éclat to anyone?'[9]

Alongside, Anne kept up correspondence with her old friends. On their return journey, she wrote to Mariana from Lyons about how she *and* Ann had ascended the Pic du Midi: 'If you know anybody that knows anything about it, you will believe it next to impossible that Adney should have scrambled to the top. Our life at the Pyrenees was a perpetual scramble... Addio! God bless you, my dearest Mary! A.L.'[10] This prompted Mariana to reply to Anne admiringly, or perhaps sardonically, about Ann's mountaineering achievement: 'You must have brought her back a little Hercules, for no strength less than this could have carried her up to the top of the Pic de Midi.'[11]

After further travels in France, with short stays in Paris and London, Anne and Ann eventually made their way home to England. They arrived back at Shibden Hall on 27 November.

*

While they were away, social and political change, unwelcome to both of them, had taken place. Since the Chartists' Six Point Charter had been published, a Great Northern Union had been formed at Leeds, and in July, a meeting was held to form a Northern Union in Halifax, at which none other than Feargus O'Connor spoke. Ben Rushton formally moved support of the People's Charter, declaring passionately 'that they should make one simultaneous rush towards the citadel and usurp power'.[12] O'Connor extravagantly proclaimed: 'When presenting this petition, we, five thousand fighting men, demand justice at your hands' (cheers). Then in October, a great Chartist meeting was held at Peep Green near Dewsbury. The Halifax contingent processed behind two bands and would have marched along the very edge of the Shibden estate. Their demand was for political reform, by physical force if necessary.[13]

As well as political discontent, there was dramatic social change too. Anne's letter to Lady Stuart written shortly after she returned to Shibden highlighted these shifts:

> The influence of the railroad is already felt. What will it be, by and by, when even such old-fashioned-going people as I begin to follow in the train? Posting [i.e. travel by coach] will be knocked up and we shall do all by steam, from carrying ourselves to boiling our potatoes. But they must have coal to have steam, and some good may come of every great change that we are at present undergoing.[14]

Anne was canny enough a businesswoman to know there was no steam power without coal mines such as hers. Listerwick was progressing well. James Holt's 'hurrying gates', three feet six inches high, offered just room enough for 'the boys (hurriers)' pulling corves of coal underground. Such child labour was soon to be exposed by the *Children's Employment Commission Report* (1842).[15]

Houses also required heating with coal fires. Winter 1838–39 was freezing cold. Snowstorms and bitterly cold temperatures meant that Shibden extravagantly burned a dozen house fires. In September 1838, while Anne and Ann were still away, Emily Brontë from nearby Haworth had arrived to teach at Law Hill in Southowram. By winter, with the thermometers seldom above freezing, life at Law Hill must have been scarcely bearable. Emily wrote little during that school term: probably she was just too cold to write. Although they both enjoyed walking, the two women never met: certainly Anne Lister did not mix with lowly schoolteachers.[16] Rather, on returning to Shibden, she was immediately immersed in entrepreneurial bustle, mainly at Listerwick

Also on Anne's mind were the unhappy tensions with Ann, still often about money and inheritance. In December Ann had drawn £300 from the bank and put half in a little parcel which, 'with a look of pleasure', she gave to Anne. Yet Anne still had other ideas:

> I had thought it would be a saving to A~, and enough for me, if she would keep the establishment [i.e. Shibden household] as I had mentioned before... To my surprise she said she could not do that and do for her estate [Cliff Hill], which was in worse order than mine... She cried and said it was very hard – she had no comforts herself. This upset me... I left her about eleven, declining her invitation to sleep with her. My mind was made up to leave her. I longed for a nutshell to live quietly in, and yet the thought of her and the parting distressed me.[17]

*

By spring 1839 the icy weather might have softened; but the dangerous Chartists were now unstoppable. On Whit Monday another great West Riding demonstration was held, again at Peep Green. Ben Wilson recalled later how the very large Halifax procession 'marched by Godley Lane and Hipperholme' to meet up with contingents from Bradford and elsewhere. In other words, the Chartists did indeed march along the very edge of Anne Lister's ancient acres.[18] And by this time, Anne and Ann were back in residence.

However, Anne had not forgotten her ambition, inspired by Captain Cochrane's *Pedestrian Journey*, of travelling to Russia. Within just six weeks of this Chartist procession, in June 1839, Anne and Ann left Halifax and set sail towards Moscow.[19]

As is now well known, Anne Lister died in the remote Russian province of Western Georgia on 22 September 1840. It fell to the bereaved Ann Walker to arrange for the coffin to be brought back for burial in Halifax Parish Church, which journey took six months. Eventually, on 17 April 1841, Anne Lister's will was proved on oath by Ann Walker and Gray, the trustees. Thirteen pages long, it bequeathed a life-tenancy of Shibden Hall and the estate 'unto my friend Ann Walker', to be forfeited 'thenceforth' should she marry; and to be held in trust for John Lister of Swansea, Anne's indirect descendant.

*

The tragic and melodramatic story that ensued has often been told. In 1843 Ann Walker, held to be of 'unsound mind', was moved from Shibden, according to a plan of Elizabeth Sutherland, helped by Robert Parker and Dr Belcombe. Designated 'a lunatic', Ann was taken to a private asylum near York. Meanwhile Captain Sutherland shared with John Lister his deep suspicions about Anne Lister's motives in having instilled 'a mistrust and hatred of her closest relatives', to the financial benefit of Anne herself. Poor Ann, a truly tragic Victorian 'madwoman in the attic', died in 1854.[20]

The Listers were always a dynastically fragile family. Marian Lister, a rather ghostly figure, died in 1882 aged 84. Shibden had by then long been inherited by the distant Lister family. Their son, John Lister, who contributed so substantially to what we know of the magnificent Anne Lister diaries, published his selections in the *Halifax Guardian*. And about 1892, with fellow antiquarian Arthur Burrell, he managed to crack the code. The diaries were then seemingly placed back behind panels at Shibden Hall – and a forty-year silence followed.

It was only after John Lister's own death in 1933 that the diaries fell to Halifax Borough and so to the care of its librarian. The elderly Burrell wrote to him, warning him darkly of 'what old Halifax scandal knows about Miss Lister'.[21] Meanwhile, the Walkers' Crow Nest estate fell into disrepair and the main house was eventually demolished. Its grounds became a golf course. By the 1990s, when I first visited the site, it was as if all sign of the daringly clandestine marriage between Anne and Ann had been completely grassed over. I ended the Epilogue of *Female Fortune* (1998) with 'it is as if Ann Walker never was'.[22] However, since 2019 and the global impact of Sally Wainwright's *Gentleman Jack*, that sentence has sparked rebellion; there has been a phenomenal growth of interest in the complex Ann Walker story, with impressive research both at Lightcliffe and on social media.[23]

AFTERWORD

Since *Gentleman Jack*, Anne Lister's readership across the globe has grown hugely and is now widely diverse. An Anne Lister Society was formed and held its first conference in Halifax during ALBW in April 2022.[1] We now live in a post-*Gentleman Jack* world. Not only are there two books with this title, there is now also one called *The Gentleman Jack Effect* (2021), subtitled 'Lessons in Breaking Rules and Living Out Loud'. A sculpture in the Halifax Piece Hall of Anne Lister was unveiled in autumn 2021 by Sally Wainwright and Suranne Jones; movingly, it is not the jaunty woman of *Gentleman Jack*, but rather a contemplative solitary Anne. Most *Gentleman Jack* fans are also hugely enthusiastic Anne Lister fans; others are critical of her.[2] Readers will by now have formed their own judgements.[3]

Here, with the focus on the 1836–38 diaries, I ask: did Anne's writing form an organic whole, a consistent self-portrait? I suggest that it comprised three slightly different, interwoven narratives. The first, the major proportion of the journals, is in her own handwriting. These lengthy sections record day by day, indeed hour by hour, her phenomenal energy and achievements, particularly in the public sphere. Secondly, Anne's own letters, mainly written to her elite friends, present a version of herself to these titled women. Finally, there is the smaller portion of the diary written in Anne's own secret code. For 1836–38 this mainly details her relationship with Ann Walker. And it is, of course, these coded passages that particularly help us address the key question: was it 'as good as a marriage'?

*

In the sections in her own handwriting Anne recorded her impressive work on the estate, both landscape and architectural embellishments, and her entrepreneurial zeal, especially in developing her own coal mines and seeing off the industrial competition, notably the Rawsons. These sections also record her intellectual activity, notably her phenomenally wide reading, everything from the latest guide on coalmining engineering to Captain Cochrane's *Pedestrian Journey through Russia*.

Anne's diaries were like having a recording device trained 24/7 on the Shibden Hall rooms, on her estate and on its neighbourhood, catching the multiple conversations she had with everybody she met.[4] A good oral historian will capture all the rich aspects of an interview; Anne does just that, recording the nuances of a conversation beautifully and for the permanent record. She was aided by her powerful and capacious memory, so no tricksy tenant escaped their dialogue about unpaid rents being recorded in hypnotizing detail.

An indefatigable walker, Anne knew everyone on her estate and beyond. So, her diary records in vivid detail relationships with local people, and often their warm respect for her. However, anyone who challenged her authority would live to regret it, as the Rawsons found out. Anne could also maintain her power over the skilled professionals whom she dealt with on regular business trips down into Halifax: to visit Mr McKean at the bank, or Thomas Adam or Robert Parker at their lawyers' offices. Here routine deference to a member of the landed gentry probably had something more friendly about it too. At Shibden, within her own fragile family, it was only her aunt whom Anne loved dearly: she 'gave me all she had and loved me much'.[5] After her aunt's death, Anne became the only Lister living at Shibden. She was a traditionalist: this comes across most strongly in the enormous significance she attached to her ancestors and dynasty.[6]

I have aimed to capture her prodigious achievements in developing her Shibden estate.[7] The diary vividly records how she assimilated gargantuan amounts of complex information day in, day out. There were at that time other women coal owners, but few (if any) threw themselves into their extractive enterprises with Anne's energy and competence. Listerwick pit, completed shortly before Anne and Ann set off travelling, was an economic success. Hastening its completion with a keen eye on costs, Anne knew she could rely on its income.

Anne also remained active politically both in the small Halifax and in the sprawling West Riding constituencies. Especially during the 1837 election, she doorstepped her tenants to ensure they would vote 'Blue'. Yet in neither constituency were Anne nor Ann successful against the 'Yellows'. And beyond the Whigs loomed the Radicals and the Chartists. The Chartist *Northern Star* had an eager readership around Halifax, with processions marching near Shibden. Anne would have known of this from reading the *Halifax Guardian*. Yet as a member of the local landed gentry, her gaze was firmly fixed well above this 'mobocracy'.

Inheritor of Shibden's ancient acres, no Whig nor Chartist threatened her during her lifetime. And, with no secret ballot as yet, she could exert firm authority. For landowning women such as Anne and Ann, being voteless counted for little. The only point at which women's explicit exclusion from the parliamentary franchise seemed to impact on Anne was when she suggested holding a discreet Conservative meeting at Shibden with key local 'Blue' gentlemen. This seems never to have happened. Political 'separate spheres' for men and women had embedded themselves.[8] Instead, Anne found herself having to catch up with political news from lowly local tradesmen. It is unlikely that she relished this.

The first 'Reading around the World' chapter highlighted Anne's phenomenal intellectual appetite for pre-Darwinian geology. She might have been barred from university, but she paid close attention to geologists, notably the eminent Charles Lyell. Yet Anne was a firm believer in the Bible, including the opening words of Genesis: 'In the beginning God created the heavens and the earth.'[9] She was a woman of her time, in many ways a classic traditionalist. Had she lived a generation later, it would all have been different.

Darwin's *On the Origin of Species* was eventually published in 1859. By then, educational opportunities for women were opening.[10] In the 1830s this future was beyond her ken. Yet her intellectual competence remains staggeringly impressive. Had women been allowed to study law, Anne would have made a formidable lawyer. Her handling of business challenges, such as Ann's complex Water Lane mill problems, illustrates this.

The second 'Reading around the World' chapter reflects Anne's enormous appetite for travel literature, the more remote and adventurous the better. Captain Cochrane's mesmerizing *Pedestrian Journey through Russia and Siberian Tartary* captivated Anne. I noted in the Epilogue our 2003 climb to the peak of Vignemale, as it was the only one of Anne's many magnificent accomplishments that I managed myself. Of the others, her final voyage to Moscow and down the Volga to West Georgia, I remain in distant awe.

*

The second narrative form is Anne's own letters, written mainly to her elite women friends.[11] These evidence her social aspirations, notably visiting these friends (preferably in their castles) and European travel. Ann Walker is either rendered invisible or referred to merely as 'my little friend'.[12] We see clearly how Anne wished to present herself to Lady Stuart's circle, and this suggests how extremely adept she was at forming relationships. Anne was warm and loving, yet also a consummate snob. An adroit networker, she knew that the elderly dowager Lady Stuart represented her entrée to the elite world of other interesting women, such as Lady Stuart de Rothesay. And less aristocratic women friends? For some, like Isabella Norcliffe, Anne retained loyal affection. Yet other acquaintances were cast aside.

To the woman who had been her greatest love, Mariana, Anne wrote regularly. These letters were mainly very affectionate. However, Anne also knew how to twist a blade into Mariana's heart, once saying she looked old because of all her work on her school. After the Pyrenees adventure, Anne wrote to her about how Ann had scrambled to the top of Pic du Midi. This prompted Mariana to write in response about Ann's being 'a Little Hercules'.

This, I have suggested, was meant ironically or even sardonically rather than admiringly. Yet what remains crucial here is that Anne continued to find Mariana sexually desirable.

*

Finally, there are the absolutely crucial passages of the diary written in Anne's secret code. These mainly detail her relationship with Ann Walker. Readers expecting the romantic exchanges of the earlier 1830s might well feel disappointed. These passages record frequent quarrels, tears and silences, Anne determining to 'get rid' of Ann. Yet these bleak, despairing passages are often shortly followed by happy reconciliations, with Shibden a hive of enjoyable shared activities, especially in the evenings, when they might read to each other or just *talk*. So was their relationship 'as good as a marriage ... quite as good or better'? Of course, Anne and Ann's marriage could not be like heterosexual marriages. It was recognized by neither Church nor state, nor by society. There were no guides to etiquette, no family precedents to follow. Their ceremony had to be private, solemnized by taking the sacrament together quietly at Goodramgate Church. Yet even then, the symbolic importance of this discreet ceremony was seemingly not felt equally by both. Afterwards, Anne confided to her diary: '*The first time I ever joined Miss W~ in my prayers – I had prayed that our union might be happy – she had not thought of doing so much for me.*'[13]

When they lived together on their own at Shibden, how did their marriage work?[14] My own feeling is that Ann Walker did love Anne: after all, her diary referred to Anne as 'dearest'.[15] Rather, the problem was that Anne had the experience, the worldly confidence, the *chutzpah* to view as normal (indeed, as God-given) their marriage promise. Anne was twelve years older than Ann and had been here before. Ann had not: she was inexperienced about women loving women and she had considerably less social confidence. Additionally, Ann was surrounded by inconveniently numerous relatives, especially the William Priestleys, increasingly suspicious of what was going on at Shibden and who was paying for what.

Anne, moreover, possessed other levels of self-assurance, both intellectually and in business. She networked and negotiated skilfully, few men getting the better of her, while Ann relied on Anne to redraft her letters sorting out legal difficulties. Indeed, more generally, Ann was often caught on the back foot, excluded or at least feeling excluded. This comes out most vividly when they visited London *en route* to France. Ann sat captive in the dentist's chair, while Anne visited the elegant homes of her titled friends. The one strength of Ann's that Anne coveted was, of course, money. And Anne, lacking the wherewithal to finance all her ambitious schemes, persistently tried to gain access to Ann's income stream. This had implications. Anne still entertained erotic thoughts of Mariana, and the relationship between the three of them remained oddly triangular. However, the chapter 'Mariana Lawton Visits Shibden' makes it clear that, despite her most seductive endeavours, Mariana had had to retreat. Ann had now won out: it was *she* who had the 'union' with Anne.

'Maintaining the Upper Hand – Money' records the power dynamics in their marriage. Some of this stemmed from Anne's preference for exercising authority. 'Two Fortunes are Better than One' documents how, by joining the interests of Shibden with those of Crow Nest, Anne's life was financially secured.

Meanwhile, digging deeper into the texture of their marriage reveals detailed testimony about their sexual relationship, mainly in bed. Readers will have noticed that there was less sex than previously. Just so. Many days in 'Living Married Life at Shibden' start with '*No kiss*', or less frequently '*incurred a cross thinking of M~*'. Sex was not always beguiling: '*She would have been fondling* [me], *but I was too sleepy... On her being asleep and snoring, I left her ... and went to my own bed.*' Yet it could sometimes be enjoyable: '*Good kiss last night – staid with A~ till one and a half*', though this ends with '*incurred a cross last night thinking of M~, lightly as usual.*'[16] When Anne and Ann left for London, their sexual relationship, as so often happened when travelling, warmed again: '*dawdled over getting into bed – and had a pretty good kiss and then fell asleep*'.[17] Expensive wines, particularly when drunk by Ann, also helped.

Yet out of bed, the diary pages are peppered with arguments, sometimes rows about servants: '*What a temper! She now throws the Cookson business all on to me.*' '*What a temper she has...? A vulgar pride is at the bottom of it.*' These rows sometimes appear very petty, often about money: '*Poor soul – her mind is not very large. And shall we split up on money matters at last? Well, be it so. I shall get on well, without her.*' The nub seems to have been that Anne wished the wealthier Ann to bear the expenses of *both* the Crow Nest and Shibden estates. This often drove Ann to floods of tears, despairing at being placed under such financial pressure.[18]

Intransigent, Anne documented her deep frustration with Ann's emotional outbursts and 'temper'. These accounts can sound very harsh. Yet perhaps the rows (and ensuing silences) were bad, but were not necessarily as bitter as might appear from just reading Anne's coded words. For what seems remarkable is how speedily these quarrels were patched up: Anne's determination to leave Ann (and go and live quietly in a nutshell) soon fades away, and married life continued as normal at Shibden. Anne and Ann were out in the world without a script and with precious little guidance: these coded passages surely record emotional volatility rather than necessarily a bad marriage.

*

However, it remains crucial to return Anne Lister to her pre-Victorian historical context, resisting the temptation to judge her by our own values and political correctness. These three narrative strands present differently nuanced truths about Anne. Her relationship with Ann, however, is central to this book. The chances of uncovering comparably detailed evidence about other lesbian marriages remain remote (though to discover the later volumes of Ann Walker's diary would be amazing). So the question has to be: what were most marriages like in the early nineteenth century?

We know quite a lot about conventional heterosexual marriage, both from documentary sources and from fiction. Jane Austen's *Pride and Prejudice*, published in 1813, paints a romantic story ending in a happy marriage. Written closer to Halifax, Anne Brontë's *The Tenant of Wildfell Hall*, published in 1848 just eight years after Anne's death, offers a far starker portrait of heterosexual marriage. Helen marries 'the worst kind of man', Mr Huntingdon, and from her first weeks of matrimony she finds that her cruel husband prefers drinking with his hunting friends and flirting with the wife of one of them. After one quarrel, Helen 'lock[s] myself in my own chamber'. As her husband's dissipations and long absences worsen, Helen finds solace in writing a diary at night, in her religious faith, and in doting on her young son, Arthur. However, from her dissolute husband Arthur learns 'to tipple wine like papa, to swear'. In utter despair, Helen determines to leave, seeking sanctuary in the isolated family home, indeed becoming 'the tenant of Wildfell Hall'. Her husband discovers this plan, grabs her keys and takes her money and jewels. Nevertheless, Helen leaves, taking Arthur; but her new home must remain secret, for living on her own she is unprotected.[19] Anne Brontë reminds readers that not only was divorce nigh impossible for Helen, but also that the Infant Custody Bill, permitting a wife to gain custody of her young child, had only recently become law (1839). And it was not till the 1850s that married women's property laws along with divorce legislation were considered, at which point they provoked strong opposition, on the grounds that such legislation would destroy the sanctity of the home.[20]

Anne Brontë's novel reminds us that Anne and Ann's marriage was neither as cruel as Helen Huntingdon's, nor as legally constricted. A complex system of laws enclosed wives in heterosexual marriages. For a lesbian marriage there were no legal constraints: though not being legally recognized, it might operate with freedom. So Anne and Ann's relationship was, in so many ways, 'as good as a marriage' in the early nineteenth century – when the rights of married women were very limited. Yes, Ann locked her bedroom door occasionally. One Brontë scholar wrote that 'the slamming of Helen's bedroom-door against her husband' in *The Tenant of Wildfell Hall* 'reverberated throughout Victorian England', making it an indictment of sexual double standards in conventional marriages.[21] Ann's locked bedroom door reveals, however, not the ending of a cruel marriage, but the volatility of this daring, dissident relationship. While Anne and Ann's marriage might not have been as uniformly romantic as an Austen novel, nevertheless it had many strengths, strengths that Helen Huntingdon would envy. Sex might be less frequent but was still to be enjoyed. Unlike Mr Huntingdon, Anne remained sexually faithful to Ann – even when, during her visit to Shibden, Mariana tried to entice her with languid kisses.

They enjoyed each other's company and spent happy evenings together. And they looked after each other, illnesses occurring more frequently than now. Finally, they set off together to France and the Pyrenees, sharing a joy in travelling. Anne might fantasize in code about getting rid of Ann and living on her own. But there was no *Tenant of Wildfell Hall* ending to their marriage.

So why was there such tremendous emotional volatility? Partly because they were such very different women. One was a multi-talented Renaissance woman with an elite education and formidable networking skills; the other more conventional and lacking Anne's *chutzpah*. I think that part of the explanation is that they operated in a space with no legal constraints and with unspoken social constraints, heteronormativity being the convention in early nineteenth-century society. While there were other women who were happy to enjoy a lesbian relationship with the charismatic Anne Lister, few would spurn the convenient fig leaf of a hetero-sexual marriage, with all its social rituals and expectations.[22] For Anne and Ann, there were no rules, no laws, no social conventions to guide them on how best to conduct their marriage. That together they managed to sustain and enjoy a lesbian marriage in Yorkshire in the 1830s is surely remarkable. This was not Paris or London, nor the remote countryside; this was industrializing Halifax. Anne's determination, and Ann's agreement, made this possible.

Anne's inherited social class helped immeasurably to permit this dissident relationship to be lived for most of the time 'as good as a marriage'. Quarrels, yes, but they were quickly made up. The intersection of lesbian sexual practices with money and social class remains absolutely essential to understanding how this relationship worked. And the multiple ways in which Anne achieved her ambitions remains highly impressive: as an intellectual; as a businesswoman; as a deft political operator; as a fearless traveller and mountaineer; and as a world-beating diarist, devising her own secret code, her journals now recognized by UNESCO.

*

We now live in a post-*Gentleman Jack* world, with the drama series having put lesbianism firmly on the historical map. In May 2022 the BBC broadcast a moving documentary, '*Gentleman Jack* Changed My Life'. Individual stories told of the difficulties of 'coming out to my grandparents' and of how the drama had brought two women who had separated thirty-five years earlier back together again.[23] An impressive article by Canadian scholar Chris Roulston explored the ways in which Sally Wainwright skilfully negotiated her responsibility to the archive and to historical accuracy with the demands of mainstream entertainment culture for contemporary audiences.[24]

The screening of *Gentleman Jack* season 2 in spring 2022 embedded this still further. ALBW, cancelled in 2020 and 2021 due to Covid, returned to Halifax with a bang. It was an exciting week! Undoubtedly the greatest impact was on Saturday 2 April. Halifax Minster was packed with eager fans from both sides of the Atlantic. Helena Whitbread and I spoke about our Anne Lister journeys. To our surprise, we were met with standing ovations from the audience; and at the end, a long queue of people wound its slow way up to Helena and me to have their books signed. This final photograph captures this mood of infectious excitement.[25]

8 Halifax Minster, Anne Lister Birthday Week, April 2022. Front row, seated: Helena Whitbread and Jill Liddington; standing, Rachel Lappin

Appendices

An Anne Lister glossary

Blue	Tory (soon called Conservative)
cousin	period
D.W.	measurement of area, a day's work (about two-thirds of an acre)
goit	channel for water to go to a water-powered mill
grubble	stroke, fondle, caress (*SOD*'s latest reference is 1719, but later usage may have continued in regions such as Yorkshire)
hurriers	workers (usually boys) moving coal underground
kiss	orgasm
plumper	In a two-member constituency such as Halifax an elector could vote for two candidates; if he cast just one vote, a plumper, it was more effective in strengthening a favoured candidate
Radicals	the political party of Michael Stocks and Edward Protheroe; in favour of the abolition of slavery
siding	arranging, tidying
West Riding	Yorkshire was divided into three Ridings: West, North and East. The West Riding was vast, stretching from Leeds down to Sheffield
Yellows	Whigs, believed in moderate reform (later, became Liberals)

PEOPLE AND PLACES: ANN WALKER'S FAMILY NETWORKS

Ann Walker's wealth originated in her grandfather's late eighteenth-century worsted manufacturing business. A successful merchant, William Walker built the two key family houses in Lightcliffe, Cliff Hill and Crow Nest.[1] In 1786 his eldest son, Ann's Uncle William, inherited the estate. He was a sufficiently canny entrepreneur to issue his own banknotes, probably the first person in Halifax to do so.[2] In 1809 Uncle William died unmarried. So overnight, with Ann Walker just six years old, her father, John Walker, inherited the estate.[3] The family moved into impressive Crow Nest, and this became Ann's childhood home.

However, just as significant as the Walkers' newly acquired wealth were Ann's family networks. These linked her into the elite of the Halifax area: the Edwards, the Priestleys and, of course, the Rawsons. It was these relationships, their houses and their landscapes that were so significant in Ann's life. And from 1834 onwards, living with Anne Lister at Shibden, these family networks were not neglected. When a round of formal visits was made by carriage, Anne would accompany Ann. So these people and places became highly significant to their marriage – and need to be mapped (see figure 9).

Anne Lister's own ancestors had failed to made judicious marriages which might subsequently have benefited Anne herself. The exception was her Uncle Joseph, who had prudently married his cousin Elizabeth Lister of Northgate House, thus bringing into the Shibden family this elegant house in the town centre, so significant a property to Anne.[4] But generally the Lister family was dynastically fragile, either not marrying or having children who soon died (all four of Anne's brothers died young). The Walker genealogy told a different story; and Anne, now sharing her life with Ann, rapidly absorbed the details.

There were three crucial marriages. The first was in 1776 when Ann's aunt, Elizabeth Walker of Crow Nest, married John Priestley. The Priestleys were old-established clothiers from the ancient township of Sowerby, a few miles west of Halifax. John Priestley lived at Thorpe beyond Sowerby, and Elizabeth went to live there.[5] So their son, William Priestley, though twenty-four

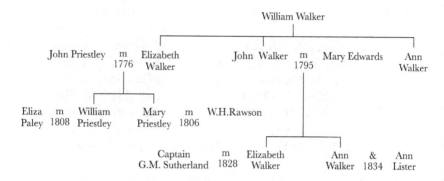

9 Ann Walker's family networks: intermarriage within the Halifax elite

years older than Ann, was her cousin. He played a particularly significant role in Ann and Anne's relationship, as he and his wife Eliza lived in Lightcliffe. Indeed, their house was situated neatly between Lidgate and Cliff Hill, and thus was well placed to keep an eye on their young cousin. Mrs Priestley and Anne Lister had been friendly, but now Eliza became watchful. One afternoon at Lidgate in autumn 1832 she had surprised Anne and Ann while they were kissing passionately. Anne recorded in her diary afterwards: '*I had jumped in time ... but Ann looked red and I pale and Mrs P~ ... looked vexed, jealous and annoyed.*'[6] With their suspicions hardening, the relationship between these Priestleys and Shibden never softened.

The second marriage was in 1795, when Ann's father John Walker married Mary Edwards of Pye Nest; it lay just to the west of Halifax, on the hillside sloping down to Sowerby Bridge. The Edwards were successful woollen manufacturers, and Pye Nest shared the same impressive elegance as Crow Nest. Their business success was a story of 'grit and determination', turning their 'ancient homestead' into a 'hive of activity, much to the disgust of the neighbouring gentry'.[7]

Ann's father died in 1823 when Ann was just 19, and her mother died shortly afterwards. Under the terms of his 48-page will, his brother-in-law Henry Edwards and his nephew William Priestley were appointed trustees.[8] This was in part to look after the interests of his two daughters, Elizabeth and Ann, protecting them against unscrupulous fortune-hunting suitors. Ann's Uncle Henry was indeed a vigilant trustee, giving Captain Sutherland a good looking-over. Both trustees, cousin William Priestley and uncle Henry Edwards, continued to be vigilant, to Anne's irritation.[9]

Finally, in 1806, Ann's older cousin Mary Priestley married William Henry Rawson, younger brother of the eminent banker Christopher Rawson. This was perhaps the trickiest of the intermarriages, triggering the fiercest feuds. Known as W. H. Rawson, he lived at Mill House beyond Sowerby, owning an old water-powered woollen mill that employed 120 workers down at Sowerby Bridge on the canal.[10]

So, in the space of just thirty years, the Walker family had married into three elite families: the Priestleys, the Edwards and the Rawsons. All shared two significant characteristics: they had all acquired wealth through traditional water-powered woollen manufacture,[11] and they all lived in the countryside near Sowerby. One key outcome was that when Ann and Anne made formal rounds of visits to Walker relatives, their carriage headed firmly west – out past Pye Nest to the ancient Sowerby township. The only exceptions were Ann's elderly aunt Walker and the William Priestleys in Lightcliffe and the Rawsons living on the edge of Halifax, who remained business rivals.[12]

Voting in the 1837 election

Shibden Hall estate: key tenants

Name	Property	Township	Constituency	Voting
Bottomley, John	Brearley Hall	Southowram	Halifax	Wortley, James
Dodgson, Henry	Lower Place	Southowram	West Riding	[blank]
Freeman, Samuel	Brier Lodge	Southowram	West Riding	Wortley, John
Hall, Samuel	Marsh	Southowram	West Riding	Wortley, John
Hardcastle, William	Roydelands	Hipperholme-cum-Brighouse	West Riding	Wortley, John
Hemingway, Abraham	Southolm	Southowram	West Riding	Wortley, John
Hepworth, Mark	Yew trees	Hipperholme-cum-Brighouse	West Riding	Wortley, John
Howarth, Charles	Ireland	Southowram	West Riding	Wortley, John
Mawson, John	Stump Cross Inn	Northowram	West Riding	Wortley, John
Naylor, George	Upper Place	Southowram	West Riding	Wortley, John
Pearson, Thomas	Denmark	Southowram	West Riding	Wortley, John
Robinson, George	Northowram	Hipperholme-cum-Brighouse	West Riding	Wortley, John
Sowden, Samuel	Sutcliffe Wood	Hipperholme-cum-Brighouse	West Riding	Wortley, John

CROW NEST ESTATE: KEY TENANTS

Name	Property	Township	Constituency	Voting
Bairstow, James	Water Lane mill	Halifax	Halifax	Protheroe & Wood
Bottomley, George	Shibden Mill	Northowram	West Riding	[blank]
Bottomley, Thomas	Shibden Mill	Northowram	West Riding	Morpeth & Strickland
Cunliffe, Thomas	Water Lane	Halifax Borough	Halifax	Protheroe & Wood
Hainsworth, Thos	Hatter's Close	Halifax	West Riding	Wortley, James
Hird, Lamplugh W.	Lidgate, Lightcliffe	Hipperholme-cum-Brighouse	West Riding	Wortley, John
Hirst, William	Moor Miers	Stainland	West Riding	Wortley, John
Outram, Benjamin	Greetland Elland	Greetland	West Riding	Morpeth & Wortley
Patterson, Matthew	Bailey Hall	Southowram	West Riding	Morpeth & Strickland
Taylor, Eli	Common Wood	Stainland	West Riding	Wortley, John
Taylor, Joseph	Hard Platts	Stainland	West Riding	Wortley, John
Tetley, Samuel	North Parade	Halifax	Halifax	Protheroe & Wood
Washington, George	Crow Nest	Hipperholme-cum-Brighouse	West Riding	Wortley, John

OTHER LOCAL ELECTORS[1]

Name	Location	Township	Constituency	Voting
Adam, Thomas	Savile Lane	Halifax	West Riding	Wortley, John
Adam, Thomas	Savile Road	Halifax	Halifax	Wortley, James
Crapper, John	Bull Green	Halifax	Halifax	Wortley, James
Holt, James	High Royd	Northowram	West Riding	Morpeth & Strickland
Jubb, Abraham	Lord Street	Halifax	Halifax	Wortley, James
Jubb, Abraham	Lord Street	Halifax	West Riding	Wortley, John
Musgrave, Rev Charles	Vicarage	Halifax	Halifax	Wortley, James
Parker, Robert	Square	Halifax	Halifax	Wortley, James
Parker, Robert	Square	Halifax	West Riding	Wortley, John
Priestley, Henry	Haugh End	Sowerby	West Riding	[blank]
Priestley, Walker	Kebroyd	Soyland	West Riding	Wortley, John
Priestley, William	Lightcliffe	Hipperholme-cum-Brighouse	West Riding	Morpeth & Strickland
Rawson, Christopher	Hope House	Halifax	Halifax	Wortley, James
Rawson, Christopher	Hope House	Halifax	West Riding	Wortley, Joseph
Rawson, Jeremiah	Halifax	Southowram	West Riding	Wortley, Joseph
Rawson, Jeremiah	Shay	Halifax	Halifax	Wortley, James
Rawson, W H.	Mill House	Sowerby	West Riding	Wortley, Joseph
Stocks, Joseph	Upper Shibden Hall	Northowram	West Riding	Morpeth & Strickland
Stocks, Michael	Skircoat	Halifax	Halifax	Protheroe & Wood
Wainhouse, Robert	Washer Lane	Halifax	Halifax	Wortley, James
Waterhouse, John	Well-head	Halifax	Halifax	Wortley, James

[1]Certain businessmen could vote in both local constituencies.

Notes

Abbreviations

AL	Anne Lister
ALBW	Anne Lister Birthday Weekend (later, Week)
AW	Ann Walker
CN	Crow Nest records
HG	John Lister (ed.), 'Some Extracts from the Diary of a Halifax Lady', *Halifax Guardian*, 1887–92
RAM	Phyllis Ramsden papers
SOD	*Shorter Oxford Dictionary*
SH	Shibden Hall records
THAS	*Transactions of the Halifax Antiquarian Society*

Preface

1 See J. Liddington, 'Who Was the Real Anne Lister?', July 2019, https://vimeo.com/348859464 (accessed 20 September 2022).
2 See Liddington, *Presenting the Past*, pp. 12–22.
3 See Liddington, *Female Fortune*, Preface, pp. xv–xx.
4 Anne Lister Codebreakers, WYAS, volunteer transcribers, project started July 2019.
5 'Ann Walker Revealed', Steve Crabtree and Diane Halford, ALBW interview, May 2020, https://www.youtube.com/watch?v=gQgjGbcJAQk (accessed 8 October 2022).
6 I later found that Marlene Oliveira in Portugal was working on the late 1830s, and we got in touch.
7 'Some Extracts of the Diary of a Halifax Lady'; see Liddington, *Presenting the Past*. This summary focuses on 1836–38.

8 See the Glossary for explanation of these arcane terms, p. 304. See also Liddington, *Presenting the Past*, p. 13.

9 Liddington, *Presenting the Past*, p. 14.

10 Liddington, *Female Fortune*, pp. 141–3.

11 He continued his 120 instalments up to the trip through Russia to Tiflis, ending on [23] May 1840.

12 Liddington, *Presenting the Past*, p. 15; John Lister was probably homosexual.

13 Liddington, *Presenting the Past*, pp. 16–18, 51–3. 1,850 AL letters survive, SH:7/ML.

14 There are also gaps for April–June 1836, August–October 1836 and 28 November 1836–3 April 1837.

15 Liddington, *Presenting the Past*, pp. 65–6.

16 Liddington, *Presenting the Past*, pp. 17, 19, 21; ironically this was just a year before the 1967 Act that decriminalized homosexuality.

17 RAM: 71–3, AL's journal, vols 19–21.

18 Halifax Borough Council effectively suppressed knowledge of these passages, lest scandal fall on the ancient Lister family; Liddington, *Presenting the Past*, pp. 19–21. Recently, Laura Johansen considered whether they were destroyed by Ramsden before her death, or shortly afterwards by a descendant. Ramsden was interviewed by the *Guardian* on 17 February 1984.

19 Quoted by Cannadine, *Aspects of Aristocracy*, p. 231.

20 Though our approaches differed, Cat and I worked together in the mid-1990s. For example, we gave a joint talk at the 1992 Women's History Conference on 'The Anne Lister Labyrinth'. The concept of intersectionality was then still new.

21 The significance of the diaries was recognized by UNESCO in 2011; Liddington, *Female Fortune*, p. xvi.

22 RAM: 6–25, Russia. See Ingham, 'Anne Lister in the Pyrenees', and Liddington, 'Anne Lister & Emily Brontë'. There are also problems with Steidele's re-translation and dense endnotes.

23 AL's travel mss were also digitized, but Green's dissertation, 'A Spirited Yorkshirewoman', has not yet been.

24 'Meet the army of code-breakers around the world working to transcribe Anne Lister's diaries', *Yorkshire Post*, 16 December 2019. See also Codebreakers, ALBW Live, January 2022, www.youtube.com/watch?v=sud1Hxy0mD8 (accessed 8 October 2022).

25 With a focus on coded passages, Euler's insights on intersectionality are often brushed aside. However, her work is not forgotten; in April 2021 'The Hunt' Facebook page put up a PDF link to her dissertation.

26 WYAS was closed from 17 March 2020.

27 Calderdale Borough Council, minutes, 24 August 2020; Calderdale Heritage Walks were also re-cancelled. However, the Happy Valley Pride talk took place on Zoom, 23 July 2020.

28 J. Liddington, *Vanishing for the Vote: Suffrage, Citizenship and the Battle for the Census*, Manchester University Press, 2014.

29 'Anne Lister Research Summit', conversation with Livia Labate, 'Packed with Potential', September 2020, https://www.youtube.com/watch?v=J6HmvX_yeH8 (accessed 20 September 2022).

30 For the discovery of Ann Walker's diary in October 2020, see Liddington, *Female Fortune*, pp. 252–7.

31 With constantly changing tiers, I used to say: 'If you think you know what's going on, you haven't been listening.'

32 Inevitably, book publishing is unlikely to be as up-to-date as Twitter. Groan!

33 Hall et al., *Legacies of British Slave-ownership*. See notably David Olusoga, 'Britain's Forgotten Slave Owners', BBC4, 2 July 2020 (first shown in 2015). See Introduction for the Sutherlands' slave ownership.

34 In the countryside beyond Leeds, the Earl of Harewood derived wealth from Caribbean slavery; Hall et al., *Legacies of British Slave-ownership*, pp. 22, 129. The only Listers linked to slavery were Anne's two great-uncles who bought about fifteen slaves; Liddington, *Female Fortune*, pp. 6, 261 n. 26.

35 Rather surprising exceptions to this were Edward Protheroe MP and John Lister's mother.

36 See https://www.ucl.ac.uk/lbs/person/view/2146650965 (accessed 20 September 2022). See Introduction.

37 Liddington, *Presenting the Past*, pp. 44–5. I have pruned this detail vigorously here.

38 https://jiangjy-713.github.io/AL_Index/html/index.html (accessed 20 September 2022) lists AL diary transcriptions by year; there are gaps especially from 1836. Thanks to Marlene Oliveira, email, 26 April 2021.

39 This is discussed in the Introduction and especially in the Afterword.

40 Esther Addley, '"A very dangerous epoch": historians try and make sense of Covid', *Guardian*, 13 February 2021, https://www.theguardian.com/world/2021/feb/13/a-very-dangerous-epoch-historians-try-make-sense-of-covid (accessed 20 September 2022). However, *The Author*, in an editorial in summer 2021, noted that 'what has most sapped authors' creativity has been a lurking feeling of triviality or irrelevance' compared to, say, an intensive-care doctor or nurse.

41 Those who have read *Female Fortune* might wish to skim the Introduction.

42 Gentleman Jack Fandom, Twitter, 30 May 2022.

INTRODUCTION

1 See Liddington, *Female Fortune*, pp. 22–3 for details; see also Liddington, *Nature's Domain*, pp. 34ff.

2 Green, 'A Spirited Yorkshirewoman', p. 418, 15 November 1831.

3 Green, 'A Spirited Yorkshirewoman', p. 433, 9 July 1832; also quoted in Green, *Miss Lister of Shibden Hall*, p. 173.

4 *HG*, pp. 125–6, 128.

5 Liddington, *Nature's Domain*, pp. 24–5, 47; map of Shibden Hall estate belonging to Mr James Lister, 1791.

6 Liddington, *Female Fortune*, pp. 34–5.

7 Will of Robert Sutherland, 1824, p. 3, notes 'Slaves Stock etc', CN:87/1, also CN:87/2 & 3, copies of RS's will, 1824. CN:103/2 suggests £24,000 per annum before emancipation of slaves. Also Halford, 'Slavery and Shibden Hall', research blog, August 2020, www.insearchofannwalker.com (accessed 8 October 2022).

8 See Liddington, *Female Fortune*, p. 66.

9 Liddington, *Nature's Domain*, pp. 63–4.

10 Liddington, *Female Fortune*, p. 65.

11 Liddington, *Female Fortune*, p. 64.

12 Liddington, *Female Fortune*, pp. 90–1, 100.

13 Liddington, *Female Fortune*, pp. 72–4; during 1833 AL travelled in Europe, including Paris and Denmark; AW visited her sister in Scotland.

14 Liddington, *Female Fortune*, pp. 92–3; see Glossary, p. 304.

15 Liddington, *Female Fortune*, pp. 93, 100. Some editors omit the final ten words, but in doing so, find themselves bemused as the relationship goes forward. The chronology seems somewhat confusing in Steidele, *Gentleman Jack*, pp. 212–18. Choma, *Gentleman Jack*, is much clearer, though it omits Anne's final words. Oddly, Ramsden's summaries of the coded passage also omit this. Sadly, the newly discovered Ann Walker diary volume does not open until two months later. In June–August 1834, AL and AW travelled abroad, climbing Mont Blanc.

16 Liddington, *Female Fortune*, p. 101.

17 Liddington, *Female Fortune*, p. 110; the rent was £100 p.a. (my thanks to Ian Philp for this information).

18 See Appendix for names and addresses of tenants.

19 He lived in a substantial farmhouse nearby, his mill at one point employing about 200 children.

20 Liddington, *Female Fortune*, pp. 51–2, August 1832.

21 Liddington, *Female Fortune*, pp. 51, 173–4, May 1835. 'Blue' was Tory (soon, Conservative); 'Yellow' was Whig.

22 CN estate documentation is much fuller from the 1840s (especially the 1867 map). For the 1830s, archival evidence is decidedly patchy. Helpful is CN:103/2/118 (July 1830). The land in Honley beyond Huddersfield is not considered here. For archival gaps concerning the vexatious litigation after Anne Lister's death in 1840, see Liddington, *Female Fortune*, pp. 238–9. Luckily, researchers are now uncovering more; see Preface, note 5.

23 The 1830s estate records are woefully patchy; however, a detailed list of tenants' rents paid at Shibden Mill at Whitsuntide 1830 is neat, legible – and revealing.

24 Here, I am especially indebted to Ian Philp, 'Elizabeth and Ann Walker's Inheritance', September 2021. http://lightcliffechurchyard.org.uk/attachments/article/137/Elizabeth%20and%20Ann%20Walker's%20Inheritance.pdf

(accessed 8 October 2022). See also plan of Crow Nest Estates, 1867 (http://www.lightcliffehistory.org.uk), which included the railway. Though dating from after AL's death, its detail remains invaluable.

25 The Crow Nest lodge was built in 1867 by Titus Salt.

26 CN:105/2, sales leaflet for Shibden Mill, 1801; scribbling preceded wool carding.

27 CN:103/2/118, rents handled by lawyer Thomas Adam.

28 Liddington, *Female Fortune*, p. 138. It was expanding along Bailey Hall, an otherwise unprepossessing strip of land on the Southowram side of the canal.

29 *HG*, p. 151, 20 November 1835; the link appears to have been that he had a cousin living near Shibden.

30 AL's and AW's diaries, 20 November 1834. For AW diary, see Liddington, *Female Fortune*, pp. 252–7.

31 Except at election time when Ann's cousin, John Edwards, was actively involved with the 'Blue' interest.

32 Whitbread, *I Know My Own Heart*, p. 15; *HG*, 1823, p. 88. Mariana's mother was related to Mary, née Page. For Haugh End, see *Halifax Courier*, 1 April 2021.

33 Liddington, *Female Fortune*, p. 151; AL told her doctor that Christopher Rawson 'had too many trades … [so] offending some influential people', 26 February 1835.

34 Liddington, *Female Fortune*, pp. 133, 180–1.

35 Liddington, *Female Fortune*, p. 140. The tenant was Aquilla Green, Mytholm, that is, in the West Riding constituency. AL and AW both had more tenants here of course. However, the Whig ascendancy (and the large electorate) in the West Riding meant that their small-scale efforts had far great impact in compact Halifax.

36 Liddington, *Female Fortune*, p. 141.

37 Liddington, *Female Fortune*, pp. 143–6.

38 Liddington, *Female Fortune*, p. 169, 29 April 1835.

39 The word 'casino' had not yet acquired its later louche associations, then meaning a public function room for dancing and music. The Deardens lived at the Hollins (probably above Sowerby Bridge).

40 Liddington, *Female Fortune*, pp. 170–1, 2 and 5 May 1835.

41 Liddington, *Female Fortune*, p. 188, 26 August 1835; p. 190, 22 September 1835 (master builder: Mr Husband).

42 As an elite York lawyer, how much did he know?

43 Liddington, *Female Fortune*, pp. 190–2, Meanwhile, the Northgate workmen, after a very good dinner, got drunk and 'said the Blues were the best'.

44 Liddington, *Female Fortune*, pp. 147, 135.

45 Ann's cousin Mary had married Christopher's younger brother, W. H. Rawson. See Appendix, p. 307.

46 I missed CN:33/18 (32 pages long) when I originally did my research. One reason for this is that back then there was less interest in Ann Walker. The

other is that the Crow Nest mss for the 1830s are complex and patchy. The date on the title page of CN:33/18 is 1861, hence my inattention.

47 Legacies of Slave Ownership, https://www.ucl.ac.uk/lbs/person/view/2146650965 (accessed 23 June 2020). See Halford, 'Slavery and Shibden Hall', research blog, August 2020, www.insearchofannwalker.com (accessed 8 October 2022).

48 CN:33/18, p. 13.

49 CN:33/18, p. 15. The document then jumps (p. 16) to 1847.

50 The amounts of money involved are too complex to follow in detail.

51 Liddington, *Female Fortune*, p. 218; it was reported in the *Halifax Guardian*.

52 Liddington, *Female Fortune*, p. 221.

53 Liddington, *Female Fortune*, p. 221. For Branwell Brontë and effigy-burning etc., see Barker, *The Brontës*, p. 270.

54 Liddington, *Female Fortune*, pp. 221, 227, 3 April 1836.

55 Liddington, *Female Fortune*, pp. 233–4; also the signing of their wills, despite AW being plagued by doubts.

56 In 1815, when Anne Lister moved into Shibden, her parents and sister Marian went to live near Market Weighton; Liddington, *Female Fortune*, pp. 8, 11. The family links were the Inmans.

NOTE ON THE TEXT

1 My 1990 calculation was four million words; later, five million words was suggested. Ruth Cummins, WYAS Archivist Calderdale, calculates that the final total could be about 4.8 million words. However, until the final diary transcriptions are confirmed, it will not be possible to offer a definite total. There are 24 main hardback diaries (March 1817–August 1840); for earlier, there are loose pages (1806–1814), and two notebooks (1816–March 1817). WYAS email, 19 August 2022. I am extremely grateful to Ruth for her work here.

2 Where Anne's letters are inserted into the text, these are usually placed at the end of that day, so as not to interrupt the diary flow.

3 Some of these have been noted in the Introduction. Significant gaps in the 1830s include CN:103/1 & 2 (correspondence); MAC:89, FW:120/28 & SH:2/CM. Taken together, they are an archivists' nightmare.

4 Roughly 459,000 words.

5 135,00 words, of which perhaps 110,000 are diary. With extracts from other sources (notably from AL's letters), the average daily total of her words here is longer.

6 For AW's diary, see Liddington, *Female Fortune*, pp. 252–7.

7 For more recent transcription (notably, Codebreakers, Packed with Potential), see Preface.

8 Not everyone will agree with me here. Some AL fans hold that every word that she wrote was gripping.

9 Mainly page and volume numbers; also her weather measurements, recording of times, and routine Sunday church attendances.

10 However, ellipses are not used at the start or end of each daily diary entry.

11 I decided not to write 'marriage' but rather marriage. Even though unrecognized by Church or state, it aimed to be 'as good as a marriage' in Anne Lister's eyes.

12 See Appendix, 'Voting in the 1837 Election'. For *Gentleman Jack*, see Roulston, 'From Text to Screen'.

13 I have modernized some place names; for example, Cliff hill becomes Cliff Hill.

14 Repeated time measurements have been omitted. However, measurements of land are given, such as D.W., that is, a day's work (roughly two-thirds of an acre).

THE ANNE LISTER DIARIES
MAY 1836

1 And undoubtedly AL now received *all* the Shibden rents herself, assisted by Samuel Washington.

2 See Davidoff and Hall, *Family Fortunes*, for gendered roles.

3 *SOD* gives date of Bucellas (Portuguese white wine) as 1836, so it was very cutting-edge!

4 Unusually, prayers were held not with the servants. Anne probably wanted to get rid of any link to trade by burning the account books; see Liddington, *Female Fortune*, p. 159 (burning Uncle Joseph's old trade books).

5 The oranges are a sign of sophisticated hospitality.

6 Unlike around Sowerby, this was not an area AL knew well. It was unusual for her to make mistakes, but she possibly confused Stainland and Greetland. My thanks to Ian Philp for this suggestion.

7 This suggests that Ann's uncle William Walker had expanded the Crow Nest estate out to Stainland; he died in 1809.

8 Readers will chuckle at the reference to 'Ainley top'. It now has only one meaning: the roundabout off the M62 motorway, between Huddersfield and Halifax.

9 Other properties lay even further out, beyond Halifax parish (e.g. Honley).

10 SH:7/ML/AC/26, 17 May 1836. Best remembered for Wainhouse Tower!

11 AL had earlier trusted Hinscliffe; Liddington, *Female Fortune*, p. 147. However, she now suspected he might side with the Rawsons.

12 Without Marian, was the household growing rather disorganized?

13 Was this melancholy partly because, despite their dynastic ambitions, they knew they could not produce an heir? If so, this was probably more keenly felt by AW.

14 This letter not in SH:7/ML but appears in the diary.

15 Undoubtedly an oblique complaint about Marian.

16 Liddington, *Female Fortune*, pp. 92–3.
17 Lidgate had been let on a long (i.e. ten-year) lease.
18 To pay for Lower Crow Nest land purchase.
19 'Special constables', sworn in by local magistrates, helped to keep law and order. The Poor Law made many working-class families fear ending up in a new 'workhouse'. Dorothy and Edward Thompson, 'Halifax as a Chartist Centre', pp. 13–15, note several years of sharp political conflict before middle-class radicalism (Michael Stocks, Edward Protheroe) and Chartism became entwined.
20 This was unusual for AL, who was perhaps irked by Samuel Washington's forgetting the note, so giving the impression to Halifax magistrates that she was unreliable.
21 Thompson, *The Chartists*, p. 322.
22 11 July was AW's next rent day.
23 The line of code is inserted, so is almost illegible. Cantharides (or dried beetle) may have been an aphrodisiac.
24 Also known as devil's dung; see Liddington, *Female Fortune*, p. 223.

June 1836

1 Line of code (inserted) omitted as almost illegible.
2 Eclipses were right up AL's street as she was a scientist.
3 'As usual'? Perhaps her enthusiasm for children didn't last long.
4 Suspicion of servants' drinking was prevalent.
5 For image of AL's Russian passport, 1839, see Hargreaves, *Halifax*, p. 79.
6 Robert Bakewell's *An Introduction to Geology* was Lyell's introduction to geology.
7 So, AL believed that if AW started menstruating again, it would help heal their sexual relationship.
8 Bowling was by Bradford.
9 This would be an industrial hamlet down at Mytholm, so not visible from Shibden Hall. 'Housefire coal' presumably commanded a higher price.
10 Also, SH:7/LL/403, Marian to her aunt, settled in lodging, chatty letter; Marian owned Holt's High Roydes.
11 Was this a reference back to the 1834 betrothal? Or did 'blessed' here refer to producing an heir?
12 'Leave here' might also make sense.
13 Some people assert that AW was 'neurotic' or weak. But given the deaths in her family, and especially given the public humiliations of the 1835 mock marriage 'outing' and more recent effigy-burning, could an Austen or Brontë heroine have got their head round such a huge challenge?
14 Possibly her casino was not developing as well as hoped? Given that Samuel Washington had bungled getting special constables sworn in, she discussed with Adam whether she should get Parker, an experienced lawyer, to be her business steward.

15 This must be the Lidgate pew rented by Lamplugh Hird.

16 Close relatives of Ann Walker's late mother; probably Anne Edwards, recently widowed (John Edwards, d. 1835); she was Anne Waterhouse before marriage.

17 See Liddington, *Female Fortune*, p. 159, 2 April 1835.

18 See Brears, 'John Harper at Shibden', p. 61. Also Liddington, *Female Fortune*, pp. 173–4, 230–1.

19 Walker Priestley was younger brother of William Priestley; he lived at Kebroyd, Sowerby.

20 Liddington, *Female Fortune*, p. 147; also SH:7/ML/AC/26 and 28 May 1836.

21 So back to late April 1836, that is, the death of her father and exile of her sister.

22 Oops! The letter has suddenly gone from 'I' to 'we'. What would Lady Stuart assume?

23 SH:7/ML/940; Green, 'A Spirited Yorkshirewoman', p. 489.

24 SH:7/ML/942; Green, 'A Spirited Yorkshirewoman', p. 490 offers just a brief selection.

25 Achnacarry is in the Scottish Highlands, to the east of Skye; Clan Cameron.

26 Eminent geologist Charles Lyell is fully introduced in February 1837.

27 AL note on envelope: answered on 1 August (i.e. she waited a month!)

JULY 1836

1 See Liddington, *Female Fortune*, pp. 219–20.

2 Contrast Mr Briggs's conversation at Cliff Hill when AL encountered him there. The idea of the railway station as high up as Northgate is now laughable.

3 Also, work on the Lodge was completed, with the masons celebrating at Stump Cross Inn; Brears, 'John Harper at Shibden', p. 62.

4 Was near neighbour Thomas Greenwood a favoured tenant?

5 See Map II and Ann Walker's family networks, Appendix, p. 305.

6 SH:7/ML/943/1 & 2; scarcely legible, and not in Green, 'A Spirited Yorkshire-woman'. Highcliffe Castle on the Dorset coast was built in 1831–36 by Lord Stuart de Rothesay in Gothic revival style. See Liddington, *Female Fortune*, p. 198, for AL's dream.

7 Matty embodied practical domestic skills.

8 Possibly because her husband kept her short of money.

9 This sounds rather furtive just for a tart. Perhaps because AW was not confident about baking?

10 Presumably this copy of the letter was for AL's archive.

11 SH:7/M/945 (not in Green, 'A Spirited Yorkshirewoman', p. 490). A very disingenuous letter. Knew that Mariana was short of money? Charles doesn't give her enough? All rather odd.

12 Interesting about conventional female domestic skills, even for a woman with servants.

13 Erotic thoughts about AW?

14 SH:7/ML/947 & 948, a longer and friendlier if illegible letter from Lady Stuart de Rothesay. Earlier editors leave gaps here, for example Green, 'A Spirited Yorkshirewoman', no letters until 12 August; also RAM: 71.

AUGUST 1836

1 Oastler came from Fixby, then in the vast Halifax parish. AL's tenant George Robinson's wire mill (reputedly) employed about 200 children. See also *Halifax Guardian*, 13 August, letter from Oastler.
2 Thompson and Thompson, 'Halifax as a Chartist Centre', p. 15.
3 Also 8 August, AW borrowed £2,500 from her aunt.
4 These new flags enabled them to enjoy the garden without getting their feet wet.
5 Presumably the walk down to the *chaumière*.
6 Green, 'A Spirited Yorkshirewoman', p. 491, SH:7/ML/951.
7 Brears, 'John Harper at Shibden', p. 60.

SEPTEMBER 1836

1 SH:7/ML/957. Eliza had been AL's schoolgirl lover, and subsequently lived in an asylum.
2 Downton – with a difference: no butler and no large servants' hall.
3 Probably Miss Inman.
4 As their aunt neared death, AL would have been sharply reminded that it was only Marian (and not herself) who could provide Shibden with a direct heir.

OCTOBER 1836

1 Ling Roth, *Banking in Halifax*, p. 29. The manager was Andrew McKean; its branch was at 4 Cheapside.
2 Quite a long hike!
3 Such a low height underground suggests it would be suitable mainly for boys.
4 Liddington, *Female Fortune*, pp. 133, 138–43; Protheroe had, of course, lost to the 'Blue' candidate Wortley by a single vote. See also August 1836, introduction.
5 Also, AL 'had' Charlotte Booth; her story set out in stark detail the scant options open to a young working-class girl. Unless she was very lucky, she would always remain dependent on the goodwill of better-placed women.
6 See SH drawing 1836, p. 89. Nelson had worked on Northgate casino; Liddington, *Female Fortune*, pp. 190–1.

7 The formality of Anne's note suggests a coolness towards Cliff Hill.

8 SH:7/ML/AC/27.

9 Liddington, *Female Fortune*, p. 147.

10 The Pollards presumably moved into the new Lodge so Conery could be used for the kitchen garden.

11 Hurry: to carry, convey, drive fast, *SOD*.

12 Was one pit an air shaft?

13 Did AL lament the loss of her sister Marian at moments like this?

14 Sutherland of the 92nd Highlanders certainly had a motive.

15 Despite rapid industrialization, the local leech woman was still relied upon.

16 Horse gin: a drum for winding or pumping.

17 Thompson and Thompson, 'Halifax as a Chartist Centre', pp. 15–16, quoting *Halifax Guardian*, 8 October 1836; they suggest that Protheroe's radicalism was half-hearted, and 'it was O'Connor who stole the thunder', lashing the Poor Law and supporting the 10-Hour Bill.

18 A popular book then widely read; my thanks to Mike Leeder for this information.

19 What is noticeable is that AL included a copy of her letter to Lady Stuart *before* recording her aunt's death in her own diary.

20 Did AL exaggerate how much the Shibden 'improvements' were at her aunt's behest so as to strengthen Anne's dynastic identity?

21 Had they known each other all their lives?

22 Sexton: church officer responsible for gravedigging etc.

23 Mutes: professional funeral attendants.

24 Also Robert Rawlinson, gardener, Conery, who moved in after the Pollards moved out.

25 SH:3/FN/30/4, 10 and 13 October 1836.

26 This was the first time that this was necessary; always before, aunt (and father and Marian) remained at Shibden.

27 Liddington, *Female Fortune*, p. 4.

28 Looks like 'genealogical map', but that can't be right.

29 AL did not record what they talked of during the 25 minutes walking on the flags.

30 See Brears, 'John Harper at Shibden'. AL planned to build some new shops on the street by Northgate?

31 There are various potential explanations for why AW is not very present here: AL did not wish AW to see her weeping, a sign of weakness; or AW's attempts to console AL were unsatisfactory.

32 Green, 'A Spirited Yorkshirewoman', pp. 491–2. The letters to newspapers were probably obituary notices.

33 A servants' hall appears to be new.

34 So Rawson still seemed interested in coal up near Shibden.

35 AL seems to talk of AW rather as if she were a child.

36 AL also wrote to John Lister, her legal next of kin, in London.

37 Unusually, AL repeated herself, understandably given the circumstances.

38 950 words selected here.

NOVEMBER 1836

1 Green, 'A Spirited Yorkshirewoman', pp. 492–3, 1 November 1836.
2 'Conservative Dinner', *Halifax Guardian*, 2 November 1836. See also Davidoff and Hall, *Family Fortunes*, p. 440, on gender in the public sphere of politics.
3 Replying to Vere's letter of 30 September, that is, before her aunt's death.
4 The late Sibella Maclean was Vere's aunt. 'Widening circle' probably refers to new children.
5 Willoughy Crewe, an unusual and charming man, lived near the Lawtons. He was not only a trustee but also a sympathetic friend to Mariana in her difficult marriage. Yet Mariana had earlier told AL that she liked *her* more than Willoughby Crewe.
6 Probably a Cheshire neighbour.
7 Here, 'Mrs' signifies not married status but seniority.
8 The rocks above the Hall were a key part of Shibden's landscape improvements.
9 Schools were, of course, a common charitable cause for women with money and time.
10 She was related to AW's mother's family.
11 Or perhaps AW wished to assert her sexual relationship with AL?
12 Some Methodist chapels, under the guise of sermons, talked radical politics, possibly including Pule Nick, Northowram. Ben Rushton, a handloom weaver who became a local Chartist, preached in Methodist chapels.
13 Mourning rings to remember the dead were carefully graded. Poor Marian was not even named. Mrs Veitch was a local friend.
14 Often it was the most remote rural millowners who defied the Act.
15 AL writes 'A~', but must mean Mariana.
16 Of course, Mariana's mother was related to Mrs Priestley; see Introduction, p. 5.
17 Mariana, who had no children of her own, probably had a special affection for her niece; also mixed into this row were Mariana's complex finances.
18 Presumably Charles's lack of hospitality was because he suspected the true nature of Anne's relationship with Ann Walker, not because the Walkers came from 'trade'.
19 SH:7/ML/967. See also AL's diary, 29 November 1836.

DECEMBER 1836

1 Was AL, now in her mid-forties, wondering about the menopause?
2 Lord Wharton's charity, founded in 1696, provided Bibles for children and young people.
3 Would AL's next four years have been different had he been dangerously ill?
4 AL did so, that is, she wrote a note.

5 Probably advertising for quarrying.

6 SH:7/ML/C/3, 5 December 1836, business letters. 'The Lady' undoubtedly referred to the Misses Preston, Halifax.

7 Letter, SH:7/ML/C/3, business letters.

8 *HG*, p. 145, lists just five Halifax banks open in 1836.

9 It is at such moments that the reader wishes to hear AW's voice to know what she was really thinking about both MacKenzie and money.

10 This included the Conservatives' slogan 'the Church in danger' (i.e. fomenting anti-Irish feeling), spurred by alarm about Radicalism, the dramatic growth of local Conservative Associations, and Robert Peel's keenness on the registration of Blue voters. Peel was Prime Minister for just five months (December 1834–April 1835); Lord Melbourne, Whig, was the current Prime Minister (1835–41).

11 Railway planning was still in its infancy; Halifax was high above the River Calder, unlike Sowerby Bridge.

12 AL swapped from code in mid-sentence.

13 The final few weeks of 1836 were largely ignored by earlier editors. They have my sympathy. Other than for economic historians, the financial and legal complexities can appear baffling.

14 Liddington, *Female Fortune*, p. 218. Confusing: Bairstow and/or Barstow?

15 See Liddington, *Female Fortune*, pp. 233–4, when they signed their wills at York (though AW had been reluctant).

16 As it happens, two Misses Preston had married Rawsons. AL would surely have been aware of this? The tenancies mortgaged included Staups, plus probably Upper and Lower Place and Southholme.

17 'Barstow' may be different from 'Bairstow'.

18 Christmas is a good example of Anne as a traditionalist. Likewise, for Dickens fans, Christmas then was more *Pickwick Papers* (1836–37) than *A Christmas Carol* (1843), published seven years later.

19 SH:7/ML/970/1.

20 The costs related especially to the Incline (from Listerwick up to Godley), a sloping roadway along which coal was dragged by boys called 'hurriers'.

21 This was similar to an earlier complaint about AW supervising servants.

22 See June 1836. Again, whether Barstow or Bairstow is confusing.

23 The Incline would have a gradient of 1 in 6, with corves (i.e. carts) on rails, helped by a chain system. Dragging these corves was very hard work.

24 See 11 November 1836, when both Mariana and AW had opposed building the East tower.

25 In fact, it was about six months earlier.

26 See, for example, 3 and 29 December 1836, Address from the Working People of Bradford, the Operative Conservatives, to the Bishop of Ripon.

27 Liddington, *Nature's Domain*, p. 104; Liddington, *Female Fortune*, p. 138.

28 I originally transcribed this on 31 May 1994, on to a disc. No use any more! Thanks to Rachel for retyping, 26 May 2020, twenty-six years later.

29 The implication was that navigation shares were slowly losing value.

JANUARY 1837

1 The Poor Law Commissioners had arrived in Huddersfield; see Thompson and Thompson, 'Halifax as a Chartist Centre', pp. 15–17; and Thompson, *Early Chartists*, p. 11.
2 *Halifax Guardian*, 7, 14, 21 and 28 January 1837.
3 Presumably John Greenwood, Northgate tenant and ropemaker; possibly related to Thomas Greenwood, Park Farm.
4 AL did like to show off about her travels!
5 Presumably, AL was 'forced' to open Listerwick because Walker pit was too close to Rawson's colliery for comfort? (This was surely only a partial truth!)
6 John Greenwood voted for Protheroe and Wood (i.e. the Whigs) in the 1837 election.
7 AL received her Christmas rents on 2 January, £602, SH:7/ML/AC/28.
8 However, public scrutiny of the underground working conditions of miners still lay four years away.
9 For Walker Priestley, see Priestley–Walker intermarriage, Appendix, p. 305.
10 Samuel Freeman owned three acres, mainly stone quarrying (1833).
11 In 1833 he paid 4 guineas rent (Mytholm), and now had two mills!
12 See 20 December 1836; also SH:7/ML/AC/28.
13 The impression given is that AL and AW now slept in separate bedrooms.
14 Freeman was being very helpful to Anne. Why? Certainly, he had voted for Wortley in 1835, and stone was increasingly valuable. Did he just want to ingratiate himself with Shibden?
15 Probably on the Crow Nest estate.
16 SH:7/ML/AC/28, 9 January, Freeman's £1,000 received; 10 January, received from AW £100 (her rents £515.13.6).
17 For Robert, see 5 November 1836.
18 Undoubtedly Catherine, Stansfield's daughter.
19 *Halifax Guardian*, 14, 21 and 28 January 1837.
20 SH:7/ML/972.
21 A tenant could gain a vote in the counties if his rent was over £50.
22 Bowling Dyke Mills was just below North Bridge.
23 Presumably for a new tenant, after Joseph Hall's widow.
24 Compare this to the advances made to AW by two hopeful male suitors. Also, this is just two years after the 'mock marriage' announcement.
25 Miss Patchett was undoubtedly Elizabeth Patchett of Law Hill; see Liddington, 'Anne Lister & Emily Brontë'.
26 AL had enjoyed Lady de Hagemann's company in Denmark in 1833.

FEBRUARY 1837

1 At Coquimbo, just north of Valparaiso.
2 The Conservatives' slogan, 'the Church in danger' was a useful rallying cry, blending with anti-Irish politics.

3 Though given by the King, this was of course the political programme of Melbourne's Whig government.

4 This seems odd, since Mr Holroyde was Conservative. Probably AL did not like these intrusive state procedures, which undermined traditional philanthropy.

5 The meeting was called by Michael Stocks and William Dearden; Henry Rawson said the new Poor Law was so aristocratic that the Radicals would have nothing to do with it; *Halifax Guardian*, 4 February 1837, quoted in Thompson and Thompson, 'Halifax as a Chartist Centre'.

6 Poor Anne: the indignity of relief from constipation taking a whole hour!

7 AL bought this on 16 September 1834; *Principles of Geology* was published in April 1833, so she read it shortly after publication. Lyell constantly updated it, geology being then so fast-moving. AL, as a devout Anglican, was more akin to Lyell than to Darwin. Lyell had *believed* the explanation of shingle terraces, Darwin could *prove it.* (See Darwin's *Journal*, first published in 1845, too late for AL.) Women were not admitted to the Geological Society until 1919. I am particularly grateful to Mike Leeder here.

8 It is unclear how this relates to the £1,000 AL took down to Old Bank earlier, from Freeman,

9 Why was AW delaying joining AL in bed?

10 Despite apparently having refused a loan.

11 Probably for Hipperholme-cum-Brighouse township. What did Samuel Washington think about being 'told'?

12 AL would not normally 'know' industrialists, but, given the loan, she might have seen things differently now.

13 Probably George Higham, a Brighouse lawyer.

14 C106/60, 15 February 1837, receipt for £1,000, to Wainhouse, Washer Lane, Halifax.

15 According to Mike Leeder, such titles were semi-popular books, widely circulated then.

16 Code looks more like 'east' but was more likely 'west tower'.

17 Golcar was near Huddersfield; interesting that this was written in code.

MARCH 1837

1 See *Children's Employment in Mines*, 1842, Halifax section, pp. 77–80. Staith is a term used in the north of England for a wharf.

2 In fact, in the 1837 election, Holt voted Whig. Had the 'Yellows' got to him first?

3 How many of these were her books and how many belonged to her ancestors?

4 Deference or AL's reputation for intensive reading? Interestingly, AL could visit the library, but seemed not to attend the Society's meetings.

5 Miss Patchett was Emily Brontë's employer at her Law Hill school during winter 1838–39; see Liddington, 'Anne Lister & Emily Brontë'; it was probably Southowram church.

6 For fossil-finding in coal seams, see Lyell, *Principles of Geology*, vol. III, p. 222, on discovering mammal bones in coal-beds. See also 'Section of the Shibden Hall Colliery', SH:2/M/4, a useful cross-section.

7 Construction of the Suez Canal did not start for another two decades.

8 Was autumn 1838 when Listerwick would become profitable, or when she calculated she would run out of money?

9 SH:7/ML/AC/28; this was mixed with colliery costs!

10 Had Ann become more emotionally committed to her school recently?

11 Subtitled *A Winter in Lower Styria*; Styria is a mountainous region of Austria.

12 Compare this to the letter to Mariana on the death of her mother a few months previously.

13 The masons were organized into an early trade union.

14 Halifax did have a Mechanics' Institute, founded in 1825, but it had led a peripatetic existence for its first few decades; Hargreaves, *Halifax*, p. 85. Horner was a Peelite Tory, AL a Wellington Tory.

15 Barker, *The Brontës*, pp. 265–9: Patrick Brontë opposed the Poor Law.

16 Little did AL know what was coming from Stansfield Rawson, see pp. 256–7.

17 Interesting (and rare) reference to AL's beaver-fur hat and boots.

18 How much did AL correlate this?

19 Liddington, *Female Fortune*, pp. 92–3.

20 Monte Carlo's casino did not open until the 1860s. And perhaps a Mechanics' Institute was still more like a library-cum-museum (after all, AL read 'mechanics').

21 'Them' must refer to the Institute's sponsors.

22 This was prompted by the arrival of the Poor Law Commissioners in northern industrial towns such as Halifax.

23 *Halifax Guardian*, 1 April 1837; Thompson and Thompson, 'Halifax as a Chartist Centre', p 17.

24 Would Listerwick mill be just for corn grinding or also for textiles?

25 Was Henry Priestley being naïve in believing that water-powered mills up side valleys had an economic future? Mills up Cragg Vale, even more remote than in Stainland, became notorious for ruthlessly exploiting child labour; see Thompson, *The Making*, pp. 382–3.

26 W. M. Higgins, *The Earth: its Physical Condition & Most Remarkable Phenomenon*. The earliest known publication date is 1838, so AL was probably reading the very latest work. Higgins was a rather *obscure* geologist!

27 And this was *all* tenants, rather than just enfranchised ones.

28 It is unclear why Liverpool: were they planning to 'steam it' from Scotland, so avoiding lengthy travel by road?

April 1837

1 Shugden was (high) up in Northowram township, tenanted by William Illingworth, and valuable mainly for its coal.

2 SH:7/ML/976; Green, 'A Spirited Yorkshirewoman', pp. 494–5. The letter offers a valuable (if caricatured) political summary.

3 AL remained self-conscious (and hence discreet) about menstruation purchases.

4 Dionysius Lardner, *The Steam Engine Explained & Illustrated*, Taylor and Watson, 1836; the book included steam power's application to railways.

5 Very unusual that no '*no kiss*' reference appears on Friday, Saturday or Sunday. AL was clearly very ill!

6 Did Jubb believe this? The kitchen chamber was a comfortable room above the kitchen.

7 Though in the Halifax area, swift-flowing tributaries into the Calder continued to power water-powered mills.

8 Little is known of this book.

9 *SOD*, yoni: symbol of the female sexual organ, venerated by Hindus and others. AL's use of code here is tricky to transcribe; she seems understandably to muddle some letters. According to the *Dictionary of Historical Slang*, 'flute' was the male member, but this perhaps makes less sense?

10 Dr Adam Clark (1762–1832), a British Methodist, was a theologian and biblical scholar.

11 *SOD:* long in use, vulgar etc.

12 Etymologies: the origins and development of words.

13 No love lost between Anne and Jonathan Akroyd!

14 The newspaper for British travellers in Europe.

15 Had AL stopped '*no kiss*' for good?

16 Master builder at Northgate.

17 William Buckland, *Geology and Mineralogy considered with reference to natural theology* (1836); he attempted (in vain) to reconcile geology and religion. (If he struggled, how could AL be expected to succeed?)

18 *Halifax Guardian* reported election news, 26 April 1837. SH:7/ML/979, Green, 'A Spirited Yorkshirewoman', pp. 495–6.

19 C106/60, 29 April 1837: AL was mortgaging titles to some of her freehold and copyhold land, securing a loan at 4% interest.

20 Ironically, in paying a formal call to the elderly Mrs Rawson at Stoney Royde, AL must have walked through the most controversial piece of AW's property: Water Lane and Bailey Hall. What were her thoughts?

MAY 1837

1 SH:7/ML/AC/28, 1 May 1837.

2 C106/60, £1,000, 15 February and 1 May 1837.

3 See Brontë, *The Tenant of Wildfell Hall*, p. 223. See Afterword.

4 Mr Gray overstaying his welcome at Shibden? But useful to consult on interior design.

5 Interesting that her period is masculinized.

6 This was the loan from the Misses Preston, C106/60; see 27 May 1837.

7 Days no longer started with '*no kiss*'; it became very amicable.
8 This must have been quite innovative then.
9 *Halifax Guardian*, 23 May 1837. Peep Green, Hartshead Moor, was beyond Brighouse (now by the M62).
10 Did AL put his fee in code because it sounded like Shibden extravagance?
11 So very different from AW's birthday. Such celebrations before 1850 were not common.
12 Mercantile associations: were such new money links a reason why AL did not go to Crow Nest?
13 There were sadly few employment options for such children.
14 Stocks's estate lay at the head of Shibden valley; see Liddington, *Female Fortune*, p. 54.
15 C106/60, 27 May 1837, £6,851.13.6d credit paid into AL's Yorkshire District Bank (from the Misses Preston; see 24 December 1836, £7,000 mortgage).
16 *HG*, p. 153, 31 May 1837.

JUNE 1837

1 In 1837 he gave a plumper for Wortley.
2 Equivalent to 30 pence a week.
3 So why was this draft correspondence in code? Was it travel plans she did not want AW to see?
4 Liddington, *Female Fortune*, p. 4.
5 Coney (i.e. a reference to rabbits) was Conery, developed as a kitchen garden. Swan Banks was the Rawsons' colliery, with brickworks alongside.
6 This letter is not in Green's thesis, nor in SH:7/ML; Achnacarry is in the western Highlands, near Skye.
7 The Norrises were 'Blue' but were urban professionals – unlike, say, the Waterhouses. William IV had no fewer than ten illegitimate children.
8 A fairly rare empathetic comment in AL's diaries about a child.
9 Did she regret that Lidgate had been let on a ten-year lease?
10 See AW's diary, Liddington, *Female Fortune*, Afterword.
11 Dove House was near John Oates's primitive coal pit at Pump.
12 Possibly the moss hut (scarcely mentioned since 1832) or a hut by the meer?
13 For Hinscliffe, a local coal operator, see p. 55.
14 After all, she suspected Briggs of the 'mock marriage' announcement; see Introduction, p. 15.
15 There were many Stephensons locally, so it was probably not *the* George Stephenson.
16 Myers' map, of which AL and AW had bought two copies (31 December 1836), had already sketched an optimistic yet speculative route for the railway through Halifax parish.
17 Finger glasses (for rinsing fingers after a meal) were the height of genteel society.

18 Yet AL had mentioned in a letter that her hair was going grey with all her estate business.

19 AL now found AW so irritatingly 'ungracious' that she even made small errors when writing in code.

20 A good instance of the smallest transaction offering an opportunity to secure a vote.

21 Perhaps inspired by Vere's Scottish estate?

22 If he is the John Priestley who married AW's aunt Elizabeth in 1776, they would be very elderly.

23 That is 23 oranges! An exotic treat, or a folk remedy for constipation?

24 Probably John Hinton, expert watchmaker and probably a Tory voter.

25 It was surely rather odd to apologize about her aunt's death (which had occurred about nine months earlier)?

26 Major Priestley, West Yorkshire Militia, died 28 April 1837, aged 46.

27 AW's cousin Mary Priestley married W. H. Rawson. *HG*, p. 20, notes that Dysons intermarried with Edwardses. There were many other visits.

28 Special treatment for expensive wine?

29 Thomas Maurice (1754–1824) was an oriental scholar and historian.

30 Halifax summer fair was a big agricultural event.

31 If Rawson did want to sell, it might have been due to the dangerous mining conditions at Swan Banks, with many deaths caused by fire damp explosions.

July 1837

1 This is what it says; no comment at all from AL. The Bellamys were a clerical family.

2 Probably this was Francis Carter. Washington was surely highly efficient.

3 Again, shades of *The Tenant of Wildfell Hall*; see Afterword.

4 See Liddington, 'Gender, Authority and Mining', p. 77.

5 Never alienate your lawyer!

6 Yet significantly, AL did not write this in code.

7 Did anything ever come of it? John Lister suggested not, and he should know!

8 Probably so that AW could live there. See below.

9 Samuel Washington's family lived in at least one wing of this great mansion. It had seven main bedrooms, plus four in each wing (and lofts, probably for servants).

10 This was a rare example of AW being vivacious at the dinner table, as during Mariana's visit.

11 At Jonathan Mallinson's pub at Mytholm; SH:2/SHE/8, half-yearly rents, £740.16.3d. Even Samuel Sowden, previously truculent, was now compliant.

12 AL had been disappointed with Husband as clerk-of-works.

13 Hothouses were the height of luxury.

14 Charles Howarth, Ireland, a joiner and tenant.

15 Parker (as with Water Lane mill well in 1836) had a quick temper.

16 Sough: horizontal opening to drain a mine.

17 Probably Thomas Greenwood, timber merchant, Old Market.

18 For 'a plumper', see Glossary, p. 304. John Bairstow, worsted spinner; Samuel Tetley and Thomas Cunliffe, both machine-makers.

19 His local links were via intermarriage with the Waterhouse family. AL had met him in 1825, when he called upon her uncle; she deemed him 'gentlemanly enough'.

20 Quoted in Thompson, *Dignity of Chartism*, p. 87.

21 John Mallinson lived at Woolshops, near Hatters Fold.

22 James Norris, secretary of the Halifax District of West Riding election committee, 1835.

23 Perhaps Anne feared that Mrs Heap might pick up gossip about them and pass it on to the Sutherlands.

24 Probably John Ogden, butcher, Woolshops.

25 When AW referred to 'home' did she mean Shibden, or the Shibden/Cliff Hill neighbourhood?

26 An odd question. However, her home, Haugh End, was scarcely altered, even two centuries later.

27 Plump, that is, not give Protheroe their second vote.

28 The Deardens were old-established rural magistrates. Thomas Holmes, probably West Grove, Halifax.

29 See *HG*, p. 157, which quotes much of this letter; and his opening page quoted these final lines. This letter is not in Green, 'A Spirited Yorkshirewoman', and there are few 1837 letters in SH:7/ML.

30 Probably of the Mallinson family, Woolshops.

31 *Halifax Guardian*, 18 July 1837.

32 Hemingway: Southolm, 42 acres. Holland: a Brighouse manufacturer, undoubtedly a strong Whig.

33 But can she completely trust Holt?

34 This was just before Emily Brontë came to work at the school there.

35 Charles Norris: listed in the 1837 *Poll Book* as a merchant. The clerk was a key commercial post.

36 Of course, crucially, in the boroughs, £10 householders could now vote, whereas in county constituencies, the bar was £50 for tenant farmers.

37 They were all 'small' men, not all of whom can be tracked accurately (as this was five years before the 1841 census).

38 John Lister selected these 1837 diary passages to open his 'Social and Political Life in Halifax Fifty Years Ago'; no wonder he looked back with distaste at his 'Blue' ancestor's politics. The 1872 Secret Ballot Act was long in coming.

39 So, Anne rewrote Ann's letter, even when it concerned Walker inheritance. Mary Walker had died in 1822; the letter concerned how much AW stood to inherit by her aunt Ann's death.

40 Was the blue room, as opposed to the kitchen chamber, a more permanent bedroom?

41 Difficult to identify Matthew Booth (so many Booths in Halifax).

42 Of course, the main emigration from Ireland, triggered by the Famine, was a few years later.

43 *Halifax Guardian*, 23 July 1837.

44 Throp, nurseryman in Halifax, was not listed in the *Poll Book*, and doesn't appear to have been an elector.

45 An unpopular move, and he thus jeopardized his political prospects in this key slavery port. He was Halifax MP, 1837–47. See index of MPs in Hall et al., *Legacies of British Slave-ownership* and website. The abolition of slavery seems to have been the one key moral issue about which Protheroe stuck out his political neck. He did, however, come from a slave-owning family. His father been a partner in a West Indian merchant firm. His son could still claim 72 slaves in Trinidad. Both were awarded £3,590.13.10d as compensation under the terms of the Emancipation Act. See Dresser, *Slavery Obscured*. He also spoke out for Irish political rights.

46 These Nelsons are difficult to trace.

47 466 electors split their votes for both Protheroe and Wood, with only 276 'plumping' for Wortley.

48 AL's diary (unusually) runs from one day into the next.

AUGUST 1837

1 Barker, *The Brontës*, p. 270; Driver, *Tory Radical*, pp. 361–3. *Halifax Guardian*, 1 August 1837, 'Terrible Riot'. There is a well-informed account in Euler, 'Moving between Worlds', pp. 260–1.

2 1837 *Poll Book*, John Crapper, ropemaker: plumper for Wortley. Mallinsons: none plumped for Protheroe.

3 Landowners would not wish for a legal challenge from an aggrieved tenant, particularly if it went to court.

4 Dennison had not voted for Wortley; this was a rather daring tactic by AL.

5 AL wrote 'shaffling'; maybe Yorkshire dialect?

6 AL sounded inconsistent with Mrs Dodgson, perhaps because she was growing politically desperate.

7 Aquilla seems not to be in the West Riding *Poll Book*, 1837.

8 Probably John Barber, Stump Cross; gave a plumper for Wortley.

9 No wonder that, half-a-century later, John Lister (*HG*, p. 1) had lots to say about these August days!

10 Possibly John Schofield, Sawood House, gave a plumper for Wortley.

11 This was probably the total of West Riding 'Blue' votes in the Halifax polling district.

12 Did AL make up his rent to £50, so his vote was above board?

13 Henry Dodgson, Lower Place, did not vote.

14 Undoubtedly John Whitely, Stainland: voted for Morpeth and Strickland.

15 No comment on intimacy or lack of it. Their sharing a bed now becomes more frequent.
16 Adelman, *Peel*, p. 22.
17 This letter does not appear in SH:7/ML and Green still has a long gap. It was probably a lament for both her nephews; AL did not reply for ten days.
18 *HG*, 9 August 1837, pp. 157, 146. Probably Thomas Hainsworth, Hatter's Close, gave a plumper for Wortley.
19 Even though the William Priestleys were near neighbours of Cliff Hill.
20 Probably the West Riding *Poll Book*.
21 AL effortlessly combined intellectual and business literature. Even though she had just bought the *Poll Book*, she did not immediately read it, which suggests that she already knew how her tenants had voted!
22 Why write this in code? Was it tricky to write about election defeats?
23 *Halifax Guardian*, 15 August 1837; Thompson, *Dignity of Chartism*, p. 87.
24 The implication is that AW had long planned to leave Shibden and live at Crow Nest.
25 A rein is not as coercive as a whip, but even so…
26 The village of Coley was within walking distance north-east of Hipperholme; see Map I. The church is well worth visiting; the Stocks plaque is up the left aisle, high on a wall.
27 Bradley had designed Crow Nest in 1788; Liddington, *Female Fortune*, p. 27.
28 Warrington, 'The Stocks Family', anti-slavery, p. 75. Stocks had died in November 1836.
29 A word not much used in the diary recently: see Glossary, p. 304.
30 Why had the mention of Standeven affected AW's temper? This coded passage, squashed at the foot of the page, is not very clear.
31 *Halifax Guardian*, 22 August 1837.

SEPTEMBER 1837

1 Liddington, *Female Fortune*, p. 101.
2 This was obviously an oblique reference to AL, and struck a similar note to Captain Sutherland's letter to Robert Parker ('interested selfish & wicked motives'), 20 July 1835; Liddington, *Female Fortune*, pp. 184–5.
3 Liddington, *Nature's Domain*, p. 76.
4 1841 census, aged 85 years.
5 The enquiry was for Willoughby Crewe's boys; Germany had developed an excellent reputation for education.
6 No wonder earlier editors skimmed so rapidly over these pages. Apart from the letter to Mariana, the barrowing and carting detail is oppressive.
7 Craven would have been fully aware that politics was now a male sphere.
8 Though there was no need to repeat this after the 1837 election, when they comfortably won Halifax.
9 And, unlike party politics, it continued to rumble on.

OCTOBER 1837

1 This was a view that Emily Brontë would soon come to know well. Rawson's quarries at Marsh included his small colliery.
2 Strict mourning could be relaxed after a year.
3 Michael Stocks's son, Joseph.
4 Probably below Lower Place, near Red Beck. See Map I.
5 SH:7/ML/991.
6 Liddington, *Female Fortune*, pp. 171–2, May 1835.
7 See Liddington, 'Anne Lister & Emily Brontë', pp. 59–62.
8 *HG*, p 158.
9 Her pony had earlier been a source of friction.
10 Next verse: 'For it is God which worketh in you both to will and to do of his good pleasure'. See also Revd Jane Finn, ALBW interview, 7 August 2021, on AL's unmediated theology (i.e. direct relationship with God), www.youtube.com/watch?v=3rDg8LRey_Q (accessed 8 October 2022).
11 Code unclear, suggesting that AL remained perturbed.
12 Thomas Maurice, *Indian Antiquities, or Dissertations Relative to … the Pure System of Primeval Theology*, 7 vols, 1793–1800.
13 *HG*, p. 158.
14 *Halifax Guardian*, 31 October 1837. In Hebden Bridge, 200–300 weavers assembled, demanding increased wages; Thompson, *Dignity of Chartism*, p. 88.

NOVEMBER 1837

1 Chase, *Chartism*, pp 16–17.
2 Clear confirmation that AW still wrote her diary.
3 This mainly concerned various Crow Nest properties.
4 Was this another rather tactless suggestion, or more of a pilgrimage?
5 SH:7/ML/993.
6 Something of a pattern here? In York, did AW take part in just some of AL's social life?
7 Anne then wrote in code about the Northgate rent to be paid,. This was surely because this rental would be crucial to her attempt for more financial independence.
8 Unclear who they are. Again, AW was left behind, while AL explored York's social circles.
9 It seems that AW was more likely to write her journal when away from Shibden.
10 Chase, *Chartism*, pp. 16–17; by January 1838 it was selling about 10,000 copies weekly. Thompson, *Early Chartists*, p. 13.
11 AL was her own highly organized archivist.

12 Was this to suggest a semblance of AL's financial independence, at least to the bank manager?

13 Highcliffe, on the Dorset–Hampshire border, built by Lord Charles Stuart de Rothesay.

14 Achnacarry, in the west Highlands, of Clan Cameron; the castle was rebuilt in 1802.

15 SH:7/ML/996; Green, 'A Spirited Yorkshirewoman', pp. 497–8. In her diary, Anne summarized the letter as a 'deserved eulogy on Lady Stuart de Rothesay's taste in landscape gardening – her judgement that of an artist'.

16 *Poll Book*, Northowram township.

17 Undoubtedly getting water for Akroyd's steam engines.

18 Crosslands of the Golden Lion, Halifax.

19 Is Harper handling this lease (rather than Parker) because he had hotel business experience?

20 *Halifax Guardian*, 21 and 28 November 1837.

21 *HG*, p. 158, 29 November 1837.

DECEMBER 1837

1 AW's estate, Northowram.

2 Earlier editors say little of the next fortnight, with gaps through December.

3 Robert Walsh, *Narrative of a Journey from Constantinople to England*, Westley and Davis, 1828.

4 So the Crow Nest estate was now supplying trees for Shibden.

5 Mining was a very dangerous occupation, with local flooding a constant threat.

6 AL consulted a Mr Bull, engineer to the Calder and Hebble Navigation, about this water burst.

7 This probably refers to Andrew Jackson, US President to March 1837; 'Jacksonian democracy' championed the 'common man' or, as its critics would claim, 'King Mob'.

8 SH:7/ML/997; Green, 'A Spirited Yorkshirewoman', pp. 498–9. The letter ends very abruptly; but see also 26 December.

9 AL read a book about banking and commerce in church. Dickens's *Christmas Carol* was not published until 1843.

10 Undoubtedly due to Samuel Washington's professional efficiency.

11 This could be Listerwick; or, because of proximity to Rawson's land, it might be Walker pit.

12 James B. Bernard, *Theory of the Constitution, compared with its practice in Ancient and Modern Times* (published after 1832 Reform Act).

13 'Miss' probably meaning young girls, but here it may have other overtones.

14 AL's haughty tone might relate to Vere's *chef d'oeuvres*. Given AL's dynastic ambitions, yet the absence of a direct heir, this was perhaps a sensitive subject.

15 AL presumably thought a rail tunnel should be far less expensive.

16 Also *HG*, p 159. The charging of tolls would, of course, push up the price at which AL could sell her coal.

17 E. P. Thompson notes gentry arriving fashionably late to church; 'Patricians and Plebs', *Customs in Common*, p. 45.

JANUARY 1838

1 In May the 'People's Charter' was published in London.

2 On New Year's Eve 1834, AL mused, 'Another year is gone!'; and on New Year's Day 1836, AL gave the servants' their new year's gifts; Liddington, *Female Fortune*, pp. 138, 203.

3 This was undoubtedly the loan from the Misses Preston; see 21 May 1837 ff.

4 SH:2/SHE/8, 3 January 1838.

5 This has the ring of the *Lady Chatterley* trial. Unclear why AL now goes into code.

6 In the 1837 West Riding election, Holland voted Whig; Carter voted for Wortley.

7 *HG*, p. 159, 6 March 1838, added that this 'violent opposition' was not effective.

8 This seems confusing, as Bottomley was AL's tenant. Perhaps another Bottomley? Or the significance was that AW had pent-up vexation?

9 George Harper, publican, was no relation to John Harper, York architect.

10 Henry Dodgson, Lower Place, offers a good example of women's indirect political influence.

11 Five changes of horses a day?

12 Having had his travel plans snubbed by the Admiralty, Cochrane had decided to walk across Europe and Russia, trying to reach North America; however, he ended up at the Mongolia frontier. Pedestrian here literally means 'on foot'.

13 Sunday 14 January: AW also wrote her journal.

14 In 1837 there had been rebellions in parts of Canada on the part of the French and some disaffected British and Irish.

15 SH:7/ML/1002.

16 AL was more ingenious and strategic, and more liked (contrast Rawson's treatment of his employees). Or was it inevitable, given the geography and geology?

17 Irtysh: utterly remote river near Mongolia.

18 *Halifax Guardian*, 23 January 1838. See also Thompson, *Early Chartists*, pp. 67–9.

19 Sir Humphry Davy was, of course, the scientist who invented the miners' safety lamp.

20 Cochrane, *A Pedestrian Journey*, vol. 1, starts from London, heads for Dieppe, then Paris, Berlin, and on to Moscow.

21 Probably 1833.
22 Abo: on the Swedish border near Finland. Kazan: on the River Volga, about 500 miles east of Moscow.
23 So the elderly Revd Wilkinson remained both headmaster and Lightcliffe curate.
24 Cochrane, *A Pedestrian Journey*, vol. 2, heads for the Kamtchatka Peninsula on the far east coast of Russia.
25 There is nothing in RAM:73 to indicate that AW had come round.
26 *Halifax Guardian*, 30 January 1838. In fact, Halifax railway station was not opened until 1863.

FEBRUARY 1838

1 Liddington, *Female Fortune*, pp. 92–3, February 1834.
2 How usual was it now for AW to take the sexual initiative?
3 This concerned property valuations.
4 See Liddington, *Nature's Domain*, p. 85.
5 SH:7/ML/1005; Green, 'A Spirited Yorkshirewoman', pp. 500–1.
6 Undoubtedly 'Proper Lessons to be read at Morning and Evening Prayers on Sundays and other Holy Days throughout the Year', *The Book of Common Prayer*.
7 How tantalizing not to know what AW wrote in her journal then!

MARCH 1838

1 Not quite clear why AL would be buying coal.
2 Tubbing: lining of pit shaft or tunnel with waterproof casing.
3 Holt was Marian's tenant.
4 Four feet would be sufficient height for a short man, or more likely boys.
5 C106/60 6 and 19.3.1838.
6 Abbott is seemingly last noted in the diary in 1835. Unless it was the reference to Marian (Holt was her tenant) that had jogged AL's memory.
7 Meanwhile, Mr Parker had sold five of Anne's navigation shares for £431 each.
8 With the Whigs and Lord Melbourne still in power, Peel was speaking from the opposition benches. For Peel on slavery, see Hall et al., *Legacies of British Slave-ownership*, p. 149.
9 A reminder of Mary Priestley's links to the Belcombe family.
10 The hilly journey from Sowerby to Huddersfield took nearly 1½ hours.
11 Had he realized that he had overstepped the mark, hence pressing the dinner invitation?
12 Liddington, *Nature's Domain*, pp. 63–4; and see Introduction, p. 5. But she had not been as suspicious as Mrs Priestley.

13　See Appendix, 'Ann Walker's family networks'.

14　Although Mr Jubb was probably unaware of this, Mary Rawson was about twenty years older than Ann, and had ten children plus grandchildren!

15　Fichu: triangular piece of lace or muslin covering the throat and shoulders.

16　AL trusted Oates.

17　See 29 November 1837, for Crossland lease.

18　My assumption is that AW did not know the code. Significantly, they are looking at diary pages with no code.

19　This seemed less about gender than a lesbian marriage, that is, they comprised a single household.

20　Was this part repayment of an earlier loan?

21　Presumably due to the impact of the railways.

22　AL was suspicion of Parker, thinking he had benefited the Crosslands rather than her.

23　Probably Thomas Holmes, a colliery partner of Holt.

24　When AL wrote the word 'quietly' it often seemed to have undertones of control.

25　Railways could, of course, transport very large quantities of coal up from the much larger coalfields, for example Barnsley.

APRIL 1838

1　William Rhind, *The Age of the Earth considered Geologically and Historically* (1837); Rhind (1797–1874) was a scriptural geologist.

2　If AL *had* heard of Darwin's discoveries, I think she would have noted this in her diaries. She might just have glimpsed how world-changing his new evidence and interpretations were, especially for traditionalist Anglicans like herself.

3　Probably in Northowram.

4　Bakewell, *Introduction to Geology*, earlier influential on Lyell.

5　Sir Henry De la Beche, geologist and palaeontologist.

6　SH:7/ML/1011; Green, 'A Spirited Yorkshirewoman', pp. 501–2.

7　Was this the thought of living at Cliff Hill if AL travelled on her own, or just of AW visiting her aunt?

8　*SOD*: a human being acting mechanically in a monotonous routine, 1796.

9　AL also wrote to Mariana; and then a kind letter from Vere Cameron.

10　AL's code here is understandably not clear.

11　Henry Fuseli, a Swiss painter, had spent much of his life in Britain.

12　The population of Halifax was then about 20,000. With no railway yet, it had to rely on the narrow Halifax coal measures, supplemented by collieries near Bradford.

13　See Davidoff and Hall, *Family Fortunes*, p. 440, for separate spheres at a political banquet.

14　James Hinscliffe, local coal operator.

15 Hipperholme had the advantage of a direct route down to the main canal at Brighouse.
16 AL had earlier encouraged Mr Jubb to take his wife to Europe to visit spas.
17 SH:/7/ML/C/3, AL business letters 1838. Also SH:7/ML/1013, AL's passport (1 May 1838).
18 Probably work concerning her school.

MAY 1838

1 Presumably sending in a bag by bank employee was more secure.
2 So, very unusually for Anne, the writing of one day's diary ran into the next.
3 Bluemantle Pursuivant of the Arms in Ordinary was a junior officer of the College of Arms, London. In 1838 it was George Harrison Rogers-Harrison.
4 Undress: less formal than dress coat?
5 The steep Northowram road was scarcely the most direct way to Doncaster. Surely far better to go via Hipperholme. Did AL wish to spare AW from going anywhere near her ailing aunt at Cliff Hill? Or more likely, in the excitement of at last getting off, and feeling very sleepy, AL made an uncharacteristic diary error.
6 Had AL been too preoccupied with estate business before she set off?
7 She was not unwell, though possibly still rather sleepy. And still no ref to AW!
8 Soult was former Minister of War in France. East Combe was near Greenwich.
9 Hertford Street is in the heart of Mayfair.
10 This slightly mysterious reference may be to their wintering in Rome in 1830; Liddington, *Female Fortune*, p. 23.
11 While AL had the carriage, AW visited the dentist (Friday), and wrote to her sister (Saturday).
12 Plowes: probably an Edwards relative.
13 Sources include Harrison, *Early Victorian Britain*, p. 151.

EPILOGUE

1 AL's diary, 27 and 28 May 1838.
2 Ingham, 'Anne Lister in the Pyrenees', pp. 57–61. Oddy returned home and a French maid was engaged.
3 Was this hypothyroidism, which can include intolerance of noise?
4 Jean de Charpentier, 1786–1855, German-Swiss geologist.
5 'Anne Lister, the Mountaineer', Anne Lister Research Summit 2022, https://storymaps.arcgis.com/stories/3428e82114dd43fe810e814c09610f7e (accessed 8 October 2022).
6 Ingham, 'Anne Lister in the Pyrenees', pp. 65–70.

7 *Halifax Courier*, 13 August 2003, 'Anne's fans tackle mountain challenge'. Also more recently, the Blister Sisters, AL fans, planned their own ascent (though COVID forced postponement).

8 My own reading of these passages is that the coded diaries are increasingly to let off steam, emotionally, rather than reflecting Anne's main feelings.

9 AL's diary, 17 August 1838; Livia Labate, Anne Lister Research Summit, 15 October 2020, www.annelisterresearchsummit.org/2020-summit (accessed 8 October 2022).

10 Green, 'A Spirited Yorkshirewoman', p. 505, from AL's diary, 1 November 1838; SH:7/ML/1037.

11 'From reclusive heiress to the Little Hercules of Shibden Hall', Marlene Oliveira, Anne Lister Research Summit, 4 October 2020, www.annelisterresearchsummit.org/2020-summit (accessed 8 October 2022). AW fans have read this as admiration; others as ironic, Mariana feeling jealous of AW.

12 *Halifax Guardian*, 4 August 1838; also Hargreaves, *Benjamin Rushton*, p. 19.

13 Thompson and Thompson, 'Halifax as a Chartist Centre', p. 19.

14 2 December 1838, Green, 'A Spirited Yorkshirewoman', pp. 505–6.

15 See image, p. 124.

16 Liddington, 'Anne Lister and Emily Brontë', pp. 56–8. This article also explored those Brontë writers who fancied that they *did* meet. Emily returned home during March–April 1839.

17 AL's diary, 3 December 1838.

18 Liddington, *Female Fortune*, p. 237, quoting Wilson, *Struggles*, p. 3.

19 Their Russian adventures have been told elsewhere, notably by Ramsden and Steidele.

20 There is lots on social media about AW and the Lunacy Commission, notably Steve Crabtree, 'September 1843: What Happened to Ann Walker?', research blog, March 2020, https://insearchofannwalker.com/research/september-1843-what-happened-to-ann-walker/ (accessed 8 October 2022).

21 See Liddington, *Female Fortune*, pp. 237–9; and Liddington, *Presenting the Past*, pp. 13–16.

22 Liddington, *Female Fortune*, p. 241.

23 Notably, Barker and Philp, *In the Shadow of Lightcliffe's Old Tower*. Social media includes 'In Search of Ann Walker', 2,347 followers on Twitter (January 2022).

AFTERWORD

1 The Anne Lister Society is coordinated by Professor Laurie Shannon, Department of English, North Western University, Chicago.

2 Contrast social media fandom with, say, Steidele, *Gentleman Jack*, 'a beast of a woman', p. 309.

3 See Roulston, 'From Text to Screen'.

4 Her journals may be compared to the Mass Observation project which recorded everyday life in Britain from 1937 to 1960, through volunteer observers' diaries and recordings of conversations; University of Sussex Archive.

5 2 May 1838.

6 Another example: her political feminism (for example, obtaining the vote) was only directed towards educated landed women like herself.

7 Much landscaping and economic activity detail (often laboriously repetitive) has been omitted.

8 Davidoff and Hall, *Family Fortunes*, ch. 10.

9 Most startling probably is the diary entry for 16 April 1837, when AL muses about Adam, Eve and a possible monkey.

10 In London, Queen's College for Women opened in 1848 and Bedford College in 1849.

11 These letters are mainly in SH:7/ML, and many are in Green, 'A Spirited Yorkshirewoman'.

12 Except when writing to Mariana, who is the exception here.

13 See Introduction, p. 6.

14 Aunt Anne died just months after this volume opens.

15 Liddington, *Female Fortune*, pp. 252–7.

16 See May 1837.

17 See May 1838.

18 See March 1836.

19 Brontë, *The Tenant of Wildfell Hall*, pp. 223, 245, 356, 362, 370–7, 391.

20 A classic account is Ray Strachey, *The Cause* (1928) (Virago, 1978), pp. 34–9, 72–6.

21 Introduction to the Penguin edition, 1979, by Winifred Gérin, quoting novelist May Sinclair, writing in 1913. Barker, *The Brontës*, pp. 341–2, 530, suggests that the novel was prompted by visits to Haworth parsonage by a Mrs Collins, the unfortunate wife of a drunken, profligate and debt-ridden local curate. The Revd Brontë advised her to leave him. This she did, thus saving her two children, and herself emerging as independent.

22 The Ladies of Llangollen were probably unusual in this. What did AL observe of other people's conventional marriages? Her parents' marriage was hardly a happy one. Equally, Mariana and Charles Lawton were not a united couple, and nor were the Milnes and others in the York set. Of William and Eliza Priestley we know little. One of the few happy marriages that AL observed and liked was that of Henry and Mary Priestley out in Ryburn. In other words, it seems that in AL's world there were more unhappy conventional marriages than happy ones.

23 BBC1, 24 May 2022.

24 Roulston, 'From Text to Screen'. This article will hopefully prompt other scholars to look again at the 'revisionist historical gaze' of 'post-heritage' popular TV drama. A campaign was begun in late 2022 by ALBW and more widely to secure the commissioning of *Gentleman Jack* series 3. Also, in August 2022 BBC R4 broadcast 'Mr Lucas's Diaries', offered a sobering

comparison to AL. Lucas, born in 1926 into a lower middle-class family, experienced harassment, blackmail and imprisonment as a homosexual; his diaries run to nearly 60 notebooks. The 1967 Act to legalize homosexuality came almost too late for him. He commented 'the orchard is thrown open, but the trees are dying'.

25 Pat Esgate could not travel to Halifax for medical reasons. A life-size cutout of Pat can be seen on the left of the photograph on p. 303. And unfortunately, over forty fans attending ALBW caught Covid by mid-week, including me. Most tragically, my already postponed Happy Valley Pride event scheduled for Sunday 10 April in Hebden Bridge's Little Theatre had to be re-cancelled. My least favourite verb! But I'm sure Anne Lister would have something philosophical in French to say about that!

APPENDICES

1 See Liddington, *Female Fortune*, p. 26, Crow Nest.

2 William Walker, Crow Nest, six guineas note, 1789; Ling Roth, *Banking in Halifax*.

3 About 'his great fondness for money', see Bretton, 'Walkers of Crow Nest', p. 112.

4 The other exception was her great-aunt Martha's marriage to General Fawcett, KB KCB.

5 Bretton, 'Walkers of Crow Nest', p. 111.

6 Liddington, *Female Fortune*, p. 65. Other rankling issues included church politics and property wrangles.

7 Kendal, 'Edwards Family of Pye Nest', pp. 21–2.

8 Liddington, *Female Fortune*, pp. 33–5.

9 Liddington, *Female Fortune*, pp. 90–1, 100.

10 Liddington, *Female Fortune*, p. 43, citing *Factory Inquiry Commission*, 1834. See also Porritt, 'The Rawson Family', p. 33.

11 In stark contrast to the new steam-powered mills, notably that of Jonathan Akroyd in Halifax; his mill boasted a 60-horsepower steam engine and had no fewer than 550 employees.

12 Liddington, *Female Fortune*, p. 151; AL told her doctor that Christopher Rawson 'had too many trades … [so] offending some influential people', 26 February 1835.

BIBLIOGRAPHY

ARCHIVE MATERIAL HELD IN CALDERDALE DISTRICT ARCHIVES, HALIFAX

SHIBDEN HALL RECORDS

SH:2/M – Shibden Hall estate, maps and plans
SH:2/SHE – Shibden Hall estate, accounts
SH:3/FN – Lister mss, funeral notes
SH:7/ML – Anne Lister correspondence
SH:7/ML/AC – Anne Lister account books and day books
SH:7/ML/C – Anne Lister business letters
SH:7/ML/E – Anne Lister journals

CROW NEST RECORDS

CN:33 – wills etc.
CN:87 – wills
CN:99 – accounts
CN:103 – accounts, correspondence

OTHER COLLECTIONS

RAM – Phyllis Ramsden papers
WYC:1525/7/1/5/1 – Ann Walker diary, Rawson mss

ARCHIVE MATERIAL HELD ELSEWHERE

C106/60 – Anne Lister mss, The National Archives, Kew

CONTEMPORARY REPORTS

Children's Employment in Mines, Children's Employment Commission, HMSO, 1842
Directory of the West Riding of Yorkshire, William White, Leeds and Sheffield, 1837
Halifax Borough Election, *The Poll Book*, Halifax, 1837
West Riding County Election, *The Poll Book*, 1837

BOOKS

Adelman, P., *Peel and the Conservative Party 1830–1850*, Longman, 1989
Barker, D., and Philp, I., *In the Shadow of Lightcliffe's Old Tower: Two Churches and a Churchyard*, Lightcliffe Local History Society, 2022
Barker, J., *The Brontës*, Phoenix, 1994
Bray, A., *The Friend*, University of Chicago Press, 2003
Brontë, A., *The Tenant of Wildfell Hall* (1848), Penguin, 1979
Cannadine, D., *Aspects of Aristocracy*, Penguin, 1995
Chase, M., *Chartism: A New History*, Manchester University Press, 2007
Choma, A., *Gentleman Jack*, BBC Books, 2019
Cochrane, Captain J. D., *A Pedestrian Journey through Russia and Siberian Tartary: To the Frontiers of China, the Frozen Sea, and Kamtchatka*, new edn, 2 vols, 1829
Davidoff, L., and Hall, C., *Family Fortunes: Men and Women of the English Middle Class 1780–1850*, Hutchinson, 1987
Dresser, M., *Slavery Obscured*, Leicester University Press, 2001
Driver, C., *Tory Radical: The Life of Richard Oastler*, Oxford University Press, 1946
Green, M., *Miss Lister of Shibden Hall: Selected Letters 1800–1840*, Book Guild, 1992
Hall, C., et al., *Legacies of British Slave-ownership: Colonial Slavery and the Formation of Victorian Britain*, Cambridge University Press, 2016
Hargreaves, J., *Halifax*, Edinburgh University Press, 1999
Harrison, J. F. C., *Early Victorian Britain 1832–51*, Fontana, 1979
Lea, J., *The Gentleman Jack Effect: Lessons in Breaking Rules and Living Out Loud*, Laurel House Press, 2021
Liddington, J., *Female Fortune: Land, Gender and Authority: The Anne Lister Diaries 1833–36*, Manchester University Press, 2022 (Rivers Oram Press, 1998, 2019)
Liddington, J., *Nature's Domain: Anne Lister and the Landscape of Desire*, Pennine Pens, 2019 (2003)
Liddington, J., *Presenting the Past: Anne Lister of Halifax 1791–1840*, Pennine Pens, 2010 (1994)
Ling Roth, H., *The Genesis of Banking in Halifax*, King and Sons, 1914
Lyell, C., *Principles of Geology: being an attempt to explain the former changes of the earth's surface, by reference to causes now in operation* (1833), vol III, Forgotten Books, 2018
Steidele, A., *Gentleman Jack: Regency Landowner, Seducer and Secret Diarist: A Biography of Anne Lister*, Serpent's Tail, 2018
Thompson, D., *The Chartists*, Temple Smith, 1984
Thompson, D., *The Dignity of Chartism*, Verso, 2015
Thompson, D., *The Early Chartists*, Papermac, 1971

Thompson, E. P., *Customs in Common*, Merlin Press, 1991
Thompson, E. P., *The Making of the English Working Class*, Pelican, 1968 (1963)
Whitbread, H., *I Know My Own Heart*, Virago, 1988; reissued as *The Secret Diaries of Miss Anne Lister*, Virago, 2010
Wilson, B., *The Struggles of an Old Chartist*, John Nicolson, 1887

ARTICLES AND BOOKLETS

Brears, P., 'John Harper at Shibden', *York Historian*, 1978
Bretton, R., 'Walkers of Crow Nest', *THAS*, 1971
Hargreaves, J., *Benjamin Rushton: handloom weaver and Chartist*, Halifax, 2006
Ingham, V., 'Anne Lister in the Pyrenees', *THAS*, 1969
Kendal, H. P., 'Edwards Family of Pye Nest', *THAS*, 1925
Liddington, J., 'Anne Lister & Emily Brontë 1838–39: Landscape with Figures', *Brontë Society Transactions*, 2001
Liddington, J., 'Gender, Authority and Mining in an Industrial Landscape: Anne Lister 1791–1840', *History Workshop Journal*, 42, 1996
Norton, Rictor, 'Anne Lister: The First Modern Lesbian', *Lesbian History*, 2003
Porritt, A., 'The Rawson Family', *THAS*, 1966
Roulston, C., 'From Text to Screen: "Gentleman Jack" Then and Now', *Journal of Lesbian Studies*, June 2022
Warrington, D., 'The Stocks Family of Upper Shibden Hall', *THAS*, 1971

THESES AND UNPUBLISHED TYPESCRIPTS

Euler, C., 'Moving between Worlds: Gender, Class, Politics, Sexuality and Women's Networks in the Diaries of Anne Lister of Shibden Hall, Halifax, Yorkshire, 1830–1840', DPhil, University of York, 1995
Green, M., 'A Spirited Yorkshirewoman: The Letters of Anne Lister of Shibden Hall, Halifax 1791–1840', Honours Diploma of the Library Association, 1938
Thompson, D., and E. P. Thompson, 'Halifax as a Chartist Centre', typescript, mid-1950s, Halifax Reference Library

INTERNET SOURCES

Anne Lister Birthday Week, https://www.annelisterbirthdayweek.com
Codebreakers, ALBW Live, January 2022, www.youtube.com/watch?v=sud1Hxy0mD8 (accessed 20 September 2022)
Liddington, J., 'Who Was the Real Anne Lister?', July 2019, https://vimeo.com/348859464 (accessed 20 September 2022)
Packed with Potential, https://www.packedwithpotential.org
http://www.jliddington.org.uk

INDEX

The central theme of this book is, of course, the relationship between Anne Lister and Ann Walker. This is indexed mainly under Anne Lister's name and is grouped into five broad chronological sections so that readers can easily follow their dissident relationship during 1836–38 (noticing increasingly frenzied activity as departure to France nears). Ann Walker's entries are shorter, and mainly concern her own activities and emotions.

Anne's letter-writing is indexed under the name of her correspondents (e.g. Mariana Lawton).

Estate business (e.g. coal mining and trespassing) is indexed under the name of the coal operative concerned (e.g. Rawsons). However, more general estate affairs are presented under Crow Nest and Shibden.

To keep the length of the index within reasonable limits, entries for details of minor people's activities are not given fully. Full entries are provided for key estate workers and professionals under their names (e.g. Samuel Washington, Robert Parker).

Book titles appear under the author's name.

9 781526 176417